Advances in Intelligent Systems and Computing

Volume 732

D1797559

Series editor

Janusz Kacprzyk, Polish Academy of Sciences, Warsaw, Poland
e-mail: kacprzyk@ibspan.waw.pl

The series "Advances in Intelligent Systems and Computing" contains publications on theory, applications, and design methods of Intelligent Systems and Intelligent Computing. Virtually all disciplines such as engineering, natural sciences, computer and information science, ICT, economics, business, e-commerce, environment, healthcare, life science are covered. The list of topics spans all the areas of modern intelligent systems and computing such as: computational intelligence, soft computing including neural networks, fuzzy systems, evolutionary computing and the fusion of these paradigms, social intelligence, ambient intelligence, computational neuroscience, artificial life, virtual worlds and society, cognitive science and systems, Perception and Vision, DNA and immune based systems, self-organizing and adaptive systems, e-Learning and teaching, human-centered and human-centric computing, recommender systems, intelligent control, robotics and mechatronics including human-machine teaming, knowledge-based paradigms, learning paradigms, machine ethics, intelligent data analysis, knowledge management, intelligent agents, intelligent decision making and support, intelligent network security, trust management, interactive entertainment, Web intelligence and multimedia. The publications within "Advances in Intelligent Systems and Computing" are primarily proceedings of important conferences, symposia and congresses. They cover significant recent developments in the field, both of a foundational and applicable character. An important characteristic feature of the series is the short publication time and world-wide distribution. This permits a rapid and broad dissemination of research results.

More information about this series at http://www.springer.com/series/11156

Sunil Kumar Muttoo
Editor

System and Architecture

Proceedings of CSI 2015

 Springer

Editor
Sunil Kumar Muttoo
Department of Computer Science
University of Delhi
Delhi
India

ISSN 2194-5357   ISSN 2194-5365   (electronic)
Advances in Intelligent Systems and Computing
ISBN 978-981-10-8532-1   ISBN 978-981-10-8533-8   (eBook)
https://doi.org/10.1007/978-981-10-8533-8

Library of Congress Control Number: 2018932994

Printed on acid-free paper

This Springer imprint is published by the registered company Springer Nature Singapore Pte Ltd.
part of Springer Nature
The registered company address is: 152 Beach Road, #21-01/04 Gateway East, Singapore 189721,
Singapore

Preface

The last decade has witnessed remarkable changes in IT industry, virtually in all domains. The 50th Annual Convention, CSI-2015, on the theme "Digital Life" was organized as a part of CSI@50, by CSI at Delhi, the national capital of the country, during December 02–05, 2015. Its concept was formed with an objective to keep ICT community abreast of emerging paradigms in the areas of computing technologies and more importantly looking at its impact on the society.

Information and Communication Technology (ICT) comprises of three main components: infrastructure, services, and product. These components include the Internet, infrastructure-based/infrastructure-less wireless networks, mobile terminals, and other communication mediums. ICT is gaining popularity due to rapid growth in communication capabilities for real-time-based applications. New user requirements and services entail mechanisms for enabling systems to intelligently process speech- and language-based input from human users. CSI-2015 attracted over 1500 papers from researchers and practitioners from academia, industry and government agencies, from all over the world, thereby making the job of the Programme Committee extremely difficult. After a series of tough review exercises by a team of over 700 experts, 565 papers were accepted for presentation in CSI-2015 during the 3 days of the convention under ten parallel tracks. The Programme Committee, in consultation with Springer, the world's largest publisher of scientific documents, decided to publish the proceedings of the presented papers, after the convention, in ten topical volumes, under ASIC series of the Springer, as detailed hereunder:

1. Volume # 1: ICT Based Innovations
2. Volume # 2: Next Generation Networks
3. Volume # 3: Nature Inspired Computing
4. Volume # 4: Speech and Language Processing for Human-Machine Communications
5. Volume # 5: Sensors and Image Processing
6. Volume # 6: Big Data Analytics

7. Volume # 7: Systems and Architecture
8. Volume # 8: Cyber Security
9. Volume # 9: Software Engineering
10. Volume # 10: Silicon Photonics & High Performance Computing

We are pleased to present before you the proceedings of Volume # 7 on "Systems and Architecture." The title "Systems and Architecture" covers the most important, pervasive, top-level, strategic inventions, decisions, and their associated rationales about the overall structure and associated characteristics and behavior. It provides an understanding of the architectures of our computing systems. The title also assists the readers to help them and plan the selection of a processor for a particular project.

Computer Architecture refers to those attributes of a system visible to a programmer. Computer Organization refers to the operational units and their interconnections that realize the architectural specifications. It is a blueprint and functional description of requirements and design implementations for the various parts of a computer, focusing largely on the way by which the central processing unit (CPU) performs internally and accesses addresses in memory. It addresses the challenge of selecting and interconnecting hardware components to create computers that meet functional, performance, and cost goals. It details how a set of software and hardware technologies standards can interact to form a computer system or platform. It refers to how a computer system is designed. The title "Systems and Architecture" also deals with the various innovations and improvements in computing technologies to improve the size, capacity, and performance of modern-day computing systems. This volume is designed to bring together researchers and practitioners from academia and industry to focus on extending the understanding and establishing new collaborations in these areas. It is the outcome of the hard work of the editorial team, who have relentlessly worked with the authors and steered up the same to compile this volume. It will be useful source of reference for the future researchers in this domain. Under the CSI-2015 umbrella, we received over 100 papers for this volume, out of which 32 papers are being published, after a rigorous review processes, carried out in multiple cycles.

On behalf of organizing team, it is a matter of great pleasure that CSI-2015 has received an overwhelming response from various professionals from across the country. The organizers of CSI-2015 are thankful to the members of *Advisory Committee, Programme Committee, and Organizing Committee* for their all-round guidance, encouragement and continuous support. We express our sincere gratitude to the learned *Keynote Speakers* for support and help extended to make this event a grand success. Our sincere thanks are also due to our *Review Committee Members* and the *Editorial Board* for their untiring efforts in reviewing the manuscripts, giving suggestions and valuable inputs for shaping this volume. We hope that all the participated delegates will be benefitted academically and wish them for their future endeavors.

We also take the opportunity to thank the entire team from Springer, who have worked tirelessly and made the publication of the volume a reality. Last but not least, we thank the team from Bharati Vidyapeeth's Institute of Computer Applications and Management (BVICAM), New Delhi, for their untiring support, without which the compilation of this huge volume would not have been possible.

Delhi, India   Sunil Kumar Muttoo
December 2017

The Organization of CSI-2015

Chief Patron

Padmashree Dr. R. Chidambaram, Principal Scientific Advisor, Government of India

Patrons

Prof. S. V. Raghavan, Department of Computer Science, IIT Madras, Chennai
Prof. Ashutosh Sharma, Secretary, Department of Science and Technology, Ministry of Science of Technology, Government of India

Chair, Programme Committee

Prof. K. K. Aggarwal, Founder Vice Chancellor, GGSIP University, New Delhi

Secretary, Programme Committee

Prof. M. N. Hoda, Director, Bharati Vidyapeeth's Institute of Computer Applications and Management (BVICAM), New Delhi

Advisory Committee

Padma Bhushan Dr. F. C. Kohli, Co-Founder, TCS
Mr. Ravindra Nath, CMD, National Small Industries Corporation, New Delhi
Dr. Omkar Rai, Director General, Software Technological Parks of India (STPI), New Delhi
Adv. Pavan Duggal, Noted Cyber Law Advocate, Supreme Court of India
Prof. Bipin Mehta, President, CSI
Prof. Anirban Basu, Vice President-cum-President Elect, CSI
Shri Sanjay Mohapatra, Secretary, CSI
Prof. Yogesh Singh, Vice Chancellor, Delhi Technological University, Delhi
Prof. S. K. Gupta, Department of Computer Science and Engineering, IIT Delhi
Prof. P. B. Sharma, Founder Vice Chancellor, Delhi Technological University, Delhi

Mr. Prakash Kumar, IAS, Chief Executive Officer, Goods and Services Tax Network (GSTN)

Mr. R. S. Mani, Group Head, National Knowledge Networks (NKN), NIC, Government of India, New Delhi

Editorial Board

A. K. Nayak, CSI
A. K. Saini, GGSIPU, New Delhi
R. K. Vyas, University of Delhi, Delhi
Shiv Kumar, CSI
Anukiran Jain, BVICAM, New Delhi
Parul Arora, BVICAM, New Delhi
Vishal Jain, BVICAM, New Delhi
Ritika Wason, BVICAM, New Delhi
Anupam Baliyan, BVICAM, New Delhi
Nitish Pathak, BVICAM, New Delhi
Shivendra Goel, BVICAM, New Delhi
Shalini Singh Jaspal, BVICAM, New Delhi
Vaishali Joshi, BVICAM, New Delhi

Contents

About the Editor

Prof. Sunil Kumar Muttoo is working as a Professor and Head of the Department of Computer Science, University of Delhi. He completed his M.Sc., M.Phil., Ph.D. at the University of Delhi and his M.Tech. (Computer Science and Data Processing, CSDP) at the Indian Institute of Technology Kharagpur (IIT-KGP). He is involved in research in the field of steganography and digital watermarking. He has published more than 60 papers in international/national journals and conference/workshop proceedings. He has more than 30 years of teaching and research experience.

A Mathematical AI-Based Diet Analysis and Transformation Model

L. K. Gautam and S. A. Ladhake

Abstract Inadequacies in nutritional intake can be considered as a major source of adverse effects on the growth and health of individuals in India. A proper balanced diet is essential from the very early stages of life for proper growth, development, to remain active and to reduce the risk of diseases. For those with diabetes, a proper diabetes diet is crucial which depends upon their energy requirements. So a need has been identified to develop educational software which should perform the routine task of analyzing, optimizing, and transforming diet by considering their energy requirements and medical problems. The different nutritional values present in a diet are generally affected by imprecision, which can be represented and analyzed by fuzzy logic. For diet balancing, a metaheuristic local search algorithm is proposed which works in a local search space recording the history of search to make it more effective and optimized. These proposed methods will help users to improve their nutritional intakes by providing detail analysis of their food intake, by providing an optimized diet plan and by suggesting possible changes to make their diet suitable according to their energy requirements.

Keywords Energy evaluation · Fuzzy interval · Tabu search · Mathematical AI model

1 Introduction

Inadequacies in nutritional intake can be considered as a major source of adverse effects on the growth and health of individuals in India. The common nutritional problems in India are malnutrition, low birth weight, chronic deficiency in adults, and diet related noncommunicable diseases [1, 2]. To maintain health and increase

L. K. Gautam (✉) · S. A. Ladhake
Sipna College of Engineering and Technology, Amravati, Maharashtra, India
e-mail: leenakgautam@gmail.com

S. A. Ladhake
e-mail: sladhake@yahoo.co.in

© Springer Nature Singapore Pte Ltd. 2018
S. K. Muttoo (ed.), *System and Architecture*, Advances in Intelligent Systems and Computing 732, https://doi.org/10.1007/978-981-10-8533-8_1

1

Fig. 1 Degree of health

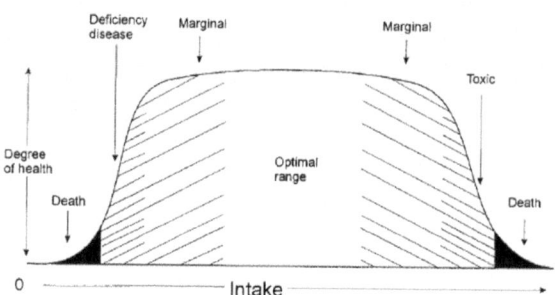

life expectancy and to decrease the frequency of cardiovascular diseases, one has to improve its dietary habits which is based on the nutrition values. Thus, a need has been identified to develop educational software which will monitor and perform the daily task of analyzing, optimizing, and correcting the user's diet at home.

The nutrition intake can be appropriately evaluated and described by employing fuzzy sets and fuzzy arithmetic. Wisram [3] evaluated the nutritional intake status assessment by comparison of intake with the official recommendation for that person. Figure 1 shows the degree of health when varying the intake of one essential nutrient and holding the rest of the diet constant at an optimal level [3].

The work proposed in this paper focuses on the development of interactive AI-based mathematical functionality as an effective solution to support continuous nutritional management. Firstly, we will discuss the general problem statement, and then, the criteria for energy evaluations are described in Sects. 4, and 5 defines some preliminaries on fuzzy sets and fuzzy interval. The background of tabu search is discussed in Sect. 6, and finally, the integration of all these sections, i.e., a proposed work is described in Sect. 7.

2   Problem Statement

A problem exists regarding the inaccurate values of nutrients in foods because the approximate amounts of nutrients available in a certain food are normally known, but there is always a question of their exact amounts. There is often a problem of imprecision with the nutrient values, i.e., their exact amount [4, 5]. This problem may increase if only partial information is available especially for industrially processed foods, but for precisely packed foods (for instance Cheese, Butter, oil, rice, biscuits, etc.), we can obtain the nutrients value precisely. For other foods, for instance vegetables and fruits (banana, apple, etc.), nutrients values varies in a large range, depending on size, growing conditions, freshness, etc.

All this values, i.e., precise and imprecise, have to be stored in a database, and a computer then needs to operate on these values. It should be able to compare these values and should perform all the arithmetic operations [1, 4, 5].

3 Energy Requirements and Its Evaluation

The amount of each nutrient needed for an individual depends upon his/her age, body weight, and physiological status which can be calculated in terms of energy [2].

RDA recommends that energy requirement must be assessed in terms of energy expenditure rather than in terms of energy intake.

$$\text{i.e. Total Energy Expenditure} = \text{Predicted Body Mass Ratio} \\ \times \text{Physical activity level (PAL)} \quad (1)$$

Physical activity ratio values for activities performed in a day can be aggregated over that period to yield the physical activity level (PAL). A detailed table of PAR values for different activities is available in the FAO/WHO/UNU 2004 report [2].

3.1 Nutrients Consideration

The primary macronutrients which are important and are considered are protein, fats, and carbohydrates which are converted into energy in different quantities, i.e., 1 g of protein contribute 17 kJ of energy, 1 g of fat constitute 37 kJ of total energy, 1 g of carbohydrates contribute 17 kJ and 1 g of dietary fiber contribute 8 kJ where 1 kJ = 0.239 kcal [3].

4 Fuzzy Arithmetic and Computation

4.1 Preliminaries

In this section, we review the fundamental notions of fuzzy set theory.

Fuzzy Interval. Definition 1. A fuzzy interval is a fuzzy set [6] of real numbers, written M, having membership function μ_M.

$$\forall \alpha \in [0, 1] \, M_\alpha = \{r | \mu_M(r) > \, = \alpha \quad \text{(the a-cut of } M) \text{ is a closed interval.} \quad (2)$$

support $S(M) = \{rj\mu_M(r) > 0\}$ is the largest membership area of x (x cannot take a value outside $S(M)$), whereas the kernel $^{\cdot}M = \{r | \, \mu_M(r) = 1\}$ is the set of the most plausible values for x, also called modal values, and membership function is unimodal and upper semicontinuous [6].

Fuzzy Computation. Extension principle [7, 8] is used for performing basic arithmetic operations on trapezoidal fuzzy numbers. Let M and N be two fuzzy

Fig. 2 Fuzzy interval

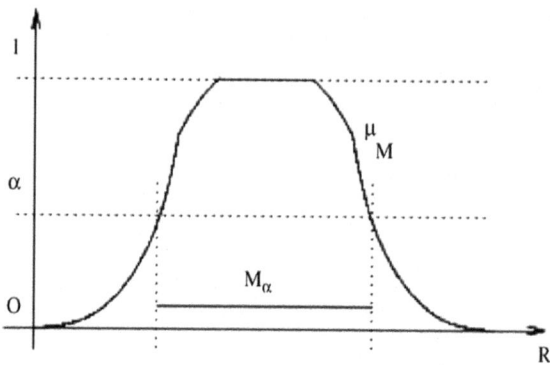

trapezoidal intervals $(\underline{m}_1, m_1, \alpha_1, \beta_1)$ and $(\underline{m}_2, m_2, \alpha_2, \beta_2)$, respectively. Addition and subtraction on M and N is given by [7, 8] (Fig. 2).

$$
\begin{aligned}
M + N &= \left(\bar{m}_1 + \underline{m}_2, \bar{m}_1 + \bar{m}_2, \alpha_1 + \alpha_2, \beta_1 + \beta_2\right)\\
M - N &= \left(\bar{m}_1 - \underline{m}_2, \bar{m}_1 - \bar{m}_2, \alpha_1 + \beta_2, \beta_1 + \alpha_2\right)
\end{aligned}
\tag{3}
$$

5   Tabu Search Background

Classical methods encounter great difficulty in solving hard optimization problems.

In several cases, we need a modified heuristic approach which provides a solution very close to optimality that tackles the difficult problems at hand and improves the computing time of local search techniques. The metaheuristic approach called tabu search (TS) was proposed by Fred Glover in 1986 to overcome local optima, which is now dramatically changing our ability to solve problems of practical significance [9, 10].

Tabu is an intelligent search process which incorporates adaptive memory and responsive exploration (an intelligent search) [11, 10]. Tabu search can be applied directly to many kinds of decision problems, without the need to transform them into mathematical formulations.

6   Proposed Work

The proposed AI-based mathematical model comprises three modules, viz. analysis module which helps the user to know the nutrients present in the selected diet and its amount. The second module is an optimized module, which gives the perfect diet planner considering the user's medical problem, and lastly the transformation module which can make small changes in the user's diet to make it well balanced while considering the requirements and possible medical problems.

6.1 Diet Analysis Module

A record for each patient is created which contains his/her physical parameters, level of physical activity, and possible medical problems. Considering these entire parameters, energy requirement is calculated by considering Eq. (1). The user is then allowed to choose a food present in a hierarchy and enter the portion for evaluation which gives the correct assessments and suggestions. This evaluation is done by using fuzzy interval which is trapezoidal mentioned in Sect. 4.1. After computing the total energy, it is compared with the prescribed norms, in order to assess whether it is compatible. Let norms and data, represented by the possibility distributions P and D, respectively. Degree of possibility of matching and degree of necessity of matching are given by $N(P, D)$ and $\pi(P, D)$

$$\pi(P, D) = \sup \, \min\big(\mu_p(\mu), \, \mu_d(\mu)\big), \; N(P, D) = 1 - \pi(P, D) \qquad (4)$$

The result of which is displayed to the user by using interfacing techniques.

6.2 Optimization Module

The food database consists of some diet plan based on different energy requirement prescribed by nutritionist. This diet plans gives total say n combinations. A measurement of appropriate energy and nutrient intake with a respect to the recommendations, or optimal intake, is evaluated by metaheuristic search logic which is further displayed in decreasing order. Optimization solutions provide assistance in the selection of a better diet plan. This module is adaptive in nature as it enhances its diet combinations from transforming module and increasing its efficiency.

6.3 Diet Transformation Module

This module aims at telling the user how he/she may modify his/her diet to make it according to his/her energy requirements and adapted to his/her possible medical problems. It is indeed a difficult task for the user to perform certain modification in their diet to make it well balanced as modifying the weight of a food, for instance, often leads to have the transformation of several nutrients modified at the same time. The diet provided by the user generates a state space which can be solved by applying minimum transformation using an algorithm. Let us assume that for each diet m in "generated diets," the following is known:

- The minimum cost of transformation from the initial diet m to noted g;
- An estimation of the cost to transform m to its closest solution g.

Proposed Transformation Algorithm 1.

```
1. Consider the initial diet m
2. searchList is empty.
3. While the stopping criteria is not satisfied do
     Check the value of meal according to energy
requirement .Generate diet m's neighbors by applying
transformations Operations by considering history and
constraints.(i.e. m')Then compute evaluation term f = g+h(goal
amount)
4. m -> m'
5. Update the search list.
6. End and return the best solution met.
```

From the above mention algorithm, a specific diet plan is generated by evaluating the required energy requirement and by applying small changes.

7   Concluding Discussion

The AI-based mathematical model for diet optimization and transformation solves the common nutritional problems of public health problems in India using fuzzy arithmetic and a search space metaheuristic algorithm.

Imprecision of data is represented by fuzzy sets, whereas fuzzy arithmetic provides all the necessary computations on these values, which are then compared with the prescribed values present in a database and can be shown to the user by using suitable interfacing techniques. A diet optimization module discussed in Sect. 6.2 gives best diet plan available according to the user's energy requirements. The contents of the daily diet BLSD (breakfast, lunch, snacks, and dinner) are already stored in the database which can be selected on the basis of constraints, preserving their eating practices by using local search metaheuristic algorithm. Finally, the proposed transformation algorithm balances the diet by developing the state space, considering the needs of user and applying minimum possible changes.

For the future, we intend to deal with optimizing diet, based on cost (price) as an additional objective function. It would enlarge the state space of metaheuristic search algorithm and would greatly help in finding more optimized solution.

Declaration

The consent from patient is not required in this paper as no patient is physically involved in this study (or during analysis). The data collected during this study are from right resources.

L. K. Gautam

References

1. Buisson, J.C.: Nutri Educ, a nutrition software application for balancing meals, using fuzzy arithmetic and heuristic algorithm. Artif. Intell. Med. **42**, 213–227 (2008)
2. Indian Council of Medical Research: Nutrient requirement and recommended dietary allowances for Indians. National Institute of Nutrition (2010)
3. Dietary Guidelines of Indians: National Institute of Hyderabad (2010)
4. Buisson, J.C.: Knowledge development expert systems and their application in nutrition. Knowledge based systems—techniques and applications. Academic Press, New York, pp. 37–65 (2000)
5. Buisson, J.C., Garel, A.: Balancing meals using fuzzy arithmetic and heuristic search algorithms. IEEE Trans. Fuzzy Syst. **2003**(11), 68–78 (2003)
6. Zadeh, L.A.: Fuzzy sets as a basis for a theory of possibility. Fuzzy sets Syst
7. Zadeh, L.A.: Fuzzy sets. Inf. Control **8**, 338–353 (1965)
8. Zimmermann, H.J.: Fuzzy set theory and applications. Academic Publisher (2001)
9. Boussaïd, I., Lepagnot, J., Siarry, P.: A survey on metaheuristics. Inform. Sci. **237**, 82–117 (2013)
10. Glover, F., Laguna, M.: Tabu Search. Kluwer Academic Publishers, Boston (1997)
11. Bluma, C., Puchingerb, J., Raidlc, G.R., Roli, A.: Hybrid metaheuristics in combinatorial optimization: a survey. Appl. Soft Comput. **11**, 4135–4151 (2011)

Energy Efficient Measures for Sustainable Development of Data Centers

Taniya Aggarwal, Saurabh Khatri and Anu Singla

Abstract Information technology (IT) industry today has become the most immense and developing industry of this era. With the growing demands of networking, storage, multimedia, computation, communication, and information, there is a need felt for setting up and maintaining the data centers. Data centers now are the biggest consumers of energy of the IT industry. The energy cost is the most driving factor of data centers. In extend to investment and maintenance price, energy efficient methods and equipment should be implemented in data centers to accomplish the overall progress of the IT sector. Energy management in these centers not only reduces the operating cost of data centers but also reduces emergence of power generation. This paper gives a comprehensive overview about the energy consumption in the data centers and provides energy efficient techniques that would contribute to the continuous and sustainable development.

Keywords Data center · Energy efficiency · Virtualization · Computer room air conditioners · Blade servers · Operation and maintenance

T. Aggarwal (✉)
School of Computer Sciences, Chitkara University, Chandigarh, Punjab, India
e-mail: taniyaaggarwal223@gmail.com

S. Khatri
School of Mechanical Engineering, Chitkara University, Chandigarh, Punjab, India
e-mail: khatri.sbh@gmail.com

A. Singla
Chitkara University Research and Innovation Network, Chitkara University, Chandigarh, Punjab, India
e-mail: anu.singla@chitkara.edu.in

© Springer Nature Singapore Pte Ltd. 2018
S. K. Muttoo (ed.), *System and Architecture*, Advances in Intelligent Systems and Computing 732, https://doi.org/10.1007/978-981-10-8533-8_2

9

1 Introduction

There have been the biggest changes in infrastructure of information technology (IT) mainly due to social media, cloud, mobility, greater computing capacity, and big data. The IT business has flourished enormously in last two decades. The rapid growth of IT activities and business has resulted in establishment of large number of data centers. Data centers are the dedicated physical and virtual IT infrastructures used by organizations to support their businesses. Data centers consist of servers, storage equipment, and networking systems. These systems are used to run application software, store, process and serve data to the client.

A data center generally requires substantial backup power supply systems, cooling systems, excessive network connections, and some policy-concerned security systems for running the organization's key applications. Energy consumption of data centers has increased manifolds. Resources reveal that if complete data centers become a nation, it will be attributed as twelfth largest user of electricity internationally. The processors, server power supplies, other server components, storage and communication equipment account for almost 52% of total consumption of a data center [1]. It has become imperative to incorporate green IT technologies in data centers [2]. The motive may be:

- Reduction in energy bills.
- Increase in business profitability and sustainability.
- Optimal utilization of hardware resources with extended useful life.
- Reduce maintenance requirements and less chances of downtime.
- Less carbon emission.

To identify site infrastructure and design topologies of different data centers, a four tiered scale is adopted (a brief provided in Table 1). Tier 4 is the most robust infrastructure for data center.

Table 1 Data center tiers [6]

No. of tier	Redundancy of capacity components	No. of power distribution paths serving IT equipment	Example
I	No	Single non-redundant	Computer room with one UPS, generator, and HVAC cooling system. No redundancy of any system component
II	Yes	Single non-redundant	Similar to Tier I. Redundant capacity components are provided in addition
III	Yes	Multiple	Similar to Tier II. But IT equipment is supplied with two distinct UPSs
IV	Yes	Multiple	Multiple paths provided to supply IT equipment. Back power support is provided by redundant generators

The paper is divided into eight sections. Section 1 provides introduction of data centers while Sect. 2 discusses the energy consumption in data centers. Sections 3 and 4 provide the scope of energy conservation by adopting energy efficient technologies and or by efficient operation and maintenance. Conclusions are drawn in Sect. 7, and the future scope is presented in Sect. 8.

2 Scope of Energy Efficient Technologies and Techniques in Data Centers

The 2% of global CO_2 emissions come from IT industry as reported in [3]. Data centers contribute one-fourth of the total CO_2 emission by IT and are growing at a faster pace. Many data centers are consuming far more energy than they need to in relation to the service they provide. This statement can be witnessed by the fact that initial setup of data center costs is only 5% of the total cost of its working for the period of nearly 15–20 years and energy being the major part of it.

Overall energy ingesting in data centers is the sum of energy consumed by several units in operation. A significant management of energy is possible with the reduction of energy usage of each unit and synchronizing the overall setup.

The paper presents the four elementary components of data centers including electrical system, cooling system, IT system and operation and maintenance of the data centers [4]. Section 3 explains the energy management for electrical system, and Sect. 4 sums up the cooling processes and the measures to be taken for energy efficient cooling process. The information for energy management of IT equipment and peripherals is carried out in Sect. 5 while energy efficient operational and maintenance strategies are discussed in Sect. 6.

3 Energy Saving in Electrical System

The electrical systems installed in data centers need to be of high efficiency benchmarks that minimize transmission and heat loses. Developing IT industry has increased the total power requirement of data centers by 5%. In this electronic age, backup and retrieval of data are invaluable. The power consumed varies for every data center and depends on the building design and its architecture. The power flow schematic in a data center is shown in Fig. 1.

The major components, their description, and energy efficiency measures are listed in Table 2.

Fig. 1 Power flow schematic in a data center [6]

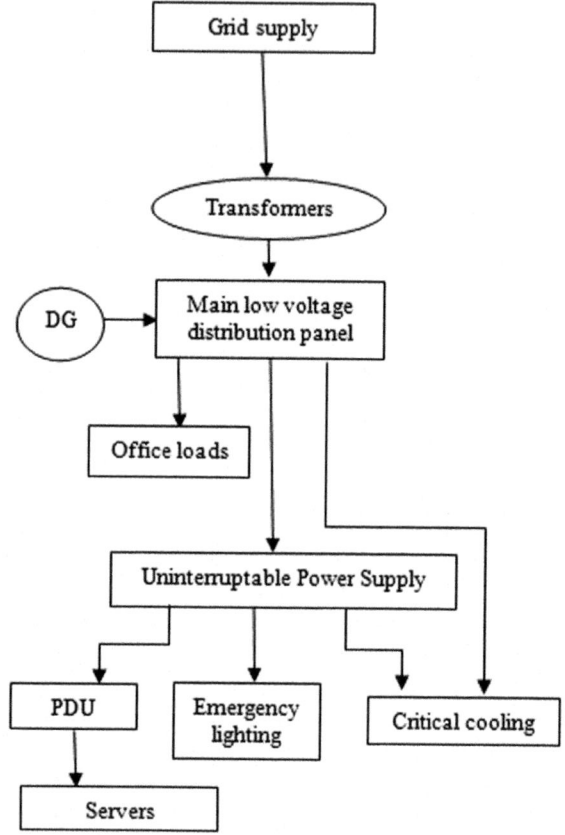

4   Cooling System

Cooling system plays an important role in effective working of data centers. Cooling system consumes 35–40% of the total power consumption. There is large potential of energy saving by adopting energy efficient technologies in cooling systems

Cooling system processes can be divided in two parts:

A. Conventional method (room cooling technique)
B. Contemporary method

Contemporary method is quite preferable energy efficient system. In this mechanism, racks are arranged in such a way that inlet face toward cold aisle gets cold air from rack and the hot air leaving rack does not go toward the outlet of other racks. Pipes flow through perforated tiles. Perforated tiles and even perforated doors can reduce energy consumption up to 83%. The working of instruments is temperature sensitive. Any increase in operating temperature limits can lead to shut

Table 2 Components of electrical system

Equipment	Description	Energy efficient measures
DG sets	Used as power backup	Steady load conditions and air filtration
Transformers	Used for stepping up/down voltage	Use K-20 over K-1 or K-13 transformers
Transient voltage surge suppressor (TVSS)	Save sensitive electronic device from voltage fluctuations	Must be installed with every PDU
Uninterrupted power supply (UPS)	Save data and devices during instable power	Optimize UPS for maintaining load more than 40%
Power distribution unit (PDU)	Distribute power to IT loads	Optimizing the load on PDU systems
Advanced power strip	Divides power and provides networking between cabinets and server racks	Regular monitoring and maintenance
Cabling	Transmit power to all the units	Maintaining them at high voltage, hence low current and heating

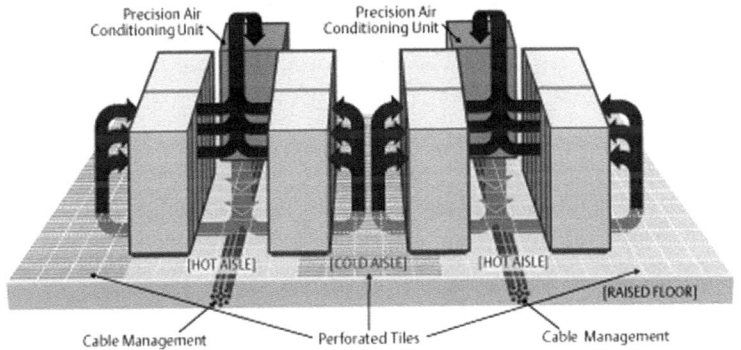

Fig. 2 Hot aisle/cold aisle configuration [6]

down of system. So this operation needs to be performed with high precision. The configuration of hot aisle and cold aisle is shown in Fig. 2.

Components of cooling system:

A. *Chilling unit*—Chilling unit is used to transfer energy from one surface to other. Chilling unit used in cooling system can be of different types. Table 3 shows the brief energy efficient strategies for direct expansion system and chilled water system:

Table 3 Savings observed with cold aisle containment (CAC) unit implementation [6]

Savings observed in direct expansion system	Traditional approach	With aisle containment (%)	With integrated CAC (%)
	-	21	33
Saving observed in chilled water system	-	15	28

B. *Water pumping unit*—Water pumping unit is used in cooling systems with water cooling chillers to pump water. Some energy efficient measures are as follows:

- Installation of high efficiency pumps
- Entire area utilization in cooling towers
- Reducing pressure of chilled water supply
- Annual checking and calibration of the condenser water supply temperature sensors.

C. *Precision air conditioner (PAC)*—Working of cooling system under the prescribed temperatures is of utmost importance. Adoption of PAC helps in attaining this by precisely managing heating, cooling, and ventilation requirements of system.

D. *Air distribution system*—Air distribution system is responsible for distribution of cold air to data center and then recovery of hot air. The process of distributing air to system in itself contains potential to save a lot of energy. Energy efficient techniques which can be implemented are

- Taking cold air closer to heat source.
- Installing rack with low self-weight.
- Use of efficient economizers lower the energy usage intensity by 13%.
- Installation of temperature and humidity sensors for monitoring air intake conditions.

5 IT Equipment

To achieve the maximum efficient output, energy efficient IT equipment should be selected keeping the purchase cost aside. The power flow and the consumption by various equipments in typical data center are shown in Fig. 3.

The breakup of power consumed by IT equipments is shown in Fig. 4.

Fig. 3 Power consumption
by various equipment [6]

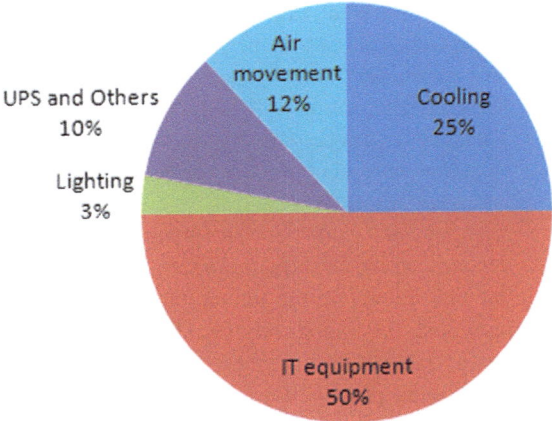

Fig. 4 Power consumption
by IT equipments [6]

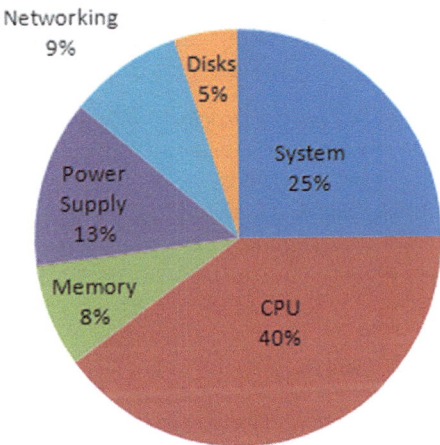

The energy efficient technologies and techniques for IT equipment are discussed below:

A. *Energy efficient server—Blade servers:*

Though servers are the most space consuming units but are also the main driving unit of IT sector. Computing servers continuously consume power for running I/O resources, buses, disks, and memory etc. [5]. Most of the servers run below 20% utilization but consume full power [6]. The internal cooling systems can be improved by using variable speed fans in place of constant speed fan for cooling, thereby saving energy. The new energy efficient technologies are developed. Blade server follows modular infrastructure that converges server, storage, and network structure [7]. It speeds up the operations performed which results in speedy delivery of applications and services running in physical and virtual environments. The modular design optimizes the use of physical space and energy consumption. It enhances the energy efficiency and performance of data center [1]. Blade servers in comparison with power edge rack servers consume around 10% less energy [1].

B. *Server virtualization:*

The data centers contain a large number of servers, but workload is distributed to a few only keeping the remaining servers idle. The unutilized expensive hardware resources not only consume power and but also require cooling arrangements and periodic maintenance. Power consumption of servers depends on the activity performed. A low-end server may consume nearly half the peak power during idle conditions [8]. It is important to decommission or repurpose the idle servers [9]. Virtualization of servers offers energy savings. Server virtualization increases resource utilization and reduces energy costs by partitioning physical servers into numerous multiple virtual servers. Each virtual server runs its own operating system and applications. The virtual servers run efficiently and reduce energy costs by 10–40% [1]. The application of dynamic reallocation of virtual machines to real-world cloud data centers minimizes energy consumption [10].

C. Following technologies may improve the data center efficiency [11]:

- *Multi-core processors*: Servers with multi-core processors are able to perform multiple tasks simultaneously in a short span of time reducing power and heat up by 40%.
- *Chip-level cooling*: In this approach, heat is moved away from the chip.
- Installing new servers over outdated ones may save the energy by 5%.
- Technique of high server density should be adopted.
- 4–5% of total power is consumed by storage systems. This consumption can be reduced by using efficient storage thin chips and by reducing redundancy of data.

A comprehensive power usage study of workloads of data centers is provided in [8].

6   Operation and Maintenance in Data Center

After the designing of data center, operation and maintenance play the major role. The extreme usage of energy can be reduced to lower levels by performing following jobs:

A. Training of officials and involving operation team in designing—Training officials working in data center easily help in bringing energy requirements of load low. By involving operation team in designing, energy in data center can be managed efficiently with help of designing considerations.

B. Regular metering—Metering different parameters at appropriate positions can help in getting information about status of energy usage thus helping in analyzing the performance of system.

C. Housekeeping—A regular housekeeping should be maintained for smooth working in data centers. Clean and dust-free environment would result in better heat transfer from equipment and thus minimize its chances of failure. It would also lead to energy saving.

D. Lighting design—Light in building has a lot of potential in saving energy. Some measures are:

- Automation of different lighting systems can lead to reduction of electricity up to 14%.
- Task-oriented lighting system shall be used.
- Using of LED lights instead of conventional bulbs.
- Regular maintenance of lighting system (cleaning etc.).

E. Routine audits—Energy audit data centers regularly so that performance can be regularly checked.

F. Preventive maintenance—A preventive maintenance would lower the chances of any breakdown of the system, but it should be scheduled at appropriate time.

G. Efficient storage techniques—A lot of energy in data center is wasted due to improper and unskilled management of storage system. A large numbers of copies of stored data should be avoided, and storage technique should be well enough to avoid usage of extra disk and drive.

Reference [12] has proposed efficient power management architecture for hardware and software in data center. The energy wastage due to variation in demand for IT services asks for power efficient configuration. The different principles of energy management system are presented in [13]. Authors of [5] have proposed energy efficient methodology named DENS based on data center network and traffic characteristics to manage energy consumption in data centers.

7 Conclusion

After studying and analyzing about the energy consumption in data centers, it can be said that on applying little efficient pathways, huge amount of energy can be conserved. Different units have different methods by which energy can be managed. The electrical supply transmission should be carried at high voltage, and optimizing loads on UPS and PDU can reduce energy consumption. Cooling consumes considerable energy in data center. This load can be reduced by using contemporary methods for direct expansion and chilled water system. IT equipment is the largest consumer of energy in data center. Using low power multi-core processors and server virtualization can reduce power wastage. Operation and maintenance team can play a leading role by focusing on some points like better housekeeping, monitoring, and auditing which can help in improving energy efficiency.

8 Future Scope

The increasing energy loads in data centers can be snapped by the continuous evolution of energy efficient technologies. Operating temperatures needs to be lowered in data centers for efficient operations. Liquid cooling has tremendous potential in cooling servers and appliances more effectively than air conditioning. Adoption of green cloud computing techniques as discussed in [14] and virtualized environment may improve the storage and power efficiency of servers.

References

1. Energy Logic: Reducing Data Center Energy Consumption by Creating Savings that Cascade Across Systems. A White Paper, Emerson Network Power, Columbus, Ohio (2008)
2. Koutitas, G., Demestichas, P.: Challenges for energy efficiency in local and regional data centers. J. Green Eng. 1–32 (2010)
3. Data Centre Energy Efficient Design Guide, Sustainable Energy Ireland. Available at http://www.seai.ie/Your_Business/Large_Energy_Users/Special_Initiatives/Special_Working_Groups/Data_Centre_Special_Working_Group_SpinI/Data%20Centre%20Energy%20Efficient%20Design%20Guide.pdf
4. Chong, F.T., Heck, M.J.R., Ranganathan, P., Saleh, A.A.M., Wassel, H.M.G.: Data center energy efficiency: improving energy efficiency in data centers beyond technology scaling. Design & Test, IEEE **31**(1), 93–104 (2014)
5. Kliazovich, D., Bouvry, P., Khan, S.U.: DENS: data center energy-efficient network-aware scheduling. In: Green Computing and Communications (GreenCom), 2010 IEEE/ACM International Conference on & International Conference on Cyber, Physical and Social Computing (CPSCom), pp. 69–75, 18–20 Dec 2010
6. Energy Efficiency Guidelines and Best Practices in Indian Data Centres. Published by Bureau of Energy Efficiency (BEE), Ministry of Power, Government of India
7. Report, FEMP Best Practices Guide for Energy-Efficient Data Center Design. National Renewable Energy Laboratory, 2010, Revised Mar 2011
8. Fan, X., Weber, W.-D., Barroso, L.A.: Power provisioning for a warehouse-sized computer. In: ISCA'07, San Diego, California, USA, 9–13 June 2007
9. Cole, D.: Data center energy efficiency-looking beyond PUE, No Limits Software, White Paper, #4 (2011)
10. Beloglazov, A., Buyya, R.: Energy efficient allocation of virtual machines in cloud data centers. In: 2010 10th IEEE/ACM International Conference on Cluster, Cloud and Grid Computing (CCGrid), pp. 577–578, 17–20 May 2010
11. Five Strategies for Cutting Data Center Energy Costs through Enhanced Cooling Efficiency. Emerson Network Power and Liebert Corporation (2007)
12. Raghavendra, R., Ranganathan, P., Talwar, V., Wang, Z., Zhu, X.: No "power" struggles: coordinated multi-level power management for the data center. In: ASPLOS'08, Seattle, Washington, USA, 1–5 Mar 2008

13. Dumitru, I., Fagarasan, I., Iliescu, S., Said, Y.H., Ploix, S.: Increasing energy efficiency in data centers using energy management. In 2011 IEEE/ACM International Conference on Green Computing and Communications (GreenCom), pp. 159–165, 4–5 Aug 2011
14. Buyya, R., Beloglazov, A., Abawajy, J.: Energy-efficient management of data center resources for cloud computing: a vision, architectural elements, and open challenges. In: Proceedings of the 2010 International Conference on Parallel and Distributed Processing Techniques and Applications (PDPTA 2010), Las Vegas, USA, 12–15 July 2010

Analysis on Multiple Combinations of Series–Parallel Connections of Super Capacitors for Maximum Energy Transferring to Load in Minimum Time

Pankaj R. Sawarkar, Akhilesh A. Nimje and Praful P. Kumbhare

Abstract High farad values of ultra capacitors (UCs) are associated with very large current during charging. This paper proposes numerous switching configurations within ultra capacitor units supplying energy to load in efficient way. This reconfiguration dealt with series–parallel connections with reference of load voltage maximum and minimum limit. By using proper switching, 99% of stored energy can be delivered to load in minimum time. In normal case, only 73% stored energy could be utilized by load. Proposed scheme shows that operation will become faster, i.e., 57.67–75.68%.

Keywords Super capacitor · Charging · Discharging · Reconnection

1 Introduction

For good performance of battery, such hybrid systems required fixed current charger and separation of battery during the process. This has been described by Jeong et al. [4]. Economical solution has been suggested by Chen and Lai [3] by using microprocessor unit switching over take place from constant current charging to constant voltage charging in electric vehicle application drive required high starting current and during regenerative braking involve high rates of discharging current. Chau and Chan [2] have reported that, which did not required voltage feedback or current feedback [1, 5]. Reconfiguration within ultra capacitor bank for reducing charging current. Simulation of MATLAB Simulink and results were

P. R. Sawarkar (✉) · A. A. Nimje (✉) · P. P. Kumbhare
Electrical Engineering, Guru Nanak Institute of Engineering and Technology,
Nagpur, India
e-mail: pankaj.sawarkar@gmail.com

A. A. Nimje
e-mail: nimjeakhilesh29@gmail.com

P. P. Kumbhare
e-mail: praf369@gmail.com

© Springer Nature Singapore Pte Ltd. 2018
S. K. Muttoo (ed.), *System and Architecture*, Advances in Intelligent Systems
and Computing 732, https://doi.org/10.1007/978-981-10-8533-8_3

21

confirmed by mathematical calculation, which indicate that during charging process using similar reconfiguration charging current can be reduced. It shows that charging time can be reduced to 330 from 480 s in constant current charging method and it is 31.35% faster. In constant voltage method, charging time reduced to 96 from 120 s and the process is 20% faster [7]. Time required to extract energy reduces to 72% in typical cases of discharging. Advantages of fast operation during charging using similar reconfiguration have also been pointed out. Typically, 20–30% faster operations are expected. The proposed reconfiguration has an additional advantage of extracting about 72% of the energy stored by the capacitor, in this reduced time period reported by Sawarkar et al. [6].

1.1 Proposed Scheme

This scheme is suggesting the use of number of capacitors for required faradays value. These capacitors will connected series and parallel for buildup required voltage level. As soon as load voltage will reduce to minimum operating voltage of load then connections of capacitors will be change in another set of series–parallel connection. This process will continue till all the capacitors connected in series. This paper has analyzed different cases which are tabled below.

Case no.	Capacitance × no. of units	Total capacitance (F)
Basic scheme	32F × 1	32
Case 1	16F × 2	32
Case 2	8F × 4	32
Case 3	4F × 8	32

Analysis is done on each case separately with percentage of energy transfer, time required, etc.

1.2 Basic Scheme

In this case, a single unit of pre-charged super capacitor is connected to the load. The capacitance of capacitor is of 32F and load resistance is of 20 Ω (Fig. 1).

Fig. 1 Series R–C circuit

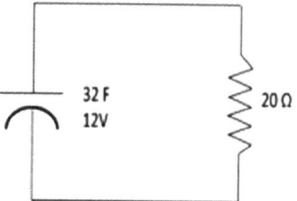

It will be series R–C circuit and time constant will be equal to 640 s. This capacitor is pre-charged at voltage 12 V. Enc is the energy available in capacitor which can be calculated by

$$Enc = \frac{1}{2}C\,V^2 = 2304\,J \qquad (1)$$

Time required to reducing capacitor voltage from 12 V to zero will be 2560 s. (2)

Figure 2 shows voltage with respect to time.

Above scheme will deliver 2304 J to load, i.e., 100% energy in 2560 s. If system is having lower voltage cutoff limit, then some percentage of energy will not supply to load. This voltage cutoff limit is considered as 6 V. The energy supplied to the load will be 1727.83 J in 443.5 s and unutilized energy will be 576.17 J which is calculated in case-1. Following graph shows variation of load voltage with system lower voltage limit.

From the above following statement can be done

$$Total\ time = 443.52\ s. \qquad (3)$$

$$Total\ Energy\ supplied\ to\ load\ in\ V_L > 6\ V\ is\ 1727.83\ J \qquad (4)$$

$$Percentage\ of\ energy\ supplied\ to\ load\ in\ V_L > 6\ V\ is\ \left(\frac{1727.83}{2304}\right) \times 100$$
$$= 74.99\% \qquad (5)$$

$$Percentage\ of\ time\ utilized \left(\frac{443.52}{2560} \times 100\right) = 17.32\% \qquad (6)$$

Refer Fig. 3 for graphical representation of voltage with respect to time.

Fig. 2 Graphical representation of voltage with respect to time

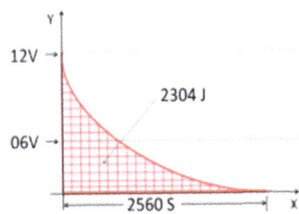

Fig. 3 Variation of voltage with respect to time

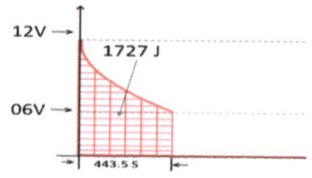

2 Case-1

In this case, two units of 16F 12 V pre-charge capacitor are used. The voltage cutoff limit is 6 V which is discussed in 1.1 and 1.2.

1.1

Pre-charged capacitors are connected in parallel to load up to 6 V (Fig. 4).
   Time required for reducing capacitor voltage from 12 to 6 V will be

$$6\,\text{V} = 12\,\text{V}\left(e^{-t1/\text{RC}}\right) = 12\left(e^{-t/640}\right) \quad \text{i.e. } t_1 = 443.52\,\text{s.} \tag{7}$$

In 443.52 s energy supplied to load will be

$$E = 7.2 \int_0^{443.52} e^{-2t/640}dt = 1727.83\,\text{J} \tag{8}$$

Refer Fig. 4 the lower limit of voltage cutoff is 6 V. During this period, energy supplied to load is 1727.83 J from Eq. (8). In 443.5 s from Eq. (7) energy remains in capacitor will be

$$(2304 - 1727.83) = 576.17\,\text{J.} \tag{9}$$

Remaining 576.17 J can be utilized only if $V_L > V/2$, this can be done by connecting capacitors in series discussed in 1.2.

Fig. 4 Circuit diagram of two capacitors connected parallel with load

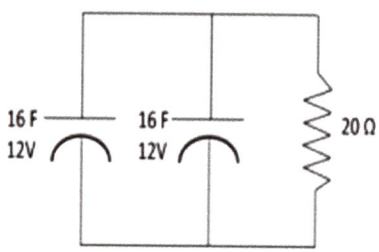

1.2

After 1.1 configuration connection will be change to series connection shown in Fig. 5.

Equivalent capacitance will be 8F, energy available will be

$$\text{Enc} = \frac{1}{2}CV2 = 576\,\text{J} \tag{10}$$

$$\text{Time constant of the circuit will be } 20 \times 8 = 160\,\text{s}. \tag{11}$$

Time required for reducing capacitor voltage from 12 to 6 V will be $t_2 = 110.9\,\text{s}$ (12)

Then energy supplied to load in t_2 s will be

$$E = 7.2 \int\limits_{0}^{110.9} e^{-2t/160} dt = 431.99\,\text{J} \tag{13}$$

Figure 6 shows the graphical representation of voltage with respect to time in above case.

Fig. 5 Circuit of capacitors is in series and connected parallel to load

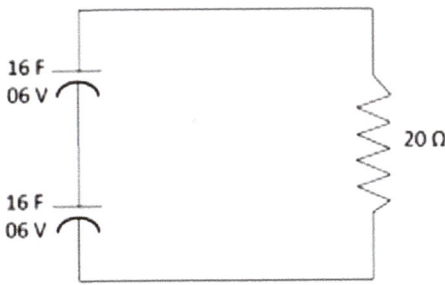

Fig. 6 Graphical representation of voltage with respect to time

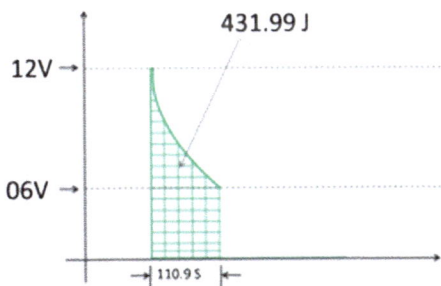

In operation described in 1.2, load is disconnected at load voltage becomes 6 V. Again energy remains in capacitor will be

$$2304 - 1727.83 - 431.99 = 144.18\,\text{J} \tag{14}$$

This 144.18 J cannot be utilized by load due to load voltage limit.

Time required for 100% energy supplied will be $4 \times 20 \times 8 = 640\,\text{s}$. (15)

1.3
From 1.1 and 1.2

$$\text{Total time} = 443.5 + 110.9 = 554.4\,\text{s}. \tag{16}$$

Total Energy supplied to load in $V_L > 6\,\text{V}$ is $1727 + 431.9 = 2158\,\text{J}$ (17)

Percentage of energy supplied to load in $V_L > 6\,\text{V}$ is $\left(\dfrac{2158}{2304}\right) \times 100 = 93.66\%$

(18)

$$\text{Percentage of time utilized} \left(\dfrac{554.4}{2560} \times 100\right) = 21.65\% \tag{19}$$

Total time consumed for 100% energy drained is $443.5 + 640 = 1083.5\,\text{s}$ (20)

Figure 7 shows the variation of voltage in 1.1 and 1.2.

Fig. 7 Graphical representation of voltage with respect to time

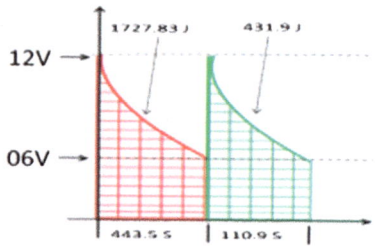

3   Case-2

In this case, 8F capacitance 12 V pre-charge capacitor is used. The capacitors connected are discussed in 2.1, 2.2, and 2.3.

2.1

Charged capacitors are connected in parallel to load up to load voltage becomes 6 V shown in Fig. 8.

From Eq. (7), t_1 = 443.52 s and from Eq. (8) 1727.83 J will supplied to load. Refer Fig. 3. Energy remains in capacitor will be 576.17. J from Eq. (9). Remaining 576.17 J can be utilized by connecting capacitors in connection discussed in 2.2.

2.2

After 2.1 configurations, connection will be changed as two capacitors will be connected in series and such two combinations will be connected in parallel with load shown in circuit diagram (Fig. 9).

From Fig. 9 Equivalent capacitance will be 8F, energy = 576 J, time constant = 20 × 8 = 160 s. From Eq. (12) t_2 = 110.9 s. From Eq. (13) energy supplied is 110.9 s will be 431.99 J. In operation described in 2.2, load is disconnected at load voltage becomes 6 V. Again energy remains in capacitor will be 144.18 J from Eq. (14) remaining 144.18 J can be utilized by applying configuration discussed in 2.3.

Fig. 8 Circuit diagram of two capacitors connected parallel with load

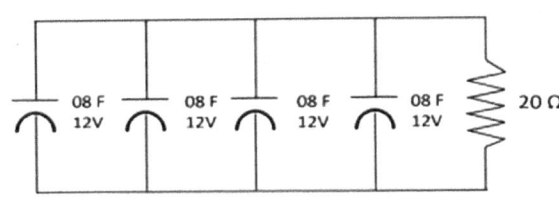

Fig. 9 Circuit diagram of two capacitors in series and connected parallel to load

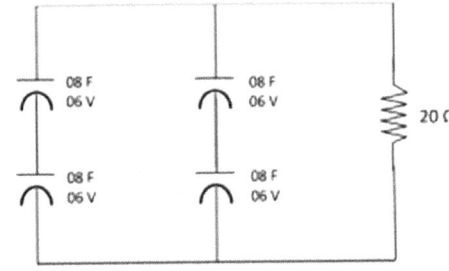

2.3

After 2.2 configurations, all capacitors will be connected in series shown in the Fig. 10.

Equivalent capacitance will be 2 F. Energy available will be 144 J   (21)

Time constant of the circuit will be $(R \times C) = 20 \times 2 = 40$ s.   (22)

Time required for reducing capacitor voltage to 6 V will be $t_3 = 27.7$ s.   (23)

Then energy supplied to load in 27.7 s. will be

$$E = 7.2 \int_0^{27.7} e^{-2t/40} dt = 107.98 \, J \tag{24}$$

Figure 11 shows the graphical representation of voltage with respect to time in above case.

In operation described in 2.3, load is disconnected at load voltage becomes 6 V. Again energy remains in capacitor will be

$$2304 - 1727.83 - 431.99 - 107.98 = 36.29 \, J \tag{25}$$

This 36.29 J cannot be utilized by load due to load voltage limit.

Time required for 100% energy supplied will be $4 \times 20 \times 2 = 160$ s.   (26)

Fig. 10 Circuit diagram of four capacitors in series with load

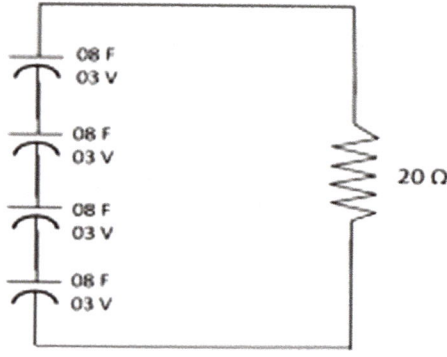

Fig. 11 Graphical representation of voltage with respect to time

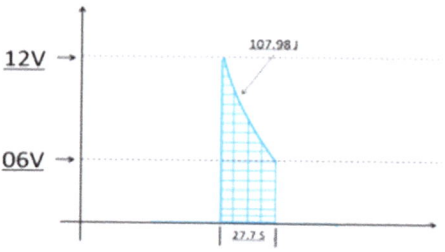

Fig. 12 Graphical representation of voltage with respect to time

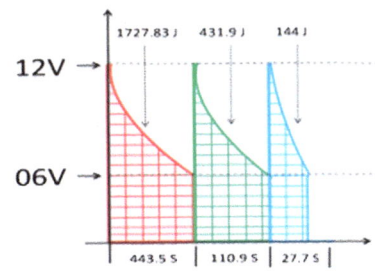

2.4

From 2.1, 2.2, and 2.3

$$\text{Total time} = 443.5 + 110.9 + 27.7 = 582.2\,\text{s}. \tag{27}$$

$$\text{Total Energy supplied to load in } V_L > 6\,\text{V is } 1727 + 431.9 + 107.98 = 2267.71\,\text{J} \tag{28}$$

$$\text{Percentage of energy supplied to load in } V_L > 6\,\text{V is} \left(\frac{2267.71}{2304}\right) \times 100 = 98.42\% \tag{29}$$

$$\text{Percentage of time utilized} \left(\frac{582.2}{2560} \times 100\right) = 22.73\% \tag{30}$$

$$\text{Total time consumed for } 100\% \text{ energy drained is } 443.5 + 110.9 + 160 = 714.4\,\text{s}. \tag{31}$$

Figure 12 shows the variation of voltage in 2.1, 2.2, and 2.3.

4 Case-3

In this case, 4F capacitance 12 V pre-charge capacitor is used. The connections are discussed in 3.1, 3.2, and 3.3.

3.1

Charged capacitors are connected in parallel to load up to load voltage becomes 6 V as shown in circuit diagram (Fig. 13).

From Eq. (7) $t_1 = 443.52$ s. From Eq. (8) energy supplied to load in 443.52 s will be 1727.83 J. Refer Fig. 3. During this period energy supplied to load is 1727.83 J from Eq. (8). Time required is 443.5 s. From Eq. (7) energy remains in

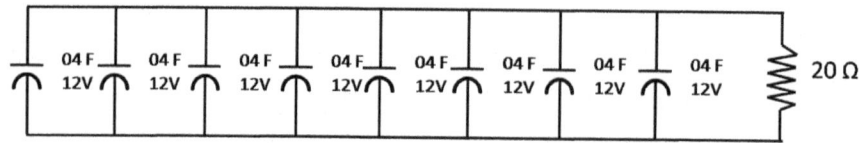

Fig. 13 Circuit diagram of eight capacitors connected parallel with load

capacitor will be 576.17 J from Eq. (9). Remaining 576.17 J can be utilized by connecting capacitors in connection discussed in 3.2.

3.2

After 3.1 configurations connection will be changed as shown in Fig. 14.

Equivalent capacitance will be 8F. Energy available will be $\text{Enc} = \frac{1}{2} C V^2 = 576 \, \text{J}$.

Time constant of the circuit will be $(R \times C) = 20 \times 8 = 160$ s. From Eq. (12) time required for reducing capacitor voltage from 12 to 6 V will be $t_2 = 110.9$ s. From Eq. (13) energy supplied to load in 110.9 s will be 431.99 J. Refer Fig. 6. Again energy remains in capacitor will be 144.18 J from Eq. (14). Remaining 144.18 J can be utilized by applying configuration discussed in 3.3.

Fig. 14 Circuit of two capacitors in series and connected parallel to load

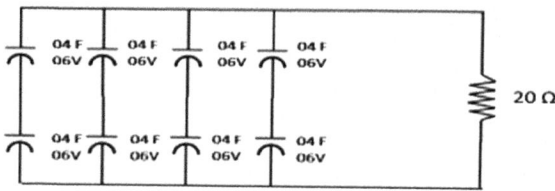

Fig. 15 Circuit of four capacitors in series and such two combinations are connected parallel to load

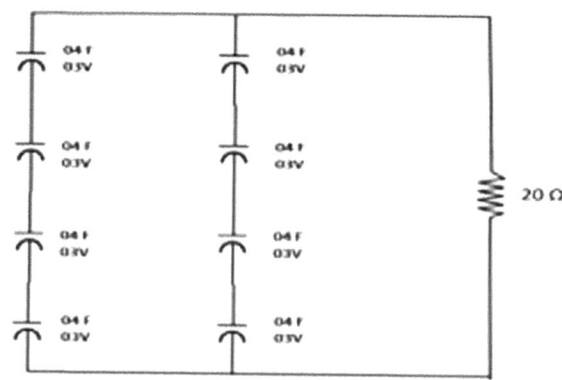

Fig. 16 Circuit of eight capacitors in series and connected parallel to load

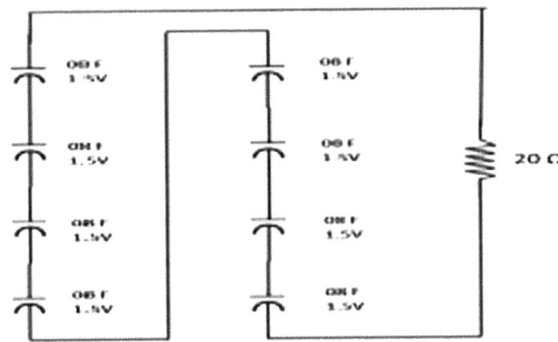

3.3

After 3.2 configurations four capacitors will be connected in series and such two branches are connected in parallel to load shown in Fig. 15.

Equivalent capacitance will be 2F. Energy available will be Enc 144 J time constant of the circuit will be 40 s. Time required for reducing capacitor voltage from 12 to 6 V will be, i.e., $t_3 = 27.7$ s. Then energy supplied to load in 27.7 s will be $E = 107.98$ J. Refer Fig. 11 by connecting capacitors in configuration as discussed in 3.4.

3.4

After 3.3 configurations connection is as shown in following circuit diagram (Fig. 16).

$$\text{Equivalent capacitance will be } 0.5\,\text{F. Energy available will be Enc} = 36\,\text{J} \quad (32)$$

$$\text{Time constant of the circuit will be } (R \times C) = 20 \times 0.5 = 10\,\text{s}. \quad (33)$$

Time required for reducing capacitor voltage from 12 to 6 V will be

$$6 = 12(e^{-t/10}),\ t_4 = 6.93\,\text{s}. \quad (34)$$

$$\text{Then energy supplied to load in 27.7 s will be } E = 7.2 \int_{0}^{6.93} e^{-2t/10} dt = 26.99\,\text{J}$$

$$(35)$$

Figure 17 shows graphical representation of voltage with respect to time in above case.

Remaining 9.3 J will be unutilized due to $V_L > V/2$ condition. Time required for 100% energy consumed will be

Fig. 17 Graphical
representation of voltage with
respect to time

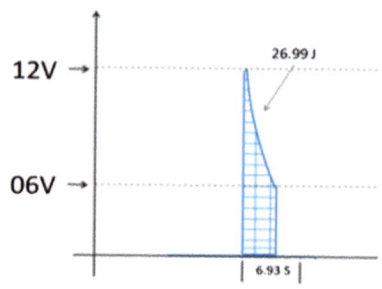

$$4 \times 20 \times 0.5 = 40\,\text{s}.\qquad(36)$$

3.5
From 3.1, 3.2, 3.3, 3.4

$$\text{Total time of discharge} = 589.09\,\text{s}.\qquad(37)$$

$$\text{Total Energy supplied to load in } V_L > 6\,\text{V is} = 2294.79\,\text{J}\qquad(38)$$

$$\text{Percentage of energy supplied to load in } V_L > 6\,\text{V is} \left(\frac{2294.79}{2304}\right) \times 100 = 99.60\%$$
$$(39)$$

$$\text{Percentage of time utilized} \left(\frac{589.09}{2560} \times 100\right) = 23.01\%\qquad(40)$$

$$\text{Total time consumed for } 100\% \text{ energy drained is} = 622.15\,\text{s}.\qquad(41)$$

Figure 18 shows the variation of voltage in 3.1, 3.2, 3.3, 3.4.

4.1
Tables 1 and 2 show consulate result obtained in all cases.

Fig. 18 Variation of voltage
with respect to time

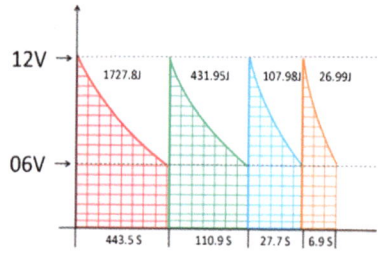

Table 1 Variation of Capacitance, Time & Energy in each case

Case	No. of capacitors used	Capacitance, time in seconds, energy supplied			
		Circuit 1	Circuit 2	Circuit 3	Circuit 4
0	01	32F, 443.5 s, 1727.83 J	NA	NA	NA
1	02	32F, 443.5 s, 1727.83 J	8F, 110.95 s, 431.99 J	NA	NA
2	04	32F, 443.5 s, 1727.83 J	8F, 110.95 s, 431.99 J	2F, 27.7 s, 107.98 J	NA
3	08	32F, 443.5 s, 1727.83 J	8F, 110.95 s, 431.99 J	2F, 27.7 s, 107.98 J	0.5F, 6.93 s, 26.99 J

Table 2 Energy supplied to load, Percentage of energy supplied to load, Percentage of time utilise, percentage of faster operation

Case	No. of capacitors used	Total energy supplied to load during Vl > 6 V (J)	% of energy supplied to load during Vl > 6 V (%)	% of time utilized by load during Vl > 6 V (%)	% of faster operation (%)
0	01	1727.83	74.81	17.32	00.00
1	02	2159.7	93.73	21.65	57.67
2	04	2267.71	98.42	22.73	72.09
3	08	2294.79	99.60	23.01	75.68

5 Conclusion

Series–parallel reconnections lead to faster processes during exchange of energy in case of multiple capacitors. It deserves attention for applying to industrial system. In industrial applications for ride-through applications in drives, and applications as short duration UPS, super capacitor banks are used. It is necessary work on prototypes', to conclude the quantitative advantages of the proposed scheme, when implemented for real-life strategic applications. Super capacitor is used for driving load with above proposed method. It is conforming that basic case to case-3 percentage of energy supplied to load during Vl > 6 V is increasing, i.e., (74.81–99.60%). Percentage of time utilized by load during Vl > 6 V is also increasing order, i.e., (17.32–23.01%), and operation will become more faster as case goes on increasing, i.e., (57.67–75.68%).

References

1. Kotsopoulos, A., Duarte, J.L., Hendlix, M.A.M.: A converter to interface ultra-capacitor energy storage to a fuel cell system. Dept. of Electrical Engineering, Technical University of Eindhoven. The Netherlands, IEEE, 4–7 May, vol. 2, pp. 827–832 (2004)
2. Chan, M.S.W., Chau, K.T., Chan, C.C.: Effective charging method for ultra capacitors. J. Asian Electric Vehicles 3(2), 771–776 (2005)
3. Chen, B.Y., Lai, Y.S.: New digital-controlled technique for battery charger with constant current and voltage control without current feedback. IEEE Trans. Ind. Electron. 59(3), 1545–1553 (2012)
4. Jeong, I.W., Kim, L.S., Guse, G.I., Rim, G.M.: Design of 35 kJ/s 25 kV capacitor charging power supply for pulsed power systems. In: IEEE Conference of the IEEE Industrial Electronics Society Busan, Korea, vol. 3, pp. 2860–2863, 2–6 Nov 2004
5. Shin, D., Kim, Y., Seo, J., Chang, N.: Battery-super capacitor hybrid system for high-rate pulsed load applications. In: EDAA, pp. 1–4, 14–18 Mar 2011
6. Sawarkar, P.R., Tarnekar, S.G., Bodkhe, S.B.: Improvement in energy transactions in ultra capacitor banks by series/parallel re-connection. Int. J. Electr. Eng. 5(5), 641–652 (2012)
7. Sawarkar, P.R.: Reduction in charging current of super capacitor by series parallel connection. Int. J. Innov. Sci. Eng. Technol. 2(4), 1015–1020 (2015)

Design and Simulation of OTA Using 45 nm Technology

Amit Sharma, Sansar Chand and Navneet Gill

Abstract OTA is very popular in electronics industry due to its large number of applications. Double gate MOSFETs are strong contenders for nanoscale region due to its better control over SCEs. In this paper, emphasis is to design low power, better phase margin OTA using double gate MOSFETs. The simulations are done at 45 nm technology.

Keywords Analog tunable circuits · Gain · Low supply voltage
Phase margin · DG MOSFETs · OTA

1 Introduction

Electronics devices based on silicon is large as like—laptops, palmtops, cellular, and many more. Due to great dealing out of silicon-based devices, silicon has made system on chip possible. A low power and voltage design to recompense increasing number of devices on chip is aimed. With the breach of 90 nm, silicon industry has moved to nanoarea to according to ITRS [1]. There are number of problems arises due scaling in conventional bulk CMOS device like SCE's [2, 3], threshold voltage, non-scaling of vertical dimensions. These problems degrade the performance and

A. Sharma (✉)
C.Sc. Department, DAV College, Jalandhar, India
e-mail: amit.hvengg@gmail.com

S. Chand · N. Gill
ECE Department, CT Institutions, Jalandhar, India
e-mail: sumisansar@gmail.com

N. Gill
e-mail: pallnavneet5@gmail.com

© Springer Nature Singapore Pte Ltd. 2018
S. K. Muttoo (ed.), *System and Architecture*, Advances in Intelligent Systems
and Computing 732, https://doi.org/10.1007/978-981-10-8533-8_4

Fig. 1 P-type and N-type double gate MOSFETs symbols

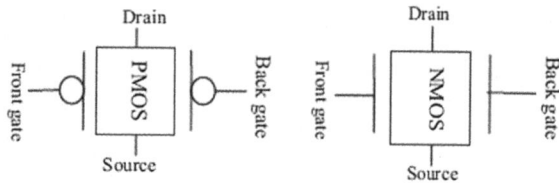

reliability of the circuits. Double Gate MOSFETs are promising devices due to better scalability in nanocircuits. With scaling down, V_{dd} and V_{gs} also decreases. It allows working in subthreshold region with increased transconductance g_m [4]. Double Gate MOSFETs have lower junction leakage and SCE's due to improved electrostatic gate control of the back gate [5]. They are also suitable for analog RF devices because of capability to handle gigahertz frequency range. By tuning of back gate, better characteristics in area, power dissipation, and speed [6] can be achieved in independent-driven mode [IDDG]. In IDDG mode two gates are separately biased. The symmetrically-driven mode (SDDG) is used in digital applications due to better I_{on}/I_{off} ratio [7]. The circuit symbols for P-type and N-type double gate MOSFETs are shown in Fig. 1. In this paper, the basic device structure using DG MOSFETs is represented, where back gate is used for the tuned circuit performance. A low power and high gain of OTA at 45 nm is designed using double gate MOSFETs. The simulations are done using spice tool.

2 Device Structure and Features

The double gates can work in two modes symmetrically-driven [SDDG] and independently driven-mode [IDDG]. The gate length is 45 nm. The device structure is shown in Fig. 2. Front and back gates are connected in the symmetrically driven mode and for analog tunable circuits. The front and back gates are biased at different voltages to achieve desired characteristics of device. The symmetrical-driven mode is better than independently-driven mode [IDDG] as discussed in [8–10].

Fig. 2 Symmetrically (SDDG) and independently-driven (IDDG) double-gate MOSFET

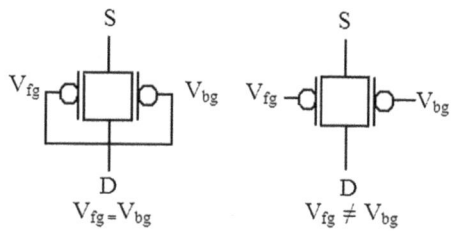

3 Operational Transconductance Amplifier

Figure 3c shows OTA-based double gate MOSFETs. The reported OTA works in independently-driven mode and shows very less gain [11]. With decreasing gate length, the channel mobility is degraded. Even for shorter channel length, output conductance is increased which will the affect the gain of OTA. The objective of OTA designed is to improve gain at 45 nm technology. Tanner EDA tool version 13.0 at 45 nm CMOS has been used for phase response, transient, and AC analysis. Existing OTA circuit works at supply voltage of V_{DD} equals to 1.16 V and V_{SS} equals to -1.16 V, respectively. The bandwidth is measured as difference between upper and lower frequency at -3 dB down from maximum gain of the circuit.

Fig. 3 **a** Block diagram of OTA, **b** symbol of OTA, **c** OTA-based double gate MOSFETs

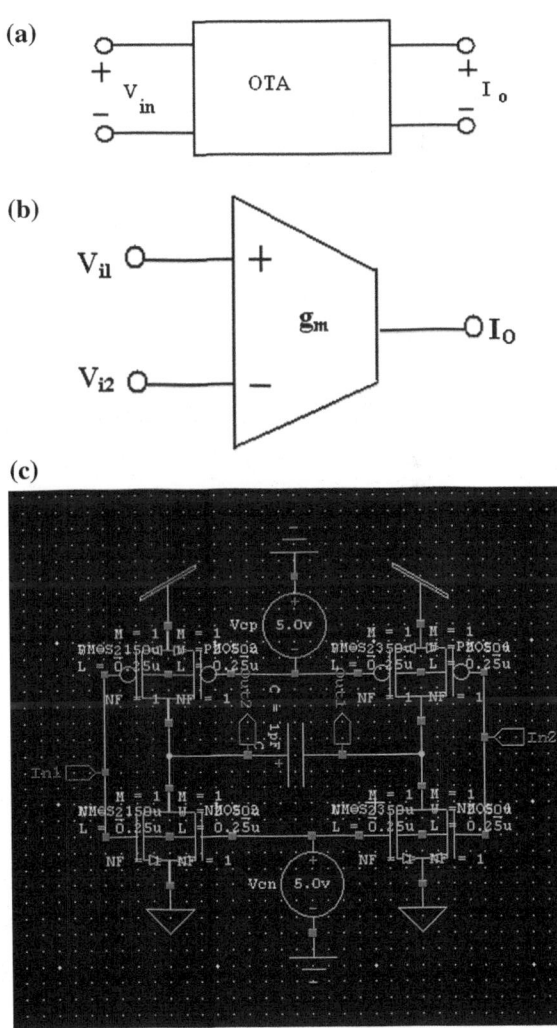

As frequency increases, the gain is decreased due to capacitive affects at high frequencies. The open loop gain is function of frequency and shown in equation:

$$A_{\mathrm{OL}}(f) = \frac{A}{\sqrt{1 + \left(\frac{f}{f_o}\right)^2}} \qquad (1)$$

where A is internal gain and f, f_o are operating frequency and cutoff frequency, respectively. The block diagram and circuit symbol is shown in Fig. 3a, b, respectively. The open loop gain of existing circuit is observed as 2.6 dB (Fig. 4).

The OTA designed works in independently-driven mode. The input V_{in1} and V_{in2} are given at back gates through inverters which are also made of double gate MOSFETs. It is an established fact that transconductance (Gm) of the input stage transistors can be changed either by altering the biasing current of the input transistors or by varying the size of the input transistors. Differential currents flow and charge a load capacitor of 0.1 fF. The load transistors act as active PMOS which

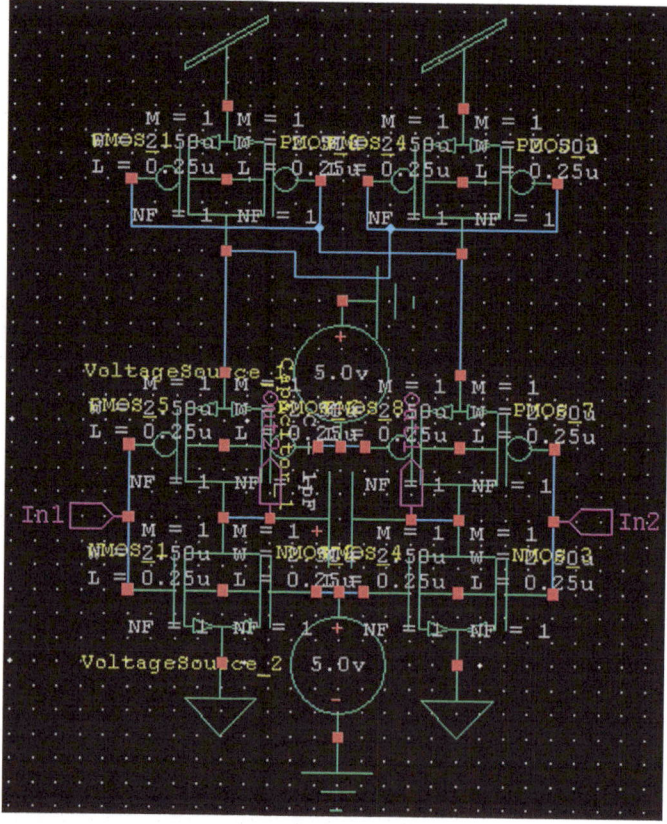

Fig. 4 Proposed OTA-based double gate MOSFETs

gives positive feedback to the circuit and increase the gain of circuit. The designed amplifier exhibits a positive feedback property. The upper transistor provides positive feedback to circuit which will increase the gain of circuit. The proposed OTA works in IDDG, i.e., independently-driven mode.

3.1 Results

The simulations are done at V_{dd} of 0.92 V and biasing at back gates is $V_{cn} = -V_{cp} = 0.1$ V. The gain is 4.85 dB as shown in Fig. 5a (Tables 1 and 2).

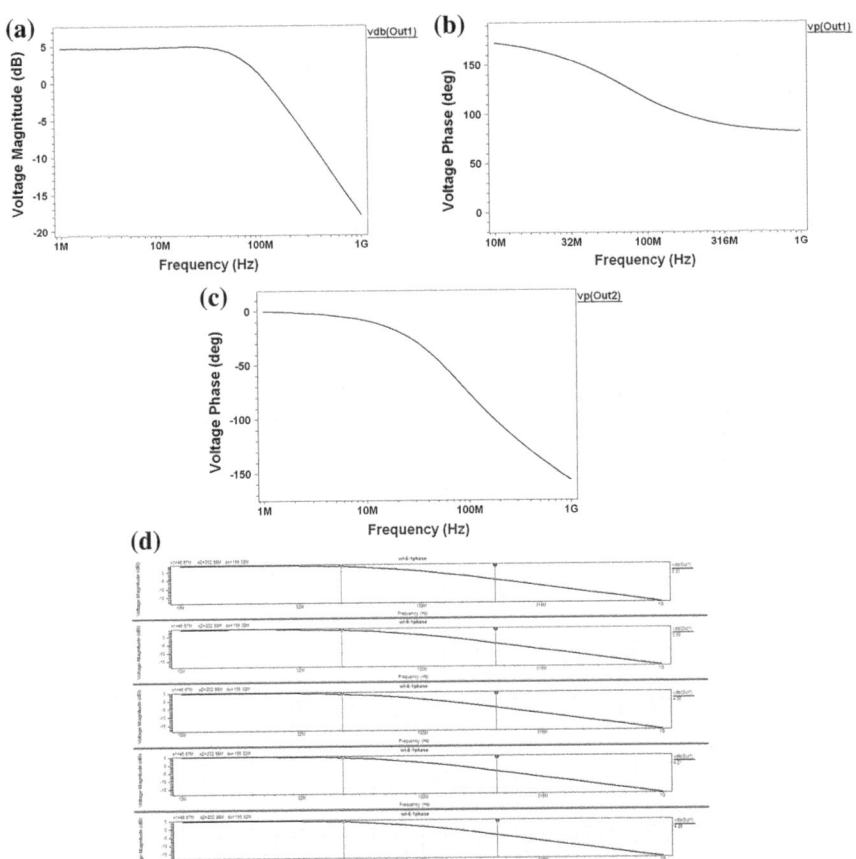

Fig. 5 **a** Differential gain of OTA, **b** phase response for input1, **c** phase response for input2, **d** gain at different temperatures

Table 1 Different parameters

Parameters	Existing OTA	Proposed OTA
C_L (fF)	0.1	0.1
Phase margin	60°	72°
Supply voltage (V)	1.16	0.92
Bandwidth (−3 db) (GHz)	0.3	0.09

Table 2 Gain at different temperatures

Temperature	Proposed OTA (Gain)
−20	3.31
−10	3.68
0	4.0
10	4.21
20	4.26

4 Conclusion

This paper shows appropriateness of double gate MOSFETs for designing of analog circuits like OTA and filters. The designed OTA shows high gain, low power dissipation. The circuit is suitable for high-frequency applications and high gain. The proposed circuit is suitable for designing analog filters consists of OTA and capacitor which are also called as integrators. As the temperature increases, the gain increases due phonon and scattering effects at higher temperature. Using double gates, further phase margin, temperature variation, and bandwidth will be explored in future.

References

1. International Technology Roadmap for Semiconductor (ITRS), WO I Version
2. Yu, B., Wang, H., Joshi, A., Xiang, Q., Ibok, E., Lin, M.-R.: 15-nm gate length planar CMOS transistor. In: Tech. Dig. IEDM, p. 937 (2001)
3. Taur, Y.: JEEE SpectruIII, vol. 36, no. 7, pp. 25–29 (1999)
4. Tosaka, T., Suzuki, K., Horie, H., Sugii, T.: Scaling parameter dependent model for sub-threshold swing S in double-gate SOI MOSFET's. IEEE Electron Device Lett. **15**(11), 466–468 (1994)
5. Wong, H.-S.P.: Beyond the conventional MOSFET. In: Proceedings of 31st European Solid-State Device Research Conference, p. 69 (2001)
6. Razavi, B.: Design of Analog CMOS Amplifier (2001)
7. Reddy, M.V.R., Sharma, D.K., Patil, M.B., Rao, V.R.: Power-area evaluation of various double-gate RF mixer topologies. IEEE Electron Devices Lett. **26**, 664 (2005)
8. Masahara, M., et al.: Demonstration, analysis, and device design considerations for independent DG MOSFETs. IEEE Trans. Electron Dev. **52**(9), 2046–2053 (2005)

9. Roy, K., Mahmoodi, H., Mukhopadhyay, S., Ananthan, H., Bansal, A., Cakici, T.: Double-Gate SOI Devices for Low-Power and High-Performance Applications. Department of Electrical and Computer Engineering, Purdue University, West Lafayette, IN School of Engineering, San Francisco State University (2005)
10. Kim, K., Fossum, J.G.: Optimal Double-Gate MOSFETs: Symmetrical or Asymmetrical Gates? IEEE (1999)
11. Kushwah, R.S., Akashe, S.: Design and analysis of tunable analog circuit using double gate MOSFET at 45 nm CMOS technology. IEEE (2013)

Design and Analysis of Microstrip Patch Antenna Using DRAF

Lohini Walia, Gaurav Walia and Umesh Pal Singh

Abstract In order to serve the users of the wireless band, a new fractal shape dual-reverse-arrow fractal is introduced in this paper. This geometry is applied at the Microstrip Patch Antenna in order to obtain the multiband and miniaturized antenna. For the sake of simplicity, the patch chosen is an equatorial triangular patch. In this paper, the design of the two triangular patches are designed with the side lengths of $a = 25$ mm and $a = 30$ mm. On the basis of antenna's performance characteristics, a comparable analysis is obtained for both the patch antennas. The results after simulation using the software HFSS demonstrates that both the designed antennas depict relatively good radiation pattern as compared to conventional antennas.

Keywords Dual-reverse-arrow fractal (DRAF) · HFSS software
Koch fractal curve · Microstrip patch · Triangular patch

L. Walia (✉)
Department of Electronics and Communication Engineering,
Seth Jai Parkash Mukand Lal Institute of Engineering and Technology,
Radaur, India
e-mail: mlohiniwalia77@gmail.com

G. Walia
Ambala College of Engineering and Applied Research, Near Mithapur,
Phalail Majra, India
e-mail: gaurav_isf@rediffmail.com

U. P. Singh
Department of Physics, Seth Jai Parkash Mukand Lal Iinstitute of Engineering
and Technology, Radaur, India
e-mail: dr.umeshsingh@jmit.ac.in

© Springer Nature Singapore Pte Ltd. 2018
S. K. Muttoo (ed.), *System and Architecture*, Advances in Intelligent Systems
and Computing 732, https://doi.org/10.1007/978-981-10-8533-8_5

1 Introduction

The wireless band is getting hectic day by day, and it is the well-known issue which has to be solved in order to serve number of users using wireless band. To serve the users, it is not only an issue to design the antenna but to design an antenna with low profile and good electric strength is also a challenge for antenna designers. Also if one wants to serve a large number of users an ultra-wide band frequency ranges are required. The work proposed in this paper provides ultra-wide bandwidth since the modern telecommunication system requires antennas with wider bandwidth and smaller dimensions than conventionally possible [1]. This demand leads the researchers to use different fractal shapes. Here in this paper, new fractal geometry dual-reverse-arrow-fractal is used. This geometry is introduced by Homayoon and Hadi in the year 2014 for the first time. They used this geometry in order to achieve a miniaturized patch. Fractals are basically nature-inspired shapes which can be referred to as space-filling contours, meaning electrically large features can be efficiently packed into small areas [2]. Here in this paper, the dual arrow fractal approach is used to design the Microstrip Patch Antenna and the patch chosen is a triangular patch with the all sides equal. The two designed patches have the side lengths $a = 25$ mm and $a = 30$ mm, on these patches, the fractal curve is applied in order to obtain the higher iterations which results in multiband antennas in order to serve number of users.

2 Antenna Design

Here in this section, the Microstrip Patch Antenna with triangular patch having side length $a = 25$ is designed firstly and then with $a = 30$ mm the antenna is designed. Both the antennas are designed using the software named HFSS (High Frequency Selective structure), and the results are also simulated using the same software.

2.1 Design of Microstrip Triangular Patch Antenna with Side Length a = 25 mm

The design starts with the construction of a simple triangular patch having the side length $a = 25$ mm. Here to design the Microstrip Antenna, FR4 substrate is used in order to differentiate the two conducting planes that are the ground and the patch.

Fig. 1 Geometrical
construction of the 0th
iteration for triangular patch
with side length *a* = 25 mm

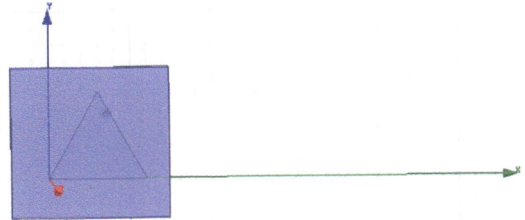

While designing the antenna, it is cured that antenna size should be less than $\lambda/4$ (λ is wave length) so that the antenna can work efficiently because if this is not cured then the radiation resistance, gain, and bandwidth is reduced, and therefore antenna size is increased [1]. Figure 1 shows the geometrical construction of the Microstrip Triangular Patch Antenna with side length *a* = 25 mm.

In order to obtain the first iteration, the dual-reverse-arrow fractal is applied at the each side of the patch. A structure shown in Fig. 2 will be inserted in the each side of the triangular patch. This structure is so obtained by combining the inward and outward Koch. The dimensions at which this structure is added in the triangle are calculated by using the simple mathematics.

In order to find the side length of the new triangle, the side length *a* = 25 mm is divided into three equal parts, that is, 8.33 mm. Now, the middle part is again divided into the three parts having new triangle side length 5.4 mm and the parameters *L1*, *L2*, *h*, and *k* represent the one-third part of the whole side length, length of the new triangle, height of the inward and outward triangle to be inserted as DRAF, and half the length of the new triangle or the point at which horizontal and vertical sections inclined, respectively.

Figure 3 represents the basic geometrical construction of the first iteration for triangular patch with side length *a* = 25 mm. Here the new inward and outward Koch triangles are also equatorial triangles. The parameters *l1*, *l2*, *h*, *k* are given by

Fig. 2 DRAF to be added in
each side of the triangle [3]

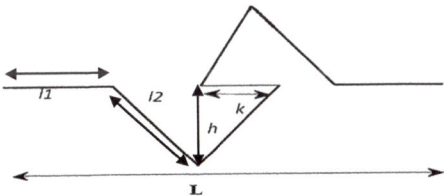

Fig. 3 Geometrical
construction of the 1st
iteration for triangular patch
with side length $a = 25$ mm

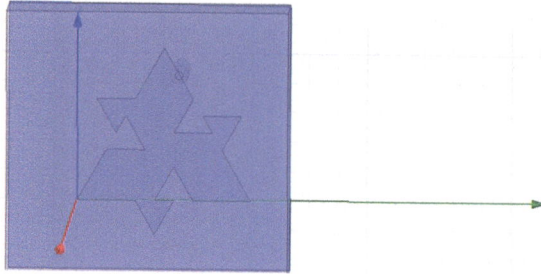

Fig. 4 Geometrical
construction of the 2nd
iteration for triangular patch
with side length $a = 25$ mm

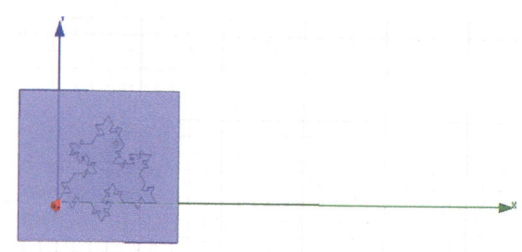

8.3 mm, 5.4 mm, 4.68 mm, and 2.7 mm. Thus, the new side length of the triangleis 5.4 mm. The height of the triangle is calculated by using the formula for height of an equatorial triangle.

Now, the second iteration can be designed in the similar way. The new parameters of the fractal that are $l3 = 1.8$ mm, $l4 = 1.2$ mm, $h1 = 1.03$, $k1 = 0.6$ mm, and $l5 = 0.9$ mm, $l6 = 0.6$ mm, $h2 = 0.51$ mm, $k2 = 0.3$ mm are to be replaced by the parameters $l1$, $l2$, h, and k in Fig. 2. These new defined parameters are added within the side length of the 5.4 mm and 2.7 mm, respectively, of the iteration so that further second iteration can be achieved. Figure 4 represents the geometrical construction of the second iteration for triangular patch with side length $a = 25$ mm.

2.2 Design of Microstrip Triangular Patch Antenna with Side Length a = 30 mm

The three geometrical constructions can be achieved by following the same way as discussed above. Here again the design will start by fragmenting the side length 30 mm into three equal parts, that is, 10 mm each. The new parameters for the

Fig. 5 Geometrical
construction of the 1st
iteration for triangular patch
with side length $a = 30$ mm

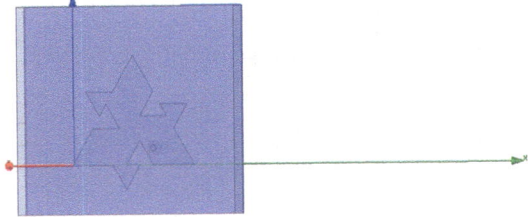

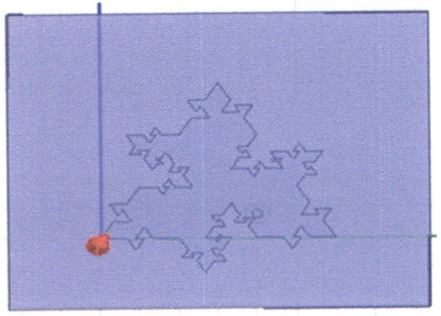

Fig. 6 Geometrical construction of the 2nd iteration for triangular patch with side length
$a = 30$ mm

inward and outward Koch triangles which are to be added now within the side
length of 10, 6.67, and 3.33 mm are given by $l1 = 10$ mm, $l2 = 6.67$ mm,
$h = 5.78$ mm, $k = 3.33$ mm; $l3 = 2.2$ mm, $l4 = 1.48$ mm, $h1 = 1.2$, $k1 = 0.6$ mm,
and $l5 = 1.1$ mm, $l6 = 0.74$ mm, $h2 = 0.64$ mm, $k2 = 0.37$ mm, respectively
(Figs. 5 and 6).

3 Simulated Results

The results are simulated using the software HFSS. Figures 7, 8 and 9 represents
the frequency for zeroth, first, and second iteration of the antenna with patch side
length $a = 25$ mm and Figs. 10, 11 and 12 depicts the 3D polar plots in terms of
radiation pattern. Similarly, the graphs can be obtained for patch with the side
length $a = 30$ mm.

Tables 1 and 2 show various simulated values in terms of resonant frequencies,
bandwidth, gain, and return losses for the antenna with patch side length
$a = 25$ mm and with patch side length $a = 30$ mm, respectively.

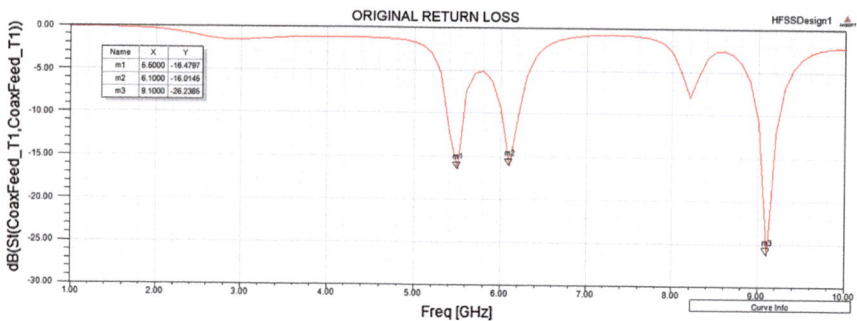

Fig. 7 Frequency response for 0th iteration of the antenna with patch side length $a = 25$ mm

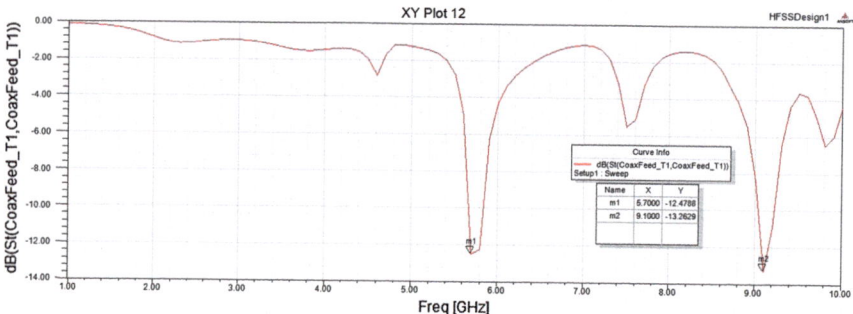

Fig. 8 Frequency response for 1st iteration of the antenna with patch side length $a = 25$ mm

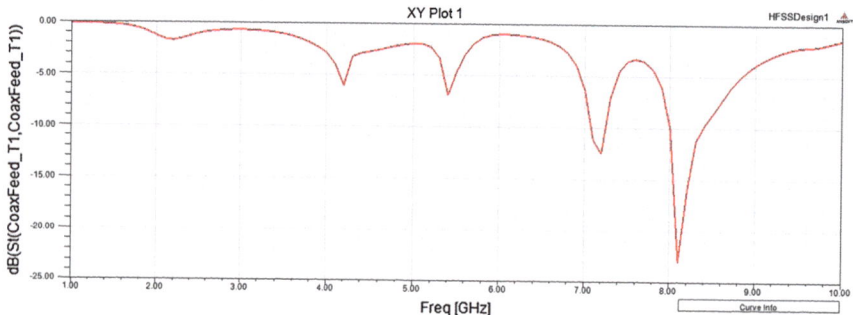

Fig. 9 Frequency response for 2nd iteration of the antenna with patch side length $a = 25$ mm

Fig. 10 3D polar plot for 0th iteration of the antenna with patch side length $a = 25$ mm

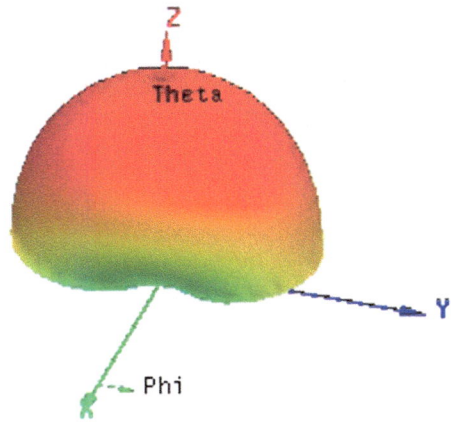

Fig. 11 3D polar plot for 1st iteration of the antenna with patch side length $a = 25$ mm

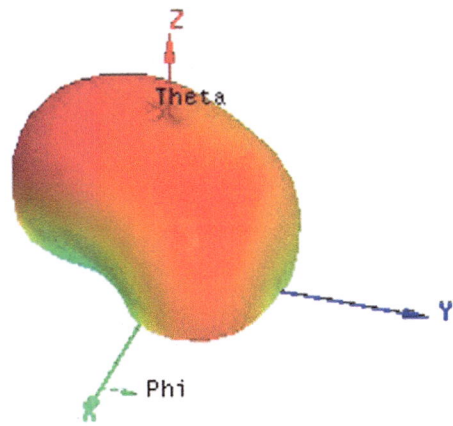

Fig. 12 3D polar plot for 2nd iteration of the antenna with patch side length $a = 25$ mm

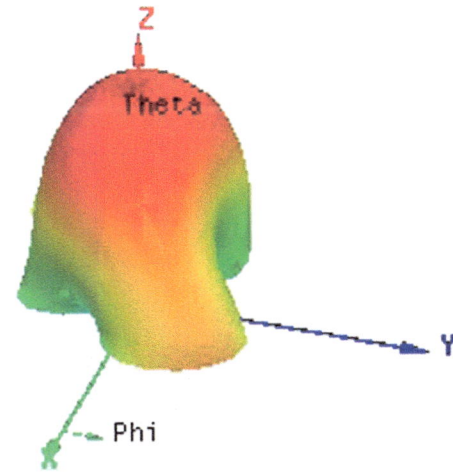

Table 1 Simulated results for the antenna with patch side length $a = 25$ mm

Iteration	S_{11} (–)	Resonating frequency (GHz)	Bandwidth (MHz)	Gain (dB)
0th	16.4, 16, 26	5.5, 6.1, 9	204.9, 187.9, 256.2	2.6
1st	12.4, 13.3	5.7, 9.1	162.2, 179.3	0.2
2nd	12, 22	7.2, 8.1	162.2, 330.6	3.1

Table 2 Simulated results for the antenna with patch side length $a = 30$ mm [3]

Iteration	S_{11} (–)	Resonating frequency (GHz)	Bandwidth (MHz)	Gain (dB)
0th	17, 21, 17	5.8, 8.3, 9	189, 256.2, 239.1	4.1
1st	17, 18, 22	4.7, 5.9, 9.3	281.8, 153.7, 529.4	0.8
2nd	18.2, 20.5, 16.3	4.3, 5.6, 7.1	159.4, 159.4, 250.5	1.5

The two tables consist of the antenna's performance characteristics such as S_{11}, bandwidth, resonating frequencies, gain. The two antennas can be compared on the basis of these two tables.

4 Conclusion

Here the two Microstrip Triangular Patch Antennas are designed with the side length of the patches $a = 25$ mm and $a = 30$ mm. Both the designed antennas are multiband that means these have more than one resonating/operating frequency. The first- and second-order iterations are obtained by applying DRAF at the each side of the patch. The antenna with patch length $a = 25$ mm resonates at the frequency band of 5.5–9.1 GHz, and the antenna with patch length $a = 30$ mm resonates at the frequency band of 4.7–9.3 GHz. Thus, the two antennas covers the ultra-wide band frequency ranges and can be used for the various interesting applications such as Wimax, WLAN, Satellite and radar applications, RLAN and in UAVs. The two proposed antennas show relatively good radiation intensity as well as high gain is obtained for the zeroth and second iteration of both the antennas. The return losses are also less as compared to the conventional antennas which are obtained by putting air gap substrate. Thus, the geometry is also not so much complex.

Acknowledgements Authors are highly grateful to the Director and Management of their respective institutes.

References

1. Azari, A., Rowhani, J.: Ultra wideband fractal microstrip antenna design. Prog. Electromagnet. Res. C **2**, 7–12 (2008)
2. Gianviff, J.P., Rahmat-Samii, Y.: A novel antenna miniaturization technique and application. IEEE Antenna's Propag. Mag. **44**(1) (2002)
3. Walia, L., Walia, G., Singh, U.P.: Design and analysis of square patch antenna using DRAF. IJRMST **3**(3) (2015)

Principal Component Analysis-Based Block Diagonalization Precoding Algorithm for MU-MIMO System

S. B. M. Priya and P. Kumar

Abstract This paper designs a new paradigm for the performance improvement in block diagonalization (BD)-based precoding algorithms for multiple-user MIMO (MU-MIMO) systems. Even though various linear precoding algorithms have been found, they are complicated in terms of receiver architecture with decoder. In order to simplify the user equipment (UE), it is necessary to design a receiver without decoder. This is consummated using principal component analysis (PCA). The PCA along with QR decomposition and minimum mean squared error (MMSE) channel inversion helps in performance improvement and avoids the decoder at the receiver system. The principal component is calculated using QR decomposition instead of traditional singular value decomposition (SVD) decomposition to reduce the computational complexity. The simulation result shows that PCA-based precoding algorithm in comparison with the existing algorithm achieves comparatively better sum rate, lower bit error rate (BER) using a simplified receiver.

Keywords BD · Lattice reduction (LR) · MMSE · MU-MIMO · PCA
Precoding · QR decomposition · Regularized block diagonalization (RBD)
Singular value decomposition (SVD)

1 Introduction

The Multiple-Input Multiple-Output (MIMO) has its own powerful performance-enhancing capability in wireless communication over the past decade [1–4]. The multiple transmit and receive antennas help in achieving significant performance

S. B. M. Priya (✉)
JJ College of Engineering and Technology, Tiruchirappalli, Tamil Nadu, India
e-mail: sbmpriya@gmail.com

P. Kumar
Department of Electronics and Communication Engineering, K S Rangasamy College
of Technology, Tiruchengode, Namakkal, Tamil Nadu, India
e-mail: kumar@ksrct.ac.in

© Springer Nature Singapore Pte Ltd. 2018
S. K. Muttoo (ed.), *System and Architecture*, Advances in Intelligent Systems
and Computing 732, https://doi.org/10.1007/978-981-10-8533-8_6

gain such as array gain, spatial diversity gain, spatial multiplexing gain by exploiting multipath fading. Recently, the researchers have focused toward MU-MIMO systems. By the spatial sharing of channel by multiple users, the MU-MIMO leads huge capacity gain over the single-user MIMO (SU-MIMO) systems [5, 6]. But unlike the SU-MIMO, it suffers from multiuser interference (MUI) along with the noise.

The precoding strategies are classified as linear and nonlinear precoding. The linear precoding algorithm or the channel inversion (CI) algorithm such as zero forcing (ZF) [7] and minimum mean squared error (MMSE) precoding can be used to cancel out MUI with reduced sum rate. The nonlinear precoding algorithms such as Dirty Paper Coding (DPC) [8] and Tomlinson–Harashima Precoding (THP) [9, 10] mitigate the MUI with high sum rate with increased complexity at transmitter and receiver compared with linear strategy.

As far as linear precoding algorithm is concerned, the generalized ZF block diagonalization (BD) [11] can be used for sum-rate maximization. But the BD shows poor performance when the noise is a dominant factor. To overcome this regularized block diagonalization (RBD) [12] with regularization factor for the noise has been proposed. As far as the algorithm implementation is concerned, the above two methods show increase in complexity for increase in number of users due to the two SVD operations involved in precoding filter computations. And the decoder adds additional computational overhead for the receiver. It can be overcome by replacing the complex SVD using any equivalent low complex matrix decomposition operations. The work on [13] implements generalized ZF channel inversion (GZI) and generalized MMSE channel inversion (GMI) algorithm which replaces first SVD operation by low complex QR decomposition. It shows less computational complexity when compared with the BD algorithm. Though the complexity is reduced in [13], the second SVD and decoder retain as in [11, 12]. It is overcome by the work [14] which devises a new algorithm LR-S-GMI-MMSE based on lattice reduction (LR). After the MUI suppression in [13], the channel gain is compressed using LR and the equivalent SU-MIMO channel is determined. Even though LR-S-GMI-MMSE results in considerable BER and sum-rate performance, the system computational complexity increases when the system dimension increases. So it is necessary to find a model order reduction algorithm which yields low complexity than LR.

In this paper, a high-performance precoding algorithm based on PCA [15] is proposed. The PCA is a simple, nonparametric method of extracting relevant information from complicated data sets [16]. A precoding filter which suppresses MUI is developed first. The resultant channel matrix is transformed into PCA vector basis. Finally, the MMSE channel inversion is applied to regulate each user's individual streams.

1.1 Organization

The paper is organized as follows. The MU-MIMO system model is detailed in Sect. 2. The proposed PCA-based precoding algorithm is presented in Sect. 3. The numerical result which depicts the performance of proposed algorithm is shown in Sect. 4. Finally, the paper is concluded in Sect. 5.

1.2 Notation

The vectors and matrices are denoted by boldface lower and uppercase letters. The inverse, pseudoinverse, transpose, and Hermitian transpose of a matrix H are denoted as H^{-1}, $H^{\dagger}$, H^{T}, H^{H}, respectively. The Frobenius norm, natural logarithm, and determinant of matrix are denoted as $\|H\|_{F}$, log (H), det (H), respectively. The symbol 'I' denotes the identity matrix, and diag $(H_1, H_2 \ldots H_k)$ denotes the block diagonal matrix.

2 MU-MIMO System Model

We consider an MU-MIMO DL model, where the BS is equipped with M transmit antennas. These M antennas simultaneously transmit over the channel H to K independent users at the receiving end and generate co-channel interference as shown in Fig. 1.

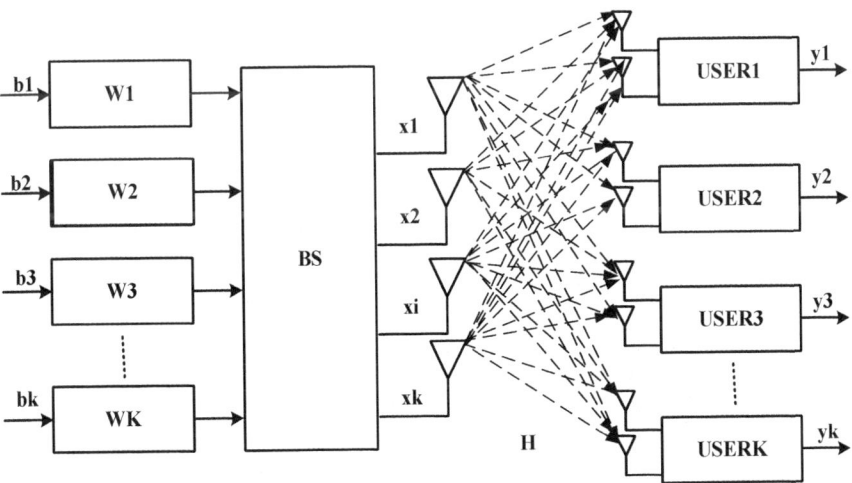

Fig. 1 MU-MIMO system model

At the receiver side, each user is equipped with N_k receive antenna. The total number of receive antennas is defined as $N = \sum_{i=1}^{K} N_k$. Let us assume independently generated data vector b, independent and identically distributed (i.i.d) zero mean, and variance σ^2 noise as n. These are expressed as:

$$b = \left[b_1^T b_2^T \ldots b_k^T\right]^T \in \mathbb{C}^{N \times 1}. \tag{1}$$

$$n = \left[n_1^T n_2^T \ldots n_k^T\right]^T \in \mathbb{C}^{N \times 1}. \tag{2}$$

The transmit data vector from BS is $x = W*b$, where the precoding matrix W is the inverse of the channel $\mathcal{H}$. If P_t is the total transmit power constraint, then $E[\| x \|^2] \leq P_t$ and $P_t \geq tr(W^H W)$. The transmit data vector from BS x is assumed to be transmitted over the flat fading channel with the channel matrix $\mathcal{H} \in \mathbb{C}^{M*N}$. These are expressed as:

$$H = \left[H_1^T H_2^T \ldots H_k^T\right]^T \in \mathbb{C}^{N \times M}. \tag{3}$$

$$W = \left[W_1^T W_2^T \ldots W_k^T\right]^T \in \mathbb{C}^{M \times N}. \tag{4}$$

The kth user channel gain and precoding matrix are represented as H_k and W_k, respectively. Finally, the received signal vector for the kth user $\tilde{y}_k$ is the summation of data vector intended for the kth user $H_k W_k b_k$, and the data vector belongs to other users $H_k \sum_{i=1, k \neq i}^{K} W_i b_i$ and the Gaussian distributed noise n_k:

$$\tilde{y}_k = H_k W_k b_k + H_k \sum_{i=1, k \neq i}^{K} W_i b_i + n_k. \tag{5}$$

The kth user receives the filtered output as written as:

$$y_k = M_k H_k W_k b_k + M_k H_k \sum_{i=1, k \neq i}^{K} W_i b_i + M_k n_k. \tag{6}$$

where M_k represents the kth user's receive decoding filter. Commonly, this additional decoding computation makes the receiver system complex.

3   Proposed PCA-Based Precoding Algorithm

In this section, the proposed PCA-MMSE-BD algorithm which employs MMSE channel inversion, QR decomposition [17], and principal component analysis is explained. The algorithm is implemented in two stages. In the first stage, a precoding matrix which suppresses MUI is defined. In the second stage, the precoding matrix which converts MU-MIMO channel into non-interfering SU-MIMO is defined using QR-PCA. The precoding matrix for the kth user is written as:

$$W_k = W_k^1 * W_k^2. \tag{7}$$

Stage1: Derive the first precoding matrix W_k^1 using QR decomposition.

Apply MMSE channel inversion on the channel matrix

$$H_{\text{mmse}}^{\dagger} = H^H \left(HH^H + \alpha I_N \right)^{-1}. \tag{8}$$

where α is the regularization factor, $\alpha = \frac{N\sigma^2}{P_t}$. The $H_{\text{mmse}}^{\dagger}$ is decomposed for individual user as:

$$H_{\text{mmse}} = [H_{1,\text{mmse}}, H_{2,\text{mmse}}, \ldots, H_{k,\text{mmse}}]. \tag{9}$$

and the kth user MMSE channel gain $H_{k,\text{mmse}}$ is designed to satisfy

$$\widetilde{H}_k H_{k,\text{mmse}} \approx 0, k = 1, 2, \ldots K. \tag{10}$$

where $\tilde{H}_k = \left[H_1^T H_2^T \ldots H_{k-1}^T H_{k+1}^T \ldots H_K^T\right]^T \in \mathbb{C}^{(N-N_k) \times M}$ is the kth user's interfering channel matrix. Decompose the $H_{k,\text{mmse}}$ using QR decomposition, we have

$$H_{k,\text{mmse}} = Q_{k,\text{mmse}} R_{k,\text{mmse}}. \tag{11}$$

where $Q_{k,\text{mmse}} \in \mathbb{C}^{M*N_k}$ is a unitary matrix and $R_{k,\text{mmse}} \in \mathbb{C}^{N_k * N_k}$ is an upper triangular matrix. Thus, (10) becomes

$$\widetilde{H}_k Q_{k,\text{mmse}} R_{k,\text{mmse}} \approx 0. \tag{12}$$

Since $R_{k,\text{mmse}}$ is invertible; (12) can be rewritten as,

$$\widetilde{H}_k Q_{k,\text{mmse}} \approx 0. \tag{13}$$

Thus, $Q_{k,\text{mmse}}$ suppresses the MUI at this stage. So the first precoding filter W_k^1 for MUI suppression is given as:

$$W_k^1 = Q_{k,\text{mmse}} \in \mathbb{C}^{M*N_k}. \tag{14}$$

Similarly, implementing the QR decomposition for K users, we get

$$W^1 = \left[W_1^{1T} W_2^{1T} \dots W_k^{1T} \right]^T \in \mathbb{C}^{M \times N}. \tag{15}$$

where W_k^1 represents the kth user's first precoding filter.

Stage 2: Derive the second precoding matrix using PCA transformation and channel inversion.

The kth user's non-interfering channel [13] is:

$$H_{\text{nint},k} = H_k W_k^1. \tag{16}$$

As defined in extended system model [18–20], the MMSE precoding is equivalent to ZF precoding of extended channel matrix. The extended non-interfering channel matrix is:

$$\underline{H}_{\text{ext},k} = \left[H_{\text{nint},k}, \sqrt{\alpha} I_{N_k} \right]^{-1}. \tag{17}$$

where $\underline{H}_{\text{ext},k} \in \mathbb{C}^{N_k \times N_k}$ and α is the regularization factor which helps to balance the MUI and noise.

For extracting the relevant information from $\underline{H}_{\text{ext}}$, we apply PCA transform. It is proved that the PCA transform can be manipulated using economic QR decomposition followed by economic SVD [21]. Before applying PCA transform, normalize the $\underline{H}_{\text{ext}}$ matrix to zero mean. Let $\underline{H}_{n\_\text{ext},k}$ be the normalized form of $\underline{H}_{\text{ext}}$, where $k = 1, 2, \dots K$. Consider $Q_{n\_\text{ext},k}$ and $R_{n\_\text{ext},k}$ are the QR decomposed matrix of $\underline{H}_{n\_\text{ext},k}$. Hence, the economic SVD of $R_{n\_\text{ext}}^H$ is computed and it results in the diagonal matrix $S_{n\_\text{ext},k} \in \mathbb{C}^{N_k, N_k}$; U and V are the complex unitary matrices, $U_{n\_\text{ext},k} \in \mathbb{C}^{2N_k, N_k}$ and $V_{n\_\text{ext},k}^T \in \mathbb{C}^{N_k, N_k}$. The principal component factor is given as:

$$PC_k = Q_{n\_\text{ext},k} * V_{n\_\text{ext},k} \in \mathbb{C}^{N_k, N_k}. \tag{18}$$

The extracted channel matrix from $\underline{H}_{n\_\text{ext},k}$ using PCA is expressed as:

$$H_{\text{pc},k} = PC_k * \underline{H}_{\text{ext},k}. \tag{19}$$

H_{pc} represents the columns of $\underline{H}_{n\_\text{ext},k}$ using the rows of PC_k. Then, the MMSE CI is obtained as:

$$W_k^2 = E H_{\text{pc},k}^H \left(H_{\text{pc},k} H_{\text{pc},k}^H \right)^{-1}. \tag{20}$$

where $E = [I_{N_k}, 0_{N_k * N_k}]$. As $EE^H = I$, it will not lead to any amplification of power in W^2 matrix. Finally, the overall second precoding matrix W^2 and overall principal component matrix PC is given by:

$$W^2 = \text{diag}\left(W_1^2, W_2^2, \ldots\ldots W_k^2\right) \text{ and } \mathbf{PC} = \text{diag}(\mathbf{PC}_1, \mathbf{PC}_2, \ldots.\mathbf{PC}_k). \qquad (21)$$

The total precoding matrix is the multiplication of W^1 and W^2 as given in (1). The received signal at the receiver is given as:

$$\tilde{y} = HWb + \sqrt{\gamma}n. \qquad (22)$$

and scaling factor $\gamma = \| Wb \|^2$. The recovered signal from the PCA vector basis is calculated by multiplying transpose of principal component with the received signal. Thus, the proposed method avoids the decoding matrix for the reconstruction of the original data. This reduces the complexity of the receiver at the user end.

4 Performance Analysis

The performance of PCA-MMSE-BD algorithm is investigated using the simulation in MATLAB. Consider a system with $M = 8$ transmit antennas and $K = 4$ users. Each user is equipped with $N_k = 2$ receive antennas. So the total number of receive antennas at the receiver is $N = K*N_k$. Assume the input data vector b is QPSK modulated and transmitted over the flat fading channel. We also assume that the BS is equipped with the perfect channel knowledge using the error-free feedback from the receiver. In the following analysis, we compare the performance of PCA-MMSE-BD with the algorithms BD with power loading (BD-PL), BD without power loading (BD-NPL), RBD, GMI, LR-S-GMI-MMSE. Figure 2 shows the sum rate of the proposed and existing algorithm. The sum rate is calculated using:

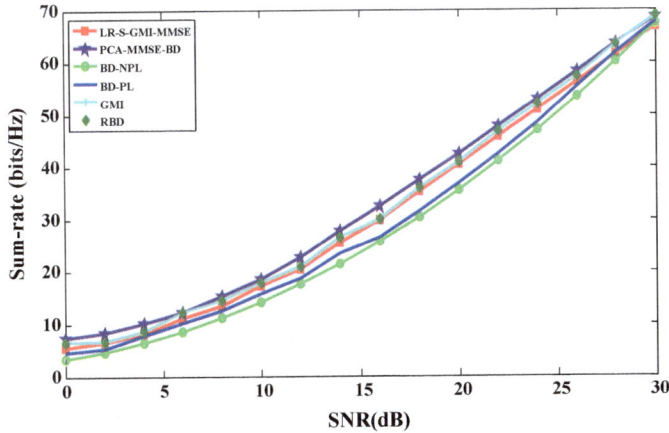

Fig. 2 Sum-rate performance for $M = 8$ and $N_k = 2$, $K = 4$, $N = 8$

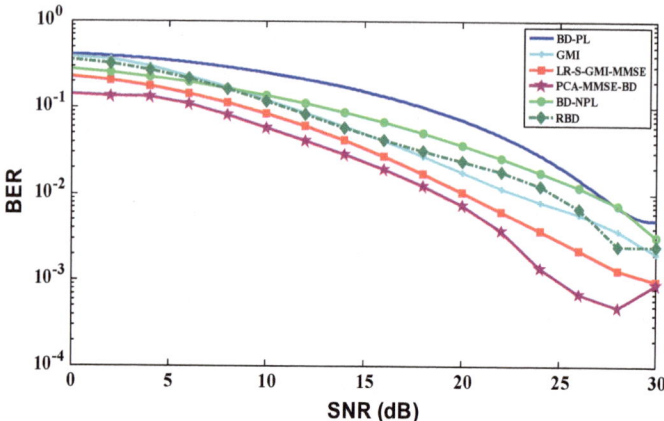

Fig. 3 BER performance for $M = 8$ and $N_k = 2$, $K = 4$, $N = 8$

$$C = \log\left(\det\left(\boldsymbol{I} + \sigma^{-2}\boldsymbol{H}\boldsymbol{W}\boldsymbol{W}^H\boldsymbol{H}^H\right)\right)\left(\frac{\text{bits}}{\text{Hz}}\right). \tag{24}$$

The performance of sum rate shows that BD-PL shows better performance than BD-NPL. But the RBD achieves more sum rate than BD-PL algorithm. The GMI and LR-S-GMI-MMSE algorithm shows almost similar performance of RBD. But the proposed PCA-MMSE-BD algorithm shows improved performance than the existing techniques. At high SNR region, the sum rate of PCA-MMSE-BD algorithm gets coincide with RBD and GMI sum rate.

The BER performance of the proposed and existing methods is shown in Fig. 3. The BD-PL shows higher BER compared to other existing algorithms. The GMI and RBD methods show almost equal BER. The LR-S-GMI-MMSE BER is lower than the above algorithms. But the proposed algorithm shows better BER performance than all other existing methods.

5   Conclusion

In this paper, the precoding algorithm for MU-MIMO based on PCA, QR decomposition, and MMSE channel inversion has been proposed. The BER, the achievable sum rate of PCA-MMSE-BD, has been analyzed and compared with the existing precoding algorithms. The performance analysis proves that the proposed algorithm results in better BER and considerable sum rate when compared with existing algorithms. The receiver without decoder makes the UE simple and less complex. As a future work, the complexity of the PCA-MMSE-BD could be analyzed in terms of floating point operations to validate the algorithm's computational efficiency.

References

1. Foschini, G.J., Gans, M.J.: On limits of wireless communications in a fading environment when using multiple antennas. Wireless Pers. Commun. **6**, 311–335 (1998)
2. Telatar, I.E.: Capacity of multi-antenna Gaussian channels. Eur. Trans. Telecommun. **10**, 585–595 (1999)
3. Paulraj, A., Nabar, R., Gore, D.: Introduction to Space-Time Wireless Communications. Cambridge University Press, Cambridge (2003)
4. Tse, D., Viswanath, P.: Fundamentals of Wireless Communications. Cambridge University Press, Cambridge (2005)
5. Vishwanath, S., Jindal, N., Goldsmith, A.: Duality, achievable rates, and sum-rate capacity of Gaussian MIMO broadcast channels. IEEE Trans. Inf. Theory **49**, 2658–2668 (2003)
6. Viswanath, P., Tse, D.N.C.: Sum capacity of the vector Gaussian broadcast channel and uplink-downlink duality. IEEE Trans. Inf. Theory **49**, 1912–1921 (2003)
7. Spencer, Q., Peel, C., Swindlehurst, A., Haardt, M.: An introduction to the multi-user MIMO downlink. IEEE Commun. Mag. **42**(10), 60–67 (2004)
8. Costa, M.: Writing on dirty paper. IEEE Trans. Inf. Theory **29**, 439–441 (1983)
9. Tomlinson, M.: New automatic equalizer employing modulo arithmetic. Electron. Lett. **7**(5), 138–139 (1971)
10. Harashima, H., Miyakawa, H.: Matched-transmission technique for channels with intersymbol interference. IEEE Trans. Commun. **20**(4), 774–780 (1972)
11. Spencer, Q.H., Swindelhurst, A.L., Haardt, M.: Zero-forcing methods for downlink spatial multiplexing in multiuser MIMO channels. IEEE Trans. Signal Process. **52**, 461–471 (2004)
12. Stankovic, V., Haardt, M.: Generalized design of multiuser MIMO precoding matrices. IEEE Trans. Wireless Commun. **7**, 953–961 (2008)
13. Sung, H., Lee, H.R., Lee, I.: Generalized channel inversion methods for multiuser MIMO systems. IEEE Trans. Commun. **57**(11), 3489–3499 (2009)
14. Zu, K., de Lamare, R.C., Haardt, M.: Generalized design of low-complexity block diagonalization type precoding algorithms for multiuser MIMO systems. IEEE Trans. Commun. **61**(10), 4232–4242 (2013)
15. Opmeer, M.R.: Model order reduction by balanced proper orthogonal decomposition and by rational interpolation. IEEE Trans. Automatic Control **57**(2), 472–477 (2012)
16. Shlens, J.: A tutorial on principal component analysis. http://www.cs.cmu.edu/ ~ elaw/papers/pca.pdf
17. Golub, G.H., Loan, C.F.V.: Matrix Computations, 3rd ed. The Johns Hopkins University Press, Baltimore (1989)
18. Hassibi, B.: An efficient square-root algorithm for BLAST. In: Proceedings of IEEE International Conference on Acoustic, Speech, Signal Processing (ICASSP), pp. 5–9, Istanbul, Turkey (2000)
19. Wubben, D., Bohnk, R., Kuhn, V., Kammeyer, K.D.: MMSE extension of V-BLAST based on sorted QR decomposition. In: Proceedings of IEEE Vehicular Technology Conference (VTC), Orlando, Florida, USA (2003)
20. Bohnk, R., Wubben, D., Kuhn, V., Kammeyer, K.D.: Reduced complexity MMSE detection for BLAST architectures. In: Proceedings of IEEE Global Communications Conference (GLOBECOM), San Francisco, California, USA (2003)
21. Sharma, A., Paliwal, K.K., Imoto, S., Miyano, S.: Principal component analysis using QR decomposition. Int. J. Mach. Learn. Cybern. **4**(6), 679–683 (2013)

Low-Power High-Performance Multitransform Architecture Using Run-Time Reconfigurable Adder for FPGA and ASIC Implementation

K. Sivanandam and P. Kumar

Abstract The multistandard transform (MST) architecture for MPEG-1/2/4, H.264 and VC-1 using common sharing distributed arithmetic (CSDA) is more popular in multimedia communications. The CSDA and multitransform architecture have more number of 12-bit and 16-bit adders. In real-time computation, more redundant input data present in the most significant bit (MSB) part. So, in this paper, a detector logic circuit is developed to distinguish unwanted and informative portion of the input data. Then, the detector logic circuit-based run-time reconfigurable adder is designed. The detector result is used to disable the unnecessary computation block within the 12-bit adder, whenever non-informative data present in the input side of the adder. Therefore, it reduces the signal-level changes in the logic gate circuits and proportionally the power consumption becomes less. This improved architecture design is used in the 2D CSDA-MST core to analyse computation speed and power consumption. The proposed adder is evaluated with 12-bit and 16-bit input length. The calculated result shows that 21.6 and 16.25% of active logic gate reduce for 12-bit and 16-bit adder, respectively. Also, synthesized result of the proposed adder-based 2D CSDA-MST core is compared with spurious power suppression technique (SPST) adder-based 2D CSDA-MST core. The major advantage of the proposed adder is less power consumption with miniature overhead of the area. So, the proposed run-time configurable adder-based 2D CSDA-MST core is suitable for low-power and high-speed multimedia applications.

Keywords Multistandard transform · Common sharing distributed arithmetic
Ripple carry adder · Spurious power suppression technique · Detector
Selected butterfly · Error-compensated error trees

K. Sivanandam (✉) · P. Kumar
Department of Electronics and Communication Engineering, K S Rangasamy College
of Technology, Tiruchengode, Namakkal, Tamil Nadu, India
e-mail: sivanandamkaliannan@gmail.com

P. Kumar
e-mail: kumar@ksrct.ac.in

© Springer Nature Singapore Pte Ltd. 2018
S. K. Muttoo (ed.), *System and Architecture*, Advances in Intelligent Systems
and Computing 732, https://doi.org/10.1007/978-981-10-8533-8_7

1   Introduction

At present, high-speed data computation device with less power utilization is the most essential parameter, to think in many embedded systems, digital signal processing systems and wireless sensor network-based multimedia applications. The adder and multiplier are the unavoidable basic building block, which is present in most of the signal processing and multimedia application systems, and the arithmetic block dominated the system performance and power consumption. In real-time image processing systems, smart video surveillance systems and video conference applications, the pixel value of the image in terms of binary number must be represented with higher order to increase the quality of the image and video. Therefore, binary representation of the data and number of bits to be processed in the computation unit are increased. As a result, it increases the data processing time in the arithmetic block and proportionally the power consumption is also increased. In the data representation part, redundant bits are present because of higher-order binary number representation for high-accuracy result. Many computation, it is crucial because of high-quality and high-accuracy data representation is required in the real world applications. On the other way, at the time of data processing in the arithmetic unit, unnecessary data bits are not influence the end result and accuracy. For this reason, we are paying attention in the processing unit, to improve the potential of the system in terms of computation time. High-throughput multitransform and DCT core are designed using common sharing distributed arithmetic for multimedia applications [1–5]. Power suppression and high-speed computation techniques are designed using run-time reconfigurable adder [6, 7]. Area-efficient DCT core is implemented to achieve high-throughput rate with less gate counts [8–12].

2   Multitransform Architecture

The multistandard transform architecture consists of a selected butterfly (SBF) module, an even part CSDA (CSDA_E), an odd part CSDA (CSDA_O), eight error-compensated error trees (ECATs) which are used to produce the transformed data. Selected butterfly module performs the eight-point butterfly model with eight multiplexers [1]. CSDA even part calculates the even part of the eight-point transform similar to the four-point transform for H.264 and VC-1 standards. Here, it consists of the two pipeline stage architecture, which is developed using the D flip-flops as pipeline registers. Similar to the even part CSDA, the odd part CSDA also consists of the two pipeline stage registers. The ECAT architecture consists of full-adder and half-adder. The ECAT has the highest accuracy with a moderate area–delay product, and therefore, it is suitable for high-speed and low-error applications [1, 5]. The spurious power suppression technique (SPST) separates the adder into two parts; one is most significant part

(MSP), and another one is least significant part (LSP). The MSP computation takes place only when it generates informative result. Otherwise, MSP computation turns off. The detection logic unit turns on/off the MSP adder based on the input data. Along with detection logic unit and adder unit, MSP consists of data latch and sign extension unit [6].

3 Proposed Adder

In the SPST-based adder, area overhead occurred due to the detection logic unit. To overcome this issue, we proposed less area overhead detection logic unit-based adder. In the proposed adder, the two operands of the MSP enter the detection logic unit, to detect redundant bit, so that the detection logic unit can decide whether to turn off the MSP computation or not. Moreover, we propose one single bit signal-based detection unit to detect the non-informative computation to reduce switching activity. The close signal indicates the input type whether it belongs to case 1 or case 2 as shown in Table 1. Along with detection unit, simple logic circuit is developed to determine the MSP part adder result, if input data lies under case 2. Boolean equations for MSP summation result of 16-bit addition are shown in Eqs. (1)–(3). Similarly, Boolean equations for MSP summation result of 12-bit addition are shown in Eqs. (4)–(6). From this point of view, the adders in the multistandard transform coding design are separated into two parts and this detection logic is introduced in the proposed adder to determine the effective ranges of the operands. Detection logic unit and sum generation unit of the proposed 12-bit adder are shown in Figs. 1 and 2, respectively. From the logic circuit shown in Fig. 1, the signal close generates '1' for the input case 1 and generates '0' for the input case 2. By generating close signal, it can able to increase the computational speed of the adder. When compared with SPST adder, the proposed adder has less number of logic gates in the detection unit and it has no data latch circuit for enabling the input data and also has no sign extension unit to compensate for the sign signals of the MSP.

The circuit shown in Fig. 2 is designed for 12-bit adder, and it will accept the 8-bit MSB only and will be enabled only if the close signal is '0', i.e. for the input case 2 to reduce the combinational delay and switching activity. If the close signal is '1', the simple 8-bit ripple carry adder will be performed (Table 2).

Table 1 16-bit adder input data for case 1 and case 2

Case 1	Case 2			
All combinations except case 2	$A_{8-15} = 00000000$ $B_{8-15} = 00000000$	$A_{8-15} = 11111111$ $B_{8-15} = 11111111$	$A_{8-15} = 11111111$ $B_{8-15} = 00000000$	$A_{8-15} = 00000000$ $B_{8-15} = 11111111$

Fig. 1 Detection logic unit
of proposed 12-bit adder

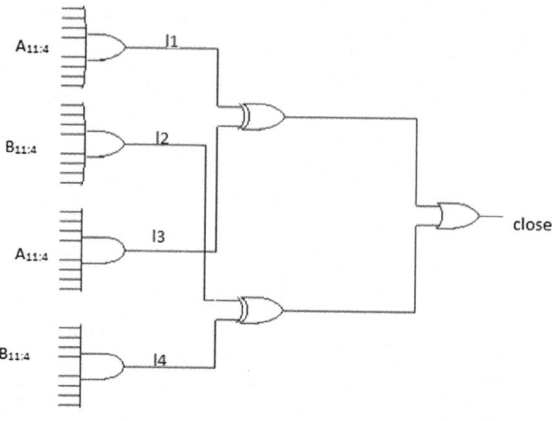

Fig. 2 Sum generation unit
of the proposed 12-bit adder

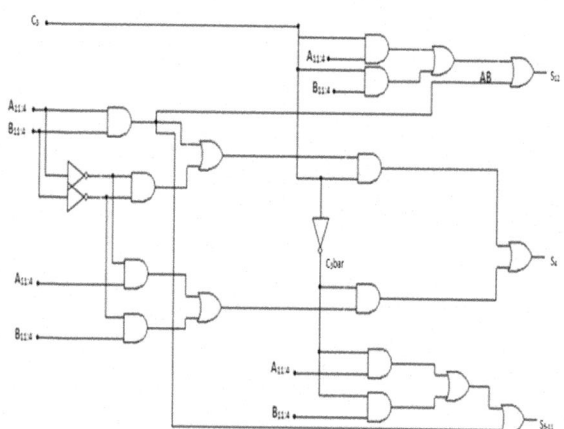

Table 2 Logic gate count analysis for 12-bit and 16-bit RCA adder

Type of adder	2 input XOR	2 input OR	2 input AND	Total no. of logic gates
12-bit RCA	12	24	24	60
16-bit RCA	16	32	32	80

Boolean equation for 16-bit adder MSP sum

$$S_8 = C_7'\left(A_{8-15}'.B_{8-15} + A_{8-15}.B_{8-15}'\right) + C_7\left(A_{8-15}'.B_{8-15}' + A_{8-15}.B_{8-15}\right) \qquad (1)$$

$$S_{9-15} = C_7'.B_{8-15} + C_7'.A_{8-15} + A_{8-15}.B_{8-15} \qquad (2)$$

$$S_{16} = A_{8-15}.B_{8-15} + C_7.B_{8-15} + C_7.A_{8-15} \qquad (3)$$

Boolean equation for 12-bit adder MSP sum

$$S_4 = C_3' \left(A_{4-11}' . B_{4-11} + A_{4-11} . B_{4-11}' \right) + C_3 \left(A_{4-11}' . B_{4-11}' + A_{4-11} . B_{4-11} \right) \quad (4)$$

$$S_{5-11} = C_3' . B_{4-11} + C_3' . A_{4-11} + A_{4-11} . B_{4-11} \quad (5)$$

$$S_{12} = A_{4-11} . B_{4-11} + C_3 . B_{4-11} + C_3 . A_{4-11} \quad (6)$$

where A = input 1, B = input 2, C = carry and S = sum

From Table 3 for the data set size as 100, if the probability that 70% of input lies in case 1 and 30% of data lies in case 2, there is an increase of 1.25% in active gate count. If the probability that 65% of input lies in case 1 and 35% of data lies in case 2, it meets the mid-point zero. If the probability that 60% of input lies in case 1 and 40% of data lies in case 2, there is a decrease of 1.25% in active gate count. Similarly, it keeps decreasing up to 11.25% for only 20% of input lies in case 1 and 80% data lies in case 2. The efficient theoretical analysis of data with both 12-bit and 16-bit proposed detection unit has only less increment in active gate count variation in case 1 and huge decrement in active gate count variation in case 2 as shown in Table 4. The tabulated result shows that the proposed adder achieves better results when compared with SPST adder.

For the RMS titanic video sequence with 55 frames, the total number of pixels is calculated as 3520 and the number of pixels less than value 16 is calculated as 2873. Therefore, there are 81.61% of data which lies in case 2 which is shown in Table 5 and active gate count variation shown in Table 6. Probability-based analysis shows that active gate count will reduce if more than 35% of data lies in case 2. So, theoretical analysis confirms that RMS titanic video sequence will consume less power due to 11.654% reduction in active gate count.

Table 3 Probability-based analysis for 16-bit adder with input data set size of 100

% of input in case (1)	% of input in case (2)	No. of active gates with detection unit			No. of active gates without detection unit	Variation in active gates (%)
70	30	6090	2010	8100	8000	1.25↑
65	35	5655	2345	8000	8000	0
60	40	5220	2680	7900	8000	1.25↓
50	50	4350	3350	7700	8000	3.75↓
40	60	3480	4020	7500	8000	6.25↓
30	70	2610	4690	7300	8000	8.75↓
20	80	1740	5360	7100	8000	11.25↓

Table 4 Active gate count comparison for 12-bit and 16-bit proposed adder with 12-bit and 16-bit SPST adder

Type of adder	Possibility of input data (A, B)	Total no. of active logic gates	Variation in active gates (%)
12-bit proposed adder	case 1*	67	11.6 ↑
	case 2*	47	21.6 ↓
16-bit proposed adder	case 1*	87	8.75 ↑
	case 2*	67	16.25 ↓
12-bit SPST adder	case 1*	110	83.3 ↑
	case 2*	54	10↓
16-bit SPST adder	case 1*	130	62.5 ↑
	case 2*	74	7.5↓

Table 5 Pixel value-based computation analysis for RMS titanic video sequence

Name of the video sequence	No. of frames	No. of pixels less than value 16	Total no. of pixels	% of computation lies in case 2
RMS titanic sequence	55	2873	3520	81.61%

Table 6 Active gate count variation for RMS titanic sequence

No. of input data in case (1)	No. of input data in case (2)	No. of active gates with detection unit			No. of active gates without detection unit	Variation in active gates (%)
		case 1	case 2	Total		
647	2873	56289	192491	248780	281600	11.654↓

4 Performance Evaluation and Comparison

4.1 FPGA Implementation

The proposed adder-based and SPST adder-based 2D CSDA-MST core design is done using Verilog coding style, simulated and synthesized using Xilinx ISE 13.4 tool, and implementation result has been realized with Virtex-4 FPGA family device XC4VLX100. We evaluated the performance of the design based on the combinational path delay for the 12-bit and 16-bit SPST adder and 12-bit and 16-bit proposed adder. The combinational path delay for both adders is shown in Table 7, and its comparison chart is shown in Fig. 3.

By considering input size as 12-bit for SPST adder, there is a delay of 21.031 ns in combinational path, and for 12-bit proposed adder, there is a delay of 19.666 ns in combinational path; hence, there is a decrease of 6.49% in delay. Similarly, for the 16-bit SPST adder and proposed adder, there is a delay of 25.790 and 24.682 ns in combinational path; hence, there is a decrease of 4.296% in delay.

Table 7 Combinational path delay

Input size	Type of adder	Combinational path delay (ns)
12-bit	SPST adder	21.031
	Proposed adder	19.666
16-bit	SPST adder	25.790
	Proposed adder	24.682

Fig. 3 Comparison chart for combinational path delay

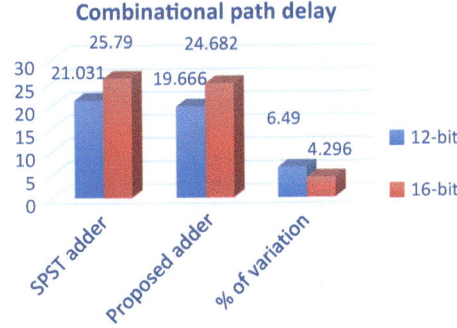

4.2 ASIC Implementation

The proposed adder and SPST adder-equipped 2D CSDA-MST core design is simulated using Synopsys VCS and synthesized using the Synopsys Design Compiler tool with 90 nm Standard Cell library. We analysed the performance of the design based on the area and power for the 12-bit and 16-bit SPST adder and 12-bit and 16-bit proposed adder. The area and power report is shown in Table 8. The area is calculated with the combinational area, non-combinational area and net interconnect area. The power is calculated based on the dynamic and internal power. The comparison chart for area and power is shown in Figs. 4 and 5, respectively. By considering input size as 12-bit, the area occupied by the SPST adder is 1830.889 and the area occupied by the proposed adder is 1044.707; hence, there is a decrease of 42.94% in area. Similarly, the 16-bit SPST adder occupies the area of 2154.362 and the area occupied by the proposed adder is 1325.201; hence, there is a decrease of 38.48% in area. By considering input size as 12-bit, the power consumed by the SPST adder is 17.318 and the power consumed by the proposed

Table 8 Power and area report comparison for 12-bit, 16-bit SPST and 12-bit, 16-bit proposed adder

Input size	Type of adder	Area (μm^2)	Power (μW)
12-bit	SPST adder	1830.889	17.318
	Proposed adder	1044.707	15.112
16-bit	SPST adder	2154.362	20.141
	Proposed adder	1325.201	18.524

Fig. 4 Comparison chart for
area

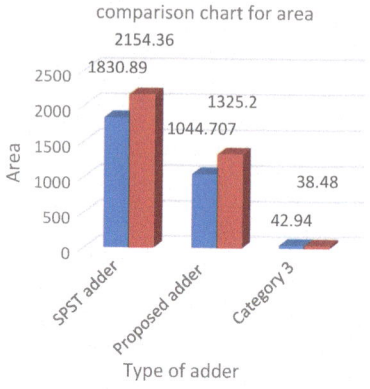

Fig. 5 Comparison chart for
power

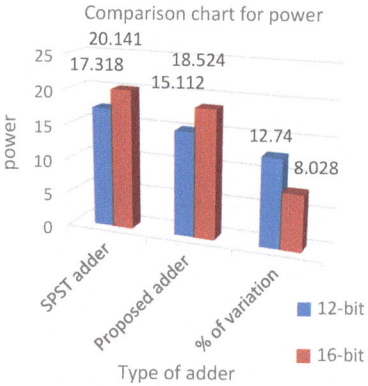

adder is 15.112; hence, there is a decrease of 12.74% in power. Similarly, the 16-bit
SPST adder consumes the power of 20.141 and the power consumed by the proposed adder is 18.524; hence, there is a decrease of 8.028% in power.

The area and power report for 2D CSDA-MST with proposed adder and ripple
carry adder is shown in Table 9. The synthesis result shows that proposed 2D
CSDA-MST architecture can save 31.3% of power with 11.73% of area overhead.

Table 9 Power and area report comparison for 2D CSDA-MST with proposed adder and RCA

Input size	Design	Area (μm^2)	Power (mW)
12-bit	2D CSDA-MST with RCA	205505.9334	2.8920
	2D CSDA-MST with proposed adder	229614.0127	1.9868

5 Conclusion and Future Scope

We have proposed a low-power high-performance run-time reconfigurable adder with detection unit. The improved architecture design is used in the 2D CSDA-MST core, which is at the bottom of MPEG-1/2/4, H.264 and VC-1 multistandard transform and analysed computation speed and power consumption. The proposed adder-based and SPST adder-based 2D CSDA-MST core is synthesized using the Synopsys Design Compiler tool with 90 nm Standard Cell library and Virtex-4 FPGA family device XC4VLX100. The proposed adder involves the detection unit which is used to detect the redundant bit at the input side of MSB bit in order to reduce the switching activity and area. The proposed core is tested using RMS titanic video as input sequence; 11.654% of active gate can be saved for computing the single 12-bit adder. The major advantage of the proposed adder is that it consumes less power when compared with SPST adder. The power consumed by 12-bit proposed adder is 15.1118 µW and for 12-bit SPST adder is 17.318 µW. Similarly, the power consumed by 16-bit proposed adder is 18.524 µW and for 16-bit SPST adder is 20.141 µW. So, the proposed run-time configurable adder-based 2D CSDA-MST core is suitable for low-power and high-speed multimedia applications. In future, the proposed adder can be used in any architecture, which consists of more number of adder units and more than 8-bit addition.

Acknowledgements We would like to thank the Centre for VLSI Design, Department of Electronics and Communication Engineering, K. S. Rangasamy College of Technology, Tiruchengode, Tamil Nadu, for providing the Synopsys EDA tools and various Xilinx FPGA kits.

References

1. Chen, Y.-H., Chen, J.-N., Chang, T.-Y., Lu, C.-W.: High-throughput multistandard transform core supporting MPEG/H.264/VC-1 using common sharing distributed arithmetic. IEEE Trans. Very Large Scale Integr. (VLSI) Syst. **22**(3) (2014)
2. El-Hadedy, M., Purohit, S., Margala, M., Knapskog, S.J.: Low Latency Transpose Memory for High Throughput Signal Processing. Norwegian University of Science and Technology, Trondheim, Norway (2010)
3. Shams, A.M., Chidanandan, A., Pan, W., Bayoumi, M.A.: NEDA: a low-power high-performance DCT architecture. IEEE Trans. Signal Process. **54**(3) (2006)
4. Yu, S., Swartzlander, E.E.: DCT implementation with distributed arithmetic. IEEE Trans. Comput. **50**(9) (2001)
5. Hwangbo, W., Kyung, C.-M.: A Multitransform architecture for H.264/AVC high-profile coders. IEEE Trans. Multimedia **12**(3) (2010)
6. Chen, K.-H., Chu, Y.-S.: A spurious-power suppression technique for multimedia/DSP applications. IEEE Trans. Circ. Syst. I Regular Papers **56**(1) (2009)
7. Sivanandam, K., Kumar, P.: Run time reconfigurable modified vedic multiplier for high speed multimedia applications. In: 2nd International Conference on Computing for Sustainable Global Development, 11th–13th Mar 2015

8. Chen, Y.-H., Chang, T.-Y., Li, C.-Y.: High throughput DA-based DCT with high accuracy error-compensated adder tree. IEEE Trans. Very Large Scale Integr. (VLSI) Syst. **19**(4) (2011)

9. Chen, K.-H., Guo, J.-I., Wang, J.-S., Yeh, C.-W., Chen, J.-W.: An energy-aware IP core design for the variable-length DCT/IDCT targeting at MPEG4 shape-adaptive transforms. IEEE Trans. Circ. Syst. Video Technol. **15**(5) (2005)

10. Fan, C.-P., Su, G.-A.: Fast algorithm and low-cost hardware-sharing design of multiple integer transforms for VC-1. IEEE Trans. Circ. Syst. II Express Briefs **56**(10) (2009)

11. Lin, C.-T., Yu, Y.-C., Van, L.-D.: Cost-effective triple-mode reconfigurable pipeline FFT/IFFT/2-D DCT processor. IEEE Trans. Very Large Scale Integr. (VLSI) Syst. **16**(8) (2008)

12. Xie, J., Meher, P.K.: Hardware-efficient realization of prime-length DCT based on distributed arithmetic. IEEE Trans. Comput. **62**(6) (2013)

A Review of Dynamic Scheduling Algorithms for Homogeneous and Heterogeneous Systems

Mahfooz Alam, Asif Khan and Ankur K. Varshney

Abstract The dynamic scheduling algorithms are widely used to evaluate the performance of homogeneous and heterogeneous systems in terms of QoS parameters such as scheduling length, execution time, load imbalance factor and many more. Over the time, many dynamic scheduling policies were introduced which are designed to achieve their goal such as efficient utilization of process elements, minimization of resources idleness, or determining the total execution time. In this paper, we analyzed different aspects in dynamic scheduling algorithm and numerous issues in various levels of the homogeneous and heterogeneous systems.

Keywords Parallel processing · Multiprocessor system · Static and dynamic scheduling · Heterogeneous and homogeneous systems

1 Introduction

Scheduling is a process of comparable tasks to the resources at specific times. A scheduling algorithm (SA) is used to find out a schedule for a set of task on the bases of task's deadline and recourse requirements specified. The prospective speedup of applications has motivated the extensive use of multiprocessors in current years [1–5]. In multiprocessor, scheduling algorithms developed for uniprocessor can be applied if we consider each core of the multiprocessor as an

M. Alam (✉)
Department of Computer Science, Al-Barkaat College of Graduate Studies, Aligarh, India
e-mail: mahfoozalam.amu@gmail.com

A. Khan
University of Electronic Science and Technology of China, Chengdu, China
e-mail: asif05amu@gmail.com

A. K. Varshney
Institute of Technology & Management, Aligarh, India
e-mail: ankur.varshn@gmail.com

© Springer Nature Singapore Pte Ltd. 2018
S. K. Muttoo (ed.), *System and Architecture*, Advances in Intelligent Systems and Computing 732, https://doi.org/10.1007/978-981-10-8533-8_8

isolated core, which is a uniprocessor [6–8]. However, in multiprocessor scheduling the complexity of varying the execution of different tasks on multiple cores does not interfere with each other and also determining which tasks should be given to a certain core increases the complexity greatly as compared to uniprocessor scheduling. The two main approaches for SA on multiprocessors are global scheduling and partitioning scheduling [9–12]. But the point of emphasis of scheduling is always to reduce the execution time, schedule length (or makespan), and maximization of speedup. Besides this, it is clear that the multiprocessor scheduling suffers from NP-complete problem in its many variants excluding some interpreted conditions. The SA can be categorized as *off-line* (static or deterministic) SA and *on-line* (dynamic or nondeterministic) SA.

In off-line scheduling, all scheduling decisions are taken before the system starts and the scheduler has an exact knowledge of the all task properties and behaviors are therefore needed. During runtime, the tasks are executed in a predetermined order. The static task scheduling problem is known as NP-complete [2]; that is, task list is not updated with new ordering at runtime. There are two kinds of static scheduling algorithms (SSA): one is Heuristic Based (HB) and another is Guided Random Search-Based (GRSB). HB algorithm can be further subdivided into three categories: List Scheduling, Cluster Scheduling, and Task Duplication-Based Scheduling (TDBS) algorithms.

An on-line scheduling algorithm takes its scheduling decisions during the operation of the application. In other words, on-line scheduling tasks can be real-located to other processors during runtime [3]. On-line scheduling is supple and very faster than the static scheduling algorithms. The key point of on-line scheduling is to map tasks in parallel on the multiprocessor and arrange their execution so that a minimal makespan is given in the bound of task priority necessities. Dynamic scheduling algorithm can be further subdivided into three

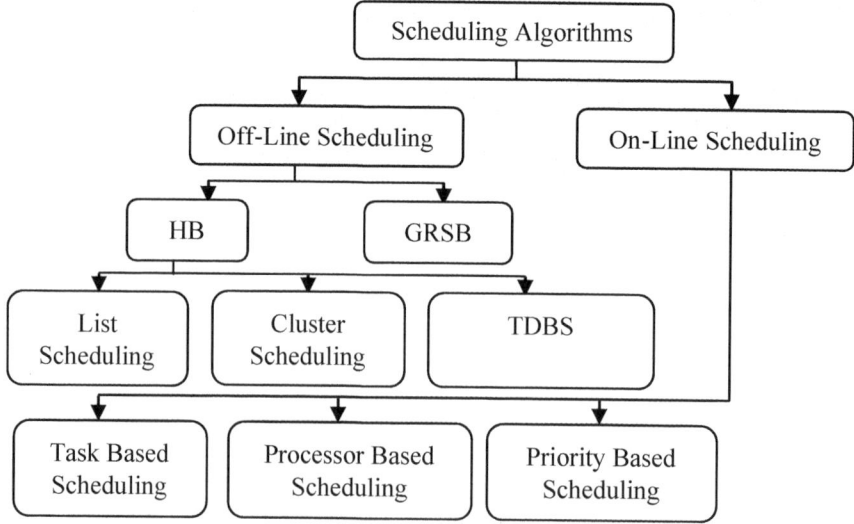

Fig. 1 Taxonomy of scheduling algorithms

kinds: Task-Based Scheduling (TBS) Algorithms, Processor-Based Scheduling (PBS) Algorithms, and Priority-Based Scheduling (PRBS) Algorithms (Fig. 1).

2 Homogeneous and Heterogeneous Systems

A multiprocessor system is either homogeneous (HM) or heterogeneous (HT). Heterogeneous and homogeneous systems are explained as under.

2.1 Heterogeneous System

Heterogeneous systems (HTS) consist of different processors that are capable of performing different tasks. HTS become the latest thing in both client and cloud. Scheduling a parallel program is critical step in inefficiently harnessing the complexity power of a HTS. Heterogeneity in parallel systems introduces an extra degree of complexity to the scheduling difficulty that is variable speed of processors. The difficulty of the problem rise when task scheduling is to be done in heterogeneous nature, where the computational nodes in the system may not be equal and different amount of time to execute the same task. Heterogeneity can be proposed in two types, namely functional-level and performance-level heterogeneity [4, 5]. All tasks may not be running on all functional units. One of the key concepts of HTS is schedule problem. To achieve high performance, the efficient scheduling of the tasks of a function is needed.

2.2 Homogeneous System

Homogeneous systems (HMS) consist of the processors identical in terms of their functionality [2]. The characteristics of homogeneous multiprocessor system are replication effect, memory dominant, less performance, data parallelism, shared memory and dynamic task mapping. HMS is all exactly the identical: cache sizes, equivalent frequencies, functions, etc., while every core in a HTS may have a unlike function, memory model, frequency, etc. So, it is easier to develop software for HMS. However, in homogeneous processor, system typically requires additional registers for "special instructions" such as Single Instruction Multiple Data likes MMX, SSE, while a HTS can implement unlike types of hardware for unlike instructions/uses.

This paper is classified as follows: Sect. 2 presents HMS and HTS, and Sect. 3 reviews the dynamic scheduling algorithms. Section 4 presents comparison of algorithm with factors, and Sect. 5 presents conclusions and suggests possible avenues for future research.

3   Review of Dynamic Scheduling Algorithms (DSA)

In dynamic scheduling the decision about how to schedule tasks priorities which are either assigned dynamically or statically? Many research works investigated the DSA problem in different aspects and the problems faced in various levels of the HMS and HTS. Then important contributions of DSA in HMS and HTS are discussed in this section.

3.1   The Earliest Time First (ETF) Algorithm

This algorithm is alike to the Modified Critical Path Algorithm; it considers fixed node priorities and assumes only a limited number of processors. Yet, a node with superior priority may not automatically obtain scheduled earlier than the nodes with inferior priority [13]. After the computation of earliest begin times (EBT) for all the prepared nodes at each step, ETF algorithm selects the one with the lesser begin time, which is calculated by investigating the begin time of the node on all processors thoroughly. The ETF is stated below.

1. At every node, static b-level is calculated.
2. In the starting, the group of prepared nodes contains only the admission nodes. Repeat.
3. At every processor, for every node in the prepared group, the EBT is calculated.
4. Finally, joint the new prepared nodes to the prepared node group. Till all nodes are scheduled.

3.2   Dynamic Level Scheduling (DLS) Algorithm

This algorithm is alike to the Mobility Directed Algorithm; its uses as node priorities dynamically through allocating an attribute called dynamic level (DL) to unscheduled nodes at every scheduling step. The stepwise description of the DLS is given below.

1. At every node, static b-level is calculated.
2. In the beginning, the group of prepared contains only the admission nodes. Repeat.
3. The EBT is calculated at each processor for every node.
4. Pick the node processor couple that gives the biggest DL. All nodes are scheduled to the equivalent processor.
5. Finally, joint the new prepared nodes to the prepared group. Till all nodes are scheduled.

3.3 The Earliest Deadline First (EDF) Algorithm

EDF is a DSA that helps real-time operating systems in placing processes in a precedence line. When a scheduling incident arises the processor searches the line for finding out the process nearest to its limit. This process succeeds to be scheduled for execution. EDF is the finest scheduling algorithm on preemptive uniprocessor, in the following way: if a group of free jobs, each having its own arrival time, execution necessity and a limit, can be programmed in a manner that ensures all the jobs complete by their limit, the EDF will schedule this group of jobs so they all complete by their limit. With scheduling periodic processes that have limits equal to their stages, the utilization limit of EDF is 100%.

3.4 Online Scheduling of Dynamic Task Graph (OSDTG)

This algorithm stated that the OSDTG is more practical compared to conventional schemes and task graphs are subject to variation at execution time and interprocessor communications (IC) of static number (SN) of channels. Broadcast and point-to-point communication is applied in online scheduling. The key point of this algorithm is to decrease scheduling length [6].

3.5 Dynamic Load Balancing Using Task-Transfer Probabilities (DLBTTP)

This algorithm is based on the recent position of the system load; task move probabilities were calculated for every node in the system. These probabilities, represented by P_{nm}, are between a node n and each other node m. The computation and adjustment of the task move probabilities later than the move of every recently arrived task are at done at the end of every periodic interval [14].

3.6 Dynamic Task Scheduling (DTS) Algorithm

This algorithm has been proposed with a lower time complexity for homogeneous environment. This algorithm is based on DAG model, and the plan makes the entire parallel task complete at the feasible initial time; that is, response time (RT) of this parallel task is smallest [7].

3.7 DLS Algorithm with Genetic Operators (DLSAGO)

Dynamic Level Scheduling Genetic Algorithm (DLSGA) proposes to overcome the excess time for schedule. DLSGA uses a quantity known as dynamic level, which is the dissimilarity between the maximum total of calculated costs from task to a way out task, and the earliest begin run time on processor [8]. No tasks are scheduled between two earlier scheduled tasks by DLSGA. To reproduce offspring, the most favored and the fittest are selected.

3.8 Dynamic Task Graph Scheduling with Fault-Tolerant (FTDTGS)

An approach has been proposed to fault-tolerant execution of dynamic task graphs scheduled using work stealing. The work-stealing-based algorithm is applied when the data and metadata corresponding with a task get corrupted; then a task graph is mounted to enable recovery [10]. The algorithm was shown to be asymptotically optimal for graphs whose degree can be bound by a stable. In the lack of faults, the fault-tolerant edition was shown to not incur significant overheads compared to the non-fault-tolerant version.

3.9 DTS with Load Balancing (DTSLB)

DTSLB proposes to schedule a heterogeneous tasks dynamically on to corresponding processors in a distributed setup and load balancing which is a main problem in task scheduling is also measured. The nature of the tasks is free and non-preemptive. To determine the efficiency of the scheduling algorithm, a number of different tests have been performed [11]. The unique approache of this algorithm is solving the DTS using Hybrid Particle Swarm Optimization (HPSO).

3.10 Dynamic Load Balancing Using Genetic Algorithms (DLBGA)

DLBGA have been proposed for a static number of tasks; each having a task number and a length is arbitrarily generated and located in a task group from which tasks are allocated to processors [15]. As load balancing is performed by the centralized Genetic Algorithm (GA)-based method, begin with initializing, a population of probable solutions [16]. By using the sliding window technique it is achieved.

3.11 Parallel Genetic Algorithms for Heterogeneous (PGAH)

This PGAH engages a central scheduler, which has the processor lists and the task queue. The processors are heterogeneous in distributed system. The available network resources vary over time between the processors in distributed system. The possibility of every processor can vary over time. In distributed system the task which are indivisible, independent of all other tasks, arrive randomly and can be processed by any processor [17].

3.12 Global Scheduling for Mixed-Critically (GSMC)

In the context of multiprocessor mixed-criticality system, the fixed-priority algorithms can be applied globally [18]. The global Fixed-priority (FP) scheduling of mixed-criticality task sets (MCTS) are on HM multiprocessors. In this paper, there are two main ways in which an algorithm must be selected. Particularly, a priority assignment strategy to individual tasks and a feasibility testing given a specific priority assignment must be selected.

3.13 The Response Time Analysis of Global Fixed-Priority (RTAGFP)

This algorithm states a new analysis that improves over current state-of-the-art (SOA) response time analysis (RTA) by reducing its pessimism. Finally, how to improve the new response time analysis method by empirical tests with arbitrarily generated task sets [19, 20]. The RTA with Limited Carry-in (RTA-LC) [21] is the most accurate algorithm for RTA of global FP scheduling on multiprocessors. In this paper, first propose a new formula to bound the workload of carry-in jobs.

3.14 New Response Time Bounds for Fixed Priority (RTBFP)

This algorithm improves analysis precision response time for sporadic tasks on multiprocessor systems where the limits of tasks are within their periods and task systems with random limits, allowing tasks to have limits beyond the end of their periods [22]. In this paper, there are two main contribution folds such as: (1) The analysis precision has been significantly improved against previous work, and (2) To my knowledge, this is the first work to rectify the RTA problem of arbitrary-deadline systems on multiprocessors.

Table 1 Existing dynamic scheduling algorithm

Algorithms	Objectives	Merits	System types	Conclusion/ future enhancements
ETF	The initiate time reduced of a node at every step	Processor selection phase goes on side by side	HM	Heterogeneous environment
DLS	To select highest static stage and lesser time to schedule	Pair matching of nodes is performed, and highest priority node is found	HM	Heterogeneous environment
EDF	Job priority is inversely proportional to its deadline	No need to define priorities	HT	Future deadlines can be calculated
OSDTG	To minimize the makespan	IC of SN of channels	HT	Off-line
DLBTTP	Determine transferring tasks between each two nodes in the system	Well RT with a feasible amount of communication overheads	Distributed	IC and transfer delays
DTS	Lower time complexity	High speedup-dependent tasks	HM	Add fault-tolerant
DLSAGO	Overcome the spend much time and space for search	The most favored and the fittest are selected	HT	Homogeneous system
FTDTGS	To minimize overheads in the absence of faults with recovery costs	Handling recovery correctly and efficiently for dynamic task graph	HT	Recovery faults without global coordination
DTSLB	Schedule the tasks in a HTS, free and non-preemptive	Solving the DTS using PSO with fixed inertia	HT	Bounded and pre-emptive
DLBGA	Less run time, higher processor utilization, and good load balance	Threshold strategies, information switching criteria, and IC	HT	Large number of very effective tasks
PGAH	Reduce parallelization of the fitness evaluation	More scalable and extends its practicability	HT	Spends less time
GSMC	Timing controls to progress the schedulability of MCTS	Priority task policy and global schedulability tests	HM	Offers robust performance
RTAGFP	Improve the response time	Iterative analysis procedure and improve the efficiency	HM	Lead worst-case RT and good SOA

Table 1 (continued)

Algorithms	Objectives	Merits	System types	Conclusion/ future enhancements
RTBFP	Improve the analysis precision response time	Improve the RTA problem	HT	Deal with platforms and task systems
LBSCMCS	Priority-based scheduling	Better quality to the space-time partitioning approach to scheduling	HM	Study of the schedulability properties of OCBP

3.15 Load-Based Schedulability Analysis of Certificate Mixed-Criticality System (LBSCMCS)

It is apriority-based algorithm for scheduling such mixed-criticality systems on preemptive uniprocessor platforms. This paper shows that this algorithm is strictly better to prior algorithms that have been used for scheduling mixed-criticality systems needing certification [23]. The conventional real-time scheduling theory does not address the certification consideration which give rise to fundamental new resource allocation and scheduling challenges (Table 1).

4 Comparison of Dynamic Scheduling Algorithms on HMS and HTS

A Comparison of aspects influencing the homogeneous and heterogeneous environment has been done and different algorithms are discussed. Out of which, ETF and DLS were applied on homogeneous setting while OSDTG and DLBGA were applied on heterogeneous setting, although their objective were same, i.e., to minimize the execution time and makespan. DTS algorithm may be adding fault-tolerance, whereas DLSGA can be homogeneous in future. FTDTGS is useful for recovery from faults without global coordination, while DTSLB is pre-emptive and dependent in nature, yet both use HTS. The goal of RTAGFP and RTBFP improves the response time but cannot be applied on same system. The objectives, merits, and future enhancement of the algorithm have already been discussed. This review is mainly focused on the parameters such as makespan, running time, resource utilization load balancing, speedup, efficiency, and high performance.

5 Conclusion and Future Work

The paper gives a short review of DSA for HMS and HTS. In this study, we found that dynamic scheduling algorithm is important to scheduling. It helps in answering questions such as: how to minimize the execution time and makespan, how to load balance on each processor, how to manage selection of task, and how to improve performance utilization and efficiency of system. It is also analyzed that load balancing issue in HMS was found easier compare to HTS in essence of load capacity. The appliance of the dynamic scheduling algorithm is a rapidly developing research area.

Hence, on the basis of this study in future will propose a novel dynamic scheduling algorithm for homogeneous as well as heterogeneous system to better performance.

References

1. Kwok, Y.K., Ahmad, I.: Static scheduling algorithms for allocating directed task graphs to multiprocessors. ACM Comput. Surv. **31**(4), 406–471 (1999)
2. Singh, K., Alam, M., Sharma, S.K.: A survey of static scheduling algorithm for distributed computing system. Int. J. Comput. Appl. **129**(2), 25–30 (2015)
3. Singh, M.K., Tiwari, R.: A survey on scheduling of parallel program in heterogeneous system. Int. J. Advanced Research in Computer Engineering & Technology. **1**(8), 357 (2012)
4. He, Y., Liu, J., Sun, H.: Scheduling functionally heterogeneous systems with utilization balancing. In: IEEE International Parallel and Distributed Processing Symposium, pp. 1187–1198 (2011)
5. Alam, M., Varshney, A.K.: A comparative study of interconnection network. Int. J. Comput. Appl. **127**(4), 37–43 (2015)
6. Choudhury, P.: Online scheduling of dynamic task graphs with communication and contention for multiprocessors. IEEE Trans. Parallel Distrib. Syst. **23**(1), 126–133 (2012)
7. Amalarethinam, D.I.G., Joyce Mary, G.J.: A new DAG based dynamic task scheduling algorithm (DYTAS) for multiprocessor systems. Int. J. Comput. Appl. **19**(8), 24–28 (2011)
8. Kaur, P., Kaur, A.: Implementation of Dynamic Level Scheduling Algorithm Using Genetic Operators. Int. J. of Appl. or Innovation in Eng. & Manag. **2**(7), 2319–4847 (2013)
9. Khan, Z.A., Siddiqui, J., Samad, A.: Linear crossed cube (LCQ): a new interconnection network topology for massively parallel system. Int. J. Comput. Netw. Inf. Secur. **7**(3), 18–25 (2015)
10. Kurt, M.C., Krishnamoorthy, S., Agrawal, K., Agrawal, G.: Fault-tolerant dynamic task graph scheduling. In: SC14: International Conference for High Performance Computing, Networking, Storage and Analysis (2014)
11. Visalakshi, P., Sivanandam, S.N.: Dynamic Task Scheduling with Load Balancing using Hybrid Practical Swarm Optimization. Int. J. Open Problems Compt. Math. **2**(3), 475–488 (2009)
12. Khan, Z.A., Siddiqui, J., Samad, A.: A novel multiprocessor architecture for massively parallel system. Int. Conf. Parallel Distrib. Grid Comput. 466–471 (2015)
13. Kwok, Y.K., Ahmad, I.: Static scheduling algorithms for allocating directed task graphs to multiprocessors. ACM Comput. Surv. (CSUR) **31**(4) (1999)

14. Evans, D.J., Butt, W.U.N.: Dynamic load balancing using task-transfer probabilities. Parallel Comput. Elsevier North-Holland **19**, 897–916 (1993)
15. Zomaya, A.Y., Hwei, Y.: Observations on using genetic algorithms for dynamic load-balancing. Parallel Distrib. Syst. IEEE **12**(9) (2001)
16. Munetomo, M., Takai, Y., Sato, Y.: A genetic approach to dynamic load-balancing in a distributed computing system. In: Proceedings of First International Conference on Evolutionary Computation, IEEE World Congress Computational Intelligence, vol. 1, pp. 418–421 (1994)
17. Pico, C.A.G., Wainwright, R.L.: Dynamic scheduling of computer tasks using genetic algorithms. In: Proceedings of First IEEE Conference Evolutionary Computation, IEEE World Congress Computational Intelligence, vol. 2, pp. 829–833 (1994)
18. Kelly, O.R., Aydin, H.: Fixed—priority global scheduling for mixed-critically real-time system. Int. J. Embedded Syst. **6**(2/3) (2014)
19. Sun, Y., Lipariy, G., Guanzx, N., Yix, W.: Improving the Response Time Analysis of Global Fixed-Priority Multiprocessor Scheduling. Embedded and Real-Time IEEE Xplore (2014)
20. Davis, R.I., Burns, A.: Improved priority assignment for global fixed priority pre-emptive scheduling in multiprocessor real-time systems. Real-Time Syst. **47**(1), 1–40 (2011)
21. Guan, N., Stigge, M., Yi, W., G.: New response time bounds for fixed priority multiprocessor scheduling. In: 30th IEEE on Real-Time Systems Symposium, 2009, RTSS 2009, pp. 387–397. IEEE (2009)
22. Guan, N., Stigge, M., Yi, W., Yu, G.: New Response Time Bounds for Fixed Priority Multiprocessor Scheduling. In Real-Time Systems Symposium, RTSS 2009. 387–397 IEEE, (2009)
23. Li, H., Baruah, S.: Load-based schedulability analysis of certifiable mixed-criticality systems. In: Proceedings of the 10th ACM International Conference on Embedded Software (2010)

Effective Information Retrieval Algorithm for Linear Multiprocessor Architecture

Zaki Ahmad Khan, Jamshed Siddiqui and Abdus Samad

Abstract Information retrieval is magnetizing important interest due to exponential development of the quantity of information accessible in different formats such as textual, numeric and image formats. A number of applications can be downloaded in parallel by several servers available on net using downloading applications. These applications may vary depending upon the mechanism used to improve to downloading time. One of the methods to speedup downloading is to incorporate concurrency. In this paper, a new approach for downloading files is proposed that uses a parallel architecture as a server. The server named as Linear-Crossed Cube (LCQ) is based on linear topology with all desirable topological properties. The load on the server balances dynamically. The proposed downloading algorithm is implemented, and downloading time is evaluated for number of queries. A comparative simulation study has been carried out along with the execution time to download file. The simulation results show significant improvement in the downloading time by using the proposed system.

Keywords Information retrieval · Multiprocessor architecture · Server
Download · Load balancing

1 Introduction

Information retrieval is the technological restraint that refers to the analysis, design, and implementation of computerized systems that tackle the illustration, company of, as well as retrieve to huge amounts information from the Internet in form of file,

Z. A. Khan (✉) · J. Siddiqui
Department of Computer Science, Faculty of Science, Aligarh Muslim University,
Aligarh 202002, India
e-mail: jmi.amu1@gmail.com

A. Samad
University Women's Polytechnic, Aligarh Muslim University, Aligarh 202002, India

© Springer Nature Singapore Pte Ltd. 2018
S. K. Muttoo (ed.), *System and Architecture*, Advances in Intelligent Systems
and Computing 732, https://doi.org/10.1007/978-981-10-8533-8_9

Web pages, etc. [1]. The Internet has been a source of significant development in Web traffic and also reputation of data access. As a result, widely used Web and ftp sites suffer from weighty loads. However, user's expectations have improved: to ensure that the preferred information ought to be downloaded rapidly, in the shortest feasible time. Consequently, within this situation, the relevant hardware and software products are developed [2]. Nevertheless, the crucial concern is how to deal with the issue of a sufficient design of the system to be able to attain the preferred performance [3–5].

A vital aspect of a textual document information retrieval system is retrieving the documents which could quench you the information requirements of a user from a huge number of documents. For several years, the evolution of multiprocessing has been influenced by several factors including: (i) speedup by incorporating parallelism; (ii) scalability; and (iii) flexibility. Moreover, the success of a multiprocessor system depends on the interconnection topology and load balancing mechanism [6, 7]. Many networks have emerged as attractive interconnection topologies for distributed memory multiprocessor systems such as hypercube, crossed cube network, star, star cube, star-crossed cube, and LEC networks [8–11]. In this paper, a Linear-Crossed Cube (LCQ) has been chosen as a server. This server is used for storing and maintaining the database and retrieving information concurrently. However, selecting the best server to get the maximum performance is a trivial task for the end users, and a bad choice may provide poor end user experience that ultimately results in poor download time. Therefore, the multiprocessing approach is the most generalized and flexible one as it incorporates the maximum concurrency. The scheduling algorithms play an essential role in multiprocessor systems while allocation of load and to obtain the load balancing among the available processors. To evaluate the proposed server performance, the standard dynamic scheduling scheme is implemented [12, 13]. Recently the various parallel downloading algorithms have been reported by a number of researchers in the literature [14–16]. They proposed a dynamic parallel-access scheme to access multiple mirror servers. They showed that their dynamic parallel download scheme achieves significant downloading speedup with respect to a single server. However, the main disadvantage is that there are many requests and response packets exchanged between the client and server, and thus performance varies on different division number [17].

In a similar way, an adaptive parallel downloading technique that can manage for modify of server efficiency has been revealed [18]. This process breaks a file into a number of equivalent bits as well as every block is ordered from another server in parallel. The subsequent block is allocated every time a server coating a downloading process and also gets idle. The scaled-down every block is extra versatility to improvement in efficiency among servers is received; however, downloading time is often massive while the rounded trip time between a server and a client is comparatively massive. In addition, there is an issue that the appropriate block dimensions will modify based on the temporal network condition, which technique ought to determine the splitting amount beforehand. The proposed algorithm contains the salient properties of the above-revealed strategies. They are definitely improved and also implemented to ensure that the round trip time between nodes is decreased. This algorithm has been outlined in Sect. 3.

The rest of the paper is organized as follows. Section 2 describes the server and its characteristics. Section 3 is devoted to the proposed algorithm for information retrieval. In Sect. 4, the relative performance of the download algorithm is evaluated. Finally, concluded the paper in Sect. 5.

2 The LCQ Server

The proposed LCQ network is undirected graph and grows linearly in cube-like shape. Let q be the set of designated processor of Q, and thus, $q = \{P_i\}$, $0 \leq i \leq N - 1$. The link functions E_1 and E_2 define the mapping from q to Q as.

$$E_1(P_i) = P(i+2)\text{Mod}N, \quad \forall P_i \text{ in } q$$

$$E_2(P_i) = P(i + 3)\text{Mod}N$$

The two functions E_1 and E_2 indicate the links between various processors in the network.

Let Z be a set of N identical processors, represented as

$$Z = \{P_0, P_1, P_2 \ldots P_{N-1}\}$$

The total number of processor in the network is given by

$$N = \sum_{k=1}^{n} K,$$

where n is the depth of the network. For different depth, network having 1, 3, 6, 10, 15, 21... processors are possible.

In order to define the link functions, we denote each processor in a set K as P_{in}, n being the level/depth in LCQ, where the processor P_i resides. As per the LCQ extension policy, one or two processors exist at level/depth n. Thus at level 1, P_0 and P_1 exist, and similarly at level 2, P_2 and P_3 exist as shown in Fig. 1.

Properties of the LCQ Server

Some properties of the LCQ server like number of nodes, degree of nodes, etc., have been compared with LEC network, SCQ, CQ, and hypercube networks and shown in Table 1.

Fig. 1 Linear-Crossed Cube (LCQ)

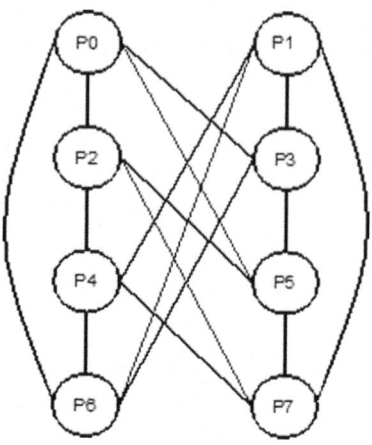

Table 1 Summary of properties of multiprocessor architectures

Parameter	CQ	SCQ	LEC	LCQ
Nodes	$2n$	$n!2\ m$	$2n$	$\sum k$
Diameter	n	$\lceil (m+1)/2 \rceil + \lfloor 3(n1)/2 \rfloor$	$\lfloor n \rfloor$	$\lfloor \sqrt{N} \rfloor$
Degree	$\lceil n+1/ \rceil$	$m+n-1$	4	4
Cost	$n \lceil n+1 \rceil$	$m+n \lceil [m+1]/2 \rceil + \lfloor 3[n-1]/2 \rfloor$	$4 \lfloor n \rfloor$	$4 \lfloor \sqrt{N} \rfloor$

3   System Model

Internet is an enormous and also abundant content material helpful to countless users. Consequently, it is extremely hard to examine and categorize the entire information offered on the Internet. Even though search engines like Google have resolved certain issues of information retrieval from the Internet. Nevertheless, extra issues are shown in search engine, for instance, information overloading which minimizes the proficiency. In case the retrieval of information is massive, it brings about the holdup in downloading the information. The proposed server attempts to categorize the gathered information of its database, which classification is made in such a way that each time any specific information is retrieved from the database, it is retrieved almost instantly. For the purpose of simulation, we have considered only textual file. The proposed model, however, could be extended for other file formats. If the needed information is unavailable, a link for the identical is searched for additional linked servers. The entire retrieval system includes three points, i.e., an analyzer, indexer, and a user interface along with the database, as shown in Fig. 2.

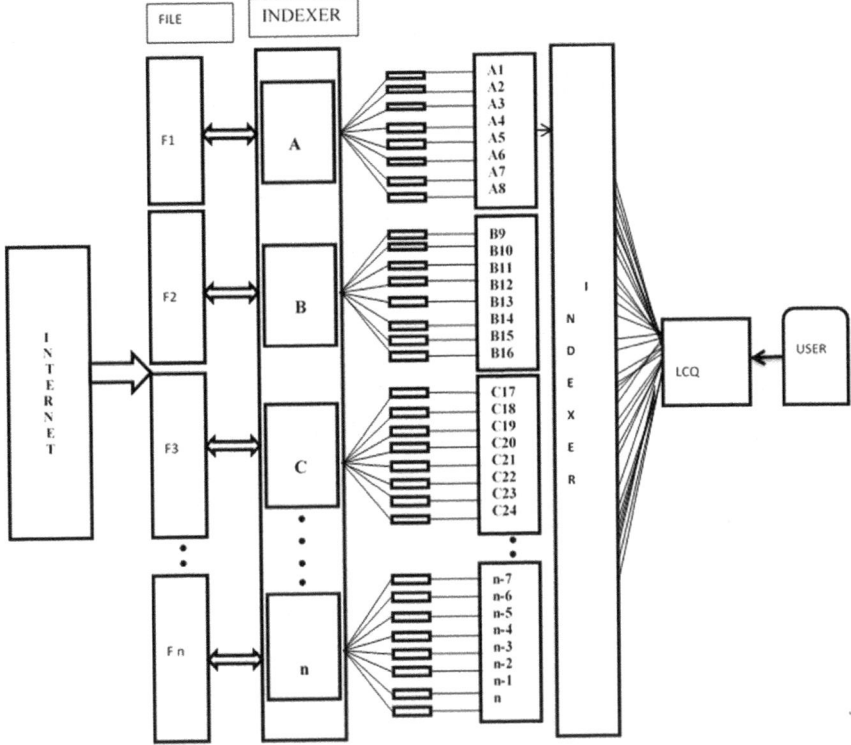

Fig. 2 Proposed system model

3.1 The Proposed Algorithm

The workflow of the proposed algorithm is as follows: The server collects information in the form of Web pages or files from the Internet. Each file when loaded into the database of the server is first analyzed in terms of its size, and ID is assigned and the file is divided into several parts (or packets) of equal sizes. Each packet is again designated by its ID and loaded into the database. The addresses of packets in the database along with their IDs are recorded in a table, which is shared by all the nodes of the server and updated frequently. This table may be viewed as the indexer which indexes the data as shown in Fig. 2. The ID of each packet is recorded in the table in such a way that the vector address of the table corresponds to the packet ID.

A specialized searching technique is useful when detailed or high specific information about a subject area is needed. It can match the personal requirements better than a general search engine. Keeping the same in view, an information

Table 2 Pseudocode of proposed scheduling algorithm

```
Prepare the Document List {
Public static void main (String args []) {
PrepareDocumentList Pd = New PrepareDocumentList ();
DataIndexer di = New DataIndexer ();
If (di.conn! = Null)
di.closeSession (); }
Int rand = (int) (Math. Random ()*1000);
DocIdRandom dir = new DocIdRandom ();
dir.setDocId (rand);
If (lstrnd.add (rand); }
Return lstrnd;}
Merge Packet {
Private static int limit = 10;
Private static final ExecutorService executor = Executors.NewFixedThreadPool (limit);
Public void mergeData (List<DocumentDetails> lstdoc, DocSummary ds) {
Completion Service<DocumentDetails> completionService = New ExecutorCompletion-
Service<DocumentDetails> (executor);
FileData = new byte [(int) ds.getSize () +1];
Int i=0;
For (DocumentDetails docDetails: lstdoc) {
IF (docDetails! =Null) {
Final DocumentDetails dd = docDetails;
Final String ip = "10.0.17.4";
CompletionService. Submit (New Callable<DocumentDetails>(){
Public DocumentDetails call () {
HttpSendGet HttpGet = New HttpSendGet ();
DocumentDetails d = New DocumentDetails ();
Try {
d = HttpGet.sendGet (ip, dd);   }
Return d;   }}); }}
IF (! executor.isShutdown ())
Executor. Shutdown ();}
Manage Indexer {
Private Int packetSize1 = 8;
Public void createDocIndex (String docName, double size, String type, byte [] data)   {
String sqlMaxDocID = "select max (doc_id) as max from tbl_doc_indexer";
DataIndexer di = New DataIndexer ();
Statement stmt = Null;
Try {
Stmt = di.conn.createStatement ();
Result Set docId = Stmt.executeQuery (sqlMaxDocID);
Int dId=0;
While (docId.next ())
If (docId==null)
DId = 1;
Else
DId = docId.getInt ("max") + 1;
Prepared Statement PS = null;
PS = di.conn.prepareStatement ("insert into tbl_doc_indexer (doc_id, doc_name, doc_size, type,
doc_data) Values (?,?,?,?,?)");
Ps.setInt (1, dId);
Ps.setString (2, docName);
Ps.setDouble (3, size);
Ps.setString (4, type);
Ps.setBytes (5, data);       }
tbl_packet_indexer (packet_data, packet_size, doc_id) Values (?,?,?)");
Ps1.setBytes (1, bdata);
Ps1.setDouble (2, nsize);
```

Table 2 (continued)

```
                        Ps1.setDouble (3, dId);        }
                    Public int CheckDuplicate (String name)  {
        String sqlMaxDocID = "select doc_id from tbl_doc_indexer where doc_name=?";
                        DataIndexer di = new DataIndexer ();
                        Prepared Statement stmt = Null;
                                    Try {
                    Stmt = di.conn.prepareStatement (sqlMaxDocID);
                            Stmt.setString (1, name);
                    ResultSet docId = Stmt.executeQuery ();}
                    Retrieve the Document from the Indexer {
        Public List<DocSummary> getDocumentList (List<Integer> lstRand){
            List<DocSummary> lstDoc = new Array List<DocSummary>();
    String sqlMaxDocID = "SELECT d.doc_id, d.doc_name, d.doc_size, d.type, COUNT (p.packet_id) AS
    total packets FROM tbl_doc_indexer d, tbl_packet_indexer p WHERE d.doc_id = p.doc_id and d.doc_id =?
                            GROUP BY d.doc_id";
                        For (Integer rnd : lstRand) {
                        DataIndexer di = new DataIndexer ();
                        Prepared Statement stmt = null;
                                    try {
                    Stmt = di.conn.prepareStatement (sqlMaxDocID);
                            stmt.setInt (1, rnd.intValue ());
                    ResultSet docId = stmt.executeQuery ();
                                    Int dId=0;
                            While (docId.next ())  {
                        DocSummary ds = new DocSummary ();
                        ds.setDocId (docId.getInt ("doc_id"));
                    ds.setDocName (docId.getString ("doc_name"));
                        ds.setSize (docId.getLong ("doc_size"));
            ds.setTotalNoOfPackets (docId.getInt ("total packets"));
                            Doc.add (ds);           }
                    }    catch (Exception ex){}     }
                                Return Doc;
                                    }
```

retrieval system has been designed. To download the information rapidly and accurately, a user interface is designed that works in association with the loading mechanism. When particular information is being retrieved, it will be first searched in the packet table where its detail information is available. By using these details, the complete information is then retrieved from the existing database. Users submit a query and receive result pages instantaneously. Moreover, the model also searches the Web information resource on its own initiative and traces the change of the Web information, in order to automatically update and extend the local resource periodically. For those search requests that are not in the database, it can automatically select the commercial search engines to search information and perform classification and integration of information received from different search engines. A pseudocode of the whole algorithm is shown in Table 2.

Fig. 3 Summary of
searching time versus queries

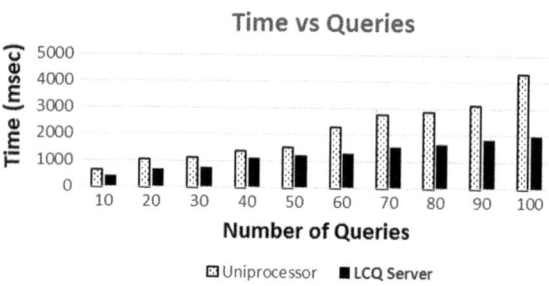

Fig. 4 Summary of
searching time versus queries

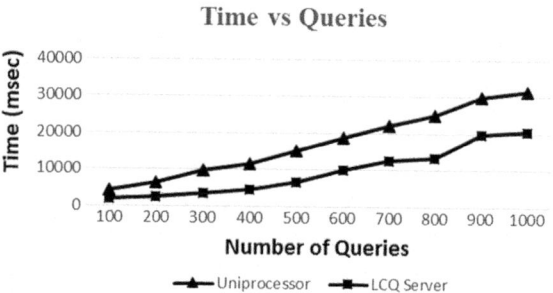

4 Result and Discussion

A comparative simulation study has been carried out to evaluate the performance of
the LCQ server as compared to ordinary system. The proposed algorithm is
implemented in the same environment for both the architectures. A number of
search queries have been examined, and the time taken to process these queries is
computed. The results so obtained are shown in Figs. 3 and 4. The curves show that
the search time for uniprocessor system is always greater than the multiprocessor
system (proposed LCQ server). As the number of queries increases, the ratio of
searching time remains constant, i.e., LCQ server takes lesser time for searching the
same number of queries in comparison to uniprocessor type server.

5 Conclusion

The LCQ server is a low cost server with eight processors and considered as a
complete multiprocessor network based on linear architecture. It exhibits better
performance in comparison to other similar type networks and also has good
topological properties. The proposed algorithm is implemented for information
retrieval using LCQ, CQ, and ordinary system. The results obtained show that the
algorithm works effectively on LCQ network. For other multiprocessor

architectures, the results are comparable. However, due to low cost of LCQ, the proposed algorithm in particular is efficient when implemented on LCQ. Results obtained indicate that the algorithm is suitable for linear type of multiprocessor architecture in general.

References

1. Canfora, G., Cerulo, L.: A taxonomy of information retrieval information models and tools. J. Comput. Inf. Technol. **12**(3), 175–194 (2004)
2. Song, H., Yin, Y., Chen, Y., Sun, X.H.: A cost-intelligent application-specific data layout scheme for parallel file systems. In: Proceedings of the 20th International Symposium on High Performance Distributed Computing, ACM, pp. 37–48 (2011)
3. Long, S., Zhao, Y., Chen, W., Tang, Y.: A prediction-based dynamic file assignment strategy for parallel file systems. Parallel Comput. **41**, pp. 1–13 (2015)
4. Cho, J.Y., Jin, H.W., Lee, M., Schwan, K.: Dynamic core affinity for high-performance file upload on hadoop distributed file system. Parallel Comput. **40**, 722–737 (2014)
5. Zhu, Y., Yu, Y., Wang, W.Y., Tan, S.S., Low, T.C.: A balanced allocation strategy for file assignment in parallel i/o systems. In: 2010 IEEE Fifth International Conference on Networking, Architecture and Storage (NAS) IEEE, pp. 257–266 (2010)
6. Rao, G.N., Nagaraj, S.: Client level framework for parallel downloading of large file systems. Int. J. Comput. Appl. **3**(2), 32–38 (2010)
7. Zeng, Z., Veeravalli, B.: Design and performance evaluation of queue-and-rate- adjustment dynamic load balancing policies for distributed networks. IEEE Trans. Comput. **55**(11), 1410–1422 (2006)
8. Khan, Z.A., Siddiqui, J., Samad, A.: Performance analysis of massively parallel architectures. BVICAM's Int. J. Inf. Tech. **5**(1), 563–568 (2013)
9. Samad, A., Rafiq, M.Q., Farooq, O.: LEC: an efficient scalable parallel interconnection network. In: Proceeding International Conference on Emerging Trends in Computer Science, Communication and Information Technology, pp. 453–458 (2010)
10. Tripathy, C.R.: Star-cube: a new fault tolerant interconnection topology for massively parallel systems. IE(I) J. ETE Div. **84**(2), 83–92 (2004)
11. Adhikari, N., Tripathy, C.R.: On a new multicomputer interconnection topology for massively parallel systems. Int. J. Distrib. Parallel Sys. (IJDPS) **2**(4) (2011)
12. Khan, Z.A., Siddiqui, J., Samad, A.: Linear crossed cube (LCQ): a new interconnection network topology for massively parallel system. Int. J. Comput. Netw. Inf. Secur. **7**(3), 18–25 (2015)
13. Khan, Z.A., Siddiqui, J., Samad, A.: A novel multiprocessor architecture for massively parallel system. In Proceeding of IEEE International Conference on Parallel, Distributed and Grid Computing, pp. 466–471 2014.
14. Rodriguez, P., Biersack, E.: Dynamic Parallel access to replicated content in the internet. IEEE/ACM Trans. Network. **10**(4) Aug 2002
15. Khan, Z.A., Siddiqui, J., Samad, A.: A novel task scheduling algorithm for parallel system. In: 3rd IEEE International Conference for sustainable Global Development, pp. 3983–3986, New-Delhi, India (2016)
16. Zeitoun, A., Jamjoom, H., El-Gendy, M.: Scalable parallel-access for mirrored servers. In 20th IASTED International Conference on Applied Informatics (AI 2002), Innsbruck, Austria, Feb 2002

17. Kharwar, C., Viyas, T., Shah, V.: Content based parallel information retrieval for text files—exploiting the multiprocessor functionality. In Proceeding of International Conference of Emerging Research in Computing, Information, Communication and Applications (ERCICA-2014), Banglore 2014

18. Guan, N., Yai, W., Deng, Q., Gu, Z., Yu, G.: Schedulability analysis for non-preemptive fixed-priority multiprocessor scheduling. J. Syst. Archit. **57**, 536–546 (2011)

Design of Energy-Efficient Random Access Memory Circuit Using Low-Voltage CMOS and High-Speed Transreceiver Logic-I I/O Standard on 28 nm FPGA

Tarun Agrawal and Vivek Srivastava

Abstract In this paper, we are designing an efficient memory using LVCMOS and HSTL-I IO Standards on 28 nm (Artix-7) FPGA. There are various families, LVCMOS and HSTL-I families are compared for finding the maximum power-efficient IO standards between them. We tested 64-bit RAM circuit at different range of frequencies of Intel Processor that are at Intel I-3 5005U 2.0 GHz, Intel I-3, 5015U 2.1 GHz, Intel I-3 5157U 2.5 GHz, Intel I-5 3380M 2.9 GHz, Intel I-5 3340U 3.1 GHz, and Intel I-7 3370K 3.5 GHz frequency range to find the most power-efficient circuit. When we migrate our design to LVCMOS from HSTL, then there is 40–60% saving in power dissipation of memory circuits.

Keywords Artix-7 · Efficient energy · RAM · Less power · LVCMOS
HSTL-I · Filed programming gate array (FPGA)

1 Introduction

Selecting the more power-efficient family among the various different families plays key role to develop a most efficient circuit. These various families are having different feature sizes (channel size of transistor). In this paper, our design is implemented on family Artix-7 having feature size of 28 nm FPGA using LVCMOS and HSTL-I family [1]. Artix-7 family of FPGA supports various families of IO standard like HSTL, LVCMOS, and SSTL [2]. The motivation behind this work is to realize a most energy-optimized designing of circuit to save the energy. In order to get the

T. Agrawal (✉) · V. Srivastava
Department of Electronics and Communication, G.L.A. University, Mathura, India
e-mail: er.tarun.ag@gmail.com

V. Srivastava
e-mail: vivek.srivastava_ec12@gla.ac.in

© Springer Nature Singapore Pte Ltd. 2018
S. K. Muttoo (ed.), *System and Architecture*, Advances in Intelligent Systems
and Computing 732, https://doi.org/10.1007/978-981-10-8533-8_10

better performance in device and also lower cost and area, manufacturer scales the geometry of IC. During scaling, manufacturer must remember one thing with each reduction parameters of IC [3]. Under the shadow of the electronic industries, day by day the semiconductor technology is booming. Low-voltage semiconductor metal oxide semiconductor (LVCMOS) supply voltage and interface standards for decreasing voltages have been defined by Joint Electron Devices Engineering Council (JEDEC) for 3.3, 3.0, 2.5, 1.5, 1.2, and 1.0 V [4]. RAM is a very essential part of any computer system. RAM is directly accessed by the Central Processing Unit [5]. It is used for both read and write operations quickly. SRAM is basically a collection of flip-flops which contains less memory cells and takes less access time [6]. DRAM is basically a collection of capacitors, contains large memory cells, and takes more time to access as compared with static RAM.

2   Block Diagram of Memory

In this work, we are implementing a 64-bit RAM circuitry with low-voltage complementary metal oxide semiconductor and HSTL-I I/O standard with size of 28 nm field programmable gate array to enhance the power consumption and to make circuit more energy efficient. Figure 2 shows the RTL schematic of 64-bit memory (Fig. 1).

2.1   Register Transfer Level Schematic of 64-Bit RAM

Register Transfer Level is used in hardware description languages like VHDL and Verilog to create high-level representation of circuit, and it also shows the implementation logic of the digital circuit. Figure 2 shows the top-level view of memory package pins of 64-bit RAM.

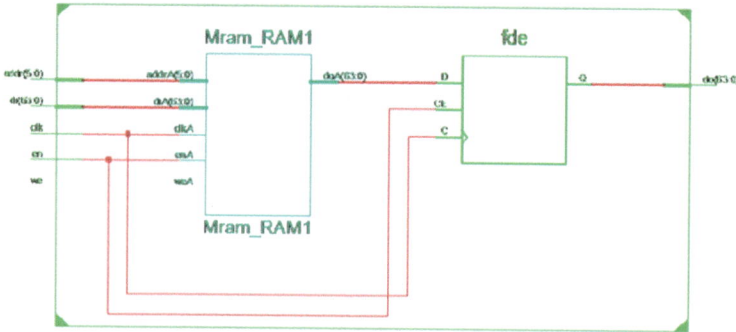

Fig. 1 Register transfer level schematic of RAM

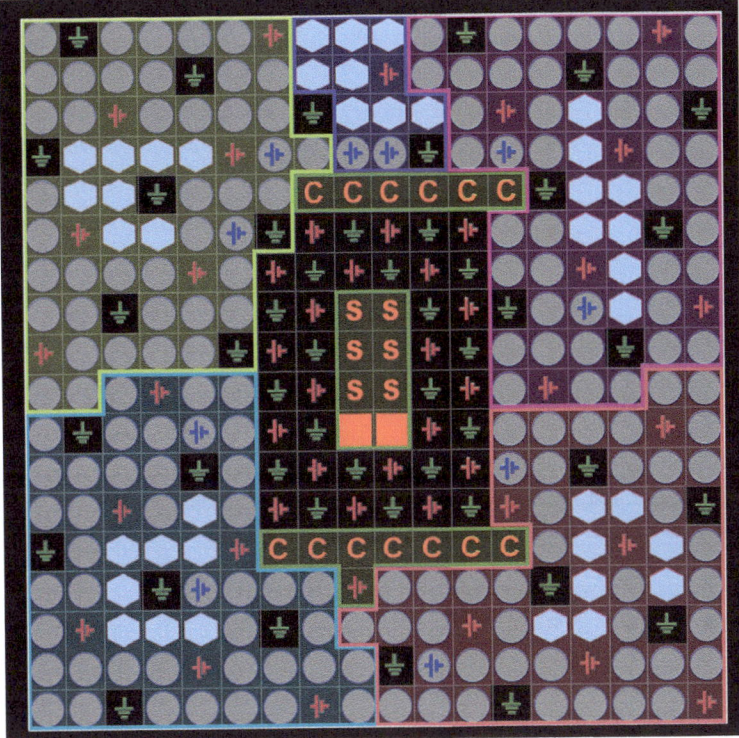

Fig. 2 64-bit random access memory package pins

2.2 Top-Level View of Random Access Memory Package Pins

See Fig. 2.

3 Analysis of Power

Power can be categorized into two types, that is, static power and dynamic power (Fig. 3).

Fig. 3 Classification of power

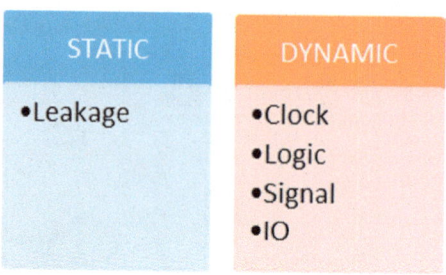

3.1 Power Consumption on 2.0 GHz Frequency

3.1.1 Using LVCMOS

In this work, our goal is to reduce the operating power and make our circuit faster, most power efficient, and cost-effective. In this experiment, we analyze the power consumption of 64-bit RAM memory at clock frequency of 2.0 GHz as of Intel I-3-5005U processor. According to our experiment, Table 1 shows that clock power is constant, i.e., 0.010 W at temperature 25 and 50 °C. Signal power is 0.026 W at 25 °C and 0.023 W at 50 °C temperature. BRAMs power is 0.144 W at 25 °C and 0.050 W at 50 °C temperature. Leakage power is 0.044 W at 25 °C and 0.077 W at 50 °C for low-voltage complementary metal oxide semiconductor technology.

3.1.2 HSTL-I

In this experiment, we analyze the power consumption of 64-bit RAM memory at clock frequency of 2.0 GHz as of Intel I-3-5015U processor. According to our experiment, Table 2 shows the Clock power is constant, i.e., 0.010 W at temperature 25 and 50 °C. Signal power is 0.026 W at 25 °C and 0.021 W at 50 °C temperature. BRAMs power is 0.144 W at 25 °C and 0.050 W at 50 °C temperature. Leakage power is 0.044 W at 25 °C and 0.079 W at 50 °C for HSTL-I technology.

Table 1 Power consumption on 2.0 GHz frequency with LVCMOS

Temp (°C)	CLK	Signal	BRAMs	IOs	Leakage	Total
25	0.010	0.026	0.114	0.451	0.044	0.646
50	0.010	0.023	0.050	0.222	0.077	0.382

Table 2 Power consumption on 2.0 GHz frequency with HSTL-I

Temp (°C)	CLK	Signal	BRAMs	IOs	Leakage	Total
25	0.010	0.026	0.144	0.649	0.044	0.843
50	0.010	0.021	0.050	0.502	0.079	0.662

As shown in Tables 1 and 2, IOs consume maximum power from these tables of LVCMOS and HSTL-I, comparing at 25 °C temperature the power consumption of clock, signal, BRAMs, and leakage power is same but IOs power is different, i.e., HSTL-I technology consumes IOs power around 1.43 times consumes power by LVCMOS technology. LVCMOS technology consumes less power as compared to HSTL-I technology. At 25 °C with Artix-7 family at 2.0 GHz LVCMOS is better as compared to HSTL-I technology. From Tables 1 and 2 of LVCMOS and HSTL-I technology at 50 °C clock power and BRAMs power is same. But signal, IOs, and leakage power are different. At 50 °C, HSTL-I technology consumes total power around 1.7 times of LVCMOS technology. Hence, it is clear that at frequency range of 2.0 GHz, the best less power consumption technology between HSTL-I and LVCMOS is LVCMOS.

3.2 Power Consumption on 2.1 GHz Frequency

3.2.1 LVCMOS

In this experiment, we analyze the power consumption of 64-bit RAM memory at clock frequency of 2.1 GHz as of Intel I-3-5015U processor. According to our experiment, Table 3 shows the clock power is constant, i.e., 0.010 W at temperature 25 and 50 °C. Signal power is 0.028 W at 25 °C and 0.024 W at 50 °C temperature. BRAMs power is 0.120 W at 25 °C and 0.053 W at 50 °C temperature. Leakage power is 0.044 W at 25 °C and 0.077 W at 50 °C for LVCMOS.

3.2.2 HSTL-I

In this experiment, we analyze the power consumption of 64-bit RAM memory at clock frequency of 2.1 GHz as of Intel I-3-5015U processor. According to our experiment, Table 4 shows the clock power is constant, i.e., 0.010 W at temperature 25 and 50 °C. Signal power is 0.027 W at 25 °C and 0.022 W at 50 °C temperature. IOs power is 0.665 W at temperature at 25 °C and 0.511 W at 50 °C temperature. BRAMs power is 0.120 W at 25 °C and 0.053 W at 50 °C temperature. Leakage power is 0.044 W at 25 °C and 0.079 W at 50 °C for HSTL-I technology.

From Tables 3 and 4, it is shown that IOs consume maximum power of LVCMOS and HSTL-I. On comparing at 25 °C temperature, the power

Table 3 Power consumption on 2.1 GHz frequency with LVCMOS

Temp (°C)	CLK	Signal	BRAMs	IOs	Leakage	Total
25	0.010	0.028	0.120	0.474	0.044	0.676
50	0.010	0.024	0.053	0.233	0.077	0.397

Table 4 Power consumption at 2.1 GHz frequency with HSTL-I

Temp (°C)	CLK	Signal	BRAMs	IOs	Leakage	Total
25	0.010	0.027	0.120	0.665	0.044	0.866
50	0.010	0.022	0.053	0.511	0.079	0.675

consumption of clock, BRAMs, and leakage power is same but signal and IOs power are different, i.e., HSTL-I technology consumes total power around 1.28 times consumes total power by LVCMOS technology. LVCMOS technology consumes less power in comparison with HSTL-I technology. At 25 °C with Artix-7 family at 2.1 GHz, LVCMOS is better as compared to HSTL-I technology. From Tables 3 and 4 of LVCMOS and HSTL-I technology, 50 °C clock power and BRAMs power are same. But signal, IOs, and leakage power are different. At 50 °C, HSTL-I technology consumes total power around 1.7 times of LVCMOS technology. Hence, it is clear that at frequency range of 2.1 GHz, the best less power consumption technology between HSTL-I and LVCMOS is also LVCMOS.

3.3 Power Consumption on 2.5 GHz Frequency

3.3.1 LVCMOS

In this experiment, we analyze the power consumption of 64-bit RAM memory at clock frequency of 2.5 GHz as of Intel I-3-5157U processor. According to our experiment, Table 5 shows the clock power is constant, i.e., 0.012 W at temperature 25 and 50 °C. Signal power is 0.033 W at 25 °C and 0.028 W at 50 °C temperature. BRAMs power is 0.143 W at 25 °C and 0.063 W at 50 °C temperature. IOs power is 0.564 W at 25 °C and 0.277 W at 50 °C temperature. Leakage power is 0.044 W at 25 °C and 0.078 W at 50 °C for LVCMOS.

3.3.2 HSTL-I

In this experiment, we analyze the power consumption of 64-bit RAM memory at clock frequency of 2.5 GHz of Intel I-3-5157U processor. According to our experiment, Table 6 shows the clock power is constant, i.e., 0.012 W at temperature 25 and 50 °C. Signal power is 0.032 W at 25 °C and 0.026 W at 50 °C temperature. IOs power is 0.729 W at temperature at 25 °C and 0.546 W at 50 °C

Table 5 Power consumption at 2.5 GHz frequency with LVCMOS

Temp (°C)	CLK	Signal	BRAMs	IOs	Leakage	Total
25	0.012	0.033	0.143	0.564	0.044	0.796
50	0.012	0.028	0.063	0.277	0.078	0.458

Table 6 Power consumption at 2.5 GHz frequency with HSTL-I

Temp (°C)	CLK	Signal	BRAMs	IOs	Leakage	Total
25	0.012	0.032	0.143	0.729	0.044	0.96
50	0.012	0.026	0.063	0.546	0.079	0.727

temperature. BRAMs power is 0.143 W at 25 °C and 0.063 W at 50 °C temperature. Leakage power is 0.044 W at 25 °C and 0.079 W at 50 °C for HSTL-I technology.

From Tables 5 and 6, it is shown that IOs consume maximum power of LVCMOS and HSTL-I. On comparing at 25 °C temperature, the power consumption of clock, BRAMs, and leakage power is same but signal and IOs power are different, i.e., HSTL-I technology consumes total power around 1.2 times consumes total power by LVCMOS technology. LVCMOS technology consumes less power as compared to HSTL-I technology. At 25 °C with Artix-7 family at 2.5 GHz LVCMOS is better as compared to HSTL-I technology. From Tables 5 and 6, LVCMOS and HSTL-I technology at 50 °C clock power and BRAMs power are same. But signal, IOs, and leakage power are different. At 50 °C, HSTL-I technology consumes total power around 1.58 times of LVCMOS technology. Hence, it is clear that at frequency range of 2.5 GHz, the best less power consumption technology between HSTL-I and LVCMOS is also LVCMOS.

3.4 Power Consumption on 2.9 GHz Frequency

3.4.1 Using LVCMOS

In this experiment, we analyze the power consumption of 64-bit RAM memory at clock frequency of 2.9 GHz as of Intel I-5, 3380M processor. According to our experiment, Table 7 shows the clock power is constant, i.e., 0.014 W at temperature 25 and 50 °C. Signal power is 0.038 W at 25 °C and 0.033 W at 50 °C temperature. BRAMs power is 0.166 W at 25 °C and 0.073 W at 50 °C temperature. IOs power is 0.659 W at 25 °C and 0.322 W at 50 °C temperature. Leakage power is 0.045 W at 25 °C and 0.078 W at 50 °C for LVCMOS.

Table 7 Power consumption at 2.9 GHz frequency with LVCMOS

Temp (°C)	CLK	Signal	BRAMs	IOs	Leakage	Total
25	0.014	0.038	0.166	0.659	0.045	0.917
50	0.014	0.033	0.073	0.322	0.078	0.579

Table 8 Power consumption at 2.9 GHz frequency with HSTL-I

Temp (°C)	CLK	Signal	BRAMs	IOs	Leakage	Total
25	0.015	0.040	0.177	0.826	0.045	1.103
50	0.015	0.032	0.078	0.519	0.080	0.804

3.4.2 Using HSTL-I

In this experiment, we analyze the power consumption of 64-bit RAM memory at clock frequency of 2.5 GHz of Intel I-5, 3380M processor. According to our experiment, Table 8 shows the clock power is constant, i.e., 0.015 W at temperature 25 and 50 °C. Signal power is 0.040 W at 25 °C and 0.032 W at 50 °C temperature. IOs power is 0.826 W at temperature at 25 °C and 0.519 W at 50 °C temperature. BRAMs power is 0.177 W at 25 °C and 0.078 W at 50 °C temperature. Leakage power is 0.045 W at 25 °C and 0.080 W at 50 °C for HSTL-I technology.

From Tables 7 and 8, it is shown that IOs consume maximum power of LVCMOS and HSTL-I. On comparing at 25 °C temperature, the power consumption of only leakage power is same and all clock, BRAMs, signal and IOs power are different, i.e., HSTL-I technology consumes total power around 1.2 times consumes total power by LVCMOS technology. LVCMOS technology consumes less power in comparison with HSTL-I technology. At 25 °C with Artix-7 family at 2.9 GHz LVCMOS is better as compared to HSTL-I technology. From Tables 7 and 8, LVCMOS and HSTL-I technology at 50 °C all power parameters are different. At 50 °C, HSTL-I technology consumes total power around 1.38 times of LVCMOS technology. Hence, it is clear that at frequency range of 2.9 GHz, the best less power consumption technology between HSTL-I and LVCMOS is also LVCMOS.

3.5   Power Consumption on 3.1 GHz Frequency

3.5.1 Using LVCMOS

In this experiment, we analyze the power consumption of 64-bit RAM memory at clock frequency of 3.1 GHz as of Intel I-5, 3340U processor. According to our experiment, Table 9 shows the clock power is constant, i.e., 0.015 W at temperature 25 and 50 °C. Signal power is 0.041 W at 25 °C and 0.035 W at 50 °C temperature. BRAMs power is 0.177 W at 25 °C and 0.078 W at 50 °C temperature. IOs power is 0.7 W at 25 °C and 0.344 W at 50 °C temperature. Leakage power is 0.045 W at 25 °C and 0.078 W at 50 °C for LVCMOS.

Table 9 Power consumption at 3.1 GHz frequency with LVCMOS

Temp (°C)	CLK	Signal	BRAMs	IOs	Leakage	Total
25	0.015	0.041	0.177	0.7	0.045	0.977
50	0.015	0.035	0.078	0.344	0.078	0.550

3.5.2 HSTL-I

In this experiment, we analyze the power consumption of 64-bit RAM memory at clock frequency of 3.1 GHz as of Intel I-5, 3340U processor. According to our experiment, Table 8 shows the clock power is constant, i.e., 0.015 W at temperature 25 and 50 °C. Signal power is 0.040 W at 25 °C and 0.032 W at 50 °C temperature. IOs power is 0.826 W at temperature at 25 °C and 0.032 W at 50 °C temperature. BRAMs power is 0.177 W at 25 °C and 0.078 W at 50 °C temperature. IOs power is 0.826 W at 25 °C and 0.519 W at 50 °C temperature. Leakage power is 0.045 W at 25 °C and 0.080 W at 50 °C for HSTL-I Technology.

From Tables 9 and 10, it is clear that IOs consume maximum power of LVCMOS and HSTL-I. On comparing at 25 °C temperature, the power consumption of clock, BRAMs, and leakage power is same but signal and IOs power are different, i.e., HSTL-I technology consumes total power around 1.12 times consumes total power by LVCMOS technology. LVCMOS technology consumes less power as compared to HSTL-I technology. At 25 °C with Artix-7 family and 3.1 GHz LVCMOS is better as compared to HSTL-I technology. From Tables 9 and 10, LVCMOS and HSTL-I technology at 50 °C clock power and BRAMs power is same. But signal, IOs, and leakage power are different. At 50 °C, HSTL-I technology consumes total power around 1.46 times of LVCMOS technology. Hence, it is clear that at frequency range of 3.1 GHz, the best less power consumption technology between HSTL-I and LVCMOS is also LVCMOS.

3.6 Power Consumption on 3.5 GHz Frequency

3.6.1 Using LVCMOS

In this experiment, we analyze the power consumption of 64-bit RAM memory at clock frequency of 3.5 GHz as of Intel I-7, 3370K processor. According to our experiment, Table 11 shows the clock power is constant, i.e., 0.017 W at temperature 25 and 50 °C. Signal power is 0.046 W at 25 °C and 0.039 W at 50 °C

Table 10 Power consumption at 3.1 GHz frequency with HSTL-I

Temp (°C)	CLK	Signal	BRAMs	IOs	Leakage	Total
25	0.015	0.040	0.177	0.826	0.045	1.103
50	0.015	0.032	0.078	0.519	0.080	0.804

Table 11 Power consumption at 3.5 GHz frequency with LVCMOS

Temp (°C)	CLK	Signal	BRAMs	IOs	Leakage	Total
25	0.017	0.046	0.2	0.79	0.045	1.098
50	0.017	0.039	0.088	0.388	0.6799	0.611

temperature. BRAMs power is 0.2 W at 25 °C and 0.088 W at 50 °C temperature. IOs power is 0.79 W at 25 °C and 0.388 W at 50 °C temperature. Leakage power is 0.045 W at 25 °C and 0.6799 W at 50 °C for LVCMOS.

3.6.2 HSTL-I

In this experiment, we analyze the power consumption of 64-bit RAM memory at clock frequency of 3.5 GHz as of Intel I-7, 3370K processor. According to our experiment, Table 12 shows the clock power is constant, i.e., 0.017 W at temperature 25 and 50 °C. Signal power is 0.045 W at 25 °C and 0.036 W at 50 °C temperature. IOs power is 0.890 W at temperature at 25 °C and 0.634 W at 50 °C temperature. BRAMs power is 0.200 W at 25 °C and 0.088 W at 50 °C temperature. IOs power is 0.890 W at 25 °C and 0.634 W at 50 °C temperature. Leakage power is 0.045 W at 25 °C and 0.080 W at 50 °C for HSTL-I Technology.

From Tables 11 and 12, it is clear that IOs consume maximum power of LVCMOS and HSTL-I. On comparing at 25 °C temperature, the power consumption of clock, BRAMs, and leakage power is same but signal and IOs power are different, i.e., HSTL-I technology consumes total power around 1.09 times consumes total power by LVCMOS technology. LVCMOS technology consumes less power as compared to HSTL-I technology. At 25 °C with Artix-7 family and 3.5 GHz LVCMOS is better as compared to HSTL-I technology. From Tables 11 and 12, LVCMOS and HSTL-I technology at 50 °C clock power and BRAMs power are same. But signal, IOs, and leakage power are different. At 50 °C, HSTL-I technology consumes total power around 1.4 times of LVCMOS technology. Hence, it is clear that at frequency range of 3.1 GHz, the best less power consumption technology between HSTL-I and LVCMOS is also LVCMOS.

Table 12 Power consumption at 3.5 GHz frequency with HSTL-I

Temp (°C)	CLK	Signal	BRAMs	IOs	Leakage	Total
25	0.017	0.045	0.2	0.890	0.045	1.198
50	0.017	0.036	0.088	0.643	0.080	0.856

4   Conclusion

LVCMOS is the most energy-efficient IO standard compared to HSTL. Energy-efficient memory design is possible if we replace HSTL with LVCMOS. Our design is compatible with the latest processor developed by leading microprocessor developer of the world like Intel, Motorola. Among different component of dynamic power, clock power is the least and IOs power is maximum in magnitude. Dynamic power reduction is larger than static power. We have also tested the thermal stability of our RAM by operating this design with two different temperatures of 25 and 50 °C. HSTL consumes approx. 40–60% more power compared to LVCMOS.

5   Future Scopes

In this work, we are using LVCMOS and HSTL IO standards in energy-efficient design of RAM. In future, we can go for other memory circuits like register, ROM, and CAM. There is also open scope to design energy-efficient memory using different IO standards like transistor–transistor logic, mobile DDR, high-speed unterminated logic, high-speed transceiver logic, stub series terminated logic, gunning transceiver logic, and peripheral component interconnect. Now, our target design is 28 nm technology-based Artix-7 FPGA. We can migrate to 3-D IC, System on Chips (SoCs), and other programmable logic devices and re-implement same memory on that. In future, we shall design high-speed memory that will be able to operate with frequency of 1 THz and beyond.

References

1. Lee, D.: Area efficient ROM-embedded SRAM cache. IEEE Trans. Very Large Scale Integr. (VLSI) Syst. **21**(9) (2013)
2. Lee, D., Fong, X.: R-MRAM: a ROM-embedded STT MRAM cache. IEEE Electron Device Lett. **34**(10) (2013)
3. Sasagawa, R., Fukushi, I., Hamaminato, M., Kawashima, S.: High-speed cascode sensing scheme for 1.0 V contact-programming mask ROM. In: Proceedings of the IEEE Symposium on VLSI Circuits Digest of Technical Papers, pp. 95–96 (1999)
4. Sweety, B.D., Pandey, B., Singh, D., Aaseri, R.: IO standard based green multiplexer design & implementation on FPGA. In: IEEE 5th International Conference on Computational Intelligence and Communication Network (CICN), 27–29 Sept 2013
5. Kalra, L., Bansal, N., Saini, R., Bansal, M., Pandey, B.: LVCMOS I/O standard based environment friendly low power ROM design on FPGA. In: International Conference on "Computing for Sustainable Global Development", 11th–13th Mar 2015

6. Khare, K., Ku, S.H., Donaton, R.A., Greco, S., Brodsky, C., Chen, X., Chou, A., DellaGuardia, R., Deshpande, S., Doris, B., Fung, S.K.H., Gabor, A., Gribelyuk, M., Holmes, S., Jamin, F.F., Lai, W.L., Lee, W.H., Li, Y., McFarland, P., Mo, R., Mittl, S., Narasimha, S., Nielsen, D., Purtell, R., Rausch, W., Sankaran, S., Snare, J., Tsou, L., Vayshenker, A., Wagner, T., Wehella-Gamage, D., Wu, E., Wu, S., Yan, W., Barth, E., Ferguson, R., Gilbert, P., Schepis, D., Sekiguchi, A., Goldblatt, R., Welser, J., Muller, W.H., Agnello, P.: A high performance 90 nm SOI technology with 0.992 μm^2 6T-SRAM cell. In: Proceedings of the IEEE IEDM Digest of Technical Papers, Dec 2002, pp. 8–11

Stub Series Terminal Logic-Based Low-Power Thermal-Aware Vedic Multiplier Design on 40-nm FPGA

Arushi Aggarwal, Bishwajeet Pandey, Sweety Dabbas, Achal Agarwal and Siddharth Saurabh

Abstract In this paper, we have proposed SSTL-based low-power energy efficient design on Vedic multiplier. SSTL is an acronym for Stub Series Terminated Logic. The paper presents the proficiency of Antyayor Dasakepi Vedic technique for multiplication that strikes a disparity in the real procedure of multiplication by itself. It allows comparable production of biased products and eliminates unnecessary steps of multiplication. The projected algorithm is represented using Verilog language, a hardware description language. Also, we analyzed how this integrated design is affected when it is operated in different regions under different temperatures: 10, 25, 40, 55, 70 °C. It is observed that at different ambient temperatures from 10 to 70 °C, there is 37.95, 58.85, 36.03, 34.84, 33.51% reduction in leakage power for SSTL2_1 as compared to SSTL2_II, SSTL15_DCI, SSTL18_DCI, there is 8.37, 8.39, 8.47, 8.50, 7.47% reduction in MAT for SSTL15_DCI as compared to SSTL2_II, SSTL2_I, SSTL18_DCI, and there is 17.29, 3.84, 6.72, 5.124, 4.135% reduction in JT for SSTL18_DCI as compared to SSTL2_II, SSTL15_DCI, SSTL2_I.

Keywords Multiplier · Vedic multiplier · SSTL · IO standard
Energy efficient · Antyayor Dasakepi

A. Aggarwal (✉) · B. Pandey · S. Dabbas
Gyancity Research Lab, Gurgaon, India
e-mail: arushi@gyancity.com

B. Pandey
e-mail: gyancity@gyancity.com

S. Dabbas
e-mail: sweety.dabas@gmail.com

A. Agarwal
Ajay Kumar Garg Engineering College, Ghaziabad, India
e-mail: agarwal.achal94@gmail.com

S. Saurabh
Giant Meterwave Radio Telescope, Khodad, Pune, India
e-mail: siddharthsaurabh1@gmail.com

© Springer Nature Singapore Pte Ltd. 2018
S. K. Muttoo (ed.), *System and Architecture*, Advances in Intelligent Systems and Computing 732, https://doi.org/10.1007/978-981-10-8533-8_11

1 Introduction

In the near beginning of twentieth century on or after ancient Indian Vedas Vedic mathematics was rediscovered. Prehistoric Indian system of mathematic has been resulted from various Vedic sutras. The predictable mathematical algorithms can be cut down and even optimized by the exercise of Vedic math [1]. A system's performance is in general resoluted by the pace of the multiplier as it is one of the very important modules in elevated speed recital systems such as IIR and FIR filters, microprocessors, digital signal processors (DSPs), and in many other systems. Multipliers consume considerable power and have long latency [2]. Hence, high-quality multiplier designing rises the effectiveness and proficiency of a system to a great extent. Vedic multiplier is one such soaring pace, low area multiplier construction.

1.1 Antyayor_Dasakepi_Sutra

This sutra signify numerals, the last digits of which are summed up to provide 10; i.e., this sutra is implemented by burgeoning of numbers; for example 62 * 28, 45 * 45, 37 * 23 make a note that in every scenario the sum of the last digit of second number to the last digit of the first number is 10. In advance, the numbers leftward to the last digits remain same. The right-hand part of the answer is obtained by multiplying the last digits. For example,

In 66 * 64, there is 6 + 4 = 10. Therefore Ekadhikena of 6 = 7;

$$66 * 64 = (6 * 7)/(6 * 4) = 42/24 = 4224.$$

In order to make the design thermal-aware [3] and energy efficient [4, 5] both, we have selected the most energy efficient IO standard in SSTL family available on FPGA [6–8]: SSTL2_1, SSTL2_11, SSTL15_DCI, SSTL18_DCI. We have used various abbreviations such as JT for junction temperature, MAT for maximum ambient temperature, IO for input–output, LP for leakage power, SSTL for Stub Series Terminal Logic.

2 Power and Thermal Analysis of Vedic Multiplier

2.1 Analysis of MAT, Junction Temperature, and Leakage Power

There is 18.59, 1.77, and 80% reduction in power, MAT, and JT temperature, respectively, as we range down ambient temperature from 10 to 70 °C for SSTL2_1 IO standard. Graphical representation is shown in Table 1 and Fig. 1.

Table 1 Analysis of leakage power, JT, and MAT for SSTL2_1

(°C)	Power	MAT	JT
10	1.950	73.1	15.3
25	2.032	72.9	32.5
40	2.132	72.6	45.8
55	2.255	72.3	61.1
70	2.406	71.8	76.5

Fig. 1 Graphical representation of MAT, JT, LP for SSTL2_1

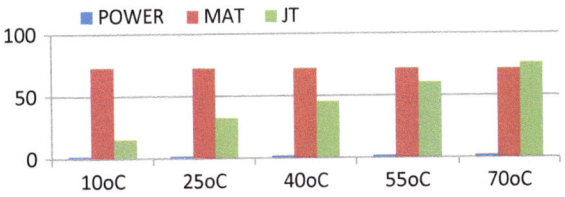

There is 17.79, 1.66, and 79.61% reduction in power, MAT, and JT temperature, respectively, as we range down ambient temperature from 10 to 70 °C for SSTL2_11 IO standard [3]. Graphical representation is shown in Table 2 and Fig. 2.

There is 17.57, 1.522, and 79.50% reduction in power, MAT, and JT temperature, respectively, as we range down ambient temperature from 10 to 70 °C for SSTL15_DCI IO standard. Graphical representation is shown in Table 3 and Fig. 3.

There is 13.15, 1.71, and 76.81% reduction in power, MAT, and JT temperature, respectively, as we range down ambient temperature from 10 to 70 °C for SSTL18_DCI IO standard. Graphical representation is shown in Table 4 and Fig. 4.

Table 2 Analysis of leakage power, JT, and MAT for SSTL2_11

(°C)	Power	MAT	JT
10	2.116	72.2	15.7
25	2.198	72.0	31.0
40	2.299	71.7	46.2
55	2.422	71.4	61.6
70	2.574	71.0	77.0

Fig. 2 Graphical representation of MAT, JT, LP for SSTL2_11

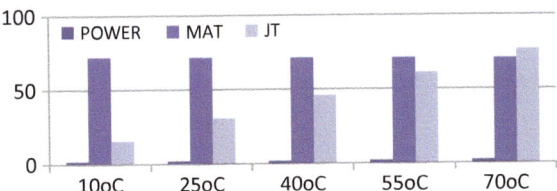

Table 3 Analysis of leakage power, JT, and MAT for SSTL15_DCI

(°C)	Power	MAT	JT
10	2.148	78.8	15.8
25	2.230	78.6	31.1
40	2.331	78.34	46.3
55	2.454	78.0	61.7
70	2.606	77.6	77.1

Fig. 3 Graphical representation of MAT, JT, LP for SSTL15_DCI

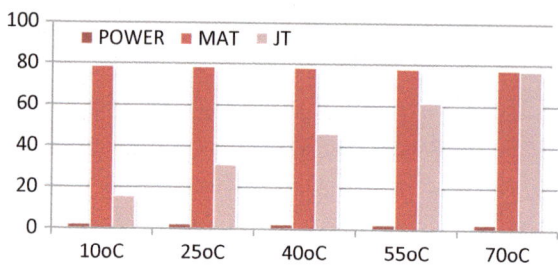

Table 4 Analysis of leakage power, JT, and MAT for SSTL18_DCI

(°C)	Power	MAT	JT
10	3.143	75.8	18.5
25	3.228	75.6	33.8
40	3.333	75.3	49.1
55	3.461	75.0	64.4
70	3.619	74.5	79.8

Fig. 4 Graphical representation of MAT, JT, LP for SSTL18_DCI

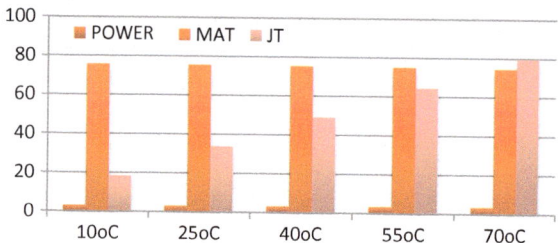

3 IO Standards

3.1 Power Analysis

At different ambient temperatures from 10 to 70 °C, there is 37.95, 58.85, 36.03, 34.84, 33.51% reduction in leakage power for SSTL2_1 as compared to SSTL2_11, SSTL15_DCI, SSTL18_DCI as shown in Table 5 and Fig. 5.

Table 5 Leakage power analysis for various IO standards

(°C)	SSTL2_1	SSTL2_11	SSTL15_DCI	SSTL18_DCI
10	1.950	2.116	2.148	3.143
25	2.032	2.198	2.230	3.228
40	2.132	2.299	2.331	3.333
55	2.255	2.422	2.454	3.461
70	2.406	2.574	2.606	3.619

Fig. 5 Graphical power analysis for various IO standards

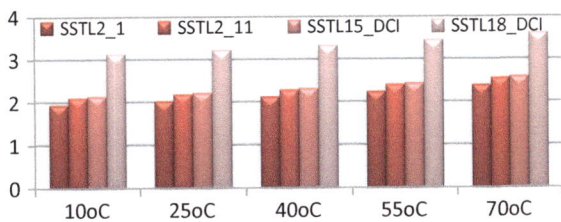

3.2 Thermal Analysis

At different ambient temperatures from 10 to 70 °C, there is 8.37, 8.39, 8.47, 8.50, 7.47% reduction in MAT for SSTL15_DCI as compared to SSTL2_11, SSTL2_1, SSTL18_DCI as shown in Table 6 and Fig. 6.

At different ambient temperatures from 10 to 70 °C, there is 17.29, 3.84, 6.72, 5.124, 4.135% reduction in JT for SSTL18_DCI as compared to SSTL2_11, SSTL15_DCI, SSTL2_1 as shown in Table 7 and Fig. 7.

Table 6 Thermal analysis in terms of MAT for various IO standards

(°C)	SSTL2_1	SSTL2_11	SSTL15_DCI	SSTL18_DCI
10	73.1	72.2	78.8	75.8
25	72.9	72.0	78.6	75.6
40	72.6	71.7	78.34	75.3
55	72.3	71.4	78.0	75.0
70	71.8	71.0	77.6	74.5

Fig. 6 Graphical thermal analysis in terms of MAT for various IO standards

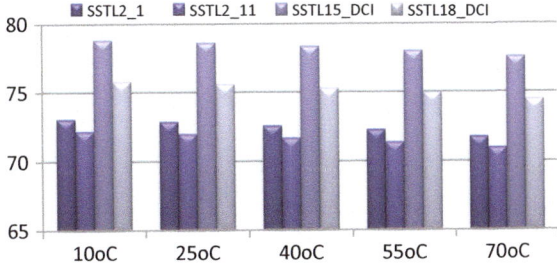

Table 7 Thermal analysis in terms of JT for various IO standards

(°C)	SSTL2_1	SSTL2_11	SSTL15_DCI	SSTL18_DCI
10	15.3	15.7	15.8	18.5
25	32.5	31.0	31.1	33.8
40	45.8	46.2	46.3	49.1
55	61.1	61.6	61.7	64.4
70	76.5	77.0	77.1	79.8

Fig. 7 Graphical thermal analysis in terms of JT for various IO standards

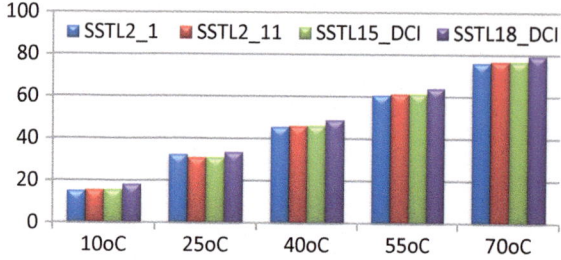

4   Conclusion

At different ambient temperatures from 10 to 70 °C, there is 37.95, 58.85, 36.03, 34.84, 33.51% reduction in leakage power for SSTL2_1 as compared to SSTL2_11, SSTL15_DCI, SSTL18_DCI, there is 8.37, 8.39, 8.47, 8.50, 7.47% reduction in MAT for SSTL15_DCI as compared to SSTL2_11, SSTL2_1, SSTL18_DCI and 17.29, 3.84, 6.72, 5.124, 4.135% reduction in JT for SSTL18_DCI as compared to SSTL2_11, SSTL15_DCI, SSTL2_1.

5   Future Scope

The execution is done successfully on Virtex-6 (40-nm) FPGA. A wide span is there to execute this device and construct power investigation on 28-nm FPGA and 45-nm FPGA like Virtex-7, Kintex-7, and Spartan-6 Field Programmable Gate Array devices. In order to examine the intend made, in terms of control and temperature using other I/O standards such as low voltage complementary metal oxide semiconductors (LVCMOS), digitally controlled impedance (DCI) and high-speed transistor logic (HSTL) are other extents to expand the implementation and put forward another squat power designs.

References

1. Munjal, A., Gita, B.: Rig Veda and the Second Law of Thermodynamics, http://creative. sulekha.com/bhagavad-gita-rig-veda-and-the-second-law-of-thermodynamics_217316_blog
2. Pandey, B., et al.: Mechanics based energy efficient FIR filter for digital signal processing. Appl. Mech. Mater. (AMM) (2014)
3. Huang, W., et al.: Compact thermal modeling for temperature-aware design. In: 41st Annual Design Automation Conference (DAC), pp. 878–883 (2004)
4. Musavi, S.H.A., Chowdhry, B.S., Kumar, T., Pandey, B., Kumar, W. (2015). IoTs enable active contour modeling based energy efficient and thermal aware object tracking on FPGA. Wirel. Pers. Commun. **85**(2), 529–543 (2015). ISSN: 1572-834X
5. Kumar, T., Pandey, B., Das, T., Chowdhry, B.S.: Mobile DDR IO standard based high performance energy efficient portable ALU design on FPGA. Wirel. Pers. Commun. Int. J. **76** (3), 569–578 (2014)
6. Kumar, T., et al.: CTHS based energy efficient thermal aware image ALU design on FPGA. Wirel. Pers. Commun. Int. J. **83**(1) (2015). ISSN: 0929-6212 (print), 1572-834X (electronic)
7. Ogras, U.Y., Hu, J., Marculescu, R.: Key research problems in NoC design: a holistic perspective. In: 3rd IEEE/ACM/IFIP International Conference on Hardware/Software Codesign and System Synthesis, pp. 69–74 (2005)
8. Uddin, A., et al.: Thermal aware energy efficient bengali unicode reader in text analysis. In: IEEE International Conference on Reliability Optimization & Information Technology (ICROIT), India (2014)

LVCMOS-Based Low-Power Thermal-Aware Energy-Proficient Vedic Multiplier Design on Different FPGAs

Arushi Aggarwal, Bishwajeet Pandey, Sweety Dabbas, Achal Agarwal and Siddharth Saurabh

Abstract In the paper, we'll be discussing about amalgamating thermal-aware intent in energy-proficient Vedic multiplier on different FPGAs. LVCMOS is a contraction for low-voltage complementary metal-oxide semiconductor. Here, we are implementing this Vedic multiplier design via three LVCMOS I/O standards they are: LVCMOS12, LVCMOS18, and LVCMOS25 which are accessible among 45, 40, and 28-nm FPGA. To check the thermal-aware of our design on the Vedic multiplier, we are analyzing the design at diverse room temperatures 20, 30, and 45 °C. Vedic Mathematics is one of the oldest processes of arithmetic that has a distinctive method of performing a calculation based on different Sutras. The techniques showed in this paper is Yavadunam Tavadunikrtya, and the recital study of these techniques is obtained as: for LVCMOS_18, as the multiplier design is migrated from 45 to 28-nm intent, there is 88.29% diminution in Leakage control of Vedic multiplier at constant temperature of 20 °C, for LVCMOS_15, as the Vedic multiplier intent is moved from 45 to 90-nm intent, there is 89.54% diminution in Leakage control of Vedic multiplier at constant temperature of 30 °C.

Keywords Thermal-aware design · Multiplier · Yavadunam Tavadunikrtya LVCMOS · Energy efficient design · IO standards

A. Aggarwal (✉) · B. Pandey · S. Dabbas
Gyancity Research Lab, Gurugram, India
e-mail: arushi@gyancity.com

B. Pandey
e-mail: gyancity@gyancity.com

S. Dabbas
e-mail: sweety.dabas@gmail.com

A. Agarwal
Ajay Kumar Garg Engineering College, Ghaziabad, India
e-mail: agarwal.achal94@gmail.com

S. Saurabh
Giant Meterwave Radio Telescope, Khodad, Pune, India
e-mail: siddharthsaurabh1@gmail.coms

© Springer Nature Singapore Pte Ltd. 2018
S. K. Muttoo (ed.), *System and Architecture*, Advances in Intelligent Systems and Computing 732, https://doi.org/10.1007/978-981-10-8533-8_12

1 Introduction

Multiplication is an imperative aspect in mathematical operations and is also used in a number of applications. As multipliers take extensive time for implementation, so there is a requirement of hasty multipliers to hoard the implementation time [1]. We are implementing this design of Vedic multiplier via three LVCMOS I/O standards they are: LVCMOS12, LVCMOS18, and LVCMOS25 which are accessible among various sizes, i.e., 45, 40, and 28-nm FPGA (Fig. 1).

To check the thermal awareness of our Vedic multiplier [2–5], we are analyzing the design at three variant room temperatures, i.e., 20, 30, and 45 °C. According to the sutra Yavadunam Tavadunikrtya whatsoever is the deficit take away that from the numeral and inscribe alongside the square of that deficit [6]. This sutra can be related to attain square of numbers close up to the base of power 10.

1.1 Example 1: Square of 8?

Here, base is 10.

The solution will be divorced into two parts by the symbol: '/'.

Deficit is $10 - 8 = 2$. Multiply the deficit by itself or square it $22 = 4$. As the deficiency is 1, subtract it from the number, i.e., $8 - 2 = 6$. Now, place 8 on left and 1 on right side of this line or slash, i.e., 6/4.

Therefore, 64 is answer.

1.2 Example 2: Square of 992?

Here, base is 1000.

Deficit will be $1000 - 992 = 8$. Square it: 64. Deficit subtracted from 994 gives $992 - 8 = 984$. Answer: 984/064 [because base is 1000].

Fig. 1 Different LVCMOS IO standards available in FPGA

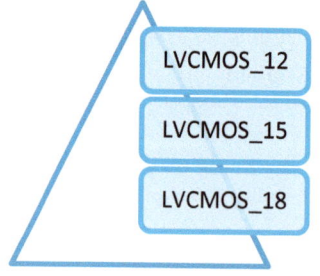

We have used various abbreviations such as JT for junction temperature, MAT for maximum ambient temperature, IO for input output, LP for Leakage Power, and LVCMOS for low-voltage complementary metal-oxide semiconductor.

2 Power Scrutiny via Scaling Thermally

In order to make it energy efficient and thermal aware both we are LVCMOS IO Standards available on FPGA [7–9].

2.1 Power Scrutiny Using LVCMOS_12 I/O Standard

Using LVCMOS_12, there is 1.98, 5.23, and 87.96% reduction in Leakage Power on 28, 45, and 40 nm in that order as displayed in Table 1 and Fig. 2, as we range down atmospheric temperature from 45 to 20 °C. The graphical representation is shown in Fig. 2.

Table 1 Analysis of leakage control for LVCMOS_12 on 3 different FPGAs

	28 nm	45 nm	40 nm
20	1.582	0.181	1.587
30	1.591	0.184	1.646
45	1.614	0.191	0.191

Fig. 2 Leakage Power on variant ambient temperature using LVCMOS12

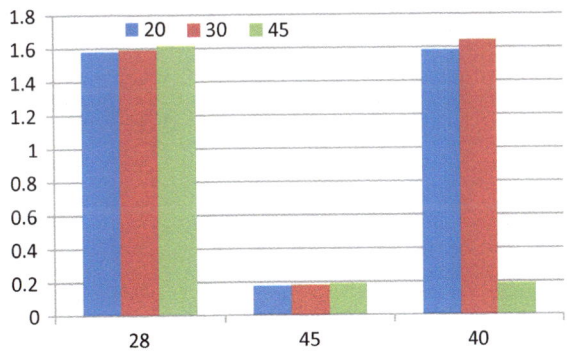

118

A. Aggarwal et al.

2.2 Power Scrutiny Using LVCMOS15 IO Standard

Using LVCMOS15, there is 9.71, 4.90, and 8.33% diminution in Leakage Power on 28, 40, and 45 nm in that order as shown in Table 2, when we level down ambient temperature from 45 to 20 °C. The graphical representation is shown in Fig. 3 and Table 3.

2.3 Power Scrutiny via LVCMOS12 I/O Standard

Using LVCMOS18, there is 7.75, 4.01, and 7.60% diminution in Leakage Power on 28, 45, and 40 nm as displayed in Table 4, as soon as we range the ambient temperature from 45 to 20 °C. The graphical representation is shown in Fig. 4.

Table 2 Scrutiny of Leakage Power for LVCMOS_15 on 3 different FPGAs

	28 nm	45 nm	40 nm
20	0.251	0.194	1.825
30	0.259	0.197	1.885
45	0.278	0.204	1.991

Fig. 3 Leakage Power on different ambient temperature using LVCMOS15

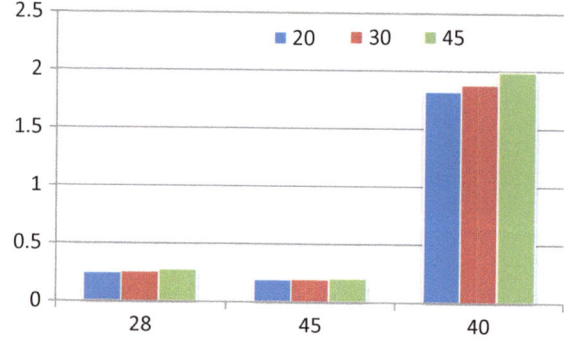

Table 3 Analysis of MAT, JT, LP for LVCMOS_33 IO standard

(°C)	MAT	JT	POWER
10	38.5	56.5	22.658
25	38.4	71.6	22.731
40	38.1	86.9	22.855
55	37.7	102.3	23.055
70	37.1	117.9	23.360

There is 3.63, 52.00, and 3.005% reduction in MAT, JT, and POWER when we range down temperature from 70 to 10 °C

Table 4 LVCMOS-rooted Leakage Power study of Vedic multiplier

	28 nm	45 nm	40 nm
20	0.321	0.239	2.041
30	0.329	0.242	2.102
45	0.348	0.249	2.209

Fig. 4 Leakage Power on different ambient temperature using LVCMOS_18

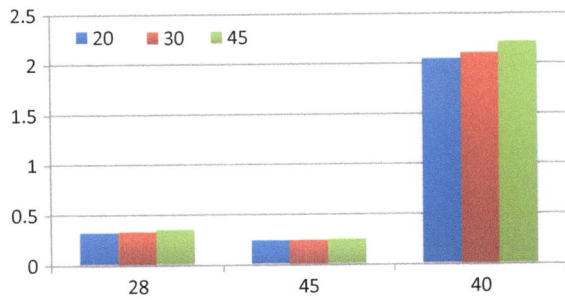

2.4 Power Scrutiny via LVCMOS I/O Set on 20 °C

For LVCMOS18, as we migrate this Vedic multiplier design is changed from 45-nm design to 28-nm design, there is 88.29% diminution in Leakage control of the design at a constant temperature of 20 °C as shown in Table 5. The graphical representation is shown in Fig. 5.

Table 5 LVCMOS-rooted Leakage Power study of Vedic multiplier

	LVCMOS_12	LVCMOS_15	LVCMOS_18
28	1.582	0.251	0.321
45	0.181	0.194	0.239
40	1.587	1.825	2.041

Fig. 5 Power on different ambient temperature on 20 °C

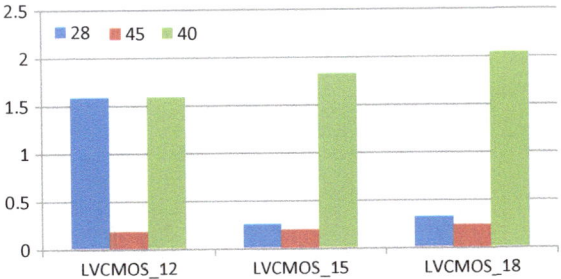

Table 6 LVCMOS-rooted Leakage Power study of Vedic multiplier

	LVCMOS_12	LVCMOS_15	LVCMOS_18
28	1.591	0.259	0.329
45	0.184	0.197	0.242
40	1.646	1.885	2.102

Fig. 6 Power on different ambient temperature on 30 °C

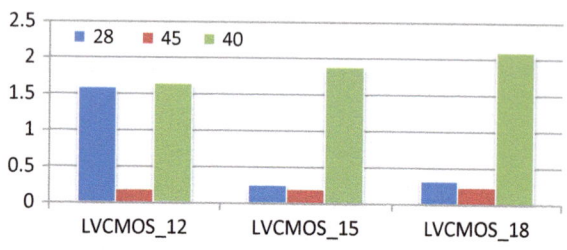

2.5 Power Scrutiny via LVCMOS I/O Set on 30 °C

For LVCMOS15, as we migrate this Vedic multiplier design from 45-nm design to 90-nm design, there is 89.54% diminution in Leakage control of the design at constant temperature of 30 °C as shown in Table 6. The graphical representation is shown in Fig. 6.

2.6 Power Scrutiny via LVCMOS I/O Set on 45 °C

For LVCMOS12, as we migrate this Vedic multiplier design from 45-nm design to 90-nm design, there is 88.16% diminution in Leakage control of the design at constant temperature of 40 °C as shown in Table 7. The graphical representation is shown in Fig. 7.

Table 7 LVCMOS-rooted Leakage Power study of Vedic multiplier

	LVCMOS_12	LVCMOS_15	LVCMOS_18
28	1.614	0.278	0.348
45	0.191	0.204	0.249
40	0.191	1.991	2.209

Fig. 7 Power on different ambient temperature on 45 °C

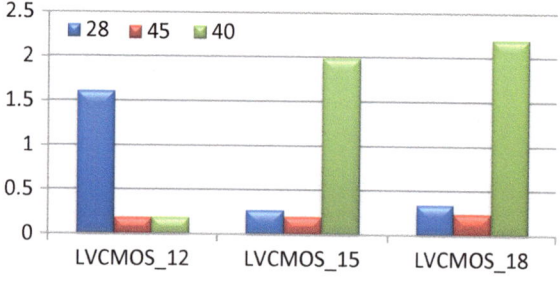

3 Conclusion

We observe that, for LVCMOS_18, as the design of Vedic multiplier is moved from 45-nm design to 28-nm design, there is 88.29% diminution in Leakage control of the design at constant temperature of 20 °C, for LVCMOS_15, when our design of Vedic multiplier is changed from 45-nm design to 90-nm design [4], there is 89.54% diminution in Leakage Power of the design when temperature is constant at 30 °C, for LVCMOS_12, when our design of Vedic multiplier is changed from 45-nm design to 90-nm design, there is 88.16% diminution in Leakage control of the design at constant temperature of 45 °C.

4 Future Scope

The Vedic multiplier design has various applications in different fields as in digital signal processing (DSP), IIR, and FIR filters, etc. High recital and speed is an inherent attribute of Vedic Mathematics [5]. As a result, we can design many complete systems such as ALUs, math coprocessors by means of time established protocols and method of Vedic math. The intent is being executed on 28, 40, and 45-nm field programmable gate array. The intent could also be established using 65, 90, and 20-nm prospect FPGAs.

References

1. Kumar, R., et al.: A novel and high performance implementation of 8×8 multiplier based on Vedic mathematics using 90 nm Hybrid PTL/CMOS logic. Int. J. Comput. Appl. 69(27)
2. Thapliyal, H., Arabnia, H.R.: A Time-area-power efficient multiplier and square architecture based on ancient Vedic mathematics. Department of Computer Science, The University of Georgia, Georgia 30602-7404, U.S.A
3. Kumar, P., Radhika, A.: FPGA implementation of high speed 8-bit Vedic multiplier using barrel shifter. In: International Conference on Energy Efficient Technologies for Sustainability (ICEETS) IEEE, Nagercoil, pp. 14–17 (2013)
4. Innocent, R., et al.: High speed Vedic multiplier for digital signal processors. IETE J. Res. 55 (6) (2009)
5. Saligram, R., et al.: Optimized reversible Vedic multipliers for high speed low power operations. In: Proceedings of IEEE Conference on Information and Communication Technologies (ICT), JeJu Island, pp. 809–814 (2013)
6. Xilinx DS571 XPS UART Lite (v1.01a), Data Sheet https://www.xilinx.com/support/documentation/ip_documentation/xps_uartlite.pdf
7. Kumar, T., et al.: CTHS based energy efficient thermal aware image ALU design on FPGA. Wirel. Pers. Commun. Int. J. 83(1) (2015). ISSN: 0929-6212 (print), 1572-834X (electronic)

8. Musavi, S.H.A., Chowdhry, B.S., Kumar, T., Pandey, B., Kumar, W.: IoTs enable active contour modeling based energy efficient and thermal aware object tracking on FPGA. Wirel. Pers. Commun. **82**(3), 1–15 (2015). ISSN: 1572-834X
9. Kumar, T., Pandey, B., Das, T., Chowdhry, B.S.: Mobile DDR IO standard based high performance energy efficient portable ALU design on FPGA. Wirel. Pers. Commun. Int. J. **76**(3), 569–578 (2014)

Timing Constraints-Based High-Performance DES Design and Implementation on 28-nm FPGA

Vandana Thind, Sujeet Pandey, D. M. Akbar Hussain, Bhagwan Das, M. F. L. Abdullah and Bishwajeet Pandey

Abstract In this work, we are going to implement DES algorithm on 28-nm Artix-7 FPGA. To achieve high-performance design goal, we are using minimum period, maximum frequency, minimum low pulse, minimum high pulse for different cases of worst-case slack, maximum delay, setup time, hold time, and data skew path. The cases on which analysis is done are like worst-case slack, best-case achievable, timing error, and timing score, which help in differentiating the amount of timing constraint at two different frequencies. We analyzed that in timing analysis, there is maximum of 19.56% of variation in worst-case slack, 0.29% change for best-case achievable, 41.17% change in timing error, and 64.12% change in timing score for two different frequencies. From this work, we also notified the delays during various signals; accordingly, we have designed our own algorithm with strong security encryption.

Keywords Timing constraints · DES algorithm · 28-nm FPGA
Pin-out report · Mapping report · Minimum period · Maximum performance
Static timing analysis

V. Thind (✉)
School of Electronics and Electrical, Chitkara University, Chandigarh, Punjab, India
e-mail: vandana@gyancity.com

S. Pandey · B. Pandey
Gyancity Research Lab, Jammu, India
e-mail: welcomesujeet@gmail.com

B. Pandey
e-mail: gyancity@gyancity.com

D. M. Akbar Hussain
Aalborg University, Esbjerg, Denmark
e-mail: akh@et.aau.dk

B. Das · M. F. L. Abdullah
UTHM, Parit Raja, Malaysia
e-mail: he130092@siswa.uthm.edu.my

M. F. L. Abdullah
e-mail: faiz@uthm.edu.my

© Springer Nature Singapore Pte Ltd. 2018
S. K. Muttoo (ed.), *System and Architecture*, Advances in Intelligent Systems and Computing 732, https://doi.org/10.1007/978-981-10-8533-8_13

1   Introduction

In this particular paper, we have worked on the pin-out report and timing analysis of DES algorithm at two different frequencies, i.e., 2.4 and 3.6 GHz. This analysis gives us detailed report about timing delay, slack, worst-case achievement, timing score, and timing errors. Slack is the difference between the required time and arrival time of signal between each connection. Worst-case achievement means maximum delay countered in our algorithm. The timing score refers to the total value constitutes the timing analysis for all constraints and by how much the constraints are failing in picoseconds where the "sum" (in picoseconds) has not met any timing constrained value at each unique endpoint. Timing score is calculated by the fact: It is equal to the sum of absolute value of all worst-case negative slack of each failing unique endpoint in picoseconds. Timing error is variation in original signal with given period of time. In this research work, we have done analysis on pin-out report, which contains detailed report about the placement of input/output data pins and operating/reference voltages on the bank of Artix-7 FPGA. We have also notified the static timing analysis, which is useful for evaluating the performance of each path, where certain violations are considered like setup time violation, when the input signal reaches late, i.e., after the clock signal is active, and hold time violation means the input signal reaches earlier than the expected time. In static timing analysis, we have considered two paths: setup and hold, where the analysis of data path delay and clock skew path for different checks like min period, min low pulse, min high pulse, setup, and hold is done. Min period is the time constraint on the clock net which generates a check for delays. From all the analyses, we notified the percentage change in all the timing constraints of different checks. This also shows us if we change frequency for DES algorithm how much variation we get.

2   Related Work

A researcher had analyzed the algorithm in perspective of total time and power utilized by DES algorithm [1], whereas we have done complete analysis on timing constraints of time delay, slack, worst-case achievement, timing score, and timing error [1]. One designer had researched on security of key bits in 16-rounded DES [2], and we have researched on complete detail of DES algorithm's pin-out report using high-performance software Xilinx [2]. Another researcher had worked on the past and future scope in addition with environmental effects [3], whereas we have done analysis on effect of timing conditions on DES algorithm at two different frequencies, i.e., 2.4 and 3.6 GHz [3]. Some researcher had tested the optimization of 4-rounded DES algorithms [4], whereas we have tested DES algorithm with 16-rounded DES algorithms [4]. One scientist had done analysis on the implementation of cryptographic algorithms on FPGA [5–7] with speed grade-4 [8] whereas we have done our analysis on Artix-7 FPGA with speed grade-3 [8]. Some other researcher had focused on bit slice architecture of DES algorithm [8], whereas here we have done complete analysis on registers and HDL synthesis of DES algorithm.

3　Pin-out Report

Pin-out report specifies the location of pseudo-component on the module when a net connects from one pin on module to a pin on another module. This report gives the detail about data of particular bit to be placed on which particular pin according to the logic of algorithm. For this particular DES algorithm, detailed pin-out report is given in the following tables. Input/output bank number is type of layout of IC with basically consisting of pin where we can provide different voltages to our board without any complication. These tables basically show us position of different data bits of plaintext, ciphertext, VCCO, reference voltages, and mixed signal voltages.

In Table 1, 64-bit plaintext is placed on different pin numbers, which are situated on different input/output banks, i.e., banks 35 and 14 of Artix-7 FPGA.

Table 2 gives the detailed pin-out report for 64-bit ciphertext which is basically encrypted output data of DES algorithm. We get ciphertext from banks 35 and 15.

Table 3 gives positions of pins which act as input as operating voltages which is provided to different sections of our Artix-7 FPGA board. Maximum of 1.50 VCCO is provided to DES algorithm.

Table 1 Pin-out report for 64-bit input data of DES algorithm

Pin number	Signal name	Data of bit	I/O bank number
A4	Plaintext	61	35
B2,B3	Plaintext	62,64	35
D2,D3	Plaintext	51,30	35
E2,E3	Plaintext	58,54	35
F4	Plaintext	25	35
G2,G6	Plaintext	52,60	35
H5	Plaintext	56	35
J2,J4	Plaintext	57,26	35
K17,K18	Plaintext	63,27	14
L6,L13,L14,L15,L16,L18	Plaintext	36,53,28,59,31,32	14
M14,M16,M17,M18	Plaintext	29,43,44,33	14
N14,N15,N16,N17	Plaintext	39,45,46,41	14
P14,P15,P17,P18	Plaintext	40,1,47,42	14
R10-R13,R15-R18	Plaintext	24,55,34,35,2,5,48,37	14
T9-T16,T18	Plaintext	22,23,13,20,3,4,6,38	14
U3,U4,U12-U14,U16-U18	Plaintext	49,50,14,21,18,11,9,10	14
V10-V17	Plaintext	16,17,15,19,7,8,12	14

Table 2 Pin-out report for 64-bit output data of DES algorithm

Pin number	Signal name	Data of bit	I/O bank number
A1,A3,A5,A6,A11, A13-A16,A18	Ciphertext	51,54,59,64,32,41,44,39,42,46	35,15
B1,B4,B6,B7,B11-14, B16-18,B15	Ciphertext	53,40,61,63,33,30,29,28,55,52,43	35,15
C4,C7,C12,C14-17	Ciphertext	38,57,31,27,50,16,17	35,15
D4,D8,D12,D13,D15, D17,D18	Ciphertext	2,62,37,36,47,10,18	35,15
E5-7,E15-18	Ciphertext	34,56,58,45,1,7,22	35,15
F3,F13-16,F18	Ciphertext	48,35,60,3,6,24	35,15
G14,G16-18	Ciphertext	8,4,14,21	15
H14-17	Ciphertext	5,13,49,11	15
J13-15,J17,J18	Ciphertext	12,15,25,20,23	15
K13,K15,K16	Ciphertext	9,26,19	15

Table 3 Pin-out report for different operating voltages in DES algorithm

Pin number	Signal name	I/O bank number	Voltages
B10	VCCO_16	35	1.50
A17	VCCO_15	15	1.50
B10	VCCO_16	16	ANY
C3	VCCO_35	35	1.50
C13	VCCO_15	15	1.50
D6	VCCO_35	35	1.50
D16	VCCO_15	15	0.75
F2	VCCO_35	35	1.50
G5	VCCO_35	35	1.50
G15	VCCO_15	15	1.50
J1	VCCO_35	35	1.50
K4	VCCO_34	34	ANY
K14	VCCO_15	15	1.50
L17	VCCO_14	14	ANY
N3	VCCO_34	34	ANY
N13	VCCO_14	14	ANY
P6	VCCO_34	34	ANY
P16	VCCO_34	14	ANY
R9	VCCO_0	0	ANY
T2	VCCO_34	34	ANY
T12	VCCO_14	14	ANY
U5	VCCO_14	14	ANY
U15	VCCO_14	14	ANY

Table 4 Pin-out report for reference voltages provided to DES algorithm	Pin number	Signal name	I/O bank number	Voltages
	D7	VREF	35	0.75
	F6	VREF	35	0.75
	L5	VREF	34	0.75
	M13	VREF	14	0.75
	R5	VREF	34	0.75
	U11	VREF	14	0.75

Table 5 Pin-out for mixed signal used in DES algorithm	Pin number	Signal name	I/O bank number
	D5	CLK	35
	F5	RST	35
	V2	ADDRESS	34
	U2	CHIP SELECT BAR	34

Table 4 reports us that 0.75 V is used as reference voltages, and maximum of six pins is provided with reference voltages. Table 5 mentions four mixed signals like clock, reset, address, chip select bar used in DES algorithm. Bank numbers used for these signals are 35 and 34.

4　Timing Analysis

This research notifies us details about time constraint of slack, worst-case achievement, best-case achievable, timing errors, and timing score. In this particular research, we have taken into consideration different checks like setup, hold, minimum period, minimum low, and high pulse, where we analyzed the percentage change of above-mentioned cases, at two different frequencies, i.e., 2.4 and 3.6 GHz.

Tables 6 and 7 give the amount of worst-case slack, best-case achievable, timing errors, and timing score for setup, hold, min period, min low pulse, and min high pulse checks. It is basically a timing analysis on DES algorithm at two different

Table 6 Timing constraint of DES algorithm at 2.4 GHz frequency

Check	Worst-case slack	Best-case achievable	Timing errors	Timing score
Setup	−2.105 ns	2.521 ns	1440	1,405,879
Hold	−0.121		34	1633
Min period	−1.176 ns	1.592 ns	1025	599,192
Min low pulse	−0.584 ns	1.000 ns	1024	598,016
Min high pulse	−0.584 ns	1.000 ns	2048	11,906,032

Table 7 Timing constraint of DES algorithm at 3.6 GHz frequency

Check	Worst-case slack	Best-case achievable	Timing errors	Timing score
Setup	−2.315 ns	2.521 ns	1440	1,678,687
Hold	−0.081		20	586
Min period	−1.315 ns	1.592 ns	1025	741,667
Min low pulse	−0.726 ns	1.003 ns	1024	744,062
Min high pulse	−0.726 ns	1.003 ns	2048	1,488,124

frequencies: 2.4 and 3.6 GHz. Percentage change in above-mentioned cases is detailed below, along with figures carrying the comparison of time constraint of different cases at different frequencies.

4.1 Worst-Case Slack in Timing Analysis of DES Algorithm

Figure 1 shows the changes of time constraint of different cases at two frequencies, i.e., 2.4 and 3.6 GHz. Percentage change of worst-case slack in setup check, hold check, min period, min low pulse, and min high pulse is 9.97, 49.38, 10.57 and 19.56 respectively.

4.2 Best Achievable Time in Timing Analysis of DES Algorithm

Figure 2 shows that there is no percentage change in setup, hold, and min period checks for both frequencies, but there is 0.29% of change in min low pulse and min high pulse check.

Fig. 1 Comparison of worst-case slack at two different frequencies

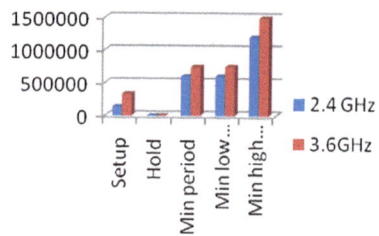

Fig. 2 Comparison of best-case achievable time at two frequencies

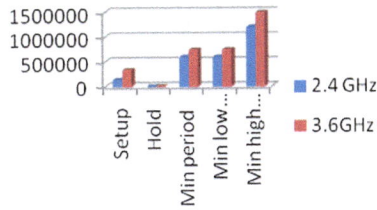

Fig. 3 Comparison of timing errors for two different frequencies

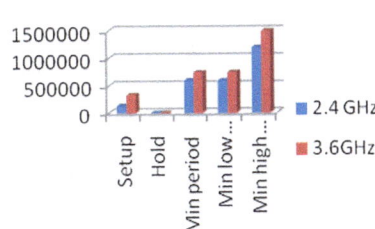

4.3 Timing Errors in Timing Analysis of DES Algorithm

Figure 3 shows that only hold check varies by 41.17% and rest of checks remain unchanged.

4.4 Timing Scores in Timing Analysis of DES Algorithm

Figure 4 shows that from two different frequencies setup, check changes by 16.25%, hold check varies by 64.12%, min period check changes by 19.21%, and both min low pulse check and min high pulse check vary by 19.62%.

Fig. 4 Comparison of timing scores for two different frequencies

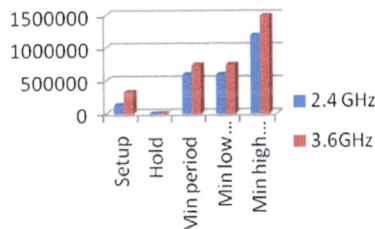

5   Static Timing Analysis

In static timing analysis, we examined the difference in setup paths and hold paths. We have taken three sources and destinations; considering them, we have varied slack, data path delay, and skew clock path. Following tables show different reading of setup paths and hold paths at two different frequencies: 2.4 and 3.6 GHz. In these analyses, a total of 3840 paths, 1440 endpoints, 5232 connections were analyzed by Xilinx software.

5.1   Setup Paths in Static Timing Analysis

From this observation, we found that setup path basically faces setup time violation, which means the signal arrives at destination too late than the time it should reach there. In Tables 8 and 9, we have done analysis on slack, data skew delay, and skew clock path, for three paths with maximum values.

Table 8 accords us with report for static timing analysis on setup path at 2.4 GHz frequency, where maximum slack has maximum data path delay and skew clock is almost the same for all three paths but in very less terms.

Table 9 subsidizes that when static timing analysis was done at 3.6 GHz frequency, for minimum slack, it is observed that data path delay (DPD) is minimum and skew clock path (SCP) is maximum.

This analysis for both frequencies is shown in Fig. 5.

Table 8 Static timing analysis on setup paths at 2.4 GHz frequency

Source	Destination	Slack	Data path delay	Skew clock path
Reg1_26	Reg1_22	−2.105	2.225	−0.261
Reg1_24	Reg1_22	−2.031	2.151	−0.261
Reg1_25	Reg1_22	−1.815	1.935	−0.261

Table 9 Static timing analysis on setup paths at 3.6 GHz frequency

Source	Destination	Slack	Data path delay	Skew clock path
Reg1_10	Reg1_10	−2.219	2.200	−0.261
Reg1_8	Reg1_30	−2.089	2.069	−0.262
Reg1_8	Reg1_16	−2.274	2.254	−0.262

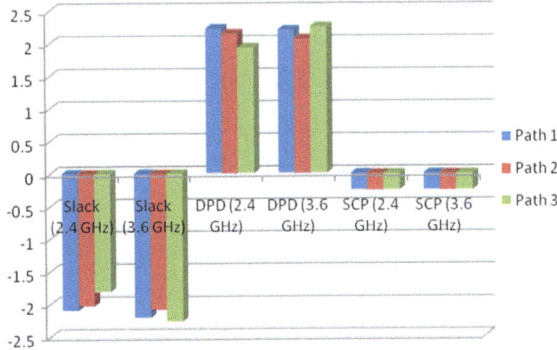

Fig. 5 Slack, data path skew, and skew clock path of setup paths

5.2 Hold Paths in Static Timing Analysis

Similar to setup path, hold path also suffers hold time violation which means that the clock signal changes earlier as soon as the clock signal gets active. Here also, analysis has been done on two different frequencies as shown in Table 10.

On observing Table 10, we see that in hold path, for maximum slack, there is minimum data path delay and maximum skew clock path.

Table 11 notifies that at 3.6 GHz frequency, for hold paths, maximum slack has minimum data path delay and minimum skew clock path. This analysis for both frequencies is shown in Fig. 6.

Table 10 Static timing analysis on hold paths at 2.4 GHz frequency

Source	Destination	Slack	Data path delay	Skew clock path
Reg1_29 right	Reg1_29 left	−0.121	0.250	0.371
Reg1_23 left	Reg1_23right	−0.119	0.251	0.370
Reg1_23 right	Reg1_23 left	−0.104	0.265	0.369

Table 11 Static timing analysis on hold paths at 3.6 GHz frequency

Source	Destination	Slack	Data path delay	Skew clock path
Reg1_4 left	Reg1_4 right	−0.081	0.289	0.370
Reg1_32right	Reg1_32left	−0.051	0.356	0.407
Reg1_15left	Reg1_32right	−0.042	0.364	0.400

Fig. 6 Slack, data path skew, and skew clock path of hold paths

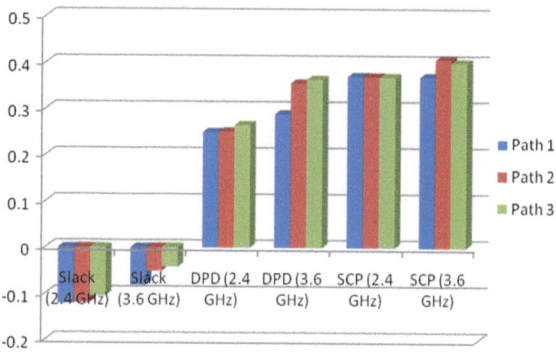

Table 12 Component switching report at 2.4 GHz frequency

Check	Slack	Value	Limit
Min period	−1.176	0.416	1.592
Min low pulse	−0.584	0.208	0.500
Min high pulse	−0.584	0.208	0.500

Table 13 Component switching report at 3.6 GHz frequency

Check	Slack	Value	Limit
Min period	−1.315	0.277	1.592
Min low pulse	−0.727	0.138	0.500
Min high pulse	−0.727	0.138	0.500

5.3 Component Switching Limits

Component switching analysis insures us that the operating voltage is supplied to the device within the range specified by the device. In this particular analysis, we analyzed the slack, limit, and check values.

From Tables 12 and 13, we noticed that for both frequencies, slack, value, and limit do not vary for min low and high pulse check; there is variation in values when we increase the frequency, i.e., 2.4–3.6 GHz; therefore, percentage change in this value is 19.6, 33.65, and 0% for slack, value, and limit, respectively.

6 Timing Report

In timing report, we examined the clock information report which tells us that at clock signal CLK, clock buffer loads the signal of quantity 1024. It also shows that speed grade of design is −3 and minimum period of design is 1.980 ns where maximum frequency is 504.974 MHz, minimum input arrival time before clock is 2.213 ns, minimum output required time after clock is 0.640 ns.

7 Mapping Report

Mapping report gives us the analysis of timing constraint, of placement and routing of components on FPGA.

In Tables 14 and 15, we analyzed the mapping report of DES algorithm at two different frequencies, i.e., 2.4 and 3.6 GHz. In this analysis, we noticed the amount of worst-case slack, best-case achievement, timing error, and timing score for five different checks. Mapping report gives us report of timing analysis which is done directly from the placement and routing of the components on the board.

7.1 Worst-Case Slack in Mapping Report of DES Algorithm

In Fig. 7, we analyzed that worst-case slack is 26.8% and there is no change for hold check. Min period check, min low pulse check, and min high pulse check vary by 10.5 and 19.5 respectively.

Table 14 Mapping report of DES algorithm at 2.4 GHz frequency

Check	Worst-case slack (ns)	Best-case achievement	Timing error	Timing score
Setup	−0.379	0.795 ns	960	138,768
Hold	0.069	–	0	0
Min period	−1.176	1.592 ns	1025	599,192
Min low pulse	−0.584	1.000 ns	1024	598,016
Min high pulse	−0.584	1.000 ns	2048	1,196,032

Table 15 Mapping report of DES algorithm at 3.6 GHz frequency

Check	Worst-case slack (ns)	Best-case achievement	Timing error	Timing score
Setup	−0.518	0.795 ns	1440	334,128
Hold	0.069	–	0	0
Min period	−1.315	1.592 ns	1025	741,667
Min low pulse	−0.726	1.003 ns	1024	744,062
Min high pulse	−0.726	1.003 ns	2048	1,488,124

Fig. 7 Component switching limit for two different frequencies

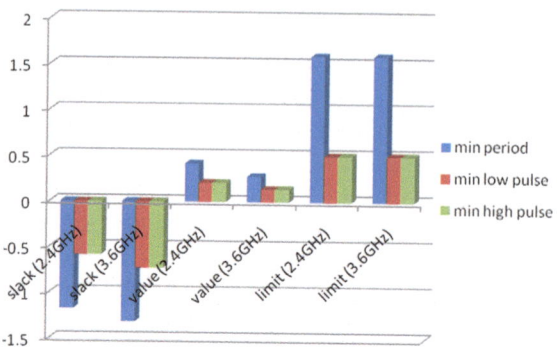

7.2 Best-Case Achievement in Mapping Report of DES Algorithm

In Fig. 8, infers that best-case achievement varies only for min low pulse check and min high pulse check, i.e., by 0.299% both. For rest of the check, there is no variation.

7.3 Timing Errors in Mapping Report of DES Algorithm

In Fig. 9, we analyzed that setup check changes by 33.33% from 2.4 to 3.6 GHz frequency. For other checks, there is no variation in timing errors.

7.4 Timing Score in Mapping Report of DES Algorithm

In Fig. 10, variation in timing score of setup check is 58.46%, and min period check, min low pulse check, and min high pulse check vary by 19.21, 19.62, and 19.62%, respectively. There is no change for hold check (Fig. 11).

Fig. 8 Variation in worst-case slack from mapping report

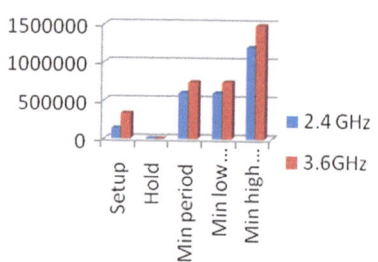

Fig. 9 Variation in best-case achievement from mapping report

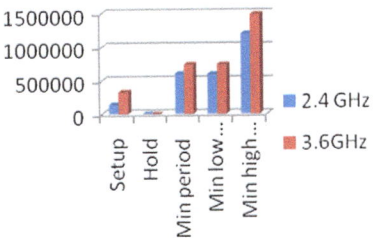

Fig. 10 Variation in timing errors from mapping report

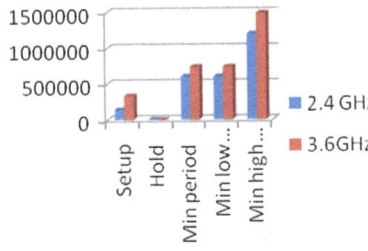

Fig. 11 Variation in timing score from mapping report

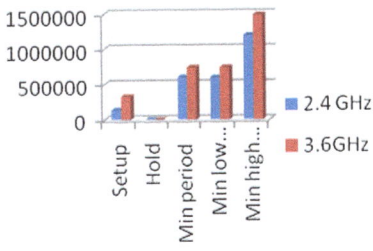

8   Generating Clock Report

In this analysis, we analyzed the amount of change in net skew and max skew of DES algorithm at two different frequencies. The difference between the loads driven by the net is called skew. Max skew is the timing constraint used to control the amount of skew on a net (Table 16).

In Fig. 12, we noticed that there is 21.94% change in the net skew and 3.91% variation in the max skew between two different frequencies 2.4 and 3.6 GHz.

Table 16 Comparison of clock report at two different frequencies

Clock net (GHz)	Fan-out	Net skew	Max
2.4	407	0.185	1.300
3.6	405	0.237	1.353

Fig. 12 Net skew and max skew for two different frequencies

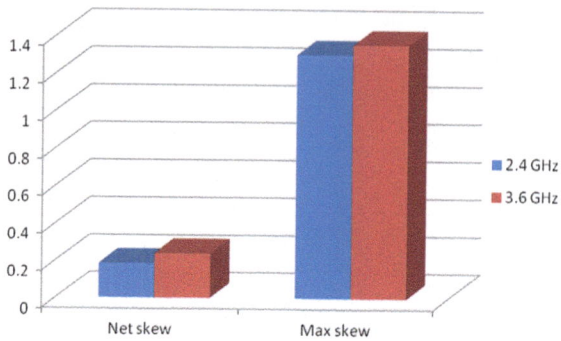

9   Conclusion

We conclude that in timing analysis, maximum changes compared to all timing constraint are found for min high pulse check, for both frequencies and hold check does not have best-case achievable.

Timing score is maximum setup check. After this, we did static timing analysis report, which infers that in setup path performance, for maximum slack, data path delay is maximum. In hold path performance, for maximum slack, we calculated maximum delay. In component switching limit, slack is maximum for min period check. With increase in frequency, low pulse and high pulse decrease. In mapping report, we can reduce the slack by interchanging worst-case slack of min high pulse by min period. Hold check does not vary for any of the cases; it remains constant.

10   Future Scope

In this particular research, we have implemented our research of timing constraint analysis on the Artix-7 FPGA, whereas in near future, we can use vertex-8, vertex-9, RC5, RC6, RC7, etc. Here, we have done timing analysis by which we come to know about the changes of different timing constraint on the two different frequencies; in near future, we can do its power analysis, from where we can eventually get idea of time and power aspects of DES algorithm. Power and timing analysis could help us replacing FPGA with any newer IC which would then come into existence to obtain better results.

References

1. Taherkhani, S., Enver, E., Gemikonakli, O.: Implementation of non-pipelined and pipelined data encryption standard (des) using xilinx virtex-6 fpga technology. In: 2010 IEEE 10th International Conference on Computer and Information Technology (CIT). IEEE (2010)
2. Matsui, M.: The first experimental cryptanalysis of the Data Encryption Standard. Advances in Cryptology—Crypto'94. Springer Berlin Heidelberg (1994)
3. Miles, E., Branstad, D.K.: Data encryption standard: past and future. Proc. IEEE **76**(5), 550–559 (1988)
4. Ghnaim, W.A.-E.: Known-ciphertext cryptanalysis approach for the Data Encryption Standard technique. In: 2010 International Conference on Computer Information Systems and Industrial Management Applications (CISIM) (2010)
5. Kumar, T., et al.: CTHS based energy efficient thermal aware image ALU design on FPGA. Wirel. Pers. Commun. Int. J. **83**(1) (2015). ISSN: 0929-6212 (print), 1572-834X (electronic)
6. Musavi, S.H.A., Chowdhry, B.S., Kumar, T., Pandey, B., Kumar, W.: IoTs enable active contour modeling based energy efficient and thermal aware object tracking on FPGA. Wirel. Pers. Commun. **85**(2), 529–543 (2015). ISSN: 1572-834X
7. Kumar, T., Pandey, B., Das, T., Chowdhry, B.S.: Mobile DDR IO standard based high performance energy efficient portable ALU design on FPGA. Wirel. Pers. Commun. Int. J. **76**(3), 569–578 (2014)
8. Arich, T., Eleuldj, M.: Hardware implementations of the data encryption standard. In: The 14th International Conference on 2002-ICM, Microelectronics. IEEE (2002)

Input–Output Standard-Based Energy Efficient UART Design on 90 nm FPGA

Rashmi Sharma, Bishwajeet Pandey, Vikas Jha, Siddharth Saurabh and Sweety Dabas

Abstract This paper illustrates the behavior of the UART in response to the various I/O standards. Research has been carried out to find out the most ideal standard for UART design which would thereby minimize the losses. Increase in power is seen as the frequency and capacitance for a standard are increased. When a relative analysis is done for the different I/O standards, it has been found out that LVCMOS18 consumes the least power and hence is the most efficient I/O standard for the UART design. Increment in power consumption has been observed within a percentage of 99.73–40% for a capacitance of 5 pF and 99.64–54.54% for a capacitance value of 50 pF. XILINX software and Verilog Hardware Description Language have been used for this purpose. The behavior for various standards has been studied to get the most energy-efficient design for the UART. This would help in increasing the output from the UART, thereby proving to be a boon in the field of electronics where power consumption is a major issue.

Keywords Input · Output · Standard · Energy efficient · UART
90 nm · FPGA

R. Sharma (✉) · B. Pandey · V. Jha
Gyancity Research Lab, Gurgaon, India
e-mail: rashmi@gyancity.com

B. Pandey
e-mail: gyancity@gyancity.com

V. Jha
e-mail: vikas.jnct@gmail.com

S. Saurabh
Giant Meterwave Radio Telescope, Khodad, Pune, India
e-mail: siddharthsaurabh1@gmail.com

S. Dabas
Maharaja Surajmal Institute, Janakpuri, India
e-mail: sweety.dabas@gmail.com

© Springer Nature Singapore Pte Ltd. 2018
S. K. Muttoo (ed.), *System and Architecture*, Advances in Intelligent Systems and Computing 732, https://doi.org/10.1007/978-981-10-8533-8_14

1 Introduction

We have majorly worked on different input/output standards to get the most energy-efficient UART design. We have analyzed the results for ten different standards of FPGA which is the most budding element in the programmable logic devices. We have studied the behavior of the UART which is the universal asynchronous receiver transmitter corresponding to different I/O standards. The analysis has been done for the 90 nm technology. UART is used for transforming the parallel data into the serial forms. The power consumption has been analyzed for various standards. After the analysis, we concluded that LVCMOS18 consumes the least power as and when compared to the other standards at different values of frequencies as well as capacitances. Therefore, this standard is the most energy efficient.

2 Related Work

A designer had been engaged in research on the LVCMOS and HSTL I/O standards in terms of impedance matching of the input and the output resistance using a Vedic multiplier. However, we have emphasized on the comparison of the power consumption by various I/O standards rather than being limited to only one of the many available I/O standards [1]. Furthermore, another researcher had aimed on designing an ALU by using the LVCMOS as the I/O standard on 28 nm FPGA since it had consumed the least power but we are more concerned about the comparative analysis of different standards on 90 nm technology [2]. Another analyst had been keenly interested in designing an I/O standard-based processor register on a very large-scale FPGA, whereas we have analyzed the results for making an energy-efficient UART [3]. A researcher had worked on simulating a fire sensor using the I/O standard SSTL, whereas we aim on making of a low-power UART on 90 nm FGPA [4]. Also, another person researched on designing a parallel integrator on the FPGA using the SSTL I/O standard; nonetheless, we have contemplated ourselves basically on the correlation between the various I/O standards [5]. To add more, another research scholar worked on the design of a multiplexer using the FPGA, whereas we have worked on making an energy-efficient UART design using 90 nm FPGA technology [6]. Additionally, a researcher had worked on output load capacitance with low power on FPGA, whereas we have dealt with various standard specifications of the UART design [7].

3 Objective

The major intent of the research is to analyze the power consumption by the various I/O standards for a UART design on the FPGA with 90 nm size. We have drawn various conclusions on the power consumption for each individual I/O standard at different values of the capacitances and the frequencies (cited in Tables 1, 2, 3, 4, 5, 6, 7, 8, 9 and 10) and have drawn a table as well as comparing the power consumption for all the I/O standards analyzed (Table 11). Every power consumption in this universe is a form of a wastage. We aim at keeping the power consumption

Table 1 Power dissipation with HSLVDCI_33

Capacitance	500 MHz	1000 MHz
5	0.212	0.216
50	0.218	0.229

Table 2 Power dissipation with LVTTL

Capacitance	500 MHz	1000 MHz
5	0.005	0.010
50	0.011	0.022

Table 3 Power dissipation with LVCMOS18

Capacitance	500 MHz	1000 MHz
5	0.003	0.006
50	0.005	0.010

Table 4 Power dissipation with PCIX

Capacitance	500 MHz	1000 MHz
5	0.005	0.009
50	0.011	0.022

Table 5 Power dissipation with GTL

Capacitance	500 MHz	1000 MHz
5	0.067	0.069
50	0.067	0.069

Table 6 Power dissipation with HSTL_I

Capacitance	500 MHz	1000 MHz
5	0.167	0.169
50	0.167	0.170

Table 7 Power dissipation with HSTL__IV

Capacitance	500 MHz	1000 MHz
5	0.238	0.240
50	0.238	0.240

Table 8 Power dissipation with SSTL__II_DCI

Capacitance	500 MHz	1000 MHz
5	1.420	1.422
50	1.421	1.424

Table 9 Power dissipation with LVDCI_15

Capacitance	500 MHz	1000 MHz
5	0.032	0.035
50	0.033	0.037

Table 10 Power dissipation with PCI33_3

Capacitance	500 MHz	1000 MHz
5	0.005	0.009
50	0.011	0.022

to the minimum. This would lessen the wastage of the resources and in turn would improve the efficiency of the corresponding device. Therefore, we are finding optimum range of the frequency, capacitance as well as the I/O standard at which the UART would consume minimum amount of power to produce the most desirable output in all respects. These viable conditions would in turn help in finding as to where would the UART be of prime usage with least extravagancy of the consumed power (Fig. 1).

Table 11 Comparison for various I/O standards

I/O standard	5 pF		50 pF	
	500 MHz	1000 MHz	500 MHz	1000 MHz
HSLVDCI_33	0.212	0.216	0.218	0.229
LVTTL	0.005	0.010	0.011	0.022
LVCMOS18	0.003	0.006	0.005	0.010
PCIX	0.005	0.009	0.011	0.022
GTL	0.067	0.069	0.067	0.069
HSTL_I	0.167	0.169	0.167	0.170
HSTL__IV	0.238	0.240	0.238	0.240
SSTL__II_DCI	1.420	1.422	1.401	1.424
LVDCI_15	0.032	0.035	0.033	0.037
PCI33_3	0.005	0.009	0.011	0.022

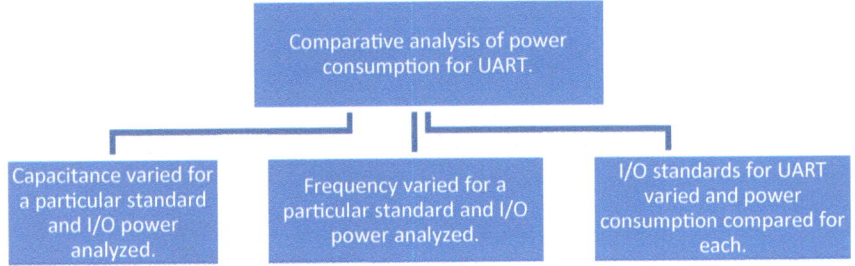

Fig. 1 Techniques for analyzing various power consumption parameters

4 Results

4.1 High-Speed Low-Voltage Digitally Controlled Impedance

There is an increase of 2.7% in I/O power as the capacitance is scaled up from 5 to 50 pF at a frequency value of 500 MHz. To add more, there is an increase of 5.6% in I/O power as the capacitance is scaled up from 5 to 50 pF at a frequency value of 1000 MHz for the HSLVDCI_33 logic as depicted in Table 1 and Fig. 2.

4.2 Low-Voltage Transistor Logic

There is an increase of 54.54% I/O power as the capacitance is scaled up from 5 to 50 pF at a frequency value of 500 MHz. To add more, there is an increase of 54.54% I/O power as the capacitance is scaled up from 5 to 50 pF at a frequency value of 1000 MHz for the LVTTL logic as depicted in Table 2 and Fig. 3.

Fig. 2 Power consumption for HSLVDCI_33 at different frequencies

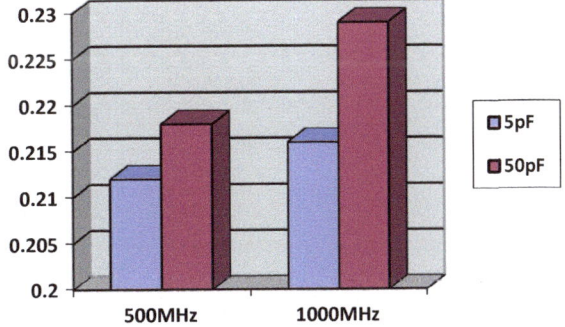

Fig. 3 Power consumption for LVTTL at different frequencies

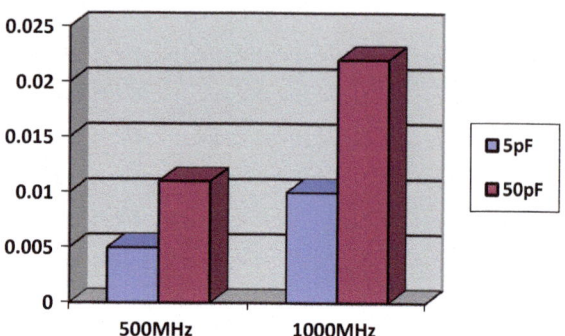

4.3 Low-Voltage Complementary Metal Oxide Semiconductor

There is an increase of 40% in I/O power as the capacitance is scaled up from 5 to 50 pF at a frequency value of 500 MHz. To add more, there is an increase of 40% in I/O power as the capacitance is scaled up from 5 to 50 pF at a frequency value of 1000 MHz for the LVCMOS18 logic as depicted in Table 3 and Fig. 4.

4.4 Peripheral Component Interconnect Extended

There is an increase of 54.54% in I/O power as the capacitance is scaled up from 5 to 50 pF at a frequency value of 500 MHz. To add more, there is an increase of 59.1% in I/O power as the capacitance is scaled up from 5 to 50 pF at a frequency value of 1000 MHz for the PCIX logic as depicted in Table 4 and Fig. 5.

Fig. 4 Power consumption for LVCMOS at different frequencies

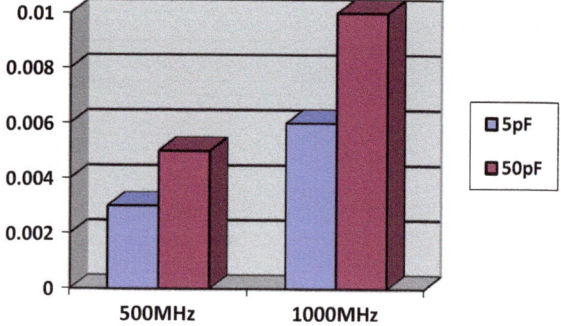

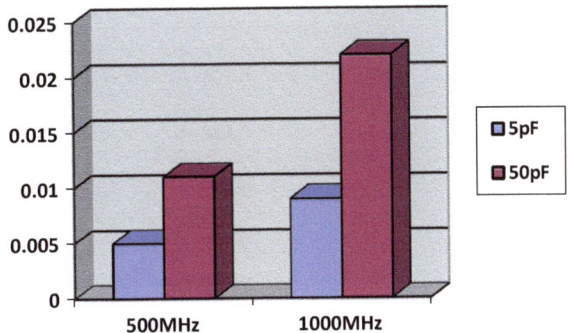

Fig. 5 Power consumption for PCIX at different frequencies

4.5   Gunning Transceiver Logic

There is no increase/decrease in the I/O power as the capacitance is raised from 5 to 50 pF for the frequency 500 MHz as well as 1000 MHz for the GTL logic as depicted in Table 5 and Fig. 6.

4.6   High-Speed Transistor Logic I

There is no increase in I/O power as the capacitance is scaled up from 5 to 50 pF at a frequency value of 500 MHz. To add more, there is an increase of 0.5% I/O power as the capacitance is scaled up from 5 to 50 pF at a frequency value of 1000 MHz for the HSTL_I logic as depicted in Table 6 and Fig. 7.

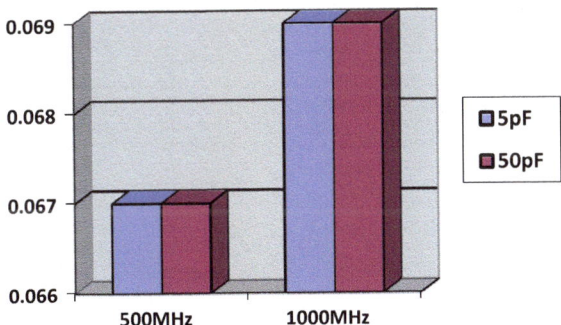

Fig. 6 Power consumption for GTL at different frequencies

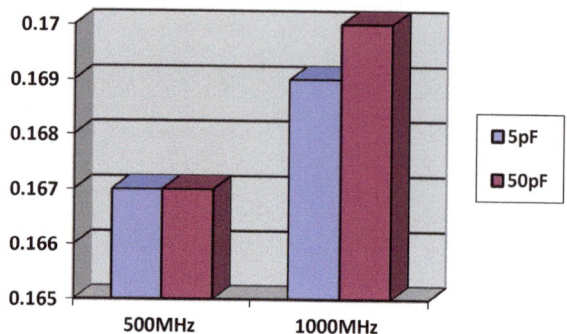

Fig. 7 Power consumption for HSTL_I at different frequencies

4.7 High-Speed Transceiver Logic IV

There is no increase/decrease in the I/O power as the capacitance is raised from 5 to 50 pF for the frequency 500 MHz as well as 1000 MHz for the HSTL_IV logic as depicted in Table 7 and Fig. 8.

4.8 Stub Series Terminated Logic_II_Digitally Controlled Impedance

There is an increase of 0.7% I/O power as the capacitance is scaled up from 5 to 50 pF at a frequency value of 500 MHz. To add more, there is an increase of 1.4% I/O power as the capacitance is scaled up from 5 to 50 pF at a frequency value of 1000 MHz for the SSTL_II_DCI logic as depicted in Table 8 and Fig. 9.

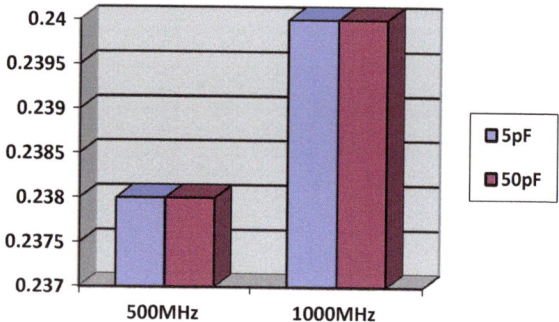

Fig. 8 Power consumption for HSTL_IV at different frequencies

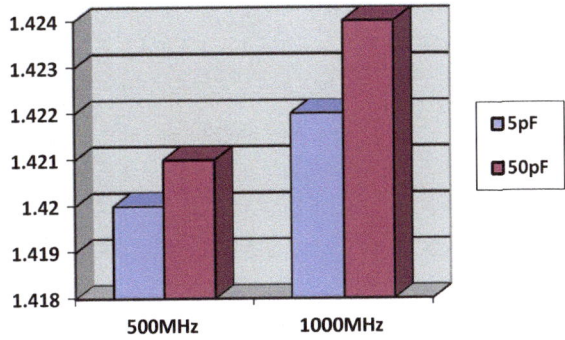

Fig. 9 Power consumption for SSTL_II_DCI at different frequencies

4.9 Low-Voltage Digitally Controlled Impedance_15

There is an increase of 3% I/O power as the capacitance is scaled up from 5 to 50 pF at a frequency value of 500 MHz. To add more, there is an increase of 5.4% I/O power as the capacitance is scaled up from 5 to 50 pF at a frequency value of 1000 MHz for the LVDCI_15 logic as depicted in Table 9 and Fig. 10.

4.10 Peripheral Component Interconnect

There is an increase of 54.54% I/O power as the capacitance is scaled up from 5 to 50 pF at a frequency value of 500 MHz. To add more, there is an increase of 59.1% I/O power as the capacitance is scaled up from 5 to 50 pF at a frequency value of 1000 MHz for the PCI33_3 logic as depicted in Table 10 and Fig. 11.

At 500 pF capacitance, the LVCMOS18 consumes the least power at 500 MHz as well as 1000 MHz. There is an increase of 95.63, 54.54, 54.54, 85.5, 94.11, 95.83, 99.29, 79.29, and 54.54% in the power consumption for HSLVDCI_33, LVTTL, PCIX, GTL, HSTL_I, HSTL_IV, SSTL_II_DCI, LVDCI_15, and

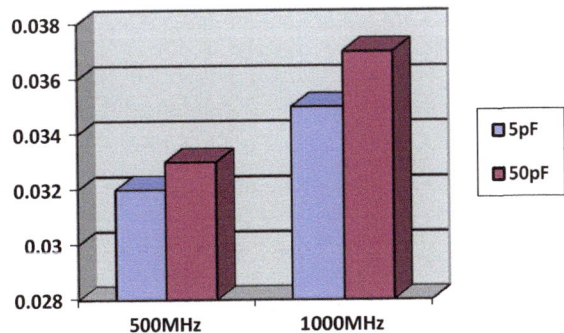

Fig. 10 Power consumption for SSTL_II_DCI at different frequencies

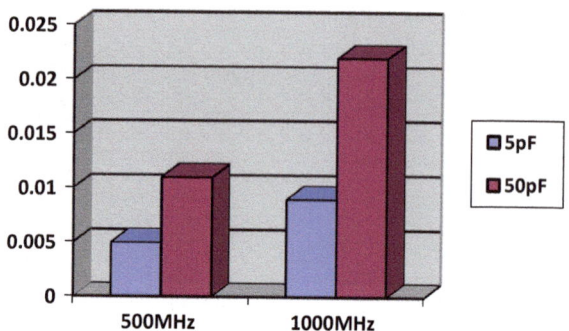

Fig. 11 Power consumption for PCI33_3 at different frequencies

PCI33_3 I/O standard at a frequency of 1000 MHz Additionally, the power consumption inflates by 97.7, 90.90, 90.90, 92.53, 97, 97.89, 99.64, 84.84, and 90.90% for HSLVDCI_33, LVTTL, PCIX, GTL, HSTL_I, HSTL_IV, SSTL_II_DCI, LVDCI_15, and PCI33_3 I/O standard at a frequency of 500 MHz as shown in Table 11 and Fig. 12.

At 5 pF capacitance, the LVCMOS18 consumes the least power at 500 MHz as well as 1000 MHz. There is an increase of 97.22, 40, 33.33, 91.3, 94.67, 97.5, 99.57, 82.85, and 33.33% in the power consumption for HSLVDCI_33, LVTTL, PCIX, GTL, HSTL_I, HSTL_IV, SSTL_II_DCI, LVDCI_15, and PCI33_3 I/O standard at a frequency of 1000 MHz Additionally, the power consumption inflates by 98.58, 40, 40, 95.52, 98.2, 98.73, 99.78, 90.62, and 40% for HSLVDCI_33, LVTTL, PCIX, GTL, HSTL_I, HSTL_IV, SSTL_II_DCI, LVDCI_15, and PCI33_3 I/O standard at a frequency of 500 MHz as shown in Fig. 13.

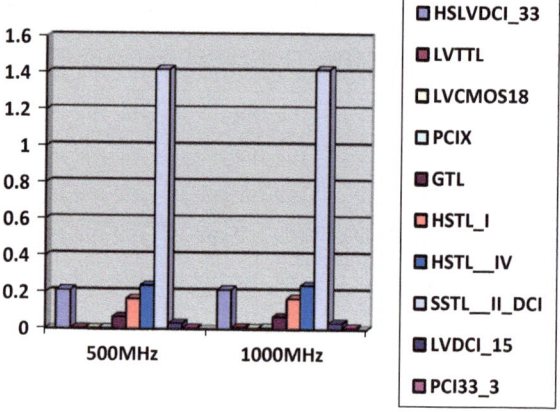

Fig. 12 Power consumption for different I/O standards at 50 pF

Fig. 13 Power consumption for different I/O standards at 5 pF

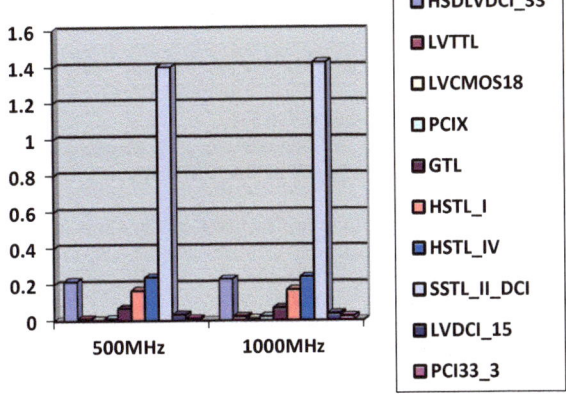

5   Conclusion

We hereby conclude that out of the various I/O standards analyzed here, the LVCMOS18 standard consumes the least power at 500 MHz as well as 1000 MHz frequency both for 5 and 500 pF capacitances. The LVCMOS18 standard is therefore the best one since it curtails the power consumption to the maximum, thereby manifesting to be the most dominant I/O standard in terms of the efficiency. Hence, if the UART is designed using this standard at 90 nm FPGA technology, we are expected to face the least amount of the power dissipation, thereby achieving maximum amount of efficiency in terms of the power wastage for the UART. This leads us to a conclusion that the LVCMOS18 standard should be used more often.

6   Future Scopes

For this analysis, we have utilized the FPGA as a PLD which is an IC in two dimensions. In the times yet to come, we could possibly be using the 3D ICs. Also here, we have worked upon the 90 nm technology; however, as the time progresses the chip size gets smaller. Hence, shortly we would be using the shorter chip sizes just as today industry mostly uses the 28 nm technology. Also, newer input/output standards would be introduced which would provide a better comparative analysis. With all this yet to come, the UART would witness a further increase in its efficiency. FPGA could also be replaced by some other hugely advanced IC taking the research work in the field of the UART a step ahead. UART could as well be replaced by some other networking devices like routers, gateways, Internet protocols as well as bridges.

References

1. Goswami, K., Pandey, B.: Energy efficient vedic multiplier design using LVCMOS and HSTL IO standard. In: 9th International Conference on Industrial and Information Systems (ICIIS), Dec 2014, pp. 1–4, 15–17
2. Pandey, B., Yadav, J., Pattanaik, M.: IO standard based energy efficient ALU design and implementation on 28 nm FPGA. 2013 Annual IEEE India Conference (INDICON). IEEE (2013)
3. Singh, P.R., et al.: I/O standard based power optimized processor register design on ultrascale FPGA. 2014 International Conference on Computing for Sustainable Global Development (INDIACom). IEEE (2014)
4. Kumar, T., et al.: Simulation of voltage based efficient fire sensor on FPGA using SSTL IO standards. In: 2014 International Conference on Robotics and Emerging Allied Technologies in Engineering (iCREATE). IEEE (2014)
5. Das, T., et al.: Simulation of SSTL IO standard based power optimized parallel integrator design on FPGA. In: 2014 International Conference on Robotics and Emerging Allied Technologies in Engineering (iCREATE). IEEE (2014)
6. Pandey, B., et al.: IO standard based green multiplexer design and implementation on FPGA. In: 2013 5th International Conference on Computational Intelligence and Communication Networks (CICN). IEEE (2013)
7. Singh, P.R., et al.: Output load capacitance based low power implementation of UART on FPGA. In: 2014 International Conference on Computer Communication and Informatics (ICCCI). IEEE (2014)

Different Configuration of Low-Power Memory Design Using Capacitance Scaling on 28-nm Field-Programmable Gate Array

Inderpreet Kaur, Lakshay Rohilla, Alisha Nagpal, Bishwajeet Pandey and Sanchit Sharma

Abstract A real capacitor will have some power dissipation, whereas an ideal capacitor will not dissipate any power. In this paper, we designed a capacitance scaling-based low-power RAM design. Our work aims to analyze how the memory circuit works using capacitance scaling does and varying temperatures. This design is implemented in Verilog. Usually, for the functioning of a device, the junction temperature is below 125 °C. If we scale down frequency from 10 to 4.5 GHz, 2.3 and 1 GHz then there is 42.96, 59.03, and 70.4% reduction, respectively, in total power at 5 pF output load. With the increase in capacitance, there should be the increase in junction temperature. But the novelty of our work is that we can control the effect of capacitance scaling on junction temperature with the help of addition airflow of 500 Linear Feet per Minute (LFM).

Keywords I/O standard · Thermal analysis · SSTL135 · Power optimized design I/Os power · FPGA · C = centigrade

I. Kaur (✉) · L. Rohilla · A. Nagpal · B. Pandey
Department of Electronics and Communications, Chitkara University, Chandigarh, Punjab, India
e-mail: inderpreet_95@yahoo.com

L. Rohilla
e-mail: bassist.lakshay@gmail.com

A. Nagpal
e-mail: alishanagpal84@gmail.com

B. Pandey
e-mail: gyancity@gyancity.com

S. Sharma
Chandigarh College of Engineering and Technology, Chandigarh, India
e-mail: sanchit2794@gmail.com

© Springer Nature Singapore Pte Ltd. 2018
S. K. Muttoo (ed.), *System and Architecture*, Advances in Intelligent Systems and Computing 732, https://doi.org/10.1007/978-981-10-8533-8_15

Fig. 1 Expression of
capacitance scaling

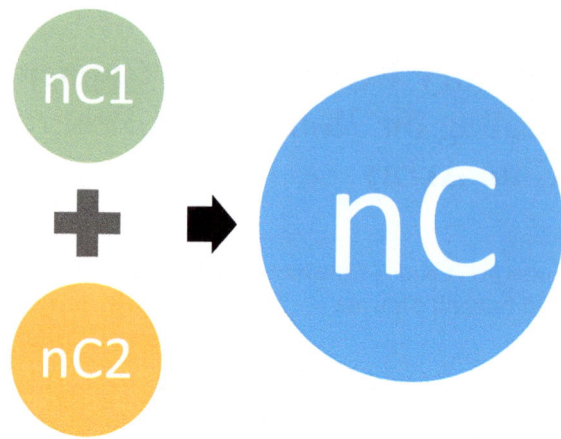

1 Introduction

A field-programmable gate array is an organized set of the gate array. Each gate array represents a specific reconfigurable logic circuitry. FPGA is used to perform design and implementation of hardware for a software application. In the place of various discrete elements, FPGA gives us flexibility by integrating millions of logic gates in one integrated circuit. Any FPGA must have memory, logic, and reconfigurable interconnect. FPGA is free from the operating system. It uses dedicated hardware to process logic. The good thing in FPGA is that different processing logic will not do a competition to get same resources because they are parallel and therefore with the addition of any processing component in the circuit puts no effect on the performance of the other processing part. Wireless sensor and actuators networks have a direct application of FPGA in both connectivity and communication. Capacitance is an ability of an object to hold the charge. The capacitor can hold many electrons for a given voltage is a measure of its capacitance. Figure 1 represents the effect of capacitance scaling on two different parts and its equivalent on overall system.

2 Related Work

Researcher inserts 128-bit IPv6 address in a RAM and transforms general RAM into the particular type of RAM, i.e., IOTs Enable RAM [1]. IOTs Enable RAM is nothing but the Internet of Thing Enable RAM. This work deals with only one configuration of RAM [1]. Whereas, we are dealing with different types of RAM. Thermal stability along with power requirement of RAM is another research area [2]. In this work, we are also analyzing junction temperature, maximum ambient temperature, and effect of capacitance on both power and heat. RAM can read and

Fig. 2 Junction and ambient temperature

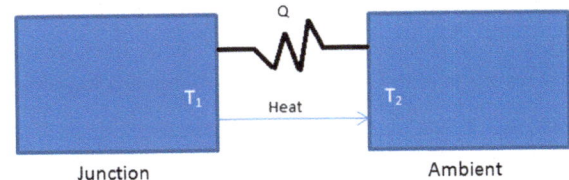

write. There are many input port as well as the output port in RAM. Therefore, selection of IO standard plays an important role to regulate power dissipation of RAM [3]. High-speed transceiver logic (HSTL) is used to design energy efficient RAM [4]. Embedded memory blocks in contemporary FPGA devices exhibit a range of sizes and control structures [5]. We have to take care of these resources to control power dissipation of the whole FPGA. Operating frequency and ambient temperature play an essential role to regulate junction temperature of the device [6].

3   Junction and Ambient Temperatures

In any electronic appliances, the maximum temperature of silicon in any corner is known as junction temperature. It tells about the durability of a device. It should be less than 125 °C.

Ambient temperature is usually referred to the standard normal temperature, that is 21 °C. Device emits heat when the silicon in the device is powered up. The ambient temperature is directly proportional to junction temperature. Heat will continue to flow from silicon to the surrounding environment according to first law of thermodynamics as shown in Fig. 2. The mathematical expression for calculating junction temperature is $T_J = T_A + R_{QJA}$ * power as shown in Fig. 3, where T_J refers to junction temperature, T_A refers to ambient temperature, and R_{QJA} refers to the junction to ambient thermal resistance.

Fig. 3 Mathematical diagram for junction temperature

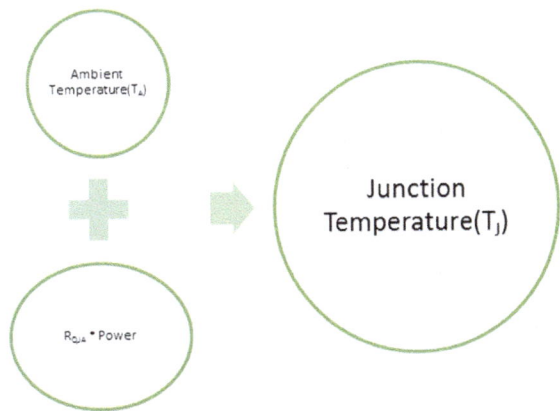

A significant increase in junction temperature leads to unreliability of IC chip. To determine an efficient airflow for the system, it is vital to calculate junction temperature of memory circuit keeping SSTL 135 as I/O standards.

4 Stub Series Terminated Logic

4.1 *Junction Temperature with SSTL135 I/O Standard for Auto RAM Style*

As the frequency increases, the junction temperature of the device also increases. In Table 1, at 1, 2.3, 4.5, and 10 GHz the junction temperature is 25.4, 25.6, 25.9, and 26.6 °C, respectively.

4.2 *Junction Temperature with SSTL135I/O Standard for Distributed RAM Style*

In Table 2, it is observed that from the frequencies 1–10 GHz, junction temperature is 25.4, 25.6, 25.9, and 26.6 °C, respectively.

4.3 *Junction Temperature with SSTL135 I/O Standard for Bufgdll BRAM*

In Table 3, it is observed that from the frequencies 1–10 GHz, junction temperature is 25.4, 25.6, 25.9, and 26.6 °C, respectively.

5 Thermal Analysis of Different RAM Styles

5.1 *For frequency Range 1–10 GHz*

As observed in Table 4, junction temperature for RAM style auto, distributed, and Bufgdll increases with increases in frequency. At 2.3 GHz, there is 0.78% increase in junction temperature compared with junction temperature at 1 GHz. At 4.5 GHz, there is 1.1% increase in junction temperature compared with junction temperature at 2.3 GHz. At 10 GHz, there is 2.7% increase in junction temperature compared with junction temperature at 4.5 GHz.

Table 1 Junction temperature (°C) with SSTL135

Frequency (GHz)	Capacitance (pF)	Airflow	Heat sink	Junc. temp.	Max. ambient temp.	Clock	Signal	IO	Total
1	5	250	MP	25.5	84.5	0.007	0.004	0.109	0.164
1	50	500	HP	25.4	84.6	0.007	0.004	0.112	0.167
2.3	5	250	MP	25.7	84.3	0.016	0.008	0.157	0.227
2.3	50	500	HP	25.6	84.4	0.016	0.008	0.157	0.226
4.5	5	250	MP	26.0	84.0	0.032	0.016	0.222	0.316
4.5	50	500	HP	25.9	84.1	0.032	0.016	0.234	0.328
10	5	250	MP	26.8	83.2	0.071	0.036	0.399	0.554
10	50	500	HP	26.6	83.4	0.071	0.036	0.426	0.581

MP medium profile, *HP* high profile, *Freq.* frequency, *Cap.* capacitance, *Junc. Temp.* junction temperature, *Max. Ambient Temp.* maximum ambient temperature, *IO* input/output

Units power—watt, airflow—linear feet per minute

Table 2 Junction temperature (°C) with SSTL135

Frequency (GHz)	Capacitance (pF)	Airflow	Heat sink	Junc. temp.	Max. ambient temp.	Clock	Signal	IO	Total
1	5	250	MP	25.5	84.5	0.007	0.004	0.109	0.164
1	50	500	HP	25.4	84.6	0.007	0.004	0.112	0.167
2.3	5	250	MP	25.7	84.3	0.016	0.008	0.157	0.227
2.3	50	500	HP	25.6	84.4	0.016	0.008	0.157	0.226
4.5	5	250	MP	26.0	84.0	0.032	0.016	0.222	0.316
4.5	50	500	HP	25.9	84.1	0.032	0.016	0.234	0.328
10	5	250	MP	26.8	83.2	0.071	0.036	0.399	0.554
10	50	500	HP	26.6	83.4	0.071	0.036	0.426	0.581

Table 3 Junction temperature (°C) with LVCMOS18

Frequency (GHz)	Capacitance (pF)	Airflow	Heat Sink	Junc. temp.	Max. ambient temp.	Clock	Signal	IO	Total
1	5	250	MP	25.5	84.5	0.007	0.004	0.109	0.164
1	50	500	HP	25.4	84.6	0.007	0.004	0.112	0.167
2.3	5	250	MP	25.7	84.3	0.016	0.008	0.157	0.227
2.3	50	500	HP	25.6	84.4	0.016	0.008	0.157	0.226
4.5	5	250	MP	26.0	84.0	0.032	0.016	0.222	0.316
4.5	50	500	HP	25.9	84.1	0.032	0.016	0.234	0.328
10	5	250	MP	26.8	83.2	0.071	0.036	0.399	0.554
10	50	500	HP	26.6	83.4	0.071	0.036	0.426	0.581

Table 4 Variation of junction temperature with SSTL135

Frequency (GHz)	Auto (°C)	Distributed (°C)	Bufgdll (°C)
1	25.4	25.4	25.4
2.3	25.6	25.6	25.6
4.5	25.9	25.9	25.9
10	26.6	26.6	26.6

Figure 4 shows a rise in temperature with frequency. For 1 GHz, junction temperature is 25.4 °C. For 2.3 GHz, junction temperature is 25.6 °C. For 4.5 GHz, junction temperature is 25.9 °C. For 10 GHz, junction temperature is 26.6 °C.

5.2 Power Consumption for Capacitance 5 pF and Airflow = 250 Linear Feet per Minute

From Table 5, it can be observed that at 1 GHz power consumed is 0.164 W, while at 2.3 GHz there is 27.7% increase in power. Similarly, at 4.5 and 10 GHz there is 28.1 and 42.9% rise in power, respectively.

Fig. 4 Variation of junction temperature at different frequencies, Junc. T— junction temperature

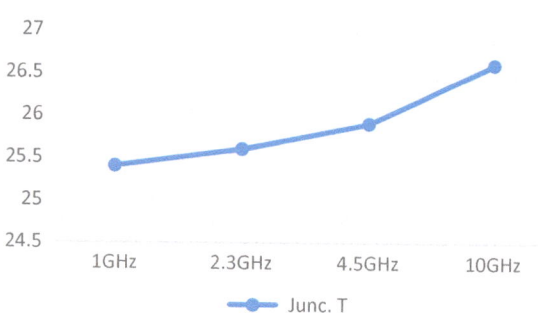

Table 5 Variation of power with SSTL135

Frequency (GHz)	Capacitance (pF)	Airflow	Total power (W)
1	5	250	0.164
2.3	5	250	0.227
4.5	5	250	0.316
10	5	250	0.554

Fig. 5 Consumption of power for cap. = 5 pF and airflow = 250

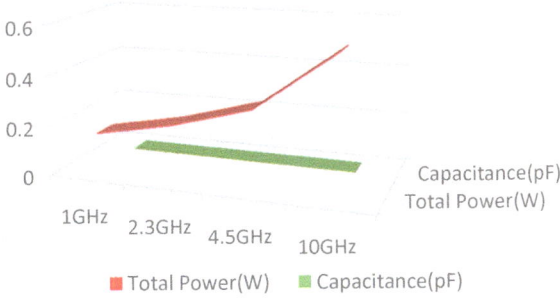

Figure 5 shows power consumption at the frequency ranging from 1 to 10 GHz at capacitance 5 pF and airflow as 250 Linear Feet per Minute. Power consumed at 1, 2.3, 4.5, and 10 GHz is 0.164, 0.227, 0.316, and 0.554 W, respectively.

5.3 Power Consumption for Capacitance 50 pF and Airflow = 500 Linear Feet per Minute

From Table 6, it can be observed that at 1 GHz power consumed is 0.167 W, while at 2.3 GHz there is 26.1% increase in power. Similarly, at 4.5 and 10 GHz there is 31.09 and 43.5% rise in power, respectively.

Figure 6 shows power consumption at the frequency ranging from 1 to 10 GHz at capacitance 50 pF and airflow as 500 Linear Feet per Minute. Power consumed at 1, 2.3, 4.5, and 10 GHz is 0.167, 0.226, 0.328, and 0.581 W, respectively.

Table 6 Variation of power with SSTL135

Frequency (GHz)	Capacitance (pF)	Airflow	Total power (W)
1	50	500	0.167
2.3	50	500	0.226
4.5	50	500	0.328
10	50	500	0.581

Fig. 6 Consumption of power for cap. = 50 pF and airflow = 500

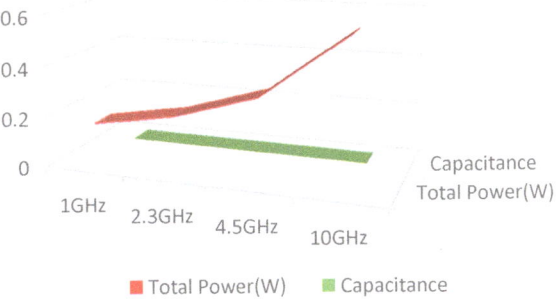

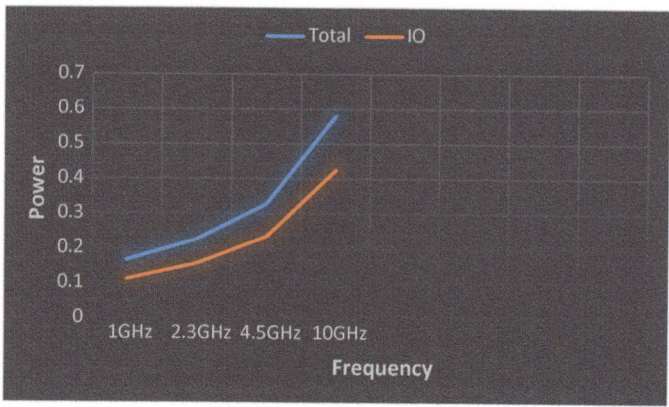

Fig. 7 Power consumption at different frequencies

5.4 Power Consumption for 1–10 GHz

From Fig. 7, we observe that at 2.3 GHz for IO power reduction is 28.6% whereas for total power reduction is 26.1%. Similarly, at 4.5 GHz IO power reduction is 32.9% whereas for total power reduction is 31.09%, and at 10 GHz IO power reduction is 45.07% whereas for total power reduction is 43.5%.

6 Conclusion

The key aim of this work was to design power-efficient memory circuit using capacitance scaling and thermal analysis. At 25.6 °C and frequency of 1, 10, 100 GHz, we observed 0.78, 1.1, and 2.63% increase in junction temperature, respectively. Also, we noted that on varying airflow and changing heat sink to high profile the junction temperature differs accordingly. It is observed that at 4.5 GHz when the capacitance is 5 pF, airflow is 250, and heat sink is medium profile, the junction and ambient temperatures are 25.7 and 84.3 °C, respectively. Whereas when the capacitance is scaled and changed to 50 pF, keeping airflow at 500 and heat sink at high profile, the junction and ambient temperatures are 25.6 and 84 °C, respectively. This shows that with scaling the capacitance junction temperature decreases whereas ambient temperature increases.

7 Future Scope

Here, 28-nm Virtex-6 FPGA is in use. We can redesign this memory circuit on Xilinx's 28-nm Artix-7, Altera's Stratix FPGA, ECP, XP, SCP/M series FPGA of Lattice, ABAX FPGA of Tabula, FPLIC series FPGA of Atmel, etc. This thermal-aware approach can be extended to different hardware like router, gateway, and another device which are specially required for green and thermal-aware communication.

References

1. Garg, K., Moudgil, A., Das, B., Abdullah, M.F.L., Pandey, B., Akbar Hussain, D.M.: GTL based internet of things enable processor specific RAM design on 65 nm FPGA. In: IEEE 57th International Symposium ELMAR-2015, 28–30 Sept 2015, Zadar, Croatia: the oldest conference in Europe
2. Verma, G., Moudgil, A., Garg, K., Pandey, B.: Thermal and power-aware internet of things enable RAM design on FPGA. In: IEEE International Conference on Computing for Sustainable Global Development (INDIACOM), Bharti Vidyapeeth, Delhi, India, Mar 2015. http://ieeexplore.ieee.org/xpl/articleDetails.jsp?tp=&arnumber=7100506
3. Pandey, B., Singh, D., Pattanaik, M.: IO standard based low power design of RAM and implementation on FPGA. In: International Conference on Information Applied Electronics (ICIAE), Colombo, Sri Lanka, 15–16 June 2013. http://www.joace.org/uploadfile/2013/0705/20130705030847941.pdf
4. Dabbas, S., Pandey, B., Kumar, T., Das, T.: Design of power optimized memory circuit using high speed transreceiver logic IO standard on 28 nm field programmable gate array. In: IEEE International Conference on Reliability Optimization & Information Technology (ICROIT), Faridabad, India, Feb 2014
5. Tessier, R., et al.: Power-aware RAM mapping for FPGA embedded memory blocks. In: Proceedings of the 2006 ACM/SIGDA 14th International Symposium on Field programmable gate arrays. ACM (2006)
6. Chowdhry, B.S., Pandey, B., Kumar, T., Das, T., Thakur, S.: Frequency, voltage and temperature sensor design for fire detection in VLSI circuit on FPGA. In: Communications in Computer and Information Science, Indexed by Elsevier: SCOPUS. ISSN: 1865-0929

Ardudroid Surveillance Bot

Himanshu Verma, Gaurav Verma, Jaswanth Yarlagadda,
Ashish Sharma and Sandeep Banarwal

Abstract A robot is an engine that is controlled and guided by CPU and electronic programming. With recent advances in mobile technology, mobile phones have shown incredible range of possible applications. Manipulation of latest robot which knows how to be proscribed using an android application should be in reach. Through this work, a robot is developed which is based on android phones that could be the basic prototype for the ground surveillance robot. Remote buttons are used in the application that is used to control the motion of the robot through the use of Bluetooth interface between app and Arduino. This robot is capable of continuously streaming photographs in the field area and uploading the picture on our cloud server in an encrypted form so as to make that it cannot be hacked or get into the wrong hands.

Keywords API's · Eclipse Juno · Arduino · Surveillance · JAVA
SDK platforms

1 Introduction

The major purpose of our work is to build up an advance mobile robot surveillance platform that can quickly be deployed in the field with minimal cost and training. In this work, the readily available commercial parts for the robot chassis as well as

H. Verma (✉) · G. Verma · J. Yarlagadda · A. Sharma · S. Banarwal
Department of Electronics and Communication Engineering, Jaypee Institute of Information
Technology, A-10, Sector-62, Noida, Uttar Pradesh, India
e-mail: himanshutechdn@gmail.com

G. Verma
e-mail: gaurav.iitkg@gmail.com

A. Sharma
e-mail: attach4ashish@gmail.com

S. Banarwal
e-mail: banarwals@gmail.com

© Springer Nature Singapore Pte Ltd. 2018
S. K. Muttoo (ed.), *System and Architecture*, Advances in Intelligent Systems
and Computing 732, https://doi.org/10.1007/978-981-10-8533-8_16

electronic components are used [1, 2]. The user interface must be carefully designed to provide an immediate sense familiarity for each use with minimal training. These days' smart devices are fetching more attraction as they are power packed with most recent processors, with enlarged storage space and additional communication methods [3]. Due to the development in wireless skills, there are numerous correlation techniques worn like GSM, Wi-fi, Zigbee, and Bluetooth to transport data. Every connection requires a different set of specifications and applications. From the above four that often implemented in this work, Bluetooth is implemented because of its suitability to the work and because of its capability. Android is an open-source platform which has been broadly worn in smart devices and has entire software parcel consists of an in use system android versions like windows is used by Microsoft for their phones, core applications, etc [4, 5]. The work has been divided into two phases: in first phase of work, we have presented and developed robots controlled by mobile phones. We have developed two modes of operation for robot to be controlled by phone which are as follows:

Button Control: We have designed an android application in which we have built buttons to control the motion of robot. If "forward" command is given to the bot, it will move forward and act according to the corresponding command.

Accelerometer Control: We have used the already developed accelerometer in your android phones to get the values to decide in which direction the robots will move and send the values to the Arduino and it act accordingly. If you tilt your phone forward, then the bot will move forward and so on.

In second phase of work, we had actually started developing our surveillance robot; till now, we have been clear about the motion of the robot through application. The objective to create surveillance bot has been achieved by using two smartphones, *first one mounted on the robot* (as it is a prototype, otherwise we can use Wi-fi camera) that will send images as required by the system. This smartphone also sends us the GPS location of the bot through our cloud server. *Second smartphone is with the user* to control the robot and to receive the images and see the location of the bot. We have added one more feature to the bot that it will be uploading the images to our secured cloud server in an encrypted form, and if any case our robot will be caught, we have our data stored in the cloud and we can download it and decrypt it. This way we are going to build our surveillance robot, and we will be providing detail on each of the aspect of the designed robot.

2 Hardware Design

Surveillance robot is designed optimally which provides mobility to the platform, as well as to the mounted camera-phone on the robot [6, 7]. In order to meet those requirements, we use following hardware parts.

2.1 Android Device

The most important part of this work is android device with inbuilt accelerometer and Bluetooth in it [8]. We have used **nexus 4** (mounted on the bot) and **nexus 5** (receiving images and controlling the bot) working right now on android version 5.0.1, i.e., lollypop. **Android** is a mobile OS (operating system) comprises of Linux kernel and at present urbanized by Google [9]. Android consumer interfaces based on straight exploitation and is premeditated largely for touch screen cellular devices such as smartphones, tablet, and computers. If we talk about the hardware platform, it is based on ARM architectures, i.e., ARM 7 or cortex series in different versions of 32- and 64-bit variants. In our work, we have used the android inbuilt capability to find and connect to peers' device through Bluetooth and also use the inbuilt accelerometer sensor in the android phone to control the motion of the robots.

2.2 Bot Chassis

To control the motion as described in this work, there are many forms of chassis available in the market. Chassis used by us in this work is shown in Fig. 1.

2.3 Microcontroller Board (Arduino UNO)

Microcontroller board used in this work is Arduino UNO which controls the robot and connects through Bluetooth module to sink with the mobile application to get commands and act accordingly. Arduino being a folks of single-board microcontrollers designed to help in building different attractive and interactive projects with very ease. Interaction with the devices in Arduino environment is very easy such that we can easily operate sensors and actuators on it. Due to its easy implementation of IDE (integrated development environment) which is applicable to almost

Fig. 1 Chassis used in the project

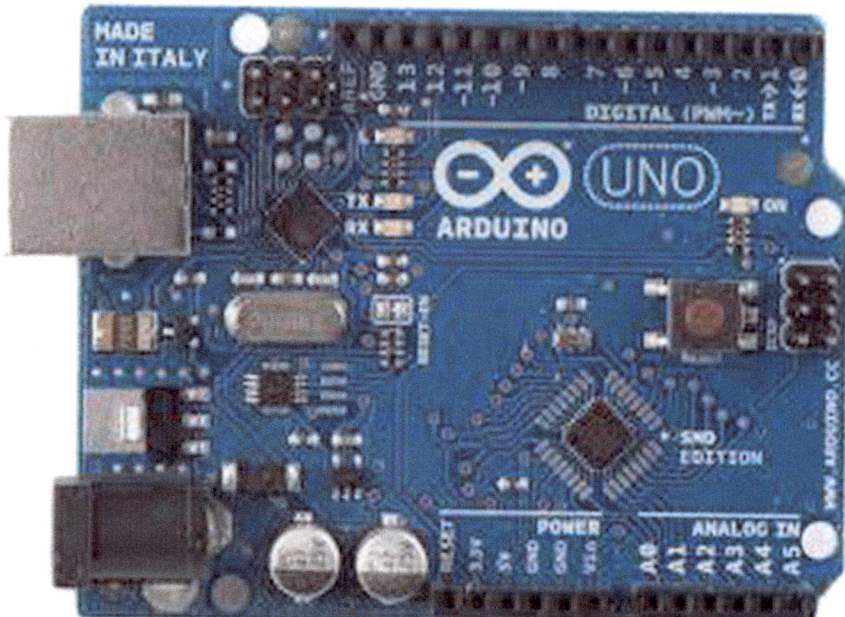

Fig. 2 Arduino UNO board

all versions of OS devices, users are free to choose programming language, i.e., C or C++. So anyone with basic background of programming language of either one of the above can easily programmed their robots or system to act accordingly and would able to see their code applying practically (Fig. 2).

2.4 Bluetooth Module

Bluetooth technology is an emerging technology and is used as wireless standards in field of communication. It uses UHF short-wavelength radio waves (frequency hopping spectrum technology included) for communication from remote or fixed devices. Transfer of data takes place in the form of packets and further addressed to designated Bluetooth channels. Module which we are using in our work is HC-06, and communication is performed on android-based platform in handset. Such platform is used to form a connection between our module and application in device. As Bluetooth serial interface and adapter being its parts, our application works in two modes, i.e., slave and master mode. TXD and RXD are two important signals which are used to establish connection such as in serial port communication devices. Our Bluetooth module can communicate computer and other smartphones

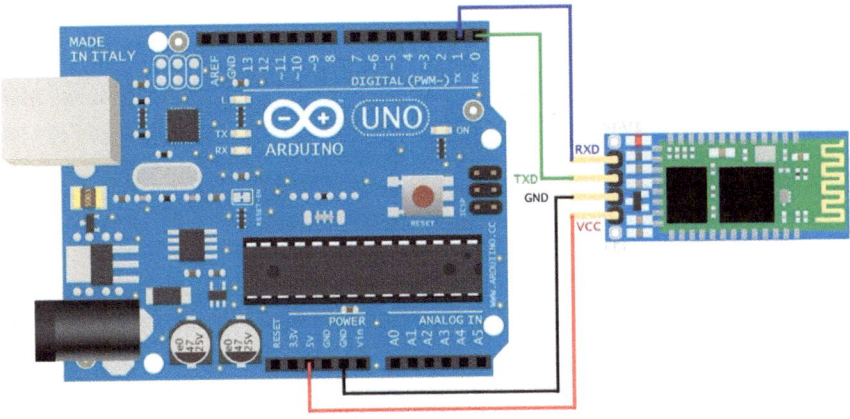

Fig. 3 Arduino and Bluetooth module connection

with the help of Bluetooth adapter. Basically, master module is used as an reference module to establish or pair connection with devices with slave module or application such that password reinforcement should be in proper order (Fig. 3).

2.5 *Motor Driver Board*

L293D consists of two H-bridges which is an electronic circuit that can be described as the circuit which provides enabling voltage that can be provided to load in direction we want. This circuitry is used in robotics applications to enhance capability of DC motors to pursue operation in forward and backward motions. I have used a L293D H-bridge circuit to control the dc motor to be controlled by Arduino board. It is intended to afford bidirectional currents of up and about 600 mA and voltages around 4.5–36 V.

2.6 *DC Motor*

To make any mechanical movement is made possible through the use of electric motors. Motors obtain electrical energy and turn out mechanical energy which in through provides mechanical movements in different motions. We can see many examples of usage of electric motors in automobiles, robots, handover control implements, and many more such applications exist today.

3 Electronics of the System

Arduino and Bluetooth are connected through there RX and TX pins to make them serially communicate and make sure that you will give power supply voltage not more than 3 V to the Bluetooth module. To connect motor to Arduino, we use Arduino motor driver shield for this we connect 4 pins from any of the 13 pins to the driver board to which motors are connected. Connect your TXD pin of Arduino to RXD pin of Bluetooth module and RXD pin of Arduino to TXD pin of Bluetooth module (Fig. 4).

Now power the Bluetooth module through Arduino 3 V pin (recommended) and provide ground through Arduino to the Bluetooth module which completes the configuration between Arduino and Bluetooth module. Now connect four pins (say 6, 7 and 10, 11) from Arduino to the motor driver board pins M1 and M2 (two each). Now connect the motors to the driver board in the given pins directly. This will complete the configuration of Arduino and driver board. Assemble all this system on your chassis, and see your hardware design completed. In our work, we did not change our hardware to great extent; there is a very small change that we have embedded a mobile phone on our chassis to get the images and videos, and for that, we have to change our chassis only, otherwise all the above-mentioned connections are same. Above the chassis another platform is made to hold the phone at place, and we kept battery here also to power the Arduino.

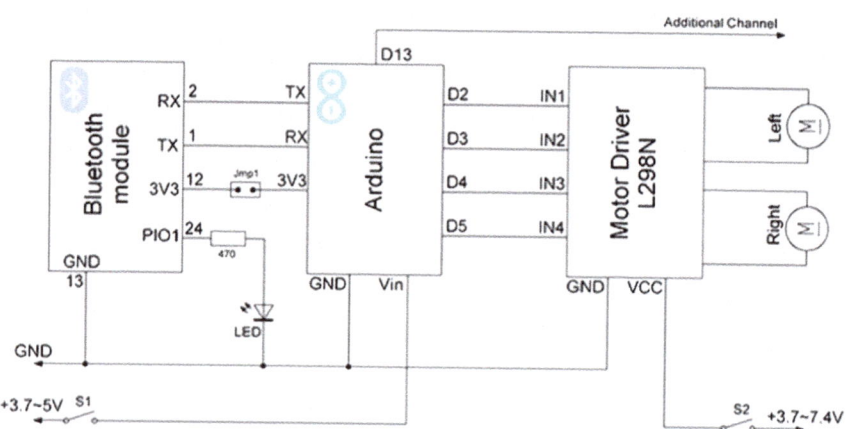

Fig. 4 Circuit diagram of work

4 Software Implementation

We have programmed for android application to control the motion of the robot through its connection through Bluetooth and also programmed in Arduino on the basis of the value getting from the application through Bluetooth. We make an app in Eclipse to pair with Bluetooth module attached to Arduino and send and receive data serially using Bluetooth of android device. This software uses JAVA coding. For most reachability and updated functions to use, we code the android app in API 17 and use the SDK manager to download the files required. We have used SDK manager to download the android directories for the Eclipse, android drivers, and an emulator to test the app in laptop before using in an android phone. Viewpoint of Eclipse software can be described as compilation of editor region and views regarding it. Different windows of Eclipse may have different persona open, but at one point of time only one viewpoint is right. Appearance of Eclipse window can be controlled by viewpoint window and can have several editors restricting to condition that only one window is active at one point of time (Fig. 5).

To design the UI for this work, you need to know how to create text fields, buttons, layouts and menu. Whole code will be in **activity_main.xml**. We use **View**

Fig. 5 Master application view

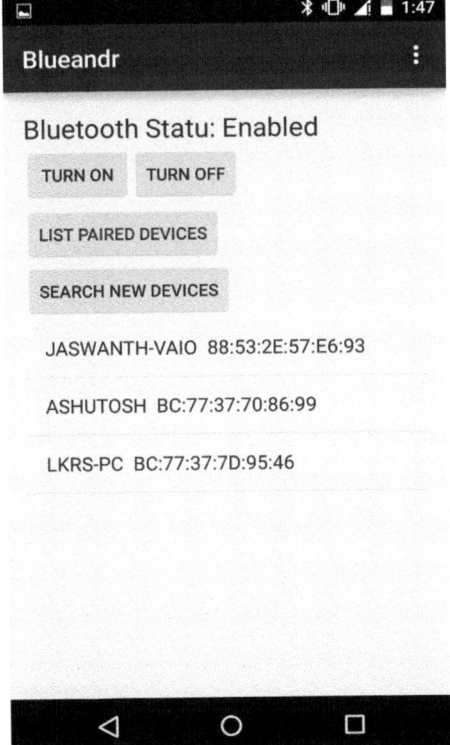

Flipper in xml file to change different frames while user interfaces with the app and **Linear Layout** in xml file to place many objects linearly in the layout. We have used functions like "onCreate", "setOnClickListener", "setOnItemClickListener", BluetoothAdapter, SensorManager. While talking about the **accelerometer** part, for this we have used magnetometer and accelerometer sensors collectively and send both the data to rotation matrix (pre-defined) to receive the angle of the mobile phone (Fig. 6).

Magnetometer tells the direction of magnetic field, and accelerometer tells the acceleration at X, Y, Z axis of the mobile phone at a point in space. Note that the BluetoothAdapter function does not work in emulator because it is not possible to virtually simulate Bluetooth in the emulator. But other activities like the layout and buttons can be tested. Export the app into an android device with minimum version of 4.2. In our work, we have used another smartphone mounted on the top of the bot

Fig. 6 Slave application view

acting as wireless camera and GPS provider. We have to develop another application called "slave" app which is going to upload the images in our secure cloud server after encrypting it using our algorithm and sends us the location of the bot. The main application "blueandr" is added with extra features to download it on the user mobile and decrypt it and also shows the current location of the bot. In this application, I have used Amazon Web services to store data on the cloud. The credentials used in the app are our private data. For encoding and decoding, I have used blowfish algorithm. For capture of the photograph, we have used hardware camera, and for GPS, we have used location manager.

Blowfish algorithm is used for our secure image transmission from one source to other source. Its code is mentioned in EncryptFile.java of this application. In our

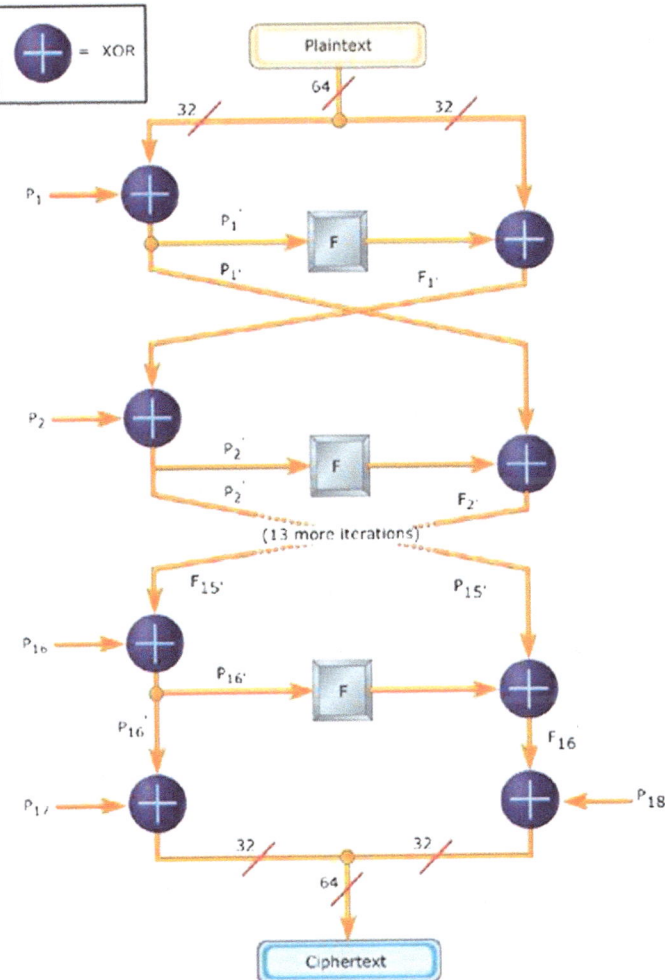

Fig. 7 Steps of blowfish algorithm

work, selected image has to be passed through the blowfish algorithm twice; that is, when the selected first image is encrypted and we get the encrypted image, then again it is passed again through the algorithm and we get our final encrypted image which gets uploaded and same when we are downloading the image, it has to be passed twice through the algorithm to get finally decrypted image. This algorithm comprises of two parts as Data Encryption and key Expansion. Around 448 key parts are converted into subarrays in key Expansion part. Data Encryption has a role to play as 16 times of a network iteration is performed. Each of the rounds consists of permutation dependent on the key and substitution of key and data-dependent. Generally, operations used in Data Encryption are performed on 32-bit words in additive and XOR's circuits (Fig. 7).

5   Conclusion and Significance

The distant manage function by smart handset provides aid and support particularly for surveillance teams in the outer field. Different pliant types of acquaintances are intended as endorsement acquaintances to the structure. The GUIs of the applications are synchronized to the control board, and system is designed such that it is user-friendly interface. This bot can be used as a surveillance drone on the ground and be used to get the surveillance of the surrounding without knowing anybody giving an advantage to the search teams in India to navigate the whole arena and get a hold of any tricky situation. As this is not as costly as drone, it can be used more often and it is more effective on ground. By adding an infrared or ultrasonic sensor, an autonomous mode can be implemented and the robot will drive around collecting data. This application can be run over Wi-fi that make it easier to connect to a Web site; this will allow to make multiple robots driving around a facility giving a better surveillance. The phone's microphone can be used to detect and transmit audio to alert the user.

References

1. Gupta, T., Verma, G.: Area & power optimization of VPB peripheral memory for ARM7TDMI based microcontrollers. In: International Conference on Cognitive Computing and Information Processing (CCIP-2015), 3–4 Mar 2015, JSSATEN, Noida, India
2. Verma, G., Verma, V., Jhambhulkar, S., Verma, H.: Design of a lead-lag compensator for position loop control of a gimbaled payload. Paper presented at the International Conference on Signal Processing and Integrated Networks (SPIN-2015), 19–20 Feb 2015, Amity University, Noida, India
3. Wong, E.M.C.: A phone-based remote controller for home and office automation. IEEE Trans. Consum. Electron. **40**(1), 28–34 (1994)
4. Chang, T.-W.: Android/OSGi-based vehicular network management system. In; 2010 the 12th International Conference on Advanced Communication Technology (ICACT), vol. 2, pp. 1644–1649, Feb 2010

5. Fuchs, A., Chaudhuri, A., Foster, J.S.: Scan Droid: Automated Security Certification of Android Applications. Technical Report, University of Maryland, College Park (2009)
6. Kaur, I.: Microcontroller based home automation system with security. Int. J. Adv. Comput. Sci. Appl. **1**(6), 60–65 (2010)
7. Das, S.R., et al.: Home automation and security for mobile devices. IEEE PERCOM Workshops, pp. 141–146 (2011)
8. Monson, H.: Bluetooth Technology and Implementation. Wiley, New York (1999)
9. Smart phone operated robot, http://www.sooxmatechnologies.com

Development of Cross-Toolchain and Linux Device Driver

Gaurav Verma, Mohammad Imdad, Sandeep Banarwal, Himanshu Verma and Ashish Sharma

Abstract An embedded system is a combination of hardware and software program. Embedded systems have a very wide range varying from a simple 8051 microcontroller device to high-speed processor devices, which are even capable of running operating systems. Depending on the hardware design and architecture, an embedded system may run a simple C program or even an operating system. The trending IOT (Internet of Things) and automation applications require high-performance systems which can also support high definition graphics. An embedded OS is a running approach for embedded computer systems. These running methods are designed to be small, efficient optimized, and strict in using resources, simply known as RTOS. The machine running an embedded working system could be very constrained in resources akin to RAM and ROM, and for that reason programs made for embedded hardware are very distinct in their performance. Because of reminiscence obstacles, embedded working programs are commonly written in meeting language, however for some excessive-finish hardware, some of them are additionally written in additional transportable languages, like C.

Keywords RTOS · IoT · Cross-compiler · Toolchain

G. Verma (✉) · M. Imdad · S. Banarwal · H. Verma · A. Sharma
Department of Electronics and Communication Engineering, Jaypee Institute of Information Technology, A-10, Sector-62, Noida, Uttar Pradesh, India
e-mail: gaurav.iitkg@gmail.com

M. Imdad
e-mail: imdad92@live.com

S. Banarwal
e-mail: banarwals@gmail.com

H. Verma
e-mail: himanshutechdn@gmail.com

A. Sharma
e-mail: attach4ashish@gmail.com

© Springer Nature Singapore Pte Ltd. 2018
S. K. Muttoo (ed.), *System and Architecture*, Advances in Intelligent Systems and Computing 732, https://doi.org/10.1007/978-981-10-8533-8_17

1 Introduction

A compiler is a program that turns source code into an executable. A particular compiler compiles the program on a host computer and the executable file it generate can be executed on unique form of computer [1, 2]. A toolchain is the set of compiler, linker, libraries plus other tools that are needed to produce the executable like shared libraries. A debugger or IDE can also be regarded as part of a toolchain. A simple application progress toolchain can include a compiler and a linker to convert the source code into an executable application, libraries to provide interfaces to the operating system, and a debugger.

2 Cross-Toolchain

Every Linux installation requires these three commands very frequently. Generally, we get Linux software in the tarball format (tgz). These files have to be decompressed using tar command. If we have a new tarball by the name Linux.tgz, then we need to type the following commands:

1. $ tar xfv lmnx, tgz
2. $./some-path/configure
3. $make

The end result is a makefile as shown in Fig. 1.

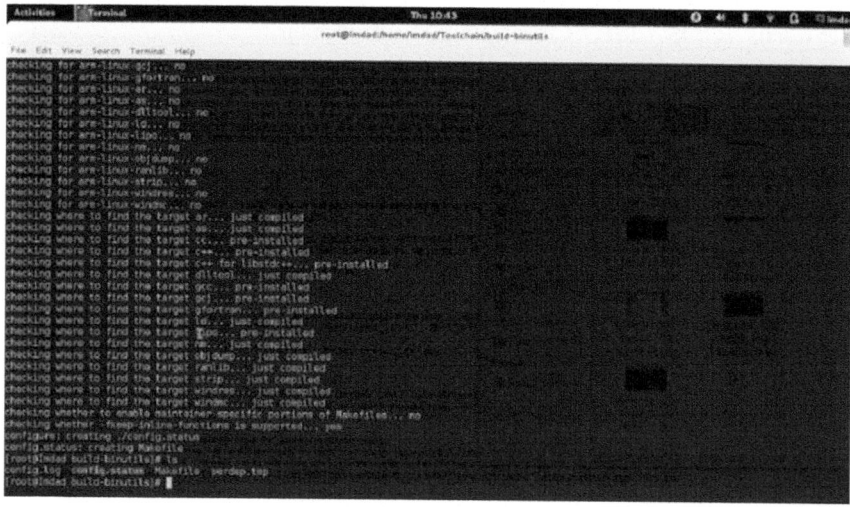

Fig. 1 End result of configure command for binutils is a makefile

The install section is the part where the executables and other required files created during 'make' and copied into the required final directories. For example, the executable file that runs may be copied to the/use/local/bin so that all users are able to run the software. Similarly, all the other files are also copied to the standard directories in Linux. When make is in execution, all the executables are created in the temporary directory where we had unzipped original tarball. So when 'make install' is executed, these executables are copied to the final directories.

2.1 Building a Cross-Compiler Toolchain

Building GCC involves fetching the sources, getting them ready for compilation, and then executing them as per procedure. While building a toolchain, we encountered some compatibility issues which were due to some versions of toolchain resources that were unable to work together. So, it is mandatory to use all the packages that support and are compatible with other packages. But this can only be realized by analyzing errors while building tools means it is a hit- and trial-based analysis.

Steps required for building a GCC cross-compiler are as follows:

- Download the packages
- Setting the build environment
- Build the binutils
- Getting the kernel headers
- Build a bootstrap GCC
- Using the bootstrap GCC to build the glibc library
- Building the final GCC

Install using cross-toolchain: Firstly, we need to download all the desired packages for the toolchain [3, 4]. We used the following packages for building our toolchain:

- Binutils-2.10.1.tar.gz
- Glihc-213 with glibc-ports-2.9
- GCC-4.3.2 with gmp, mpfr and mpc packages
- Linux kernel 2.6.32.63

After downloading all the required packages, unzip all the packages in toolchain directory and move gmp, mpc, and mpfr packages to GCC directory and glibc-ports in glibc, and then followed these steps:

- Choose a target name
- Setting up the directory structure
- Build binutils
- Kernel headers
- Building bootstrap GCC
- Build glibs
- Building the final GCC

3   Porting Linux on Mini2440

To install Linux, we need a bootloader, image of a Linux kernel (2.6.32 is supported by mini2440) and image of root file system. The root file system image and kernel image are no longer available on Friendlyarm.net [5, 6]. Hence, we had to try various third-party images that were downloaded from different blogs, forums, etc. Finally, the resources downloaded from bi11.sfonnn worked. We also tried to make an image of kernel by kernel compilation, but our compiled image was of much bigger size than the readily available image. So, the board would crash every time we tried to use our image. The steps for installing Linux are given as follows: connect serial port of mini2440 to USB port of laptop via serial to USB connector [7], install virtual machine or take another PC which has Windows-XP, and connect a USB port from PC to mini2440 board. We need DNW and PuTTY running on our systems; the DNW tool requires Windows-XP, and no version of PuTTY is compatible with Window-XP. So we used PuTTY on our Windows 8 system along with DNW in Windows-XP which was running on a virtual machine simultaneously. After all, connections have been made, connect power and switch S2 to NOR as shown in Fig. 2. Now switch on the power (Figs. 3 and 4).

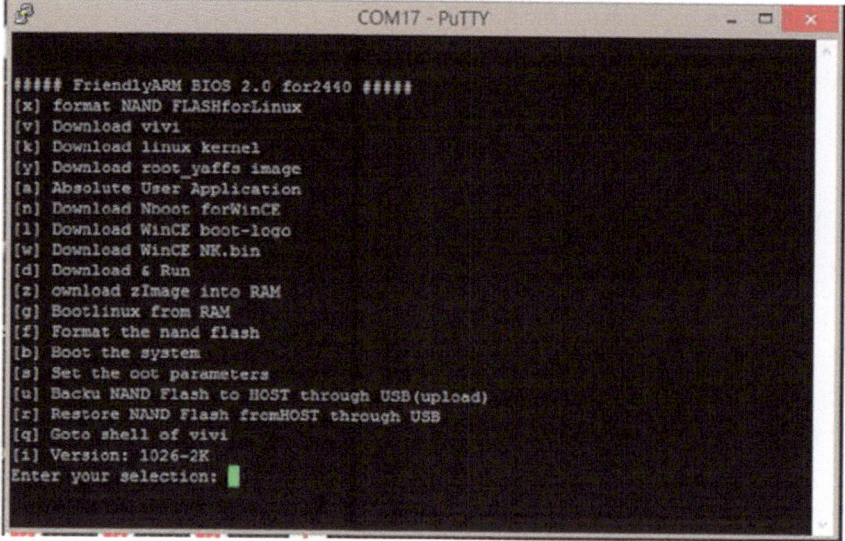

Fig. 2 Snapshot of NOR boot menu

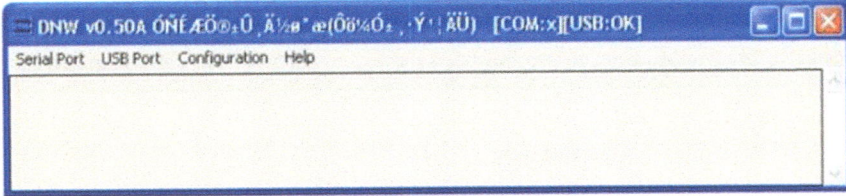

Fig. 3 Snapshot of DNW tool

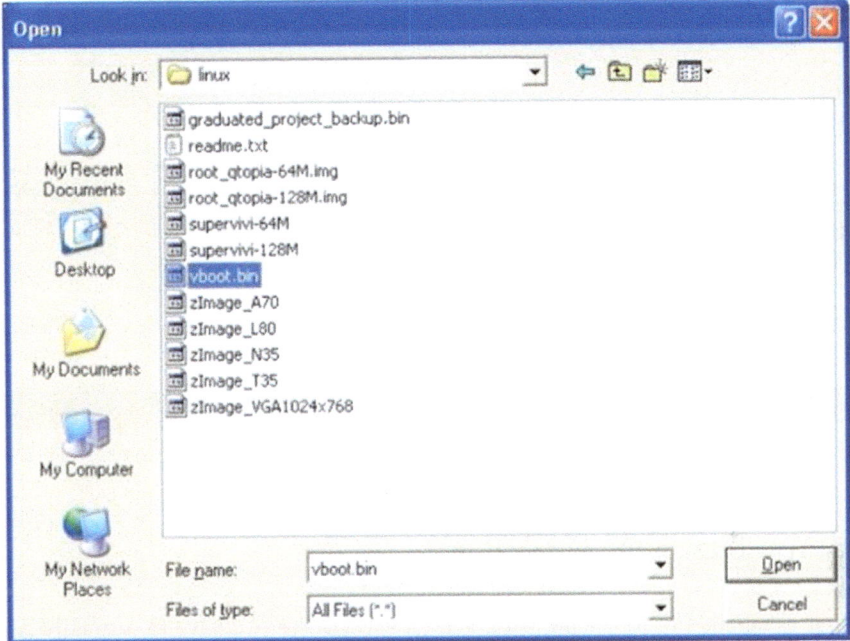

Fig. 4 Snapshot of DNW tool when transmit/restore is clicked

Step for creating an image :

• Go in the directory of Linux kernel.
• Run#make menu configure the terminal as shown in Fig. 5.

This menu is used to customize the tools and drivers required in the kernel. After selection, appropriate option exits the menu (Fig. 6).

• Run#make image after 10–12 min of compilation, it will give the image in directory arch/arm/boot. This image is a compressed version of kernel.

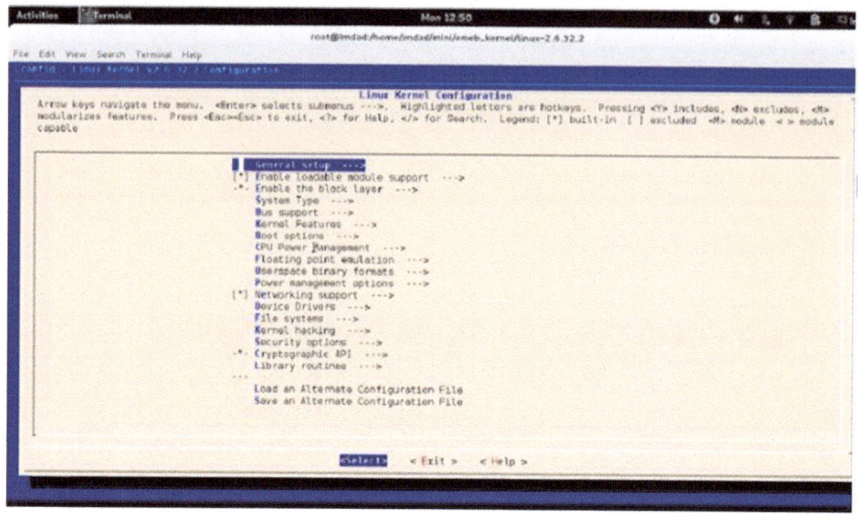

Fig. 5 Kernel configuration menu

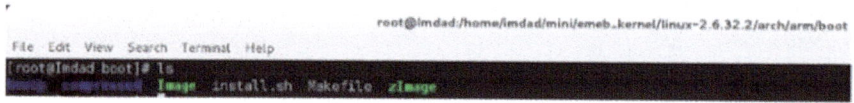

Fig. 6 Image destination directory

4 Working on Qt Applications

After installation of toolchain, tslib, and Qt-everywhere, we have to manually add the cross-compiled toolchain along with the version of Qt-everywhere as shown in Figs. 7 and 8.

After setting up the environment for cross-compilation, we started working on a simple application, which would control the RGB led's according to our choice of color. Unfortunately, we could not get the GPIO pins and network drivers running, so we had to limit our application to a simple touch screen application. However, we intend to continue this project further on a beaglebone board (Fig. 9).

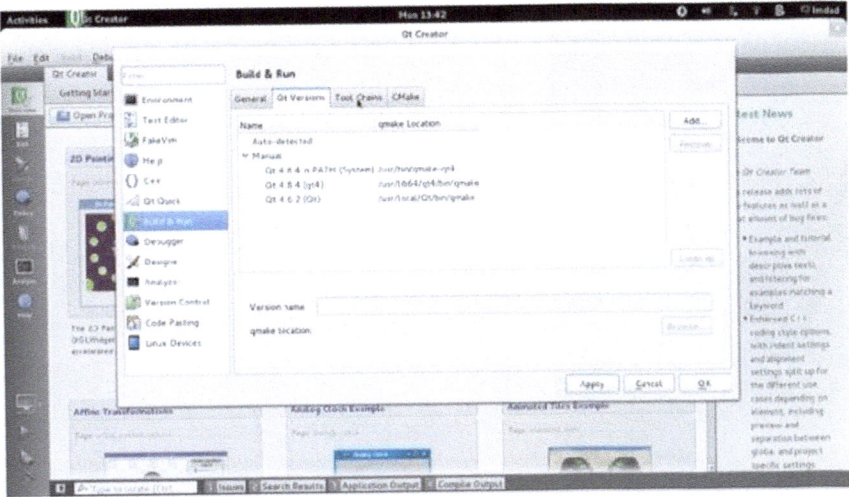

Fig. 7 Different QT versions for desktop and board application

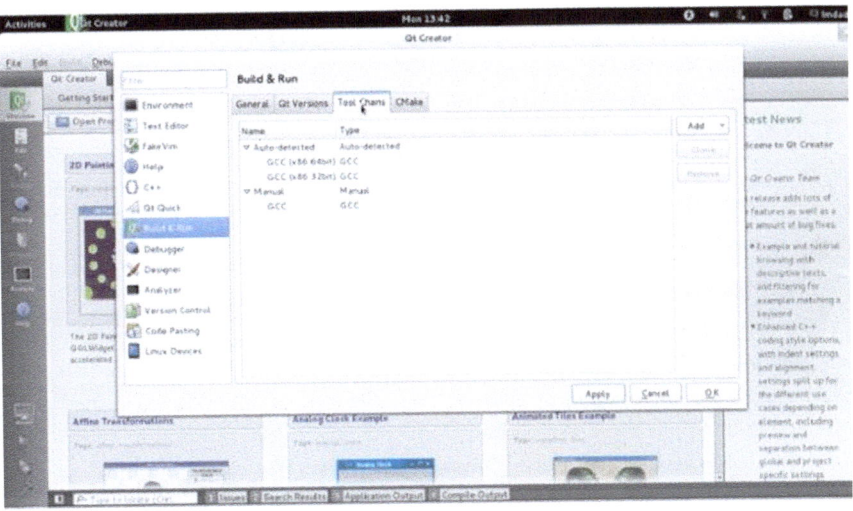

Fig. 8 Manually added cross-toolchain and other default toolchain in system

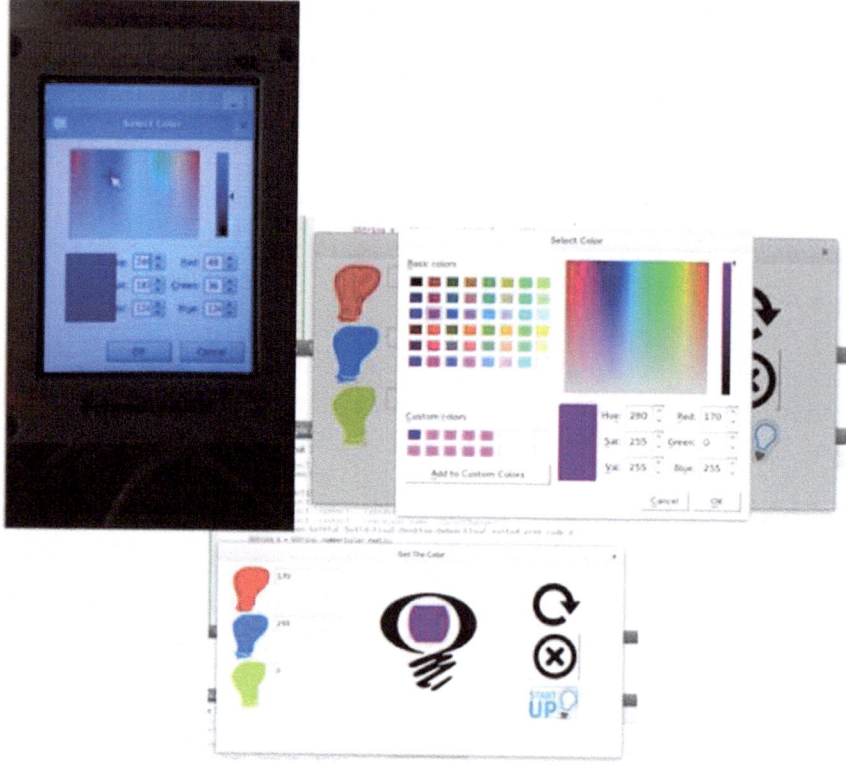

Fig. 9 Snapshots of application. **a** (i) The color chooser window on the board, (ii) complete view of color chooser window. **b** The color on the center is the color chosen from **a**(ii)

5 Implementation of Character Driver

A character driver implements various routines like read, write, and seek [8]. These routine calls are mapped in a structure type of file_operations. When a system call is invoked in an application, the control from user space is transferred to kernel space through a node in file system and these routines are executed as per input given to the application. But to make a driver functional it needs to be initialized, i.e. it should be inserted into kernel so that kernel should know about its presence and manage the control accordingly (Fig. 10).

Fig. 10 Map of interaction at different levels

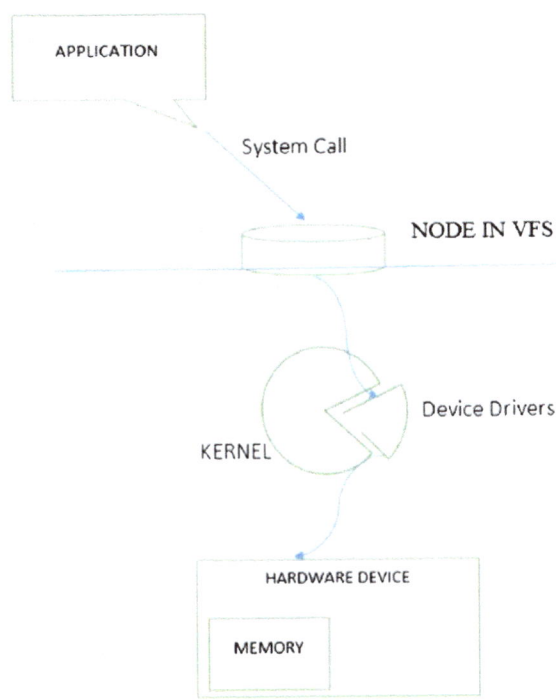

6 Sockets

Sockets are one side terminals of a two-way correspondence connection between two systems over the network. A socket is a combination of an IP address and a port number. Every 2-way connection can be uniquely identified by socket addresses. We have used a socket-based application to test driver where different clients will communicate through sockets and the texts will be handled by our driver as shown in Fig. 11.

7 Results and Conclusion

In this paper, Qt framework is used for building the applications, which is standard platform for building high-performance applications for embedded devices [9, 10]. Qt uses standard C++ libraries and has many libraries of its own which are also written in C++. We also configured a GCC cross-toolchain to understand the components of a toolchain. A cross-compiler is needed, if we have to build applications for a system that is different from the system that we are using to build. The compiler is given the desired target platform. We have configured Qt to buildcross-compiled applications for our board. Then we installed Qualia,

Fig. 11 Architectural overview of socket communication

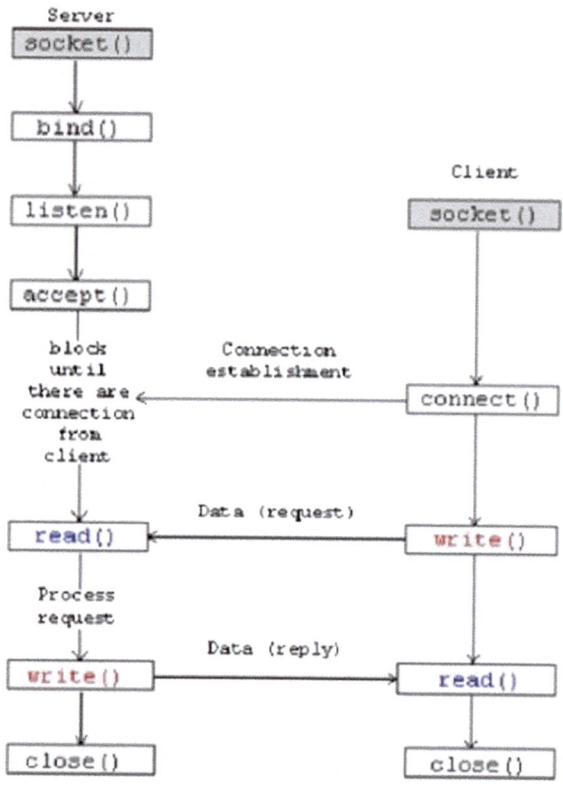

Linux-based operating system on the board. Then libraries have been compiled for touch screen and Qt and copied them on the board to support cross-compiled applications. Further, a character driver is implemented in which open, close, read, and write routines are mapped. Then a socket-based application is developed to test the driver.

References

1. Gupta, T., Verma, G.: Area and power optimization of VPB peripheral memory for ARM7TDMI based microcontrollers. In: International Conference on Cognitive Computing and Information Processing (CCIP-2015), JSSATEN, Noida, India, 3–4 Mar 2015
2. Verma, G., Verma, V., Jhambhulkar, S., Verma, H.: Design of a lead-lag compensator for position loop control of a gimballed payload. Paper Presented at the International Conference on Signal Processing and Integrated Networks (SPIN-2015), Amity University, Noida, India, 19–20 Feb 2015
3. http://importgeek.wordpress.com/2012103122/setting-up-cross-compilarion-toolchaion-to-compile-kemel-and-vivi-for-mini-2440
4. http://www.aleph1.co.uk/armlinux/thebook.html

5. http://www.arm9.net
6. http://www.friendlyarm.net
7. http://www.mini2440vietnam.blogspot.in
8. Corbett, J., Rubini, A., Kroah-Harrman, G.: Linux Device Drivers, 3rd edn., pp. 1–72. O'Reilly (2005)
9. Verma, G., et al.: Low power techniques for digital system design. Indian J. Sci. Technol. 8 (17) (2015) (IPL063)
10. Sally, G.: Pro Linux Embedded Systems, pp. 107–140. Apress (2010)

Design and Implementation of a Green Traffic Light Controller on FPGA Using VHDL

**Saumil Sachdeva, Sarthak Chowdhury, Sushant Shekhar
and Gaurav Verma**

Abstract A traffic light system ensures that the flow of traffic remains smooth and balanced. For this purpose, a combination of various signs and devices is included in the system. A traffic light controller can be designed using either a microcontroller or a field programmable gate array, but since FPGA's are more flexible and fast than a microcontroller, the traffic light controller presented in this paper has been implemented on FPGA using VHDL. A modern traffic light system needs to be even more power efficient than the previous versions. So to reduce the power dissipation, the clock gating technique is applied in the design. Clock gating enables the clock only for those portions of circuitry that are active, thus reducing the dynamic power.

Keywords VHDL · FPGA · Traffic light · Clock gating

1 Introduction

Field programmable gate array, as the name suggests, is a programmable device which can be programmed by a user using a hardware description language such as VHSIC hardware description language. FPGA consists of a matrix of configurable logic blocks (CLBs) connected via reconfigurable interconnects [1]. These logic blocks can then be programmed to perform various complex as well as simple

S. Sachdeva (✉) · S. Chowdhury · S. Shekhar · G. Verma
Department of Electronics and Communication Engineering,
Jaypee Institute of Information Technology, A-10, Sector-62, Noida, Uttar Pradesh, India
e-mail: saumil.sachdeva@gmail.com

S. Chowdhury
e-mail: sarthakchowdhury@ymail.com

S. Shekhar
e-mail: sushantshekhar09@gmail.com

G. Verma
e-mail: gaurav.iitkg@gmail.com

© Springer Nature Singapore Pte Ltd. 2018
S. K. Muttoo (ed.), *System and Architecture*, Advances in Intelligent Systems
and Computing 732, https://doi.org/10.1007/978-981-10-8533-8_18

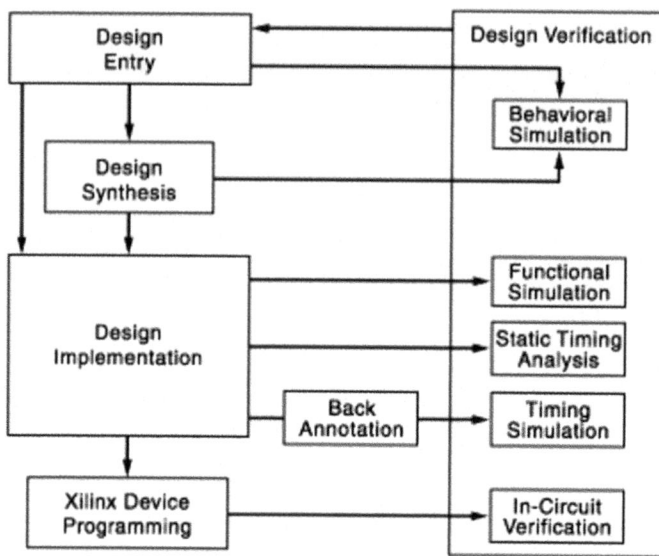

Fig. 1 Design flow for VHDL

functions. A FPGA holds certain advantages over a microcontroller or an application-specific integrated circuit (ASIC). FPGA is reprogrammable thus making it more useful than an ASIC. Also as compared with a microcontroller, FPGA's are more flexible, that is, functionality can be added or removed from it as required. Also FPGA's are hard-wired and have longer lifetime than a microcontroller. The traffic light controller was designed using VHDL in Xilinx ISE. It follows the design flow as shown in Fig. 1.

2 Traffic Light Design

The flow of the TLC design presented in this paper is as shown in Fig. 2. Three LEDs are used to indicate Red, Yellow and Green lights, whereas a seven segment is used to implement the counter that runs between each light. At RESET condition, no traffic light is on. The TLC then starts with RED light being switched on for 10 s followed by YELLOW light being switched on for 5 s, and then the GREEN light switched on for 10 s. The process then repeats itself.

Fig. 2 Design flow for TLC

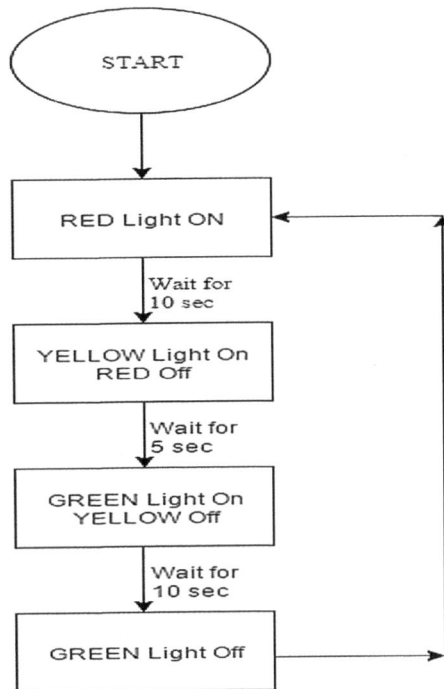

3 Clock Gating

Clock gating is a popular technique which can be used for reducing power dissipation in synchronous circuits [2]. Clock gating process uses an enable signal to enable clock for only those modules that are in use at the time of execution of process. This reduces the dynamic power consumption without affecting the functionality of the design. The clock gating technique presented in this process uses AND gates. In a two-input AND Gate, one input is taken as clock, whereas other input is an enable signal. Only when the enable signal is high, the clock passes through the AND gate to the sequential block of the circuit that is in function for the duration, as shown in Fig. 3.

Initially, without clock gating, the clock was being passed to all blocks Red, Yellow, and Green even when one of them was not active, as shown in Fig. 4. But with the application of clock gating, clock was enabled only on those blocks that were active for the duration, as shown in Fig. 5.

Fig. 3 Clock Gating using a
two-input AND Gate

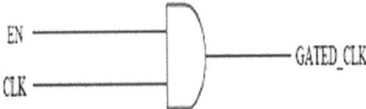

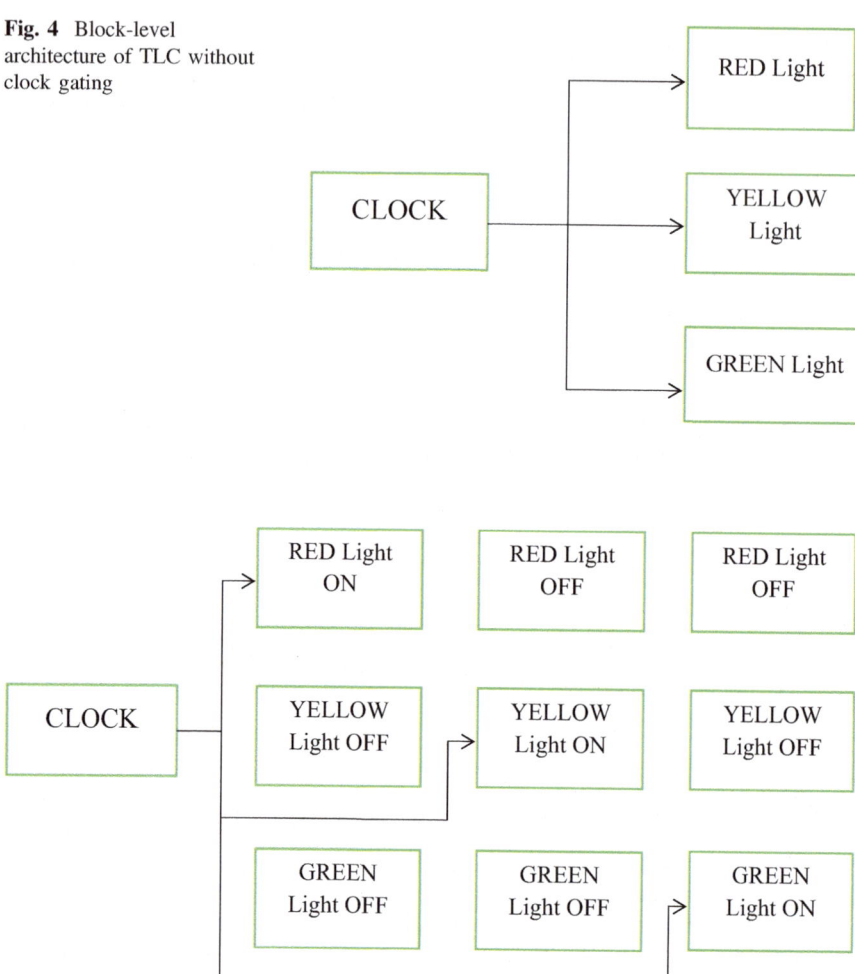

Fig. 4 Block-level architecture of TLC without clock gating

Fig. 5 Block-level architecture of TLC with clock gating

4 XPower Analyser Results

1. Without Clock Gating

Frequency	Leakage power (W)	Active power (W)				T. power (W)
		Clocks	Logics	Signals	IOs	
100 MHz	1.293	0.004	0.000	0.000	0.017	1.316
500 MHz	1.295	0.017	0.002	0.002	0.086	1.402
1 GHz	1.297	0.034	0.003	0.004	0.173	1.510
2 GHz	1.302	0.062	0.006	0.007	0.345	1.729

2. With Clock Gating

Frequency	Leakage power (W)	Active power (W)				T. power (W)
		Clocks	Logics	Signals	IOs	
100 MHz	1.293	0.003	0.000	0.000	0.006	1.303
500 MHz	1.294	0.017	0.002	0.002	0.030	1.344
1 GHz	1.295	0.035	0.004	0.004	0.059	1.397
2 GHz	1.297	0.068	0.07	0.008	0.118	1.498

The Power distribution results of the design implemented on Vertex 6 family FPGA clearly show us that when clock gating is applied, the power reduces significantly. As the frequency range increases, the power reduction is even more evident. At frequencies of 2 GHz and nearer, there is a reduction of almost 230 mW of active power.

5 Simulation Results

Simulation of the behavioural model shows the functionality of the traffic light controller, which is also verified with a Vertex 6 FPGA.

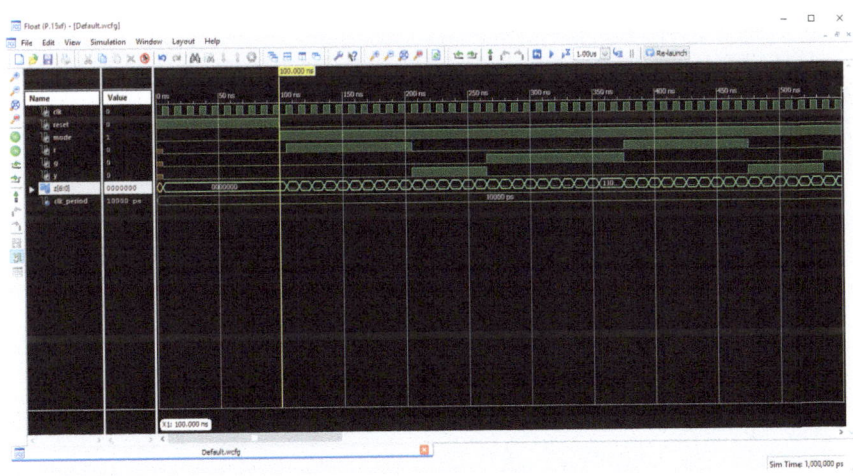

Fig. 6 Output waveforms for TLC

6 Conclusion

There is an ever-increasing demand of low-power devices in current technological environment, from cell phones to low-power appliances. Thus, traffic lights which can be found in every corner of the world needs to be converted into low-power systems too. This paper presents a viable solution to address the above problem. If applied collectively, the green traffic light could reduce power usage to a huge extent.

References

1. Field programmable gate array. (www.xilinx.com/training/fpga/fpga-field-programmable-gate-array.htm)
2. Verma, G., et al.: Low power techniques for digital system design. IJSNT **8**(17), IPL063 (2015)
3. Dilip, B., Alekhya, Y., Divya Bharathi, P.: FPGA implementation of an advanced traffic light controller using Verilog HDL. IJARCET **1**(7) (2012)

Suboptimal Controller Design for Power System Model

Shabana Urooj and Abeer Z. Alalmaie

Abstract This paper proposes a design of a suboptimal controller for a power system model. The system chosen is of order five and is reduced to models of orders four and three due to the reason that the implementation of suboptimal control demands the measurement of all the state variables of the system which is not practically feasible. The aggregation technique is employed for the reduction of order of the model. The aggregation matrix can be obtained using continued fraction expansion technique. The computational complexity is reduced by using the model order reduction techniques because the resulting suboptimal controllers are based on models with reduced orders. The performance analysis of the original system which is of the order of five is carried out in terms of several parameters.

Keywords Aggregation technique · Optimal control · Stability

1 Introduction

The area of system control involves, in most practical situations, a highly complex and high-order system model. These systems of higher orders are usually represented in terms of state variables. The solutions of these high-order models become time-consuming, and it becomes difficult to handle such systems during computer simulations and controller design. The preliminary design and optimal control policy of such systems can often be accomplished with great ease using appropriately selected lower-order models. The resulting suboptimal model retains all the important features of the original system. In practice, most of the state variables are

S. Urooj (✉)
Electrical Engineering Department, School of Engineering,
Gautam Buddha University, Greater Noida, Uttar Pradesh, India
e-mail: shabanaurooj@ieee.org

A. Z. Alalmaie
Community College of Regal Alma, King Khalid University, Abha,
Kingdom of Saudi Arabia

© Springer Nature Singapore Pte Ltd. 2018
S. K. Muttoo (ed.), *System and Architecture*, Advances in Intelligent Systems and Computing 732, https://doi.org/10.1007/978-981-10-8533-8_19

193

found to be inaccessible to measurement and thus the implement requires the realization of a filter or an observer. The suboptimal controllers improve the stability and the transient performance of the system to almost the same level as that of the optimal controllers. It is observed that the use of suboptimal controllers results in a simplified structure because the number of states to be measured is much less than those in the optimal controllers [1]. To tackle this problem, it is desirable to design suboptimal controllers for linear time-invariant systems so as to yield a system performance within an acceptable degradation limit [2]. The model reduction techniques are of fundamental importance for the design of controllers in control engineering [3] and filters for harmonic convergence [4]. Thus, using aggregation-based techniques, a suboptimal controller design is proposed for linear time-invariant systems. Simulation and modeling of dynamic systems is a task of primary importance in engineering, and differential equations are one of the most effective tools of modeling such systems. The mathematical model obtained using the first principle approach is often very complicated and time-consuming for computation and thus of very little use in practice. However, certain important aspects of these systems, in some cases, can be represented using models of significantly lower orders. This technique of obtaining a lower-order model, so that some important features of the system are retained, is known as model order reduction [5]. In the design of control systems, the sensitivity considerations are often very important [6]. In the area of control engineering when a controller is set for an optimal performance, the control system is highly sensitive to variations in the parameters which thus requires a controller setting that is not fully optimal with respect to the system performance but which compromises or makes a trade-off between sensitivity and the performance [7]. An analytical method has been presented to derive an optimal feedback control subject to sensitivity constraints [8] assuming small parameter variations. "Robust" control schemes have been proposed to resolve the sensitivity problem [9, 10]. In this approach, steady-state output regulation and asymptotic stability are obtained under variations in plant and feedback gain parameters.

2 Aggregation Technique

An aggregated model of a system is referred to the case when the system is described by a coarser set of variables.

This method is used to obtain a lower-order model of dynamic system with a state vector of higher dimensions. The model is derived by aggregating the original system's state vector into lower dimension vector. The aggregation technique can be represented in terms of pictorial representation [11].

Consider continuous linear time-invariant time dynamic system given by [12]

$$\dot{X}(t) = AX(t) + BU(t) \tag{1}$$

$$Y(t) = CX(t) \tag{2}$$

where

$A = n \times n$ system matrix.
$X = n \times n$ state vector.
$U = m \times m$ control input vector.
$Y = p \times p$ output vector.

Comparing the standard form given in Eqs. 1 and 2 with the original/nominal case data given by state variable representation as

$$\begin{bmatrix} \dot{x}1 \\ \dot{x}2 \\ \dot{x}3 \\ \dot{x}4 \\ \dot{x}5 \end{bmatrix} = \begin{bmatrix} -0.188 & 0 & 0.227 & 0 & 0 \\ 0 & 0 & 1 & 0 & 0 \\ -1.815 & -0.570 & -0.5 & 1 & 0 \\ 0 & 0 & 0 & 0 & 1 \\ 0 & 0 & -1 & -20 & -12 \end{bmatrix} \begin{bmatrix} x1 \\ x2 \\ x3 \\ x4 \\ x5 \end{bmatrix} + \begin{bmatrix} 1 \\ 0 \\ 0 \\ 0 \\ 0 \end{bmatrix} U$$

$$[y] = [0.49 \quad -0.233 \quad 0 \quad 0 \quad 0] \begin{bmatrix} x1 \\ x2 \\ x3 \\ x4 \\ x5 \end{bmatrix}$$

Now assuming X is directly observed and system is controllable, whereas the original system is of large dimension and an un-aggregated system. The original system is obtained by substituting the value of matrices A, B, X, and U in Eq. 1.

3   Results and Discussion

Consider an aggregated linear time-invariant model for same large-scale system

$$dZ/dt = FZ + GU \tag{3}$$

where Z is dimensional aggregated state vector.
F and G are $k \times k$ and $k \times m$ dimensional constant matrices, respectively.

The aggregation condition of the system model is

$$Z = QX \tag{4}$$

where $Q = k \times n$ constant aggregation matrix of A.
$K < n$, and rank Q is assumed to be k.
The aggregated control matrix G is given by

$$G = QB \tag{5}$$

$$FQQ^{\mathrm{T}} = QAQ^{\mathrm{T}} \tag{6}$$

The matrix for the reduced-order model is given by

$$F = (QAQ^{\mathrm{T}})(QQ^{\mathrm{T}})^{-1} \tag{7}$$

The system performance is studied based on response plots of different state variables using MATLAB scripts and computation of eigenvalues for open-loop and closed-loop systems for the original and aggregated model system.

The calculated aggregated matrix is

$$F = \begin{bmatrix} -2.3012 & 0.9539 & 0.8482 \\ -2.8517 & 1.1510 & 1.2417 \\ -4.1819 & 1.7000 & 0.6344 \end{bmatrix}$$

$$G = \begin{bmatrix} 25.1025 \\ 0 \\ 0 \end{bmatrix}$$

Gain matrix K for the original system is

$$K = \begin{bmatrix} 1.8592 & -0.4069 & -0.8693 & -0.4749 & -0.0380 \end{bmatrix}$$

The gain matrix KK for the aggregated system is

$$KK = \begin{bmatrix} 1.2063 & -1.5616 & -0.9653 \end{bmatrix}$$

The response plots of power system model are shown in Figs. 1, 2, 3, 4, 5 and 6. The original system is aggregated to two reduced-order models: One is aggregated from fifth to fourth, and other is aggregated from fifth- to third-order model.

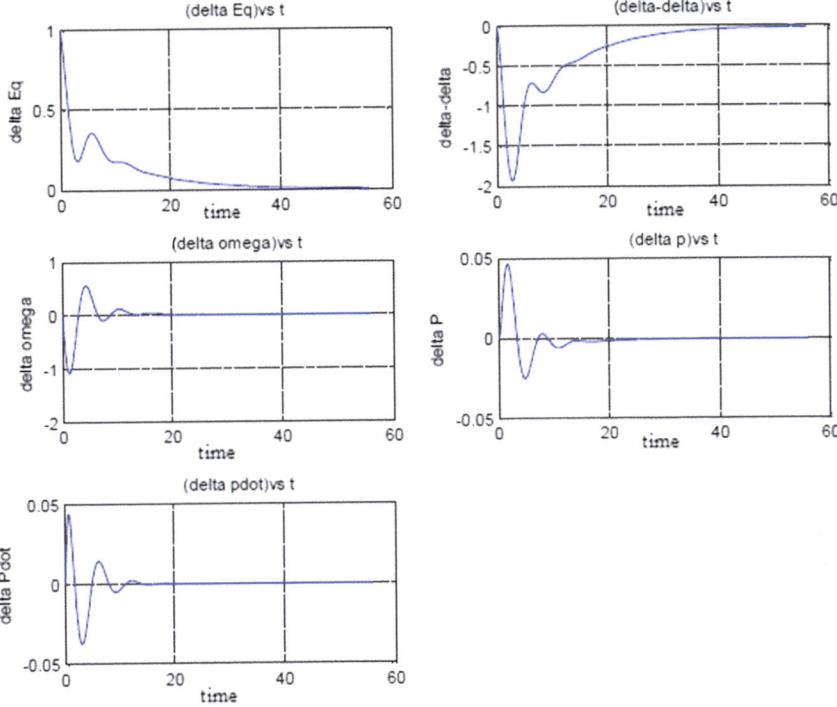

Fig. 1 Uncontrolled response of power system model

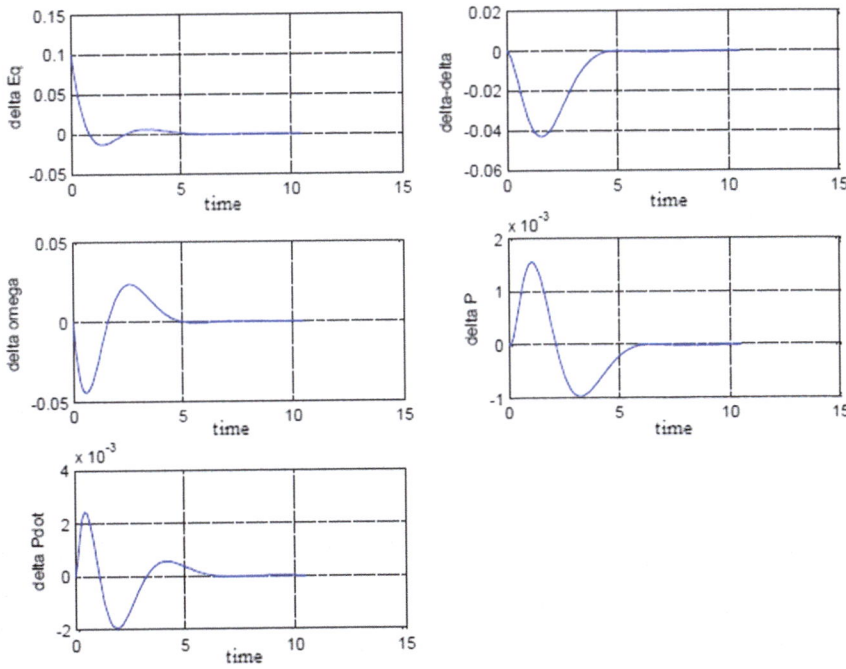

Fig. 2 Controlled response of power system model

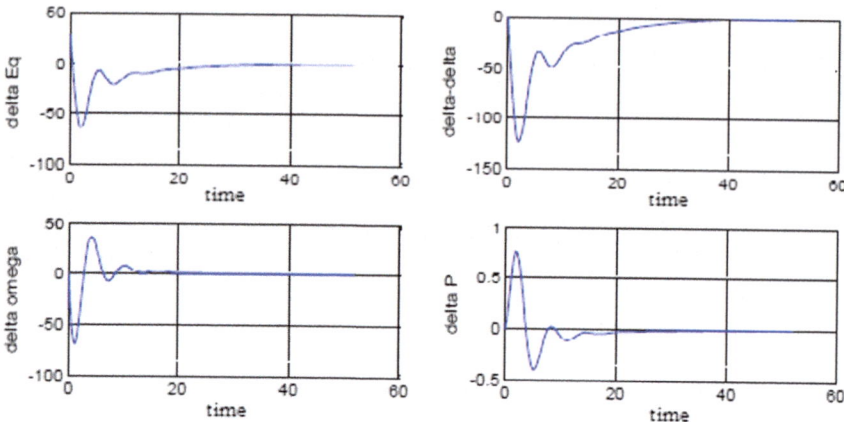

Fig. 3 Uncontrolled response of aggregated power system model reduced from fifth to fourth order

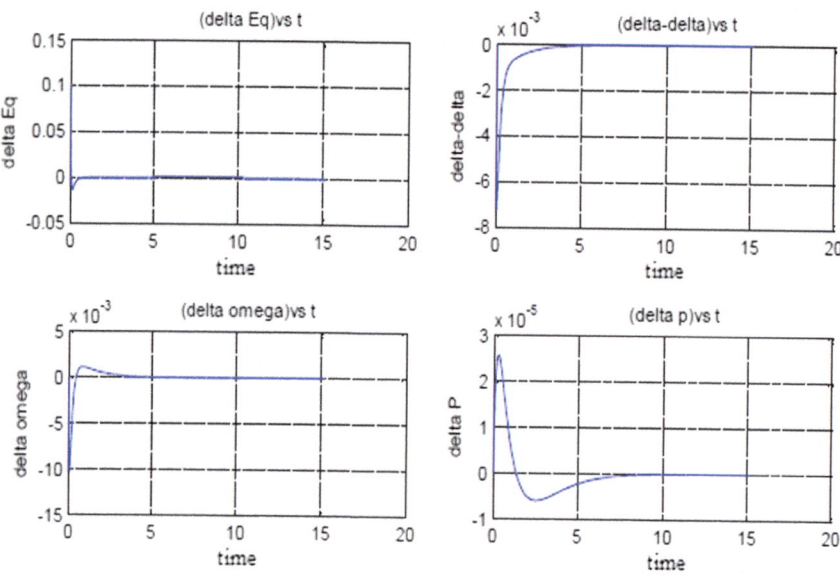

Fig. 4 Controlled response of aggregated power system model reduced from fifth to fourth order

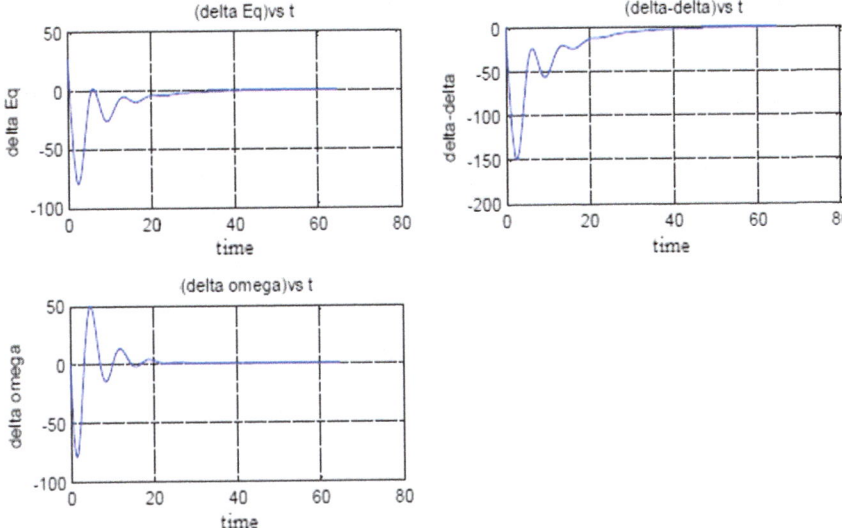

Fig. 5 Uncontrolled response of aggregated power system model reduced from fifth to third order

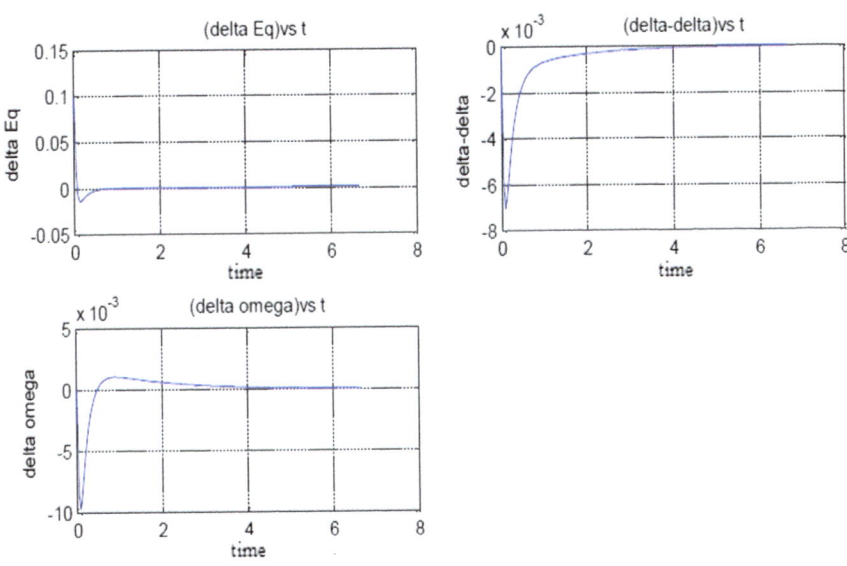

Fig. 6 Controlled response of aggregated power system model reduced from fifth to third order

4 Conclusion

The suboptimal controller is obtained for a large system which improves the stability and transient performance of the system. A sensitivity analysis is carried out for single parameter variation in inertia constant "M", damping constant "D", and time constant "T_{do}". In case of inertia constant "M", the stability of original system is increased for +50% perturbation in both the cases and the same is with 4×4 aggregated open-loop system, but for closed-loop system model, the stability is increased for −50% perturbation in 3×3 aggregated system, and in open-loop system, the stability is increased for +50% of the original value and vice versa for closed loop. In case of damping constant "D", the open-loop original system is more stable toward −50% perturbation, whereas closed-loop original system is tending toward stability at +50%, and in the aggregated cases, 4×4 and 3×3, the stability is increased toward +50% for closed loop and vice versa. For time constant "T_{do}", the nominal system model is more stable at −50% perturbations and the same is observed for aggregated 4×4 and 3×3 system model. The stability of reduced models is not guaranteed even if the original system is stable. Open-loop and closed-loop aggregated responses are shown for the original system as well as for the reduced models.

References

1. Elangovan, S., Kuppurajulu, A.: Suboptimal control of power systems using simplified models. IEEE Proc., 911–919 (1970)
2. Kousut, R.L.: Suboptimal control system subjected to control structure constraints. IEEE Proc. 15(5), 557–563 (1970)
3. Ibraheem, D., Kumar, P., Naqvi, S.: Aggregation by continued fraction method of model reduction: an application to SISO system. Int. J. Eng. Manag. Res. 2(3) (2012)
4. Urooj, S., Das, S.: Harmonic convergence for balanced and unbalanced nonlinear load using hybrid filter. Int. J. Convergence Comput. 1(2), 109–117 (2014). https://doi.org/10.1504/ijconvc.2014.063740
5. Philip, B., Pal, J.: An evolutionary computation based approach for reduced order modelling of linear systems. IEEE Proc. 10, 978–982 (2010)
6. Kuo, B.C.: Automatic Control System. Prentice Hall of India Pvt Ltd, New Delhi (1997)
7. Davison, E.J.: A method of simplifying linear dynamic systems. IEEE Proc. 11(1), 93–101 (1996)
8. Graupe, D.: Optimal control subject to sensitivity constraints. IEEE Proc., 593–594 (1974)
9. Pearson, J.B., Shield, R.W., Staats Jr., P.W.: Robust solution to linear multivariable control problem. IEEE Trans. Autom. Control 19, 508–517 (1974)
10. Davisson, E.J., Goldenberg, A.: Robust control of a general servo-mechanism problem. Automatica 11, 461–471 (1975)
11. Aoki, M.: Control of large-scale dynamic systems by aggregation. IEEE Trans. Autom. Control 13(3), 246–253 (1968)
12. Rao, S., Lamba, S., Rao, V.: Routh-approximant time-domain reduced order-models for single-input single-output systems. IEEE Proc. 125(9), 1059–1063 (1978)

Designing and Simulation of S-Shaped Dielectric Resonator Antenna with Air Gap

Ranjana Singh and Amit Kumar

Abstract Different results and effect on resonance frequency due to "air gap" present between DRA and ground are presented in this paper. This structure is inspired by rectangular DRA as rectangular DRA provides two aspect ratios. The proposed structure is a miniaturized, low-profile antenna having bandwidth of 4.1 GHz (5.8–9.9 GHz) and resonant frequency is 7.31 GHz. Simulation is done using CST Microwave Studio Suite-10, showing proposed structure has high radiation efficiency, improved gain of 5.735 dB with VSWR 1.18 at resonant frequency. Proposed antenna is excited using micro-strip line having width of only 4 mm. An air gap is introduced between S-shaped DRA and ground, and results are compared when air gap is removed (micro-strip is inserted into DRA). Proposed structure is investigated and examined at different parameters ensuring that proposed antenna is a low profile and is a good candidate for wireless systems like WLAN, WiMAX, 4G systems, and some wireless radio system.

Keywords Aspect ratio · Dielectric resonator antenna (DRA) · Radiation efficiency · Impedance bandwidth (IBW) · VSWR

1 Introduction

Dielectric resonator antennas (DRAs) have been widely investigated in microwave frequency bands because of their attractive features like small size, high radiation efficiency, lightweight, low temperature coefficient of frequency, wide impedance bandwidth, zero conduction losses, and no excitation of surface waves [1–5]. They are available in different shapes like rectangular, cylindrical, and spherical, and they

R. Singh (✉)
Communication Department, Galgotias University, Greater Noida, India
e-mail: ranjana.gcet@gmail.com

A. Kumar
SEECE, Galgotias University, Greater Noida, India
e-mail: amit.kumarc210@gmail.com

© Springer Nature Singapore Pte Ltd. 2018
S. K. Muttoo (ed.), *System and Architecture*, Advances in Intelligent Systems and Computing 732, https://doi.org/10.1007/978-981-10-8533-8_20

201

support multiband, narrowband, and wideband usage. Rectangular DRAs offer maximum design flexibility than cylindrical and spherical DRAs as rectangular DRAs have two aspect ratios providing second degree of freedom, i.e., width/height and length/height can be chosen independently [6]. Several methods and techniques have been introduced to increase the IBW such as stack DRAs [7], using collinear parasitic element [8] and so on. Many structures like P-shaped DRA [9] and H-shaped DRA [10] have been studied for wideband applications. But this S-shaped structure fed by micro-strip with air gap between DRA and ground is proposed to further improve the IBW (up to ~57%) and gain up to 5.73 dB. This antenna is theoretically designed, and its simulation is done using CST Microwave Studio. Simulated results are analyzed and discussed in terms of gain, return loss, IBW, radiation pattern and also effect of air gap on these results are presented in this paper.

2 Overview and Antenna Configuration

In rectangular DRA, fields are similar as in rectangular waveguide, and propagation modes are divided into TE and TM modes, but due to mounting of DRA over ground only TE–TE^x, TE^y, and TE^z modes are excited. The resonant frequency of these modes is a function of DRA dimensions [6]. The resonance frequency of rectangular DRA can be calculated using equation [6]:

$$f_o = \frac{c}{2\pi} \sqrt{\left\{ \frac{1}{(\varepsilon_r - 1)} [k^2 \tan^2 \left(\frac{dk_x}{2} \right) + k_x] \right\}}$$

Thus, wave number for free space can be calculated as:

$$k_o = \frac{2\pi f_o}{c}.$$

Studies on effect of introduction of air gap between DRA and ground have found that there can be significant change in resonance frequency and Q-factor, and this is also used as a method for better matching of the impedance of DRA with the feeding [11–15]. Practically, air gaps can be implemented by inserting foam spacer whose dielectric constant is equivalent to 1 [6]. The schematic diagram of proposed structure is shown in Fig. 1 in which height of antenna is 5.23 mm in z-direction.

Length is 18 mm in x-direction with breadth of 16 mm in y-direction. Dielectric constant is taken 13. Figure 2 shows the evolution of proposed antenna by removing two rectangular slots $p \times q \times h$ providing it S shape. When the volume

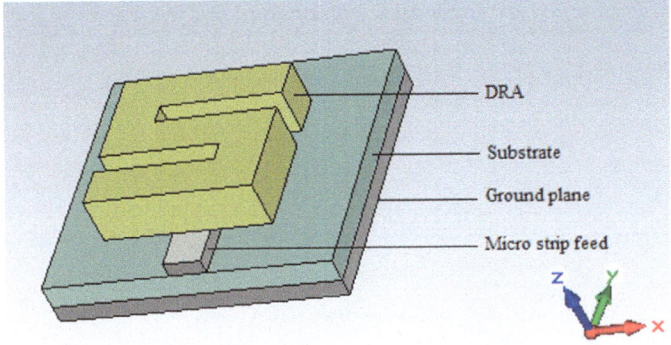

Fig. 1 Configuration of S-shaped DRA

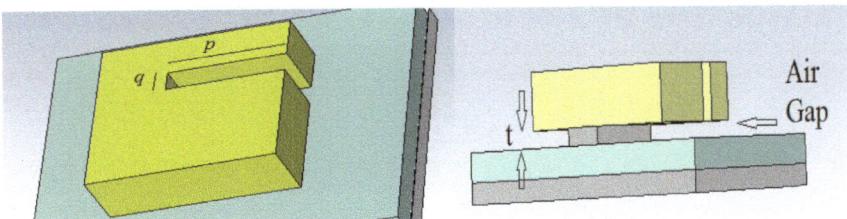

Fig. 2 Different views of proposed structure

of DRA is reduced, Q-factor is reduced resulting in increment in impedance bandwidth. Optimized dimensions of antenna are given as:

- Ground plane: $31 \times 27.5 \times 2$ mm^3
- Substrate: $31 \times 27.5 \times 2.68$ mm^3
- Micro-strip: $4 \times 12.5 \times 1.6$ mm^3
- Both slots: $13 \times 2 \times 5.23$ mm^3

Ground and micro-strip are perfect conductors, whereas substrate is of Rogers TMM (loss-free) having dielectric constant 4.5. Frequency range is chosen from 5 to 11 GHz.

3 Simulated Results and Parametric Discussion

Simulated results of both the cases (i) when air gap is present and (ii) when air gap is not present are examined and discussed in this section. Figure 3 shows the graph of return loss (in dB) versus frequency (in GHz).

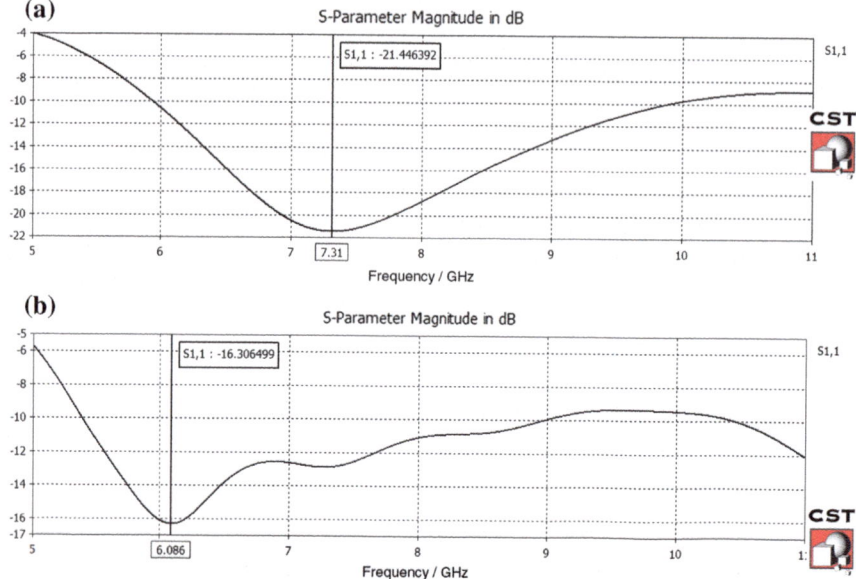

Fig. 3 **a** Return loss (dB) when air gap is present, **b** return loss (dB) when air gap is not present

S_{11} also known as return loss is the ratio of reflected power (P_r) to the incident power (P_i), defined as:

$$\text{Return loss} = \text{reflected power } (P_r)/\text{incident power } (P_i)$$

Generally, a value for return loss of −10 dB and below is acceptable. According to simulated result, resonance frequency is 7.31 GHz at which S_{11} is −21.45 dB means only 0.716% of incident power is reflected back by the terminating equipment, but when air gap is removed, S_{11} is −16.30 dB at resonance frequency 6.086 GHz means 2.34% power is reflected back. IBW is calculated according to the equation given below:

$$\text{IBW} = \text{bandwidth}/\text{resonance frequency}$$

When air gap is present, IBW is near about 57%. Figure 4 is the radiation pattern of proposed structure at resonance frequency showing gain is 5.735 dB with radiation efficiency −0.3502 dB. Whereas these values are reduced in the absence of air gap. Gain is dropped to 2.924 dB.

Figure 5 is the polar plot of far-field radiation pattern for both cases. When air gap is present, direction of main lobe is 94° with angular width of 65.6°, but this angular width of main lobe is dropped to 54.8° when air gap is removed. We can see the radiation is mainly concentrated to above-mentioned main lobe unlike the radiation pattern in Fig. 5b which is without the air gap.

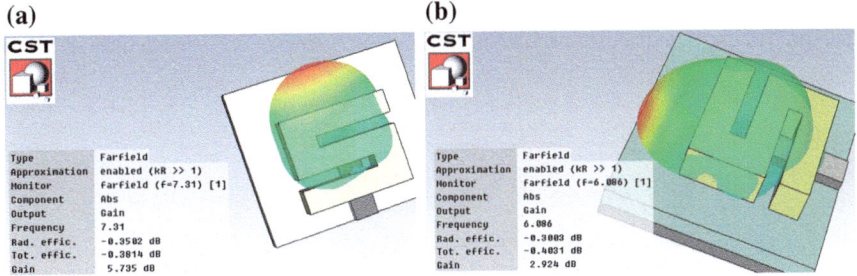

Fig. 4 Far-field radiation pattern for both cases (respectively)

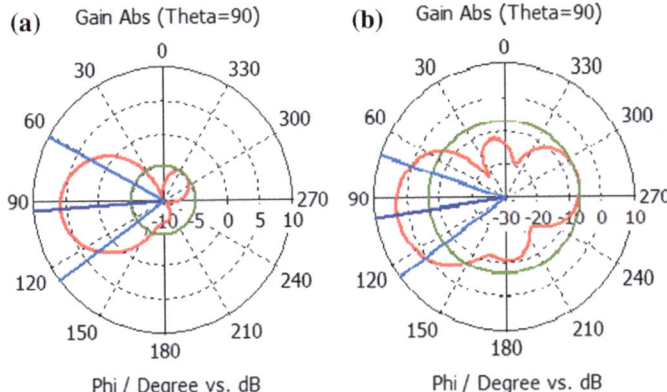

Fig. 5 Polar plot of far-field radiation pattern at resonance frequency, **a** 7.31 GHz, **b** 6.068 GHz

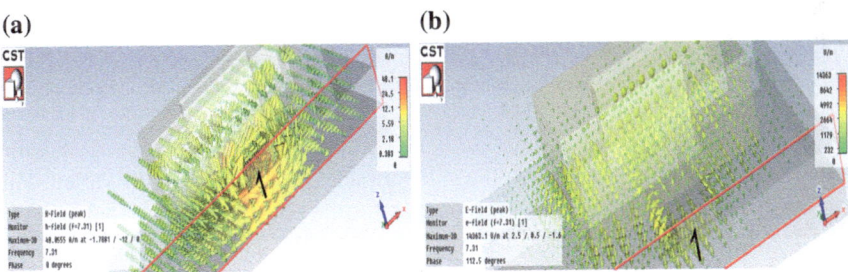

Fig. 6 **a** H-field distribution and **b** E-field distribution

The distribution of H field and E field in proposed structure is shown in Fig. 6a, b.

The H-field and E-field distribution shows that the pattern is uniform throughout the structure and converging to the simulation point showing the excitation of single mode only. Ideally, for perfect matching, input impedance should be 50 Ω.

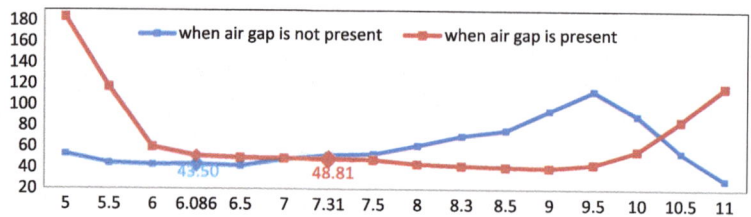

Fig. 7 Graph of input impedance (ohms) versus frequency (GHz)

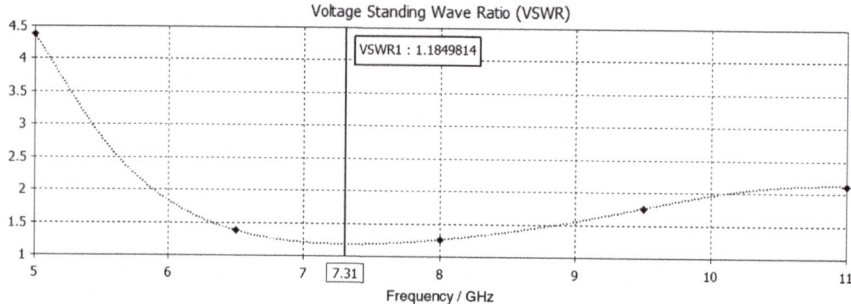

Fig. 8 VSWR of proposed structure

Figure 7 is representing the comparison of input impedance of both cases, according to simulated result at resonance frequency 7.31 GHz impedance is 48.81 Ω and at 6.086 GHz its 43.57 which clearly demonstrates that impedance is better matched when air gap is present.

Voltage standing wave ratio (VSWR) is the measure of how perfectly antenna is matched with transmission line. It is expressed as VSWR = $(1 + \Gamma)/(1 - \Gamma)$, where Γ is reflection coefficient or return loss. From Fig. 8, it is found that VSWR is 1.18 at resonance frequency 7.31 GHz.

Figure 9 is the plot of return loss (S_{11} parameter) versus frequency showing different resonance frequencies as the gap between DRA and ground is varied. This variation in gap and its result at various parameters are concluded in Table 1.

The comparison of proposed DRA on above-mentioned parameters proves that the DRA has a better response to the air gap of 1.6 mm rather than without air gap.

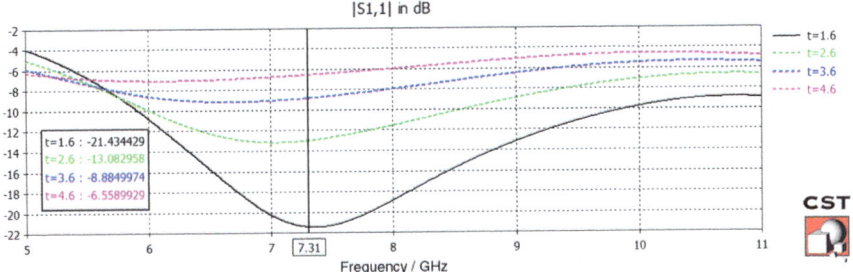

Fig. 9 Return loss (dB) versus frequency (GHz) with variation in thickness of air gap (*t* in mm)

Table 1 S_{11}-parameter and impedance bandwidth at different thickness of air gap

Air gap (mm)	Reflection coefficient (dB)	Resonant frequency (GHz)	IBW (%)
1.6	−21.43	7.31	57
2.6	−13.08	7.0	36
3.6	−8.88	6.8	NIL
4.6	−6.55	6.5	NIL

4 Conclusions

The proposed DRA has a bandwidth of 4.1 GHz ranging from 5.8 to 9.9 GHz with a gain of 5.735 dB at resonant frequency 7.31 GHz. This range lies in IEEE C-band suitable for telecommunication and radar application. This can also be a good candidate for WLAN, WiMAX, 4G systems, and some wireless radio system. The structure can further be minimized and enhanced using other DRA structure like triangular DRA.

5 Future Scope

The proposed design size can be reduced by using materials with high dielectric constants, using shorting walls and shorting pins. Planar designs with different radiator shapes can be used in which the IBW reaches 70%. These shapes include circular (BW from 2.25 to 17.25 GHz), elliptical (BW from 1.17 to 12 GHz), trapezoidal (80% BW), and roll monopoles (more than 70% BW) [16].

References

1. Kumar, J., Gupta, N.: Performance analysis of dielectric resonator antennas. Wirel. Pers. Commun. **75**, 1029–1049 (2014)
2. Luk, K.M., Leung, K.W.: Dielectric Resonator Antennas. Baldock England, Res. Studies Press (2003)
3. Petosa, A.: Dielectric resonator antenna. In: Handbook. Artech House, Norwood, MA, USA (2007)
4. Mukherjee, B., Patel, P., Mukherjee, J.: Hemispherical dielectric resonator antenna based on Apollonian gasket of circles—a fractal approach. IEEE Trans. Antennas Propag. **62**(1), 40–47 (2014)
5. Kumar, J., et al.: Compact wideband rectangular DRA with slots and air gap for C-band application. In: IEEE-ICIIS 9th International Conference, Dec 2014
6. Mongia, R.K., Bhartia, P.: Dielectric resonator antennas—a review and general design relations for resonant frequency and bandwidth. Int. J. Microw. Millimetre-Wave Comput. Aided Eng. **4**(3), 230–247 (1994)
7. Kishk, A.A., Ahn, B., Kajfez, D.: Broadband stacked dielectric resonator antennas. IEEE Electron. Lett. **25**, 1232–1233 (1989)
8. Fan, Z., Antar, Y.M.M., Ittipiboon, A., Petosa, A.: Parasitic coplanar three-element dielectric resonator antenna subarray. Electron. Lett. **32**, 789–790 (1993)
9. Khalily, M., Rahim, M.K.A., Ramlee Kamarudin, M.: A novel P-shape dielectric resonator antenna for wideband application. In: IEEE Asia-Pacific Conference on Applied Electromagnetics (APACE) (2010)
10. Liang, X.L., Denindni, T.A.: H-shaped dielectric resonator antenna for wideband applications. IEEE Antennas Wirel. Propag. Lett. **7**, 163–166 (2008)
11. Apperley, T., Okoniewski, M.: An air-gap-based frequency switching method for the dielectric resonator antenna. IEEE Antennas Wirel. Propag. Lett. **13**, 454–458 (2014)
12. Junker, G.P., et al.: Effect of an air gap on a cylindrical DRA operating in the TM_{01} Mode. IEEE Electron. Lett. **30**(2), 97–98 (1994)
13. Junker, G.P., et al.: Effect of fabrication imperfection for ground-plane-backed dielectric resonator antennas with coaxial excitation. IEEE Antenna Propag. **37**(1), 40–47 (1995)
14. Cooper, M., et al.: Investigation of dielectric resonator antennas for L-band communication. In: Symposium on Antenna Technology and applied electromagnetic ANTEM 96, Montreal, Canada, pp. 167–170, Aug 1996
15. Cooper, M., et al.: Investigation of Current and Novel Rectangular Dielectric Resonator Antennas for Broadband Application at L-Band Frequencies, M.Sc. Thesis, Carleton University (1997)
16. Chen, Z.N., Chia, M.Y.: Broadband Planar Antennas. Wiley, New York (2006)

Trajectory Generation for Driver Assistance System

Rupali Mathur, Deepika Rani Sona, Rashmi Ranjan Das and Praneet Dutta

Abstract Our project involves the generation of a path for modern driver assistant systems. It provides a cognizance of the objects ahead of the driver, which can play a major role in preventing accidents. Our algorithm is inspired from the data sets involving displacement and time. This provides the accurate position and velocity of the vehicle. To define the trajectory, polynomial equations can be used to explain this. The velocity and acceleration can be calculated according to coefficients of the polynomial equation. The number of coefficients determines the degree of the polynomial. By making use of a simulator, the trajectory generated can be studied. The objective of detection and trajectory generation is to provide a system that alerts the driver to the hurdles ahead so he/she is better placed to avoid a collision while the vehicle is moving.

Keywords Driver assistant system · Position estimation · Localization
Mapping cruise control · Decentralization · Radio detection and ranging
Lane tracking

R. Mathur (✉) · R. R. Das
School of Electrical Engineering, VIT University, Vellore 632014, India
e-mail: rupali.mathur2014@vit.ac.in

R. R. Das
e-mail: rashmiranjandas@vit.ac.in

D. R. Sona · P. Dutta
School of Electronics Engineering, VIT University, Vellore, India
e-mail: deepika.rs@vit.ac.in

P. Dutta
e-mail: praneet.dutta2012@vit.ac.in

© Springer Nature Singapore Pte Ltd. 2018
S. K. Muttoo (ed.), *System and Architecture*, Advances in Intelligent Systems
and Computing 732, https://doi.org/10.1007/978-981-10-8533-8_21

1   Introduction

As the number of vehicles rises, the road becomes increasingly accident prone. A boom in the market for high-speed cars also known as Sport-Utility Vehicles (SUVs) has encouraged increased dangerous driving at speeds over 80 km/h. The resultant rise in road accidents has spurred manufacturers to develop and improve safety systems. The driver assistant system (DAS) acts as a secondary or co-driver for a vehicle. The system was developed to minimize the large number of road accidents occurring on a daily basis due to poor driver alertness. Research is ongoing to obtain better response and accuracy. Recently, a vehicle equipped with an advanced driver assistant system (ADAS) was announced by Honda. It senses the objects, vehicles as well as nearby walkers on the pavement. The car was called Honda CR-V was released in 2014. The CR-V stands for Compact Recreational Vehicle. It boosts the following four technologies that can easily mimic the functionality of a robotic vehicle:

- Lane Keeping Assistant—Similar to the functionality of a line following robot.
- Adaptive Cruise Control—This intelligently adjusts the vehicular speed to keep an appropriate distance from the vehicle ahead.
- Collision Mitigation Braking System—Utilizing an Ultrasonic Sensor, it offers the capability to avoid objects in the path of the vehicle.
- Rearview Camera—Image processing algorithms are used to decided the route for a self parking system.

Adaptive cruise control, collision mitigation have been explained in this paper through the example of a robotic car. At lower levels, this can be implemented via a prototype model of an object avoiding robot car (including an ultrasonic sensor). Reading the data obtained from this an optimal path can be designed in order for the robot to avoid obstacles in its path. The distance obtained can be easily converted into velocity and into acceleration over time [1–3] (Fig. 1).

Fig. 1 Honda CR-V

2   Block Components and Process Implemented

2.1   Sensors

In this paper, the HC-SR04 ultrasonic sensor is used for measuring the distance. It consists of four pins. The given pins are TRIGGER, ECHO, VCC, and GND. The pins for communication of this sensor are TRIGGER and ECHO. The working principle of is graphically illustrated in Fig. 2.

The sensor's signal is sent through the TRIGGER pin. Whenever a given travelling pulse strikes an object, it is reflected and read by the ECHO pin. This pulse obtained can be manipulated and from these calculations, the distance can be derived. By utilizing these distance values at specific points with respect to time, the speed of the wave can be computed. The given specifications of this sensor are: a continuous voltage of 5 V, current of 15 mA, a frequency 40 Hz, an output signal of 0.5 V, a sentry angle not exceeding 15°, a sentry distance 2–300 cm, an accuracy within 0.3 cm, a TRIGGER signal (input). It also consists of a TTL Impulse (10 μs duration), and also an ECHO signal (TTL PWL signal) [2] (Fig. 3).

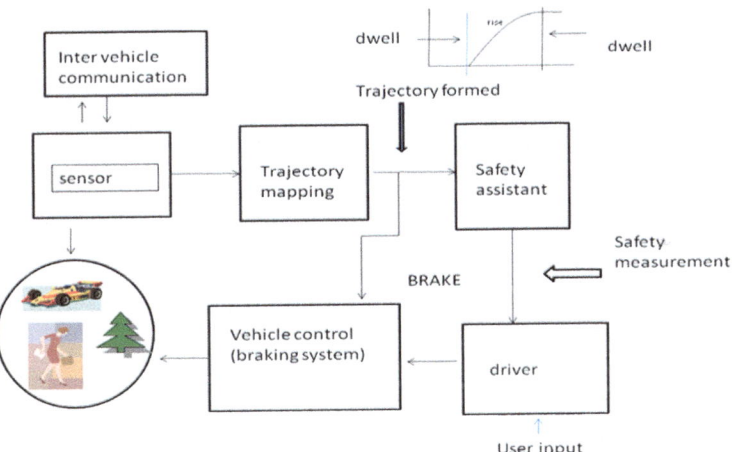

Fig. 2 Block diagram

Fig. 3 Diagram of sensor operation

2.2 Radar

The full form of radar is radio detection and ranging. In this case, radio is signified by the wave directed by the transmitter. On the other hand, detection takes place through the obstacle in the path of the transmitted wave. Finally, ranging is calculated taking into account the travelled distance of the wave. The result of the radar is derived by the use of a servomotor on which the given sensor is mounted. The angle of the sensor is varied from 0° to 180°. The distances obtained are given in Table 1 [3, 4].

When the distance falls below 10 cm, it points to the presence of an obstacle. Cubic and quantic polynomials can help plot the corresponding trajectory plot. The radar formation can be represented by Fig. 4.

The corresponding cubic polynomial for the trajectory is represented by the equation $q_0t^2 + q_1t + q_2$. This gives the distance and velocity of the object. For defining the initial acceleration of the body, the quintic polynomial is used. The trajectory of the object is graphically shown in Fig. 5 [5–7].

2.3 Intervehicle Communication

This block consists of a communication system which transmits and receives the signal via its sensors. The given data obtained are in the form of low and high signals passed on to the controller board. This in turn relays these signals to the motors of the vehicle, for forward or backward movement. The communication setup for our project is divided into four parts:

Table 1 Radar output

Angle formed	Measure distance (cm)
0	8
30	200
60	5
90	365
120	425
150	7

Fig. 4 Generation of radar formation

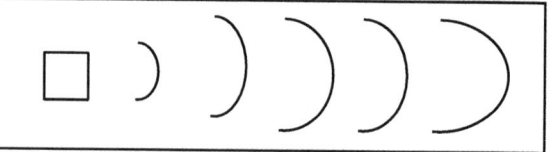

Fig. 5 Trajectory path

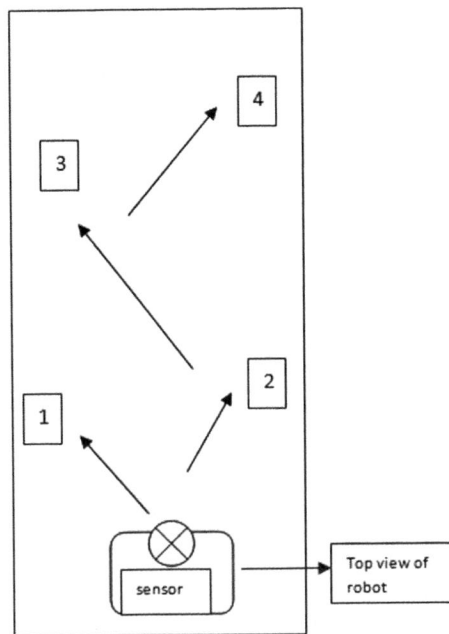

Table 2 Features of the Arduino board

Microcontroller used	ATmega328
Voltage (operating)	5 V
Recommended input voltage	7–12 V
Range of input voltage	6–20 V
Number of digital input/output pins	14 (PWM output provided by 6)
Number of input pins (analog)	6 pins
DC current of the I/O pin	40 mA
DC current for the pin drawing 3.3 V	50 mA
Memory (flash)	32 KB (ATmega328) Bootloader uses 0.5 KB
Static RAM	2 KB
Electrically erasable programmable ROM	1 KB
Clock frequency	16 MHz
Length	68.6 mm
Width	53.4 mm
Net mass	25 g

Arduino Board. ATmega328 Board is used primarily as a prototyping board. Its advantage involves the ease of programming and the interfacing between the sensor and the motor (Tables 2 and 3).

Table 3 Ultrasonic sensor electrical parameters

Working DC voltage	5 V
Operational current	15 mA
Frequency	40 Hz
Maximum range	4 m
Minimum range	2 cm
Angle of measurement	15°
Trigger signal	10 μs
TTL pulse (ECHO)	Output signal
Input TTL	Lever signal and the range in proportion

Ultrasonic sensor. Four pins are present in this:

Supply voltage of 5 V
Trigger pulse input
ECHO pulse output
Ground pin (0 V)

Interfacing. The sensors are integrated with the Arduino board in this step. The given output values are received as distance measurements. Using this setup, the results are tabulated below. These results are used to control the vehicle while the signal guides the motor in moving forward, backward, right, or left (Figs. 6 and 7).

Two algorithms are written to explain the working and planning of the trajectory path. One algorithm explains the superficial working for obstacle avoidance while the other shows in detail the working of the robot car.

Fig. 6 Setup for distance measurement

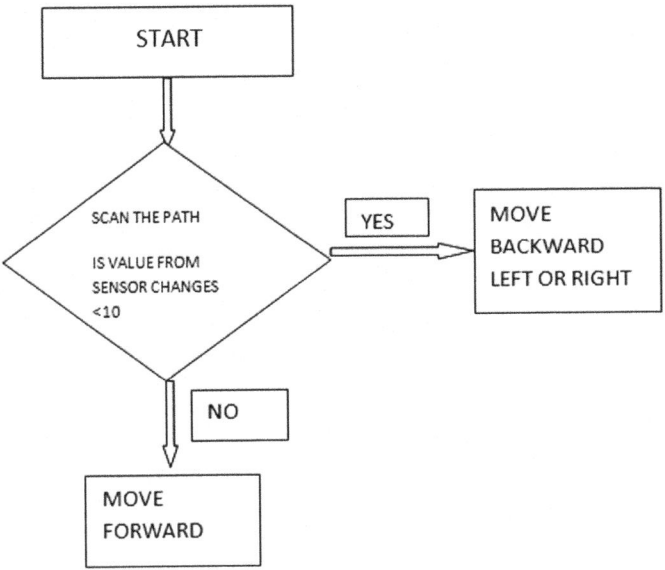

Fig. 7 Initial algorithm

3 Algorithms

When the program starts, the sensor is activated and starts sending pulses. If the distance sensed by the set up falls short of 10 cm, a signal is sent to the controller to move forward, backward, right, or left according to the programming pattern initially set.

This program is designed such that if the sensor senses a distance less than (Fig. 8).

10 cm, moves backward initially and then stops. It proceeds to scan the environment again. Based on the new findings, it takes the decision to move right or left. If the threshold is exceeded as per normal operations, the robot will move forward in that direction. In this way, an iterative scanning loop takes place to compute the distance. Using a loop statement in our program, an accurate comparison can be also performed [5, 6, 8].

4 Result

The goals in the design of the object avoidance vehicle were to simulate the adaptive cruise control technique and collision mitigation properties. The given vehicle trajectory has been shown below. The behavior of a DAS when confronted

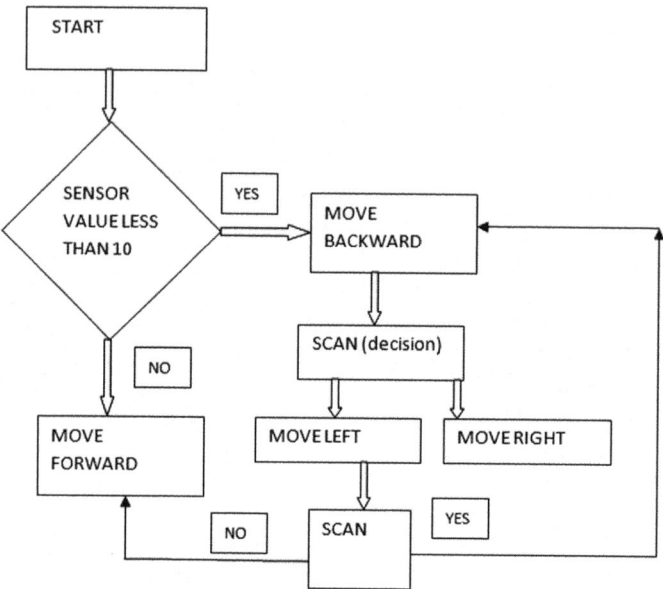

Fig. 8 Algorithm for work model

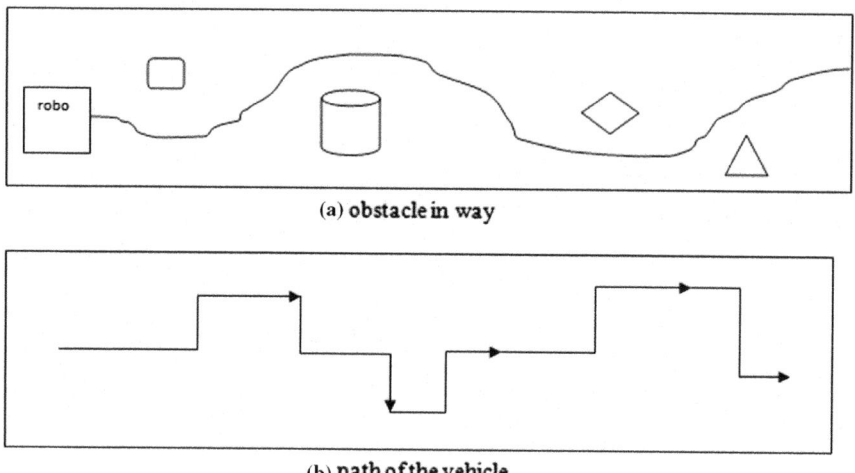

(a) obstacle in way

(b) path of the vehicle

Fig. 9 Trajectory path formed

with an obstacle has been calculated and simulated using a zigzag plot shown below. This motion shows the path taken by the robot car to avoid obstacles. This is depicted in Fig. 9.

5 Conclusion

The setup displays the accuracy obtained through use of an ultrasonic sensor. This sensor provides a wider range of data and a fast response time. The results are gathered within microseconds and relayed to the controller. The speed and acceleration of the vehicle are hence regulated.

6 Future Scope

Research for reducing the cost and heightened accuracy of DAS is particularly crucial as extension to our work. Further planning may be done for implementation of the system in smaller cars. Autonomous cars could be a long-term objective for the development of DAS [7, 9–11].

References

1. Berndt, H., Wender, S., Dietmayer, K.: Driver braking behaviour during intersection approaches and implication for strategies warning for driver assistant systems. In: IEEE Intelligent Vehicles Symposium (2007)
2. Tuner, O., Coşkun, F.: Vision based lane keeping assistance control triggered by a driver inattention monitor. IEEE, School of Computer Engineering Intelligent System Laboratory (2010)
3. Liu, H., Niar, S.: Radar signature in multiple target tracking system for driver assistant application. In: Design, Automation Test in Europe Conference Exhibition (DATE 2013), School of Electronics and Information Nantong University, Jiangshu, China, pp. 887–892 (2013)
4. García, F., de la Escalera, A., Armingol, J.M.: Enhanced obstacle detection based on data fusion for ADAS applications. In: Proceedings of the 16th international IEEE Annual Conference on Intelligent Transportation Systems (ITSC 2013), The Hague, The Netherlands, 6-9 Oct 2013
5. 16th International IEEE Annual Conference on Intelligent Transportation Systems (ITSC 2013), The Hague, Netherlands, 6–9 Oct 2013
6. García, F., de la Escalera, A., Armingol, J.M.: Enhanced obstacle detection based on data fusion for ADAS applications. Intelligent Systems Lab, Universidad Carlos III of Madrid
7. Sponge, M.W., Hutchsion, S., Vidyasagar, M.: Robot dynamics and control (2008)
8. Huo, C.L., Yu, Y.H., Syu, J.C., Sun, T.Y.: Vehicle warning system for land departure and collision avoidance: using fuzzy decision making. Department of Electrical Engineering, National Dong Hwa University (2011)
9. McCall, J., Trivedi, M.M.: Video-based lane estimation and tracking for driver assistance: survey, system, and evaluation. IEEE Trans. Intell. Transp. Syst. 7(1), 20–37 (2006)
10. Geronimo, D., Lopez, A.M., Sappa, A.D., Graf, T.: Survey of pedestrian detection for advanced driver assistance systems. IEEE Trans. Pattern Anal. Mach. Intell. 32(7) (2010)
11. Shackleton, C.J., Kala, R., Warwick, K.: Sensor-based trajectory generation for advanced driver assistance system. Robotics 2(1), 19–35 (2013)

Performance Enhancement of MRPSOC for Multimedia Applications

V. Kavitha and K. V. Ramakrishanan

Abstract There are several techniques to reconfigure the instruction set processors. One such technique is multi-reconfigurable instruction set processor system on chip (MRPSOC). Integration of MRPSOC and multigrain parallelism is done to improve the performance of SOC. By using MRPSOC, the performance of the system is increased. Multimedia application computing can be accelerated by using multi-grain parallelism. By implementing this integrated processor, extra features can be added to MRPSOC. Multiple data is packed in a single register which forms a vector; this vector of multiple data is fetched to MRPSOC at a time. Since MRPSOC is a combination of MPSOC and RISP processor, instruction-level parallelism can be implemented in MRPSOC. After the execution of operations in MRPSOC, the multiple outputs can be stored at different memory locations of same memory system simultaneously. This proposal is aimed to design MRPSOC interfaced with data-level parallelism, instruction-level parallelism, and memory transfer-level parallelism. Form this paper, it is concluded that by using both MRPSOC and multigrain parallelism in common platform, high-speed computation can be achieved for multimedia applications. Proposed design takes 28% less time to complete the task compared to MPSOC. Further completion time will be reduced for tasks having repetitive instructions.

Keywords Reconfigurable instruction set processors (RISPs) · Multigrain parallelism · Multi-reconfigurable instruction set processor system on chip (MRPSOC)

V. Kavitha (✉) · K. V. Ramakrishanan
Jain University, Bengaluru, India
e-mail: reddy.kavithav@gmail.com

K. V. Ramakrishanan
e-mail: ramradhain@yahoo.com

© Springer Nature Singapore Pte Ltd. 2018
S. K. Muttoo (ed.), *System and Architecture*, Advances in Intelligent Systems and Computing 732, https://doi.org/10.1007/978-981-10-8533-8_22

219

1 Introduction

General purpose processors (GPP) are processors which can be programmed to perform functions as per the requirements of the users. They are used in PCs, workstations, etc [1]. The most important properties are their speed, flexibility, low-cost design, and easy availability because of the large number of manufacturers, programmability, easy availability of software development tools, and a very large instruction set. In many applications such as digital processing and embedded systems where many of their functionalities are not needed, GPPs are not used due to their large size and high cost. A major drawback of GPPs is their inefficient high-performance computing [2, 3].

With the advent of embedded systems for application-specific uses, various types of microcontrollers were developed and introduced by different manufacturers to meet the market needs [4]. They reduced the size and development costs as the instruction sets were specific to the microcontrollers and saved time for the development [5].

Application-specific integrated circuits (ASICs) are customized for particular applications. Present-day ASICs have grown from 5000 gates to over a million gates [6]. They include besides microprocessors, memory blocks such as ROM, RAM, EEPROMs, and other building blocks. They are now commonly called as system on chip (SOC) [7]. The non-recurring (NRE) cost of an ASIC is very high and is preferred if the requirement is for large numbers and small sizes needed in the consumer market. Recently, application-specific instruction processors (ASIPs) were developed to perform tasks more efficiently. They reduced the production costs, simplified manufacturing processes, and are characterized by low power consumption. Instruction set is determined by the specific application. It uses general purpose registers or configuration registers. Instruction set in ASIP consists of two parts, viz. static and configurable [8]. Static logic defines minimum instruction register architecture (IRA), and configurable logic is used to introduce additional instructions depending on the application. Critical portion of an application is executed by custom function unit (CFU). It provides high programmability and flexibility. However, it gives rise to increasing algorithm complexity and high NRE cost [9]. As the algorithm complexity increases, completion time increases. We need to develop techniques to reduce the execution time without compromising on the performance.

2 Proposed System

To improve the performance and to reduce the compilation time, MRPSOC is integrated with multigrain parallelism (data-level parallelism, instruction-level parallelism, and memory transfer-level parallelism) [10]. Figure 1 describes the block diagram of proposed system. Data-level parallelism is included to fetch the data to MRPSOC; multiple data can be fetched at a time. MRPSOC processor is the main block of the system where all the operations are done [11].

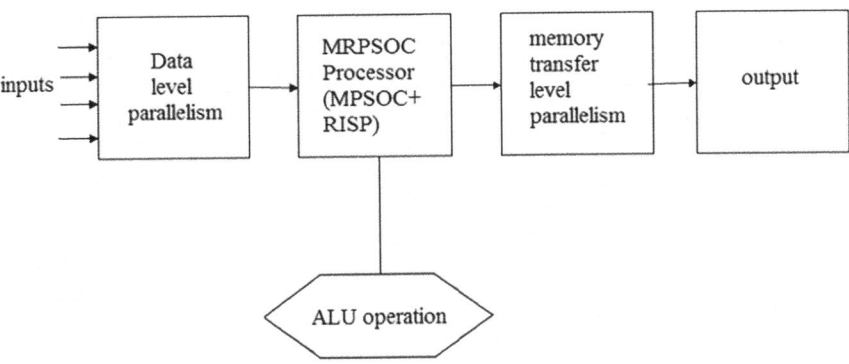

Fig. 1 Block diagram of integrated MRPSOC and multigrain parallelism

MRPSOC is the combination of MPSOC and RISP. RISP contains RFU units. The performance of the system is improved by using MRPSOC, since complex sections of program can be run on RFU unit and execution of program can be done simultaneously on ALU and RFU [12, 13]. ALU operations will be done in MRPSOC. Memory transfer-level parallelism is mainly used to store the resultant data in parallel. To store the result simultaneously, multiple numbers of memory transfer requests should be arranged in parallel before computing. To transfer the data between main memory and local storage, direct memory access (DMA) is used.

2.1 Reconfigurable Instruction Set Processor

Software flexibility and hardware efficiency are combined in RISPs [14]. To overcome the problems which are seen in ASIPs, RISPs are used. RISPs are similar to ASIPs; here, the most repetitive as well as time-consuming parts of an application are run on dynamic, adoptive functional unit called as reconfigurable functional unit (RFU). A RISP mainly contains a microprocessor core and reconfigurable logic. Processor core of RISP supplies programmability, and reconfigurable functional unit adopts specific application to the processor. Interfacing reconfigurable logic with base processor includes related issues like data transfers to and from the reconfigurable logic, and also coordination between the two elements. Design of reconfigurable logic should take care of issues like RFU granularity, interconnection between logic and processor.

2.2   Architecture of RFU

In particular, the design of RFU consumes large area. In this design, efforts are
made to decrease the size of RFU without affecting the performance. In the path of
processing data after the ALU unit, RFU structure is placed mainly to transfer the
data at a faster rate. Multiple functional units (FUs) are included in RFU structure
which can be organized as matrix. The granularity of RFU is also decided which
may be coarse-grain accelerators or fine-grain reconfigurable accelerators. This will
be depending on the type of application. Except the instructions like load, store,
multiplication, and division, the RFU supports almost all the MIPS instructions.
Input data is given to the file register in RFU and then resultant is written back to
the same file register itself (Fig. 2).

Fig. 2 RFU structure [1]

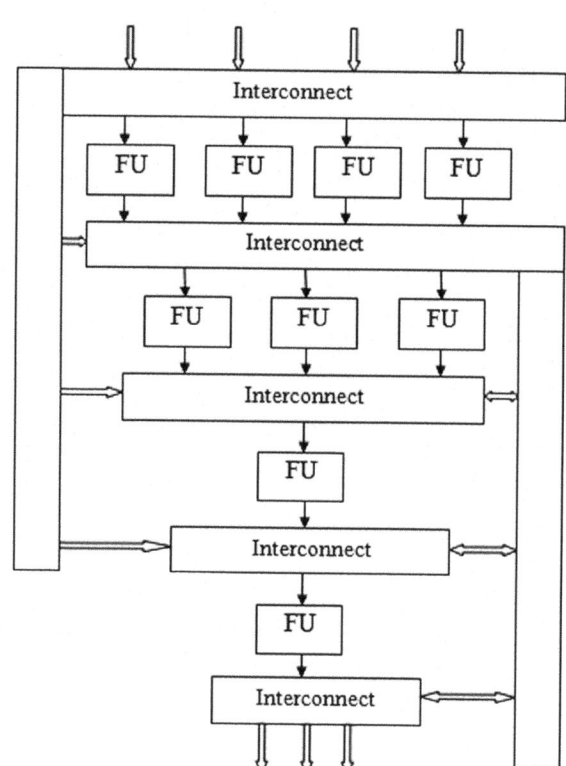

2.3 Methodology for MRPSOC

Methodology for MRPSOC is described in two steps. In the first step, processing elements are executed in parallel. In the next step, complex parts of the task are run on RFU unit. Methodology for MRPSOC is designed by using task codes, by direct acyclic graph, and by the constraints of RFU. For every task, this methodology determines which processor to select and corresponding configuration bits. Methodology for MRPSOC is described in four steps (Fig. 3):

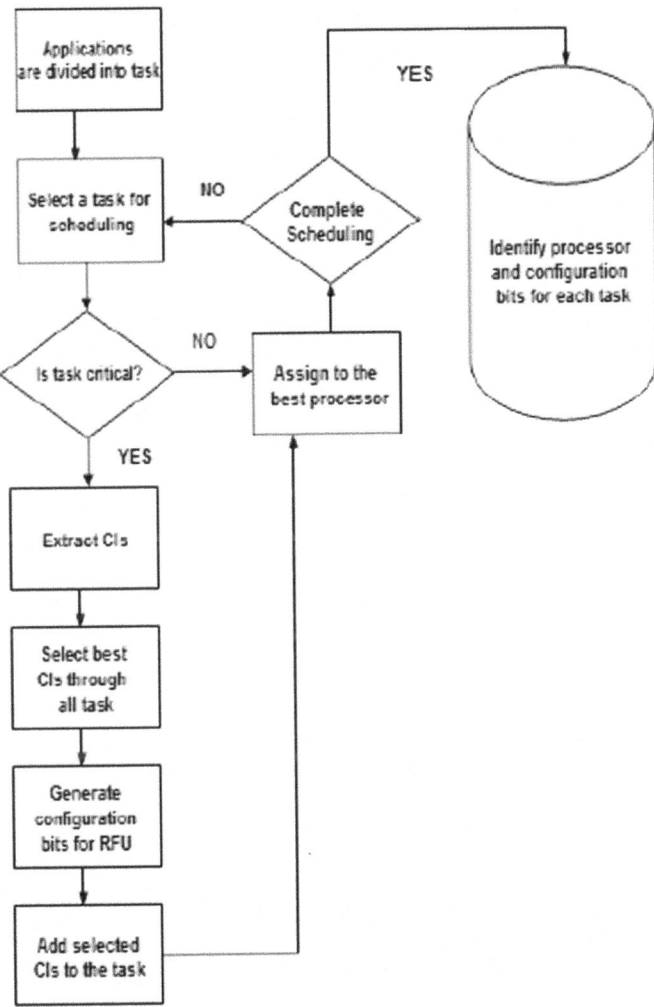

Fig. 3 Methodology for MRPSOC [1]

2.3.1 Profiling Step

This is the first step where the codes of the applications are run by direct acyclic graph on homogenous MPSOC without RFU. Identification of hot spots and execution time of particular application can be found by profiling task. Usage of any reachable solution can be done in profiling step since this step is independent of proposed methodology.

2.3.2 Identifying Step

The task which is on critical path is identified in this step. Iterative improvement process is used in this step. Tasks are scheduled in all iterations. For scheduling tasks, DCP algorithm is used. By using DCP algorithms concept, the tasks which are on critical path are identified. Absolute earliest short time (AEST) and absolute latest short time (ALST) are the two concepts which are used by DCP algorithm. If AEST is equal to ALST, then task is identified as critical one.

2.3.3 Optimization Step

If custom instructions are selected for critical task, then execution time can be reduced. But generating custom instructions itself is a complex procedure. This procedure includes searching patterns of the instruction set in a large space mainly to improve performance. So automatic tools are required to generate custom instructions or else it is difficult to generate custom instructions (CIs).

2.3.4 Assignment Step

When the selection of CIs and generation of configuration bits are finished, assignment of task to different processor is done by DCP algorithm with new execution time. For the critical task, the algorithm assigns processor to task parent; if task is not critical, then for any available task, the appropriate processor is assigned. Best CIs and the most critical tasks are selected by the algorithm in all possible iterations. But the task scheduling is affected by optimization routine custom instructions used by this will minimize completion time taken by the tasks.

2.4 Algorithm for MRPSOC

- The first step is profiling step. Here, the codes of the application are run by direct acyclic graph (DAG) on homogeneous MPSOC.
- Identification of hot spots and execution time of application are found in profiling step.

- All the tasks are initialized after profiling step.
- Then, initialized tasks are selected for scheduling.
- The task which is on critical path is identified in this step. Iterative improvement process is used in this step.
- If the task is on critical, then extract the custom instructions.
- After extraction of CIs, choose the best CIs through the entire task. The size of CIs should not exceed.
- Then, generation of bit streams for configuring RFUs is done by considering RFU limitations.
- For the selected task execution time is modified, then add the selected CIs to the task.
- This task is assigned to the best processor with new execution time.
- Then, scheduling of the task is completed for available CIs and memory.
- If the selected task is not on critical path, then by using DCP algorithm, the task is directly assigned to the best processor and scheduling of the task is completed.

2.5   Data-Level Parallelism

Data-level parallelism is one of the types of parallel computing present in multiple processors. On various parallel computing nodes, the data is distributed so that the processor need not wait for the data. Packaging of multiple data elements into single register which forms a vector can be done to exploit the data-level parallelism. At a time, the processor can run operation on the vector which is formed by data-level parallelism. Multiple ALUs can also be provided to further exploit the parallelism. If scalar-to-vector conversation of data is done, then efficiency of data-level parallelism increases.

2.6   Instruction-Level Parallelism

MRPSOC processor exploits instruction-level parallelism. In consecutive instructions, the data dependence or control dependence is not present. Parallel execution of multiple instructions is possible. Using the superscalar technology, exploitation of instruction-level parallelism is done by the processor. Execution speed is increased by using instruction-level parallelism since it allows to process more than two instructions at a time.

Concurrently, all the tasks are executed at a time. For example, (Fig. 4).

$$A = (n^*n) + (m^*m) + (o^*o)$$

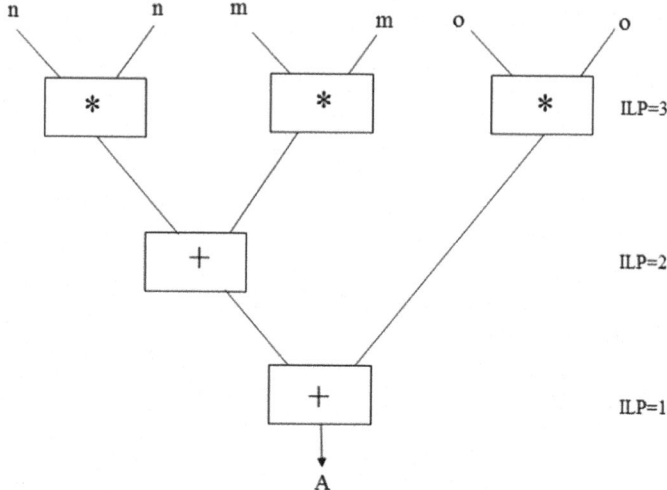

Fig. 4 Example for instruction-level parallelism

2.7 Memory-Level Parallelism

Pending operations can be done at a time by using memory-level parallelism. Pending of operations usually occurs due to any cache missing or buffer missing. By the technique of pre-fetch, memory transfer-level parallelism is achieved. Pre-fetching can be done in two ways: It may be either initiated by hardware or initiated by software. Software pre-fetching is used in this project. Identification of given application which needs a specific set of data is the basic step of software pre-fetching. By using pre-fetch, less time is consumed for instruction execution.

3 Simulation Results

In this paper, the computation speed of enhanced MRPSOC processor is examined with the set of instructions. The implemented processor is compared with MPSOC to show that integrated processor executes the instructions with 28% less completion time than MPSOC.

3.1 Simulation of MPSOC

The MPSOC takes four instructions to reset the processes that are running before. To start the execution of any processor, this is the first step. After initialization, the execution starts at pc = 5 where first instruction is fetched at 33 ns. As shown in Fig. 5a.

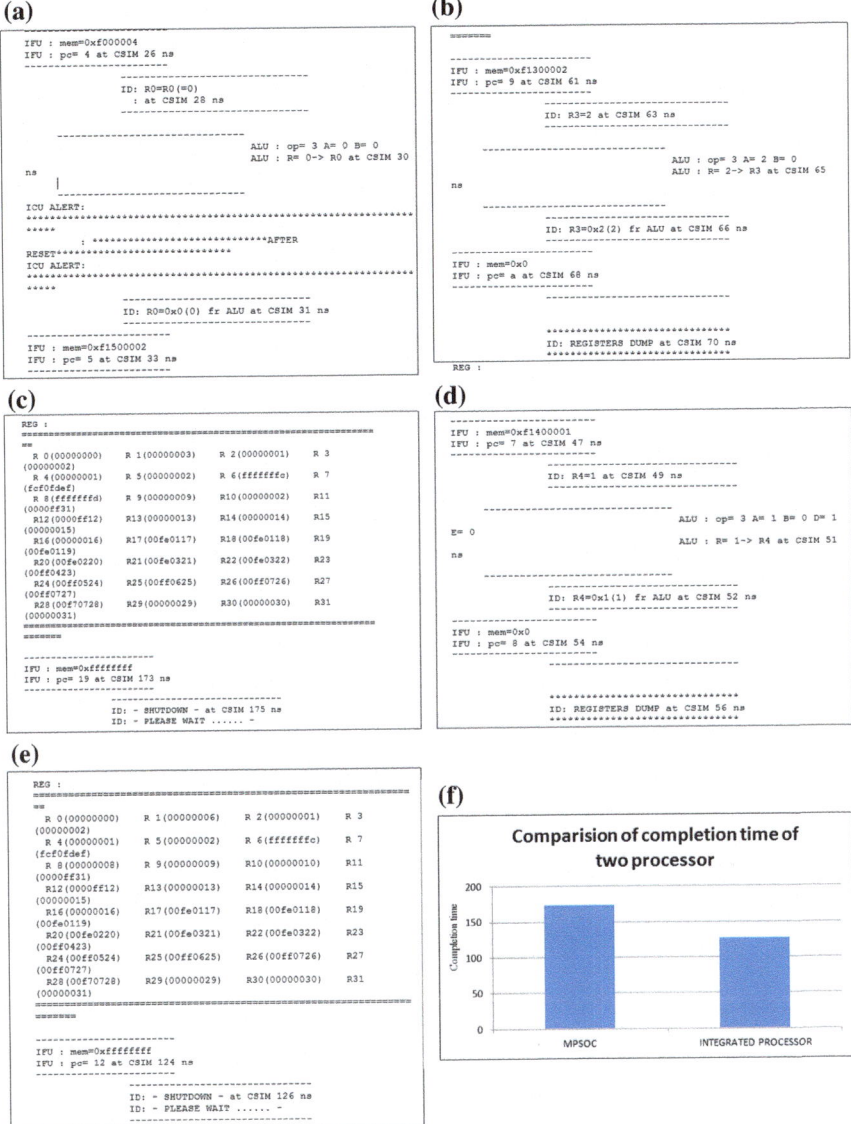

Fig. 5 **a** Initializing the instructions and fetching the instruction (at pc = 5) in MPSOC, **b** example of an instruction to show MPSOC can take two instructions at a time, **c** execution completion time in MPSOC, **d** example of an instruction to show integrated processor can take more than two instructions at a time, **e** execution completion time in integrated processor, **f** comparison of MPSOC and integrated processor with respect to completion time

In case of MPSOC, only two operands can be given to the processor at a time. For example, consider instruction which is executing at 63 ns. Here, opcode is '3' so addition operation is done. Operands are 'A' and 'B' where the value of $A = 2$ and $B = 0$. The resultant is stored in register R3. As shown in Fig. 5b.

The execution time taken by MPSOC is 173 ns after executing all the instructions which is shown in Fig. 5c. After completion of every instruction, the result is stored in registers which is also shown in Fig. 5c.

3.2 Simulation of Integrated Processor (MRPSOC and Multigrain Parallelism)

In case of integrated processor, it is possible to give more than two operands. For example, consider instruction which is executing at 51 ns. Here, opcode is '3' so addition operation is done. In this example, operation is done on four operands. Operands are 'A', 'B', 'D', and 'E' where the value of $A = 1$, $B = 0$, $D = 1$, and $E = 1$. The resultant is stored in register R3. So we can conclude that by parallelism, this processor is able to take more than four inputs (Fig. 5d).

The execution time taken by implemented processor is 126 ns after executing all the instructions which is shown in Fig. 5e. After completion of every instruction, the result is stored registers which is also shown in Fig. 5e. By the analysis of Fig. 5d, e, we can conclude that time taken by implemented processor is less than MPSOC. Due to the presence of MRPSOC, the execution speed is more in case of implemented processor when compared to MPSOC.

The above graph (Fig. 5f) shows the comparison between implemented processor and MPSOC. To execute all the instructions, MPSOC takes 175 ns whereas designed processor in the project takes 126 ns. So by analysis of the results, it is proven that integrated processor has faster speed than MPSOC.

4 Conclusion

In this paper, multigrain parallelism is integrated with MRPSOC. This adds extra feature to MRPSOC. Even though dispatch time of MRPSOC is less compared to MPSOC, still computation speed can be improved by using parallelism. Results clearly show that compared to MRPSOC processor, the designed processor is able to fetch more than two inputs simultaneously. Fetching rate is fast since at a time multiple data is fetched to the processor. Completion time of designed processor is very less compared to earlier processors. In system C, the code is written and compilation is done in Perl compiler. Cygwin is the software where the results of output can be seen.

References

1. Soleymanpour, R., Mohammadi, S.: A platform for multi reconfigurable instruction set processor system on chip. In: CSI International Symposium, 2013, pp. 99–104
2. Huang, X., Fan, X., Zhang S., Shi L.: Investigation on multi-grain parallelism in chip multiprocessor for multimedia application. In: Proceeding of IEEE 2009, Computer School, Northwestern Polytechnical University, China (2009)
3. Kuroda, I., Nishitani, T.: Multimedia processors. Proc. IEEE **86**(6), 1203–1221 (1998)
4. Barat, F., Lauwereins, R.: Reconfigurable instruction set processors: a survey. Rapid System Prototyping, 11th International Workshop, pp. 168–173 (2000)
5. Pozzi, L., Atasu, K., Ienne, P.: Exact and approximate algorithms for the extension of embedded processor instruction sets. IEEE Trans. Comput. Aided Design Integr. Circ. Syst. **25**(7), 1209–1229 (2006)
6. Huang, X., Fan, X., Zhang S.: The integration of multimedia process unit into an embedded processor. In: Proceeding of the 2007 IEEE International Conference on Integration Technology, pp. 492–495, China, March 2007
7. Lo, J.L., Eggers, S.J.: Improving balanced scheduling with compiler optimization that increase instruction level parallelism. Department of Computer Science and Engineering, University of Washington (1995)
8. Lodi, A., Toma, M., Campi, F., Cappelli, A., Canegallo, R., Guerrieri, R.: A VLIW processor with reconfigurable instruction set for embedded applications. IEEE J. Solid-State Circ. **38**(11), 1876–1886 (2003)
9. Keutzer, K., Malik, S., Newton, A.R.: From ASIC to ASIP: the next design discontinuity (2002)
10. Qasim, Y., Janga, P., Kumar, S., Alesaimi, H.: Application specific processors. Final_ECE570_ASP_2012, Project Report (2012)
11. Nohl, A., Schirrmeister, F., Jaussig, D.: Application specific processor design: architecture, design methods and tools. In: 2010 IEEE/ACM International conference on Computer_Aided Design (ICCAD), November 2010
12. Wolf, W., Jerraya, A.A., Martin, G.: Multiprocessor system on chip (MPSOC) technology. IEEE Trans. Comput. Aided Design Integr. Circ. Syst. **27**(10), 1701–1713 (2008)
13. Asokan, P.: A novel MRPSOC processor for dispatch time curtailment, Final Report (2014)
14. Grotker, T., Lio, S., Martin, G.: System design with system C. Kluwer Academic Publications (2002)

A New CPU Scheduling Algorithm Using Round-robin and Mean of the Processes

N. Sujith Kumar Reddy, H. Santhi, P. Gayathri and N. Jaisankar

Abstract This paper aims to develop the round-robin (RR) process scheduling algorithm, to get optimized waiting and turnaround time with less number of context switching for the given process. RR algorithm is the most adopted algorithm in modern computing as it overcomes the problem of starvation in first-come first-serve (FCFS) and short job first (SJF). In this article, an improved round-robin algorithm is proposed by calculating the mean of the given processes namely Check Mean with round-robin (CMRR), which reduces the average waiting time (AWT) and average turnaround time (ATT) of the given processes. The drawback of the present round-robin algorithm is that it turns to FCFS in case of large time quantum values which results in higher waiting and turnaround time of the processes. This method gives the most optimized values for scheduling the given processes reducing waiting and turnaround time comparatively. This method is more efficient if the processes burst time is in ascending order. It also reduces the number of context switches increasing the throughput.

Keywords CPU scheduling · Multiprogramming operating systems
Round-robin algorithm · FCFS · SJF · Gantt chart · Turnaround time
Waiting time · Context switches

N. Sujith Kumar Reddy (✉) · H. Santhi · P. Gayathri · N. Jaisankar
School of Computing Science and Engineering (SCSE), VIT University,
Vellore 632014, India
e-mail: naisasujith@gmail.com

H. Santhi
e-mail: hsanthi@vit.ac.in

P. Gayathri
e-mail: pgayathri@vit.ac.in

N. Jaisankar
e-mail: njaisankar@vit.ac.in

© Springer Nature Singapore Pte Ltd. 2018
S. K. Muttoo (ed.), *System and Architecture*, Advances in Intelligent Systems
and Computing 732, https://doi.org/10.1007/978-981-10-8533-8_23

1 Introduction

Operating system (OS) mainly helps user in interfacing with the memory and the CPU; in other words, it helps the user to interact with the computer hardware. Due to the advancement of operating systems, multiprogramming operating systems emerged [1, 2]. A process has the program code and the current activity, which resides in the main memory. The processes wait in ready queues for their turn of CPU utilization. In single processor systems, only one program can run at a particular time, whereas a multiprogramming OS runs several programs simultaneously, hence eliminating the shortcomings faced when using single processor systems. Given below are the five main criteria for CPU scheduling [3]:

1. *CPU Utilization*: CPU should be used all times to get good results. In general, a system is called lightly loaded if its utilization is 40% and it is called heavily loaded if it is 90% or above.
2. *Throughput*: The number of processes that are executed completely per unit time is the throughput of the system. It may vary from hours to seconds for heavy and light process, respectively.
3. *Waiting Time*: The time for which a process waits for execution is regarded as the waiting time.
4. *Turnaround Time*: The time taken by the CPU to completely execute a process is called the turnaround time of that particular process.
5. *Response Time*: A CPU turnaround time may not be good criteria, and then response time is used as parameter.

Few important scheduling algorithms are explained below [4–7]:

1. ***First-Come First-Serve (FCFS)***: This algorithm will execute the process which comes first in the ready queue(FIFO); it moves to the second process only after the complete execution of the first process, thus making a large waiting time and turnaround time. There will be less number of context switches since they are not optimized. However, it is very easy to understand and implement this algorithm.
2. ***Short Job First (SJF)***: In this scheduling algorithm, the processes are executed in the increasing order of their burst time, thereby overcoming the disadvantage of FCFS. Although a severe problem is faced when there are processes with large burst time in the ready queue, such process may not get a chance to be executed leading to "Starvation." This algorithm gives the most optimized values in all parameters like waiting, turnaround, and context switching.
3. ***Priority Scheduling***: This scheduling assigns every process with a priority number. CPU then executes the processes in decreasing order of priority regardless of their burst time. The advantage of this process is that it executes higher priority processes first making the job easier. This type of scheduling may also lead to starvation.

4. *Round-robin Scheduling (RR)*: In this algorithm, the problem of starvation is eliminated, making it an advance scheduling algorithm. Here, a time quantum is set which permits the process to utilize the CPU to its full extent, thereby giving equal importance in the ready queue. Starvation is hence eradicated due to periodic context switching making it popular. The results may not be optimized when compared to SJF. Even though the results are large, the throughput of the system is increased. Moreover by increasing the time quantum, this algorithm turns to FCFS.

The scheduling algorithms are divided into two categories: preemptive and non-preemptive. FCFS and Priority Scheduling are non-preemptive in nature, whereas round-robin is preemptive. SJF can either preemptive or non-preemptive. Literature review, terminology, related works, proposed model, flowchart, implementation with examples, discussion conclusion and future scope are followed.

2 Literature Overview

2.1 Terminology

The following are the keywords [2] used in this journal.

- Ready Queue: The queue in which all the processes wait before execution is called as ready queue.
- Multiprogramming: When several processes are run simultaneously on a single processor, it is called multiprogramming
- Average Waiting Time: Average waiting time is the ratio of the total waiting time to the number of processes. Efficiency is inversely proportional to the average waiting time.
- Average Turnaround Time: Average turnaround time is the ratio of the total completion time to the number of processes. Efficiency is inversely proportional to the average turnaround time.
- Context Switching: The process of switching the process from one to another is called context switching.

  Ex: P1 → P2 → P1, here there are two context switches.

- Mean: The ratio of total sum of observations by the number of observation is called the mean.
- Time Quantum (*T*): It is simply called as the time slice.
- Gantt Chart: It is a horizontal bar graph designed by Gantt for graphical illustration of the data.
- Throughput: The total number of tasks completed in a particular time period gives the throughput of the system.

2.2 Related Works

In [8] journal, the authors have proposed a new model named AN with dynamic time quantum with an idea of adjusting the time quantum comparing with the burst time of the process. In [3], a new scheduling algorithm using round-robin and Priority Scheduling was proposed which overcomes the problem of starvation as RR algorithm is implemented. In [9], a nonlinear mathematical model for optimum time quantum is used, such that decreasing waiting and turnaround time of the process to be executed. In [10], new algorithms for scheduling were demonstrated with examples namely IMRRSJF, SARR, ERR by comparing with FCFS, SJF, and RR.

3 Proposed Model

The proposed architecture works by calculating the mean of the given processes. It overcomes the problem of starvation as it is inspired by round-robin process [11–15].

3.1 Assumptions

- There are "Ni" number of process with same arrival time waiting in ready queue (where $i = 1, 2, 3,\dots n$).
- The burst time of all the process is known.
- A uni-processor is given.

3.2 Algorithm

1. Initially calculate the mean (add burst time of all the given processes by total number of processes).
2. Let the calculated mean be "M" (parameter).
3. Arrange the processes in increasing order of burst time.
4. Set M as the time quantum.
5. Give chance of execution in order and calculate the remaining burst time (RBT) of the process, then check:

   a) If RBT <= M give an another chance of execution with M time quantum.
   b) Else, processes should again wait in the ready queue with their remaining burst time.

6. Switch to next process and repeat the previous step until all the processes are executed once.
7. After all the processes are given one chance repeat steps 5, 6, and 7 until all the processes are executed completely (Fig. 1 explains the flow of algorithm).

3.3 Proposed Work Flow

See Fig. 1.

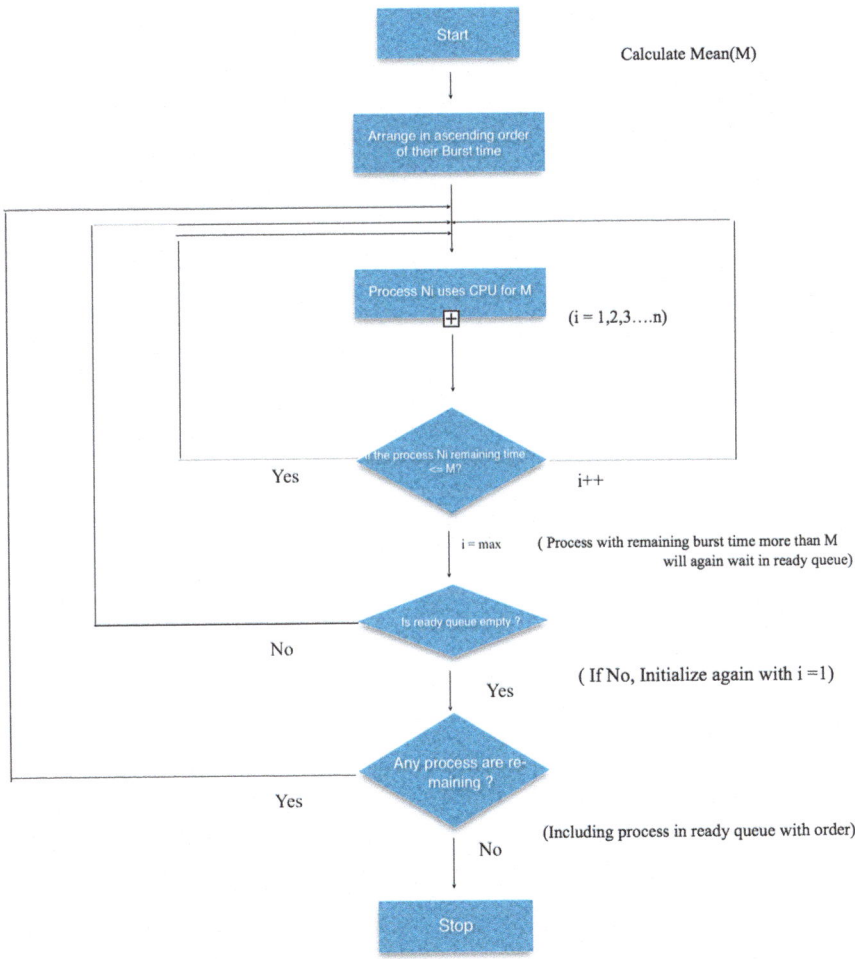

Fig. 1 Flow of the proposed CMRR algorithm

4 Illustrative Examples and Discussion

In this section, there are three solved examples for the proposed algorithm with results that are compared with other existing scheduling models.

Example 1

There are five given processes in ready queue shown in Table 1:

1. Implementing with round-robin (RR) algorithm with $T = 20$ ms.

Pro-cess_1	Pro-cess_2	Pro-cess_3	Pro-cess_4	Pro-cess_5	Pro-cess_2	Pro-cess_3	Pro-cess_4	Pro-cess_5	Pro-cess_4	Pro-cess_5	Pro-cess_5

0   11   31   51   71   91   93   108   128   148   160   180   200

AWT: $((0) + (11 + (91 - 31)) + (31 + (93 - 51)) + (51 + (108 - 71) + (148 - 128)) + (71 + (128 - 91) + (160 - 148))/5 = 74.4$ ms.
ATT: 114.4 ms.
Number of Context Switches: 11.

2. Implementing with the proposed model (CMRR)

Step 1: Calculate the mean (M) of the given process

$$\text{Mean } M = [(11 + 22 + 35 + 52 + 80)/5] = 40 \text{ ms}$$

Step 2: Arrange the given process in ascending order of burst time gives: Process_2, Process_1, Process_3, Process_4, and Process_5.

Step 3: Follow the procedure of proposed algorithm, we get Gantt chart

Process_2 (11)	Process_1 (22)	Process_3 (35)	Process_4 (40)	Process_4 (12)	Process_5 (40)	Process_5 (40)

0   11   33   68   108   120   160   200

Table 1 Processes in ready queue

Processes with same arrival time	Burst time (ms)
Process_1	22
Process_2	11
Process_3	35
Process_4	52
Process_5	80

Table 2 Comparative analysis of various scheduling algorithms

	Time slice (ms)	Average waiting time (ms)	Average turnaround time (ms)	Context switches
RR	20	74.4	114.4	11
IRR*	20	50.4	90.4	6
ERR*	20	62.4	102.4	9
SARR*	35	53.4	93.4	6
CMRR (proposed)	40	46.4	86.4	4

AWT: $(11 + 0 + 33 + 68 + 120)/5 = 46.4$ ms.

ATT: $(33 + 11 + 68 + 120 + 200)/5 = 86.4$ ms.

Number of context switches: 4.

Table 2 represents the comparative results obtained for various existing scheduling algorithms as well as the proposed scheduling algorithm. Form the result, we can observe that the proposed algorithm provides better throughput than the existing approaches.

Figure 2a–c showing the average waiting time, average turnaround time, and context switches, respectively.

Example 2

Example 2 with 15 (Table 3) process waiting in ready queue with different burst time varying hugely. The arrival time of these processes is same and arranged.

Mean $M = (10 + 20 + 30 + 40 + 50 + 60 + 70 + 80 + 90 + 100 + 110 + 120 + 130 + 140 + 150)/15 = 80$ s

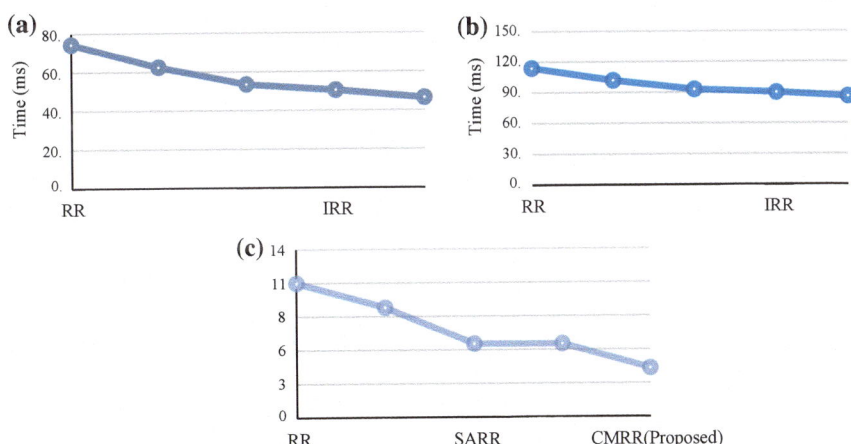

Fig. 2 **a** Average waiting time, **b** average turnaround time, **c** context switches

Table 3 Processes in ready queue

Process	Burst Time(s)
Process_1	10
Process_2	20
Process_3	30
Process_4	40
Process_5	50
Process_6	60
Process_7	70
Process_8	80
Process_9	90
Process_10	100
Process_11	110
Process_12	120
Process_13	130
Process_14	140
Process_15	150

We will solve this by both RR and CMRR with same time quantum 80 s which is mean also and check the result.

1. Implementing Round-robin (RR) algorithm with $T = 80$ s:

P1	P2	P3	P4	P5	P6	P7	P8	P9	P10	P11

0.
0   10   30   60   100   150   210   280   360   440   520   600

P12	P13	P14	P15	P9	P10	P11	P12	P13	P14	P15

600   680   760   840   920   930   950   980   1020   1070   1130   1200

AWT: $(0 + 10 + 30 + 60 + 100 + 150 + 210 + 280 + (360 + (920 - 520)) + (440 + (930 - 520)) + (520 + (950 - 600)) + (600 + (980 - 680)) + (680 + (1020 - 760)) + (760 + (1070 - 840)) + (840 + (1130 - 920)))/15 = 485.33$ s.

ATT: $(10 + 30 + 60 + 100 + 150 + 210 + 280 + 360 + 930 + 950 + 980 + 1020 + 1070 + 1130 + 1200)/15 = 565.3$ s.

Number of Context Switches: 21.

Table 4 Comparing existing RR and proposed CMRR

Time quantum 80 s	RR	CMRR
Average waiting time	485.3	370.66
Average turnaround time	565.3	450.66
Context switches	21	14

2. Implementing CMRR proposed algorithm with the mean of process as $T = 80$ s

P1	P2	P3	P4	P5	P6	P7	P8	P9	P9	P10

0   10   30   60   100   150   210   280   360   440   450   530

P10	P11	P11	P12	P12	P13	P13	P14	P14	P15	P15

530   550   630   660   740   780   860   910   990   1050   1130   1200

AWT: (0 + 10 + 30 + 60 + 100 + 150 + 210 + 280 + 360 + 450 + 550 + 660 + 780 + 910 + 1050)/15 = 370.66 s.

ATT: (10 + 30 + 60 + 100 + 150 + 210 + 280 + 360 + 450 + 550 + 660 + 780 + 910 + 1050 + 1200)/15 = 450.66 s.

Number of Context Switches: 14.

The above Table 4 is a quick analysis of the results comparing RR algorithm with proposed algorithm with same value of time quantum giving 80 s.

Example 3

Consider five process with burst time 1, 1, 2, 6, and 10, respectively for process P1, P2, P3, P4, and P5. The results are will be same in FCFS, SJF, and CMRR which are most of optimized results (AWT = 3.4 ms; ATT = 7.4 ms; Context Switches = 4) but RR (TQ = 4) gives much waiting and turnaround times. (AWT = 4.2 ms; ATT = 8.2 ms; Context Switches = 6).

5 Conclusion and Future Scope

The proposed Check Mean round-robin (CMRR) algorithm uses a mean technique to improve the round-robin (RR) algorithm since it reduces the context switches, thereby increasing the throughput of the system. This algorithm also reduces the average waiting time and average turnaround time significantly. It mainly overcomes the problem of starvation. We know SJF gives the most optimized values in scheduling, and this algorithm turns to SJF in most of the cases because of using mean as the time quantum and comparing the remaining time with the mean after every turn. This algorithm may also be used to obtain optimized values for processes in random order under certain conditions.

References

1. Silberschatz, A., Galvin, P.B., Gagne, G.: Operating Systems Concepts, 9th ed. Wiley
2. Stallings, W.: Operating Systems Internals and Design Principles, 7th ed. Prentice Hall, Pearson Publications
3. Rajput, I.S., Gupta, D.: A priority based round robin CPU scheduling algorithm for real time systems. IJIET **1**(3), 1–11 (2012)
4. Somani, M.J.S., Chhatwani, M.P.K.: Comparative study of different CPU scheduling algorithms. IJCSMC, 310–318 (2013)
5. Goel, N., Garg, R.B.: A Comparative Study of CPU Scheduling Algorithms. arXiv preprint (2013). arXiv:1307.4165
6. Dhakad, V.K., Sharma, L.: Performance analysis of round robin scheduling using adaptive approach based on smart time slice and comparison with SRR. Int. J. Adv. Eng. Technol. (2012)
7. Wang, W., Casale, G.: Evaluating weighted round robin load balancing for cloud web services. In: 2014 16th International Symposium on SYNASC. IEEE, pp. 393–400, Sept 2014
8. Noon, A., Kalakech, A., Kadry, S.: A new round robin based scheduling algorithm for operating systems: dynamic quantum using the mean average. arXiv preprint (2011). arXiv:1111.5348
9. Saeidi, S., Baktash, H.A.: Determining the optimum time quantum value in round robin process scheduling method. IJITCS **4**(10), 67 (2012)
10. Shyam, R., Nandal, S.K.: Improved mean round robin with short job first scheduling. Int. J. Adv. Res. Comput. Sci. Software Eng. (2014). ISSN: 2277 128X
11. Arora, H., Arora, D., Goel, B., Jain, P.: An Improved CPU Scheduling Algorithm
12. Ajmani, P., Sethi, M.: Proposed fuzzy CPU scheduling algorithm (PFCS) for real time operating systems. IJIT (2013)
13. Mishra, M.K., Khan, A.K.: An improved round robin CPU scheduling algorithm. J. Glob. Res. Comput. Sci. **3**(6) (2012). ISSN 2229-371X
14. Ramabhadran, S., Pasquale, J.: Stratified round robin: a low complexity packet scheduler with bandwidth fairness and bounded delay. In: Proceedings of the 2003 Conference on Applications, Technologies, Architectures, and Protocols for Computer Communications. ACM, pp. 239–250, Aug 2003
15. Jain, N., Menache, I., Naor, J.S., Yaniv, J.: Near-optimal scheduling mechanisms for deadline-sensitive jobs in large computing clusters. ACM Trans. Parallel Comput. **2**(1), 3 (2015)

Synchronization of Two Chaotic Oscillators Through Threshold Coupling

A. Chithra and I. Raja Mohamed

Abstract In this paper, the dynamic modeling of two identical oscillators which are coupled through threshold controller is proposed. Until now, most of the synchronization of chaotic systems found in literature is based on common coupling methods (unidirectional and bidirectional) that attracted the attention of researchers. To strengthen this, the idea illustrated here is to show the effectiveness of a new kind of coupling called threshold controller coupling. Using this, complete and anticipatory synchronization could be achieved. The system used is of second-order non-autonomous type. The coupled system is investigated using MATLAB–Simulink technique. The result shows that based on coupling strength, coupled system is switched among the basic synchronization, viz. lead and complete.

Keywords Modeling · Synchronization · Threshold controller
Chaotic · MATLAB–Simulink

1 Introduction

Chaos theory has one of the greatest achievement and application in secure communication over two decades. Chaotic system can produce infinite number of chaotic signals which are non-periodic and is characterized by high sensitive to parameter value and initial condition. Due to this property and broadband nature of chaotic signal, which makes particular interest in the concept of synchronization for the application of secure communication to mask the embedded message or signal becomes possible.

Synchronized chaos is a phenomenon that occurs when two or more chaotic systems adjust to common behavior due to coupling. The idea of chaos synchro-

A. Chithra · I. Raja Mohamed (✉)
Department of Physics, B. S. Abdur Rahman University, Chennai, India
e-mail: rajamohamed@bsauniv.ac.in

A. Chithra
e-mail: chithras787@gmail.com

© Springer Nature Singapore Pte Ltd. 2018
S. K. Muttoo (ed.), *System and Architecture*, Advances in Intelligent Systems
and Computing 732, https://doi.org/10.1007/978-981-10-8533-8_24

nization is where one separate identical drive system drives another system under suitable threshold coupling parameter; then the response system follows the drive asymptotically. So far, many types of synchronization and coupling methods have been reported in the literature. In this paper, a new method of achieving complete and anticipatory synchronization is proposed. The two chaotic systems with threshold nonlinearity are coupled via threshold controller coupling. To enforce synchronization, one of the signals is fed to the response side. By simply altering the coupling threshold value and coupling parameter value, the system goes through complete synchronization state from unsynchronized state.

2 Literature Overview

The concept of synchronization of chaotic oscillation is extensively studied [1]. Dutch Physicist Huygens discovered the first observation of synchronization in pendulum clock [2]. Edward Appleton and Balthasar van der Pol showed the experimental and theoretical study for this phenomenon. Then the synchronization of chaotic system which used in secure communication systems was first reported by Yamada and Fujisaka [3] followed by Pecora and Carroll [4]. Since then several interesting synchronization phenomena have been observed and reported in the literature. To initiate synchronization, the system should be coupled in a proper way. Eventually by the nature of coupling, different types of synchronization are found, viz. generalized synchronization [5], complete synchronization [6], lag and anticipatory synchronization [7], phase synchronization [8], and global synchronization [9]. Hence to achieve these types of synchronization, the commonly used coupling methods are unidirectional [10] and bidirectional [11], but rarely cascaded [12] and delay [13].

The design of flexible nonlinearity exhibiting chaos has not been much explored in the literature, and only few studies are found in this direction [14, 15]. This specific type of nonlinearity is used as coupling element in the system. Complete synchronization has been observed in Chua's oscillator [16], Lorenz and Rossler system [17], Duffing system [18], and so on. In this paper, threshold controller-based second-order chaotic system reported in Int. J. Bifuracat. Chaos; V 20 (2010) is coupled through threshold controller. The advantage of this coupling is to control the drive and response separately by altering the threshold level of threshold controller. The system will exhibit complete and anticipatory synchronization when coupling parameter value is increased.

The paper is organized as follows: The dynamic modeling of single and coupled system through threshold controller is discussed in Sect. 3. Section 4 describes the simulation result of coupled system. Summary of the result and conclusion is given finally.

3 Modeling and Simulation of Chaotic System

3.1 Dynamic Modeling of Single System

Threshold controller-based chaotic oscillator [14] is used to design dynamic modeling of coupled systems for synchronization. The dynamical differential equation of second-order non-autonomous system is as follows:

$$\frac{d^2x}{dt^2} = -\alpha \frac{dx}{dt} - \beta x + \delta G(x) + f \sin \omega t \qquad (1)$$

Here α, β, δ are constants, $x, \frac{dx}{dt}$ are the state variables of the oscillators, and G (x) is the nonlinear term used in the system called threshold controller. The control will be triggered whenever the value of dynamical variable exceeds positive $(+x^*)$ as well as negative threshold $(-x^*)$, then it will be reset to threshold value $(x^* = 0.7)$, where

$$G(x) = \begin{cases} x^*, & x > x^* \\ x, & -x \le x \le x^* \\ -x^*, & x < -x^* \end{cases} \qquad (2)$$

The standard parameter value is used for this system to make oscillate with $\alpha = 0.5$, $\beta = 1.8$, $\delta = 3.0$, where f is the amplitude of the system and ω is the angular frequency of the system. System starts to oscillate from periodic to chaotic attractor when the control parameter (f) is varied from 0.1 to 0.55. Chaotic regime is revealed at $f = 0.55$ and $\omega = 1.1$, where Fig. 1 shows the simulation result of a single system with its symmetry characteristic curve. Other characteristic confirmation of chaos in this system like bifurcation and Lyapunov exponent was reported in detail [14].

3.2 Coupled Systems Through Threshold Controller

When two identical systems are coupled in such a way, that coupling tends to make the response to follow the drive system respectively. When coupling parameter $c = 1.7$ the states of two systems coincide and vary chaotically in time [11] where the coincidence of states is preserved with time, the obtained result is complete synchronization. If $c = 1.4$, the system exhibits anticipatory synchronization with slight variation in drive system.

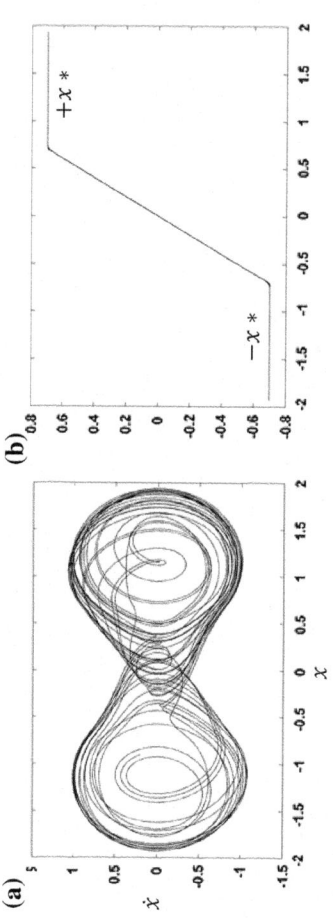

Fig. 1 Simulation output of single chaotic oscillator **a** double-scroll attractor for $f = 0.55$, $\omega = 1.1$. **b** Characteristics curve of the threshold controller

4 Simulation Result of Coupled System Through Threshold Controller Coupling

The coupled system is defined in mathematical form as follows:
Drive:

$$\frac{d^2x}{dt^2} = -\alpha\frac{dx}{dt} - \beta x + \delta G(x) + f \sin \omega t \tag{3}$$

Response:

$$\frac{d^2x'}{dt^2} = -\alpha\frac{dx'}{dt} - \beta x' + \delta G(x') + \varepsilon 1 * \varepsilon 2 * G(x - x') + f \sin \omega t \tag{4}$$

Here ε_1 and ε_2 are the coupling parameters, and when $\varepsilon > 0$, the system transits from unsynchronized to anticipatory and to complete or identical synchronization. Figure 2 shows the MATLAB–Simulink modeling of two identical oscillators' drive (D) and response (R) through threshold coupling with threshold level at $x^* = 1.4$, and other parameters values are fixed as same as drive system.

When $\varepsilon_1 = 0.55$ and $\varepsilon_2 = 1.06$, the system is in unsynchronized state. Then by gradually increasing the coupling parameter beyond $\varepsilon_1 = 0.95$ and $\varepsilon_2 = 1.06$, the system exhibits anticipatory synchronization. By further increasing the coupling parameter value, it shows complete synchronized state at $\varepsilon_1 = 1.2$ and $\varepsilon_2 = 1.06$. Figure 3 shows the time series, phase difference plot of $(x - x')$, and the simulation result is confirmed with time series analysis.

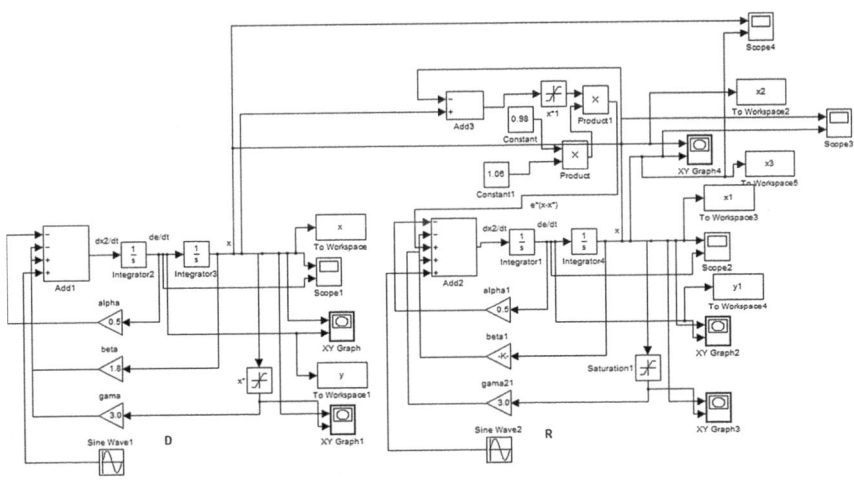

Fig. 2 Simulink modeling of two coupled systems through threshold coupling

(a)

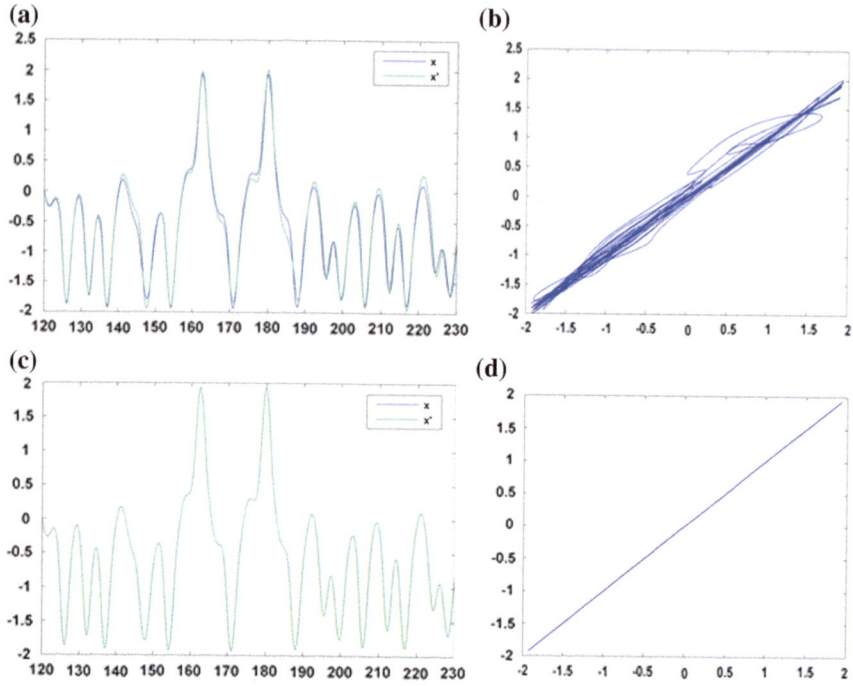

(b)

(c)

(d)

Fig. 3 Time series plot and phase difference plot. **a** and **b** are anticipatory synchronization at $\epsilon_1 = 0.98$ and $\epsilon_2 = 1.06$, $x^* = 1.4$. **c** and **d** are complete synchronization at $\epsilon_1 = 1.2$ and $\epsilon_2 = 1.06$

5 Conclusion

In this work, the dynamic modeling of two identical oscillators through threshold controller using MATLAB–Simulink technique is reported. The proposed system is based on new kind of coupling called threshold controller. The system exhibits various types of synchronization like complete and anticipatory synchronization for increasing value of coupling parameter. Further work regarding experimental proof with electronic circuit is currently being investigated.

Acknowledgements This research work is supported by SERB under project No: SR/S2/ HEP-042/2012, and authors thank SERB for providing financial support.

References

1. Pikovsky, A.S., Rosenblum, M.G., Kurths, J.: Synchronization—A Unified Approach to Nonlinear Science. Cambridge University Press, Cambridge (2001)
2. Huygen, C.: The Pendulum Clock. Iowa State University Press, Ames (1986)

3. Fujisaka, H., Yamada, T.: Stability theory of synchronized motion in coupled-oscillator systems. Prog. Theor. Phys. **69**, 32 (1983)
4. Pecora, L.M., Carroll, T.L.: Synchronization in Chaotic system. Phy. Rev. Lett. **64**, 821 (1990)
5. Abarbanel, H.D.I., Rulkov, N.F., Sushchik, M.M.: Generalized synchronization of chaos: the auxiliary system approach. Phys. Rev. E **53**, 4528–4535 (1996)
6. Lakshmanan, M., Murali, K.: Chaos in Nonlinear Oscillators: Controlling and Synchronization. World Scientific, Singapore (1996)
7. Raja Mohamed, I., Srinivasan, K.: Lag and anticipating synchronization in one way coupled Chua's circuit. In: 2nd International Conference on Devices, Circuits and Systems, (2014)
8. Pikovsky, A.S., Rosenblum, M.G., Osipov, G.V., Kurths, J.: Phase synchronization of chaotic oscillators by external driving. Phys. D **104**(3–4), 219–238 (1997)
9. Chen, H.: Global chaos synchronization of new chaotic systems via nonlinear control. Solitons Fractals **23**, 1245–1251 (2005)
10. Srinivasan, K., Senthilkumar, D.V., Raja Mohamed, I., Murali, K., Lakshmanan, M., Kurths, J.: Anticipating, complete and lag synchronization in Rc-phase-shift network based coupled Chua's circuits without delay. Chaos: An Interdisc. J. Nonlinear Sci. **22** (2012)
11. Pecora, L.M., Carroll, T.L., Johnson, G.A., Mar D.J.: Fundamentals of synchronization in chaotic systems, concepts, and applications. Chaos: Am. Inst. phys. **4** (1997)
12. Murali, K., Lakshmanan. M.: Synchronization through compound chaotic signal in Chua's circuit and Murali- Lakshmanan- Chua circuit. Int. J. Bifurcat. chaos **7**, 415 (1997)
13. Senthilkumar, D.V., Lakshmanan, M.: Transition from anticipatory to lag synchronization via complete synchronization in time–delay systems. Phys. Rev. E. **71** (2005)
14. Raja Mohamed, I., Murali, k., Sinha. S., Lindberg, E.: Design of threshold Controller based chaotic circuits. Int. J. Bifurcat. Chaos **20**, 2185 (2010)
15. Suresh, R., Srinivasan, K., Senthilkumar., V, Murali, K., Lakshmanan, M., Kurths, J.: Dynamic Environment coupling induced synchronized states in coupled time-delayed electronic circuits. Int. J. Bifurcat. Chaos **24** (2014)
16. Heagy, J.F., Carroll, T.L., Pecora, L.M.: Synchronous chaos in coupled oscillator systems. Phys. Rev. E **50**, 1874 (1994)
17. Cumo, K.M, Oppenheim, V., Stogatz, SH.: Synchronization of Lorenz-based Chaotic circuits with applications to communications IEEE Trans. Circ. Sys.-11: Analog Digit. Sig. Process. **40**(10) (1993)
18. Volos, C.K., Kyprianidis, I.M., Stouboulos, I.N.: Synchronization of two mutually coupled duffing—type circuits. Int. J Circ. Sys. Sig. Process. **1**, 274 (2007)

L3C Model of High-Performance Computing Cluster for Scientific Applications

Alpana Rajan, Brijendra Kumar Joshi and Anil Rawat

Abstract High-performance computing clusters (HPCCs) are widely used for various scientific applications. In a typical scientific research environment, software applications need large but varying number of processing elements and processor cores. To maximize throughput of a computing cluster and optimum utilization of resources, one new model has been proposed. The proposed model visualizes the computing cluster as loosely coupled cluster of clusters (L3C). Execution time for scientific applications also varies in terms of lapsed time for execution and CPU time utilized. The process scheduling algorithm maintains a list of applications to be executed along with respective number of node/core required. Using the L3C model and scheduling algorithm, multiple applications are scheduled on the computing cluster for concurrent execution. Basis for proposing L3C model along with its details is discussed in the paper. Experimental results of performance evaluation of HPC clusters were published earlier by the authors and are referred at respective places. L3C model has certain inherent advantages which are also discussed in the paper.

Keywords High-performance computing cluster · Performance evaluation
HPCC throughput · Scientific applications

A. Rajan (✉) · A. Rawat
Computer Division, Raja Ramanna Centre for Advanced Technology, Indore, India
e-mail: alpana@rrcat.gov.in

A. Rawat
e-mail: rawat@rrcat.gov.in

B. K. Joshi
Military College of Telecommunication Engineering, Mhow, India
e-mail: brijendrajoshi@yahoo.com

© Springer Nature Singapore Pte Ltd. 2018
S. K. Muttoo (ed.), *System and Architecture*, Advances in Intelligent Systems
and Computing 732, https://doi.org/10.1007/978-981-10-8533-8_25

1   Introduction

Use of computing technology for scientific research and development became popular with the advent of general purpose computers in the mid-sixties. As the computing technology progressed in terms of computing power and ease of programming, complexity of scientific codes also increased, leading to increase in workload of computing clusters [1]. In the endeavor to achieve high-performance computing at lower costs, computing clusters were built. Cluster-based computing deploys multiprocessor machines for executing scientific codes having parallel components. Interprocessor communication is supported by very high-speed interconnects. HPCCs are deployed worldwide for scientific applications demanding huge computing power.

Various software tools are available for measuring performance of clusters. Estimated performance of a cluster is a good indication for the capability of the cluster to execute computational tasks. High-performance Linpack (HPL) benchmark is a set of tools for performance evaluation of HPCC [2]. HPL is a de facto standard for measuring cluster performance; it solves a linear system by distributing data over a two-dimensional grid of processes. Peak computing power is quantified as GFlop/s.

Optimum utilization of the available resources is ensured by the architects of the computing clusters to achieve high throughput. When a cluster is built to run heterogeneous types of applications, the task becomes more complex and parameters affecting the performance are to be balanced for maximizing throughput.

2   Performance of HPCC

Performance of a computing cluster depends on components used to build it and also on the type application deployment on it. There are various software tools available for measuring the performance. Estimation of performance indicates the strength, capability, and power of a computing cluster for processing a computation-intensive task. With the advancements in technology, introduction of new system architectures, and also renewed user requirement, it is important that performance evaluation tools are also updated. In this section, the standard basic formula used for estimation is briefly described.

Let us say R_{peak} is the maximum theoretically calculated computing power of system, and R_{max} is the maximum actual computing power of system. R_{max} can be obtained by using software tools like HPL [2–4], high-performance computing challenge benchmark. R_{peak} can be calculated using the following formula:

$$R_{\text{peak}} = \text{PCS} \times \text{NC} \times \text{FPOC}$$

where PCS is processor clock speed in GHz, NC is total number of Cores X, FPOC is floating point operations/cycle.

3 Scientific Applications on HPCC

Clusters have provided a platform for execution of a wide range of applications, including supercomputing (highly processor-intensive jobs). While focusing on scientific applications, use of cluster computing is widely seen for running codes for weather forecast modeling, life sciences, computational fluid dynamics, simulation of beam tracking for accelerators, image processing, aerodynamics, astrophysics, etc. Following subsections briefly cover some popular legacy application and also include certain specific details on sequential applications and parallel applications.

Legacy Applications: Very large number of scientific codes has been written over the years, and these codes have existed for decades. They have been altered and expanded to improve them, and experiments have been conducted using these codes. Scientific community has been hesitant to replace these codes by rewritten codes, since the risk of introducing a logical error is high. Even a subtle change may result in serious consequences.

Sequential Scientific Code: Many scientific codes have been parallelized to gain on execution time using various programming tools and techniques. Tools have been developed to auto-parallelize sequential codes, although with limited success. Certain standard sequential codes are still being used by scientists and researchers.

Parallel Scientific Codes: Parallel scientific codes are either written afresh or are developed by identifying parts of the code which can be parallelized. Major improvement in performance of these codes has been achieved by computer scientists and programmers while working in tandem with scientist having required domain knowledge of the scientific codes [1, 5, 6].

4 Factors Governing Performance for Scientific Applications

Scientific codes have different characteristics as compared to codes in other application areas, as they are computationally intensive programs requiring huge resources in terms of memory, storage, etc. A large number of CPU cycles are required for completing the computations as the problems being solved are very complex in nature [7]. Typical characteristics in addition to computational requirements are computations on large data sets and large number of iterations to converge to the result. Large numbers of iterations are required before the program converges to the solution.

Impact of Number of PEs and Cores: For most of the scientific codes, parallelization is done to optimally distribute the computational part on multiple processors in such a way that the overall computational time reduces. The speedup achieved by parallelization is governed by Amdahl's law. Theoretically speaking, very large number of processing elements (PEs) and cores can be used for solving any complex problem, but there is a limitation due to other limiting factors like interconnect, interprocess communication overheads, inherent serial part of the code, etc.

Impact of Interconnect: Interconnect used for building HPCC is an important factor governing performance of the cluster. Typically, internode communication takes place using the interconnect network. Parallelized parts of code have to interact with each other for transferring the input data sets (which are generally large for scientific computing codes), for combining the output data sets for preparation of program output and at times for transferring intermediate result sets. Thus, this interprocess communication becomes one of the major factors governing performance of cluster. To provide high bandwidth and low latency, many high-end interconnects like Myrinet and Infiniband are used in HPCCs.

Process Distribution Patterns: Scientific codes being resource hungry applications, when execute on a computing cluster, will tend to exploit all the available resources. The performance governing factors like number of processors/cores, size of memory, type of interconnect, etc., depend on the budget available for building any computing cluster. After the hardware components are bought and cluster is built, optimization of algorithm and granularity of parallelism play important role in improving performance of the application. Many a times source codes of scientific applications are not available due to various reasons. It may be old legacy application or buying source code for commercially available application may be prohibitive in terms of high cost. This leaves little scope for performance improvement by changing these parameters. There is lot of scope for performance improvement of HPCC running multiple scientific codes simultaneously by optimally distributing the processes on available nodes/processors/cores. Process distribution among available nodes and cores to maximize throughput and in turn improve overall cluster performance is an area to be explored and investigated.

5 Models for Understanding HPCC Performance for Scientific Applications

Process Distribution Model: When computation in form of a software application is to be executed on a cluster, its resource requirement is assessed in terms of number of cores required, memory required, scratch area requirement, etc. Based on the assessment of requirement, applicability of available resources is carried out. Figure 1 shows a cluster having six nodes and each node is having four cores, thus total 24 cores are available for carrying out computational tasks.

Fig. 1 Process distribution model—six node cluster with 24 cores

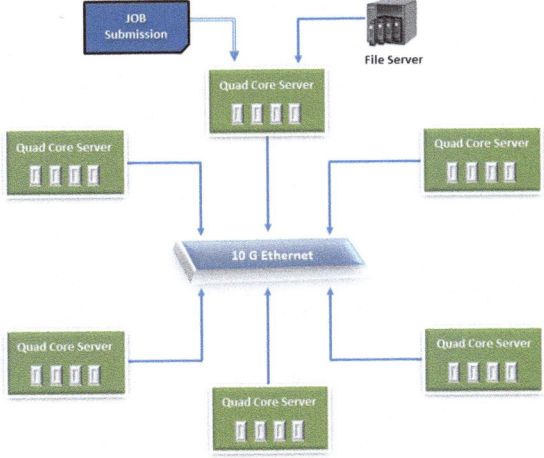

In this basic model to understand process distribution, processes are created increasingly from 6 to 36, while keeping the task size constant [8]. The cluster peak computing power increases as we deploy more cores and processors for the computational task [9]. The peak computing power deliverable by the cluster will be achieved when maximum number of available cores matches number of processes created for the computational task. Practically achieved peak computing power in each case is recorded for analysis and further explorations [8]. Using the 'process distribution model,' complexity or the size of the scientific application can be fixed for execution on the available resources.

Processor Core Usage Model: The 'processor core usage model' has been conceptualized for a finer understanding of core usage by computational tasks on clusters. The model can be viewed as two virtual models built over two different clusters differing basically in interconnect speed and also processor performance. This approach has been followed for comparative analysis purpose [10]. The model presented in previous section uses 10 G Ethernet connectivity for internode communication. To carryout comparative performance evaluation, another model built using Infiniband connectivity for internode communication is proposed. Physical realization of the model has been achieved by configuring hardware components, and the model is presented in Fig. 2.

The interconnect used to build this model is 20 Gbps Infiniband. To carryout comparative analysis, these two models are loaded with same task size and identical process creation is done for one-to-one comparative analysis [10]. The task size N in the HPL is varied in moderate range of 10,000–40,000 in steps of 10,000. A number of processes are created as a set of 1, 2, or 4 for each comparison. By using the advanced technique of HPL for distributing created multiprocesses among cores and processors, true results are obtained. For comparative analysis purpose, identical distribution of tasks on nodes and cores has been carried out on the two cluster models.

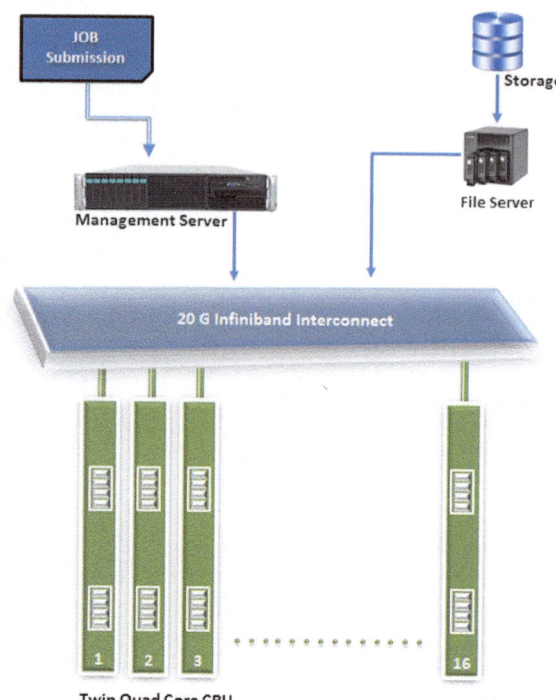

Fig. 2 Processor core usage model

In these experiments, performance is measured in terms of computing power delivered, and focus is also drawn on execution time. In both the options of this model, the created processes are forced for execution on a single processor, thus enabling interprocess communication bound to be within the processor itself. The approach uses all the cores available in the processor. The model is also investigated by distributing same size task on cores on different processor.

Figure 3 shown below represents how interprocess communication takes place using QPI when four processes are distributed on four cores of same processor. C1, C2, C3, C4 are cores of processor P1, and Proc1, Proc2, Proc3, and Proc4 are processes of an application spawned on four cores of same processor, thus the interprocess communication domain is confined to the processor itself.

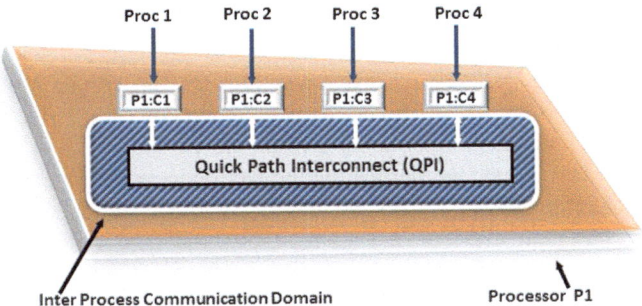

Fig. 3 Interprocess communication through QPI

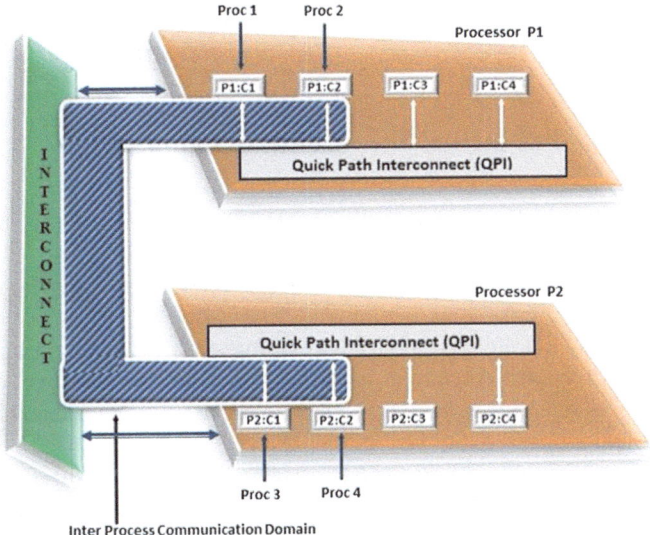

Fig. 4 Interprocess communication through interconnect

If four processes are executed on two cores of two different processors, then the interprocess communication takes place through the interconnect, as depicted in Fig. 4. In this case, Proc1 and Proc2 are spawned on C1 and C2 cores of processor P1, whereas Proc3 and Proc4 are allocated to C1 and C2 cores of processor P2. The interprocess communication domain is not confined to a single processor, instead it is through the interconnect. It is very interesting to carryout analytical studies using this model, and various experimental test runs of HPL provided set of results. Analysis of the result set revealed the behavior of cluster measured in terms of execution time for different process patterns expressed in terms of process per node (PPN). The two models discussed so far gave a clearer understanding of the cluster performance under varying processor core usage and process distribution.

Interconnect Impact Model: This model has been conceptualized to investigate impact of Infiniband interconnect. The model described in previous section is upgraded using 40 Gbps interconnect, and studies are carried out to compare the performance of clusters using 20 and 40 Gbps interconnects. Performance measured with increasing task complexity in case of 20 and 40 Gbps interconnect speed gives a clear picture of the positive impact of interconnect speed. Problem size is increased from 10,000 to 100,000 in steps of 10,000, and 24 cores have been used in three different distributive patterns. Execution time and peak computing power delivered are recorded [11, 12]. The lower latency offered by Infiniband has considerably nullified the bottleneck posed by conventional interconnects [12].

The three models described and discussed from operational requirement point of view have provided a clearer understanding of cluster performance for scientific applications. In the next section, an optimized and comprehensive model for executing multiple scientific applications concurrently on one cluster is proposed and described.

6 L3C Model of HPCC for Scientific Applications

After carrying out investigations on the three different models for scientific applications, it is logical to conceptualize an 'Optimized Model for Scientific Computing.' In a typical scientific computing scenario, the cluster is being used concurrently by multiple users for running their codes. All these scientific applications being resource hungry applications compete for available resources and at times result in resource contention, affecting the performance severely. The proposed model for scientific computing applications can be visualized as collection of multiple virtual clusters.

The current technological trends have enabled deployment of HPCCs having large number of PEs and cores. Each PE can typically have four, six, and even up to eight cores. Each node can have one, two, and even up to four PEs. This high density of PEs and cores in a single node results in availability of large number of cores for computational tasks. Application may need n number of cores, where $n < N$ (total no. of cores in the cluster), leaving some nodes unused if only one application is running. Limitation on usage of cores can come in from multiple fronts. First, there may be limitation in terms of license of the application for number of cores on which the task can be actually distributed. Second, the code may not be scalable beyond a limit and thus may leave certain cores/nodes unused. These unused cores may fruitfully be utilized by other applications.

In the proposed model, multiple scientific applications are made to utilize a subset of cores. For example, if application 1 needs 64 cores while application 2 and 3 require 32 cores each, then these three applications can coexist on the cluster without any degradation of performance. Concurrent execution of these three applications will enhance the overall throughput (along with optimum utilization of available resources) as compared to the situation where they were sequenced for execution one after another.

This concept of deploying multiple applications concurrently is in no way limited in terms of number of such applications. The limitation actually comes from the total number of cores available. All the available cores can be divided in n number of (n_1, n_2, n_3 ...) virtual clusters. Number of cores used by each virtual cluster could be different (c_1 cores by n_1 cluster, c_2 cores by n_2 cluster, and so on) as long as $c_1 + c_2 + c_2$ ... is not greater than c * n where c * n is total number of cores in the cluster.

This model can thus be termed as a loosely coupled cluster of clusters (L3C model). The model allows on-the-fly creation of clusters of varying size as per the requirement of the applications running concurrently on the cluster. We can visualize the cluster as a loosely coupled cluster of clusters.

Number of 'virtual clusters' created in this model depends on number of applications being deployed and the resources available. Thus, number of virtual clusters can vary from 1 to many, depending on size and complexity of applications being run concurrently. One can deploy multiple applications concurrently on the cluster by dedicatedly assigning/allocating x no. of cores to an application, y no. of cores to another application, and so on. It is already verified in the model (interconnect impact model) presented earlier that the 40 Gbps Infiniband interconnect ensures very high throughput for inter processor communication. This feature provided by Infiniband interconnect is exploited in L3C model to allocate cores to applications irrespective of which processor those cores belong to.

The above diagram depicts the L3C model of HPCC for a typical requirement of four applications running concurrently on HPCC. Each application requires different number of cores as shown in the Fig. 5. CE1 and CE2 are control elements, which are responsible for job distribution (scheduling among cores), access to storage (data and program files), and job submission. In the typical example depicted above, Scientific Application 1 is deployed on core C1–C64, Scientific Application 2 uses core C65 to C96, Scientific Application 3 uses another set of 16 cores from C97–C112, and Scientific Application 4 is being run on core C113–C128.

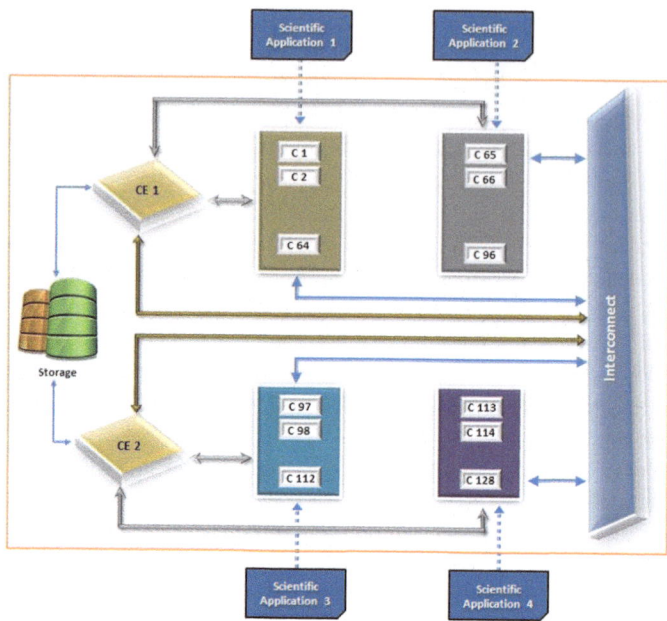

Fig. 5 Loosely coupled cluster of clusters (L3C) model

7 Implications of L3C Model

Concurrent Execution of Scientific Codes: The L3C model proposes to concurrently execute multiple scientific applications or scientific codes on computing cluster, as long as total number of cores required by all the applications put together does not exceed the total number of cores available in the computing cluster. If these multiple tasks are queued up for sequential execution one after another, all available cores may not be utilized all the time, thus resulting in wastage of computational power.

Resource Allocation Approach: A set of scientific applications requiring varied number of cores is listed in Table 1. Estimated execution time is also included in the table, which is only indicative in nature, since actual execution time depends on many other factors like size of data set, result convergence methodology, processing power of the PE, and available memory per core/per PE.

Just for an example, VORPAL, ADF, and WIEN2k_08 can coexist on a computing cluster having 128 cores. Similarly, other combination of applications is also possible, which solely depends on number of available cores, presuming other requirements like memory per core, scratch area, etc., are not constrained.

Table 1 Set of scientific applications and certain related details

Name of the scientific application	No. of cores	Estimated execution time (h)
Amsterdam density functional (ADF)	32	75
WIEN2k_08	32	200
Versatile object-oriented code for relativistic plasma analysis with laser (VORPAL)	64	400
Virtual laser plasma lab (VLPL) code	64	300
Objective ring beam injection and tracking (ORBIT_MPI)	16	24
Crystal	32	350
LS-Dyna	16	20

Optimizing Allocation of Resource: When multiple scientific applications are deployed on a computing cluster, they may end at different time, meaning they may need different execution time. This will surely render some cores free earlier as compared to cores engaged for applications requiring longer execution time. Optimization of resources as proposed in L3C model suggests scheduling those applications from the waiting queue, which can be accommodated without any overlapping of applications on cores. Thus, as soon as a set of cores is free, another application can be scheduled to occupy the free cores. The virtual cluster of clusters as visualized in L3C model thus allows an application requiring very large execution time to coexist with other applications which require comparatively smaller execution times. The state of this virtual cluster of clusters will vary dynamically depending on the scientific applications being executed concurrently at any instance of time.

8 Conclusions

The L3C model conceptualizes the division of cluster into virtual multiple clusters. Since the Infiniband interconnect ensures that there is no constrain on the inter-processor communication, thus allocation of cores to a set of concurrent applications can be done on the fly as per the demand of application, irrespective of whether the cores belong to same processor or not. Concurrent execution of the scientific applications increases HPCC utilization considerably and leads to much enhanced throughput delivered by the computing cluster.

Scientific applications require varied number of cores. Number of cores required for an application depends on the problem size being attempted and also on some other factors like software license, simulation model, etc. This concept of allocating nodes/cores to a set of applications for concurrent execution is a novel approach for enhanced utilization of computing resources.

The comprehensive L3C model proposed for scientific applications is a novel idea ensuring maximum throughput and optimum utilization of computing resources. The concept of deploying multiple applications concurrently has resulted in enhanced throughput of HPCC leading to better return on investment (RoI).

References

1. Alam, S.R., Barrett, R.F., Kuehn, J.A., Roth, P.C., Vetter, J.S.: Characterization of scientific workloads on systems with multi-core processors. In: IEEE International Symposium on Workload Characterization, pp. 225–236 (2006)
2. Dongarra, J., Luszczek, P., Petitet, A.: The LINPACK Benchmark: past, present, and future. Concurrency: Pract. Exp. **15**, 803–820 (2003)
3. Langou, J., Dongarra, J.: The problem with the Linpack benchmark matrix generator. Int. J. High Perform. Comput. Appl. **23**(1), 5–14 (2009)
4. Petitet, R.C., Whaley, J. Dongarra, A.: Cleary, HPL—a Portable Implementation of the High-Performance Linpack Benchmark for Distributed-Memory Computers. Innovative Computing Laboratory, Computer Science Department, University of Tennessee, September 2008
5. Buyya, R. (ed.): High Performance Cluster Computing: Architectures and Systems, vol. 1. Prentice Hall PTR, NJ (1999) ISBN: 0-13-013784-7
6. Buyya, R. (ed.): High Performance Cluster Computing: Programming and Applications, vol. 2. Prentice Hall PTR, NJ, USA (1999) ISBN: 0-13-013785-5
7. Hwang, K., Dongarra, J., Fox, G.: Distributed and Cloud Computing, 1st edn. Morgan Kaufmann (2011)
8. Rajan, A., Joshi, B.K., Rawat, A.: Critical analysis of HPL performance under different process distribution patterns. In: CSI 6th International Conference on Software Engineering (CONSEG 2012), Devi Ahilya Vishwavidyalaya (DAVV), Indore, MP, India, 5–7 Sept 2012
9. Vaidya, M.: Parallel processing of cluster by map reduce. Int. J. Distrib. Parallel Syst. (IJDPS) **3**(1), 167 (2012)
10. Rajan, A., Joshi, B.K., Rawat, A.: Analysis of process distribution in HPC cluster using HPL. In: The Second IEEE International Conference on Parallel, Distributed and Grid Computing 2012 (PDGC 2012), Jaypee University of Information Technology, Solan, HP, India, 6–8 Dec 2012
11. Rajan, A., Joshi, B.K., Rawat, A.: Analytical studies of peak computing power deliverable by small and mid size HPCC. In: INDIACom 2013—7th International Conference on 'Computing for Nation Development', BVICAM, New Delhi, 7–8 Mar 2013
12. Rajan, A., Joshi, B.K.: Performance comparison of 20 Gbps and 40 Gbps Infiniband Interconnect. In: IEEE International Conference on Global Sustainable Development (IndiaCom 2014), BVICAM, pp. 5–6, New Delhi, Mar 2014

Design and Development of Digital Energy Meter on FPGA

Kautilya Pachorie, Surabhi Agrawal, Varun Maheshwari, Bhagwan Das Devulapalli and A. K. Saxena

Abstract Nowadays, microprocessors and microcontrollers are widely used in the field of modern power system schemes. But these devices are slow due to their sequential approach. Field Programmable Gate Array (FPGA) works on concurrent architecture and advantage of reusability. Time delay constraint is a crucial factor in different applications of modern power system schemes such as relays, energy meters, and Phasor Measurement Unit (PMU). In this paper, different FPGA-based modules are implemented which work on pipelined architecture instead of traditional microprocessors and microcontrollers which are sequential in nature. Time delay in the sense, process, and communication cycles is reduced due to concurrent working modules of the FPGA. In this paper, various FPGA modules are implemented on GENESYS XILINX VIRTEX 5 XC5VLX50T FPGA Board for implementing digital energy meter. Modules are implemented in Very High Speed Integrated Circuit Hardware Descriptive Language (VHDL) with the help of different Intellectual Property (IP) cores. Test results are presented and communicated to the hyper-terminal.

Keywords Analog to Digital Converter (ADC) · Concurrent Architecture
FPGA Modules · IP Cores · Zero Crossing Detector (ZCD)

K. Pachorie (✉) · S. Agrawal · V. Maheshwari
Faculty of Engineering and Technology, Agra College, Agra, India
e-mail: kautilya1425@gmail.com

S. Agrawal
e-mail: surbhi084@gmail.com

V. Maheshwari
e-mail: varun_agr@yahoo.com

K. Pachorie · S. Agrawal · V. Maheshwari
Department of Electronics and Communication Engineering, Agra College, Agra, India

B. D. Devulapalli · A. K. Saxena
Department of Electrical Engineering, Dayalbagh Educational Institute, Agra, India
e-mail: dbhagwandas@gmail.com

A. K. Saxena
e-mail: aksaxena61@gmail.com

© Springer Nature Singapore Pte Ltd. 2018
S. K. Muttoo (ed.), *System and Architecture*, Advances in Intelligent Systems
and Computing 732, https://doi.org/10.1007/978-981-10-8533-8_26

1   Introduction

Due to accuracy and stability problems with electromechanical systems now-a-days microprocessors and microcontrollers are used in different power system schemes. Microprocessors/microcontrollers are also preferred for their programmability approach. Reference [1] presents microprocessor-based intelligent electronic meter. Intelligent electronic meter comprises zero crossing detector, sample and hold circuits, analog to digital converters. Only 481 samples per second are considered in the paper. Different electrical quantities such as Root-Mean-Square (RMS) voltage, RMS current, and average power are calculated. Waveform-based test results are presented in the paper. Microcontroller-based prepaid energy meter is presented by [2]. Metering and billing system are presented in this paper. Real-Time Clock (RTC), Liquid Crystal Display (LCD), and communication modules are presented for metering system and encoder; smart card and encryption module are implemented for billing system. Voltage, current, active power, and frequency measurement results are presented in the paper. Microcontroller-based impedance relay is presented in [3]. Data Acquisition Controller, Relay Function Controller, and Output Decision Controller are used in implementing impedance relay. Five microcontrollers are used to implement these modules. Sampling frequency is chosen at 960 Hz. Microprocessor-based overcurrent relay is presented in [4–6]. A microcontroller-based design for the implementation of multiple overcurrent relays is presented in [7]. However, the processing for each relay is sequential in time which results in increased computational time and thus adversely affects the overall performance of the relay.

A new PMU is implemented in [8]. The phasor measurement unit comprises of signal transformation and synchronized sampling board. The prototype is developed with the help of data acquisition card AD 512. MATLAB-based test results are presented in the paper. Reference [9] presents an improved phasor computation algorithm. The algorithm is based on QNX real-time operating system which includes measurement module and task module. Sampling rate (4800 Hz) of PMU is considered in the paper. Digital simulation and laboratory-based test results are presented in the paper.

The above-mentioned paper presents application of microprocessors/ microcontrollers in different fields of power system schemes. However, approach is slow due to sequential behavior of microprocessors/microcontrollers. To eradicate the problem, the FPGA with concurrent architecture is employed which provides the most suitable platform for different power system schemes. In this paper, different FPGA modules and IP cores have been implemented on GENESYS XILINX VIRTEX 5 XC5VLX50T FPGA Board for implementing digital energy meter. These different FPGA modules which work on concurrent architecture can be widely used in implementing various power system schemes. Some of the modules are used in implementing concurrent processing overcurrent relay in [10].

2 FPGA Architecture and Design Flow

2.1 FPGA and Its Architecture

FPGAs came into existence in the mid-1980s after the successive introduction starting from the Programmable Logic Devices (PLD's) in the mid-1970s then moving forward to Programmable Logic Array (PLA) or Programmable Array Logic (PAL) also known as Generic Array Logic (GAL) which then after collectively termed as Simple Programmable Logic Devices (SPLDs). Later on, GAL was improved to Complex PLDs (CPLDs). FPGAs and CPLDs are completely from each other considering the parameters like built-in features, architecture, basic features, and including the cost as well. FPGAs are designed to aim at the implementation of large-size and high-performance circuits [11].

FPGAs are most widely used as an alternative implementation of digital logic in systems in a simple and effective manner. FPGAs are prefabricated silicon chips that are programmed electrically to implement any sort of digital design. The first SRAM-based FPGA was introduced in 1967 by Wahlstrom in which the architecture allowed both the logic and interconnection configuration using stream of configuration bits.

The internal architecture of FPGA consists of three major components (i) Configurable Logic Blocks (CLBs), (ii) Programmable Interconnects, and (iii) Input/Output (I/O) blocks (Fig. 1).

The CLB's in an FPGA provides the basic computation and storage elements used in digital systems. The basic logic element contains some form of programmable combinational logic, a flip-flop or latch, and some fast carry logic to

Fig. 1 Internal architecture of FPGA [12]

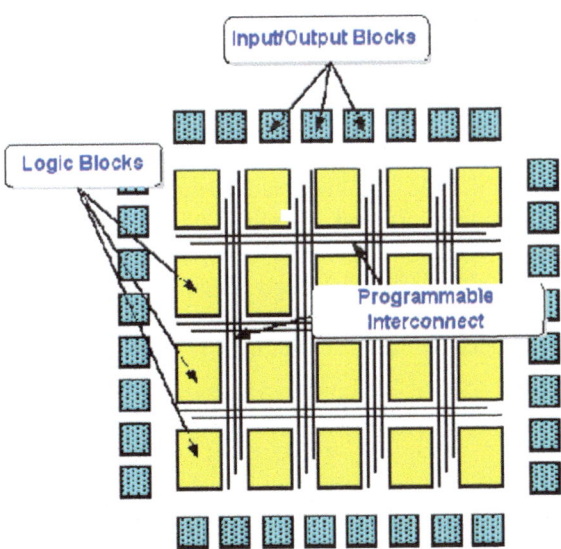

reduce area and delay cost to it could be entire processor. In many of the modern FPGAs, a heterogeneous mixture of different blocks is used which can only be used for specific functions like dedicated memory blocks, multipliers or multiplexers.

The programmable interconnects in an FPGA provide connections among configurable logic blocks and I/O blocks to complete a user-defined design. It consists of multiplexers, pass transistors, and tristate buffers, which forms the desired connection.

The I/O blocks are used as the medium to interface the configurable logic blocks and the programmable interconnects to the external components. The I/O pad and surrounding logic circuitry forming an I/O cell. These cells are important components of an FPGA and consume a significant portion of FPGAs area (approximately 40%).

2.2 FPGA Design Flow

First of all design entry is done by adding files to the project and the User Constraint File (UCF) as well. Design entry includes assignment of constraints such as area constraint, pin constraint. After the design entry is done, flow is transferred to the functional verification in which the Register Transfer Level (RTL) simulation is run and then design is synthesized to implement it. The design implementation includes translate, map and place and route processes. After the success of all of the three parts (design entry, design synthesis, and design implementation), the FPGA device is programmed by first generating a BIT file which programs the FPGA then creating a JTAG file to be used by the iMPACT that programs the FPGA through the programming cable (Fig. 2).

3 Advantages of FPGA

The major advantage of FPGA's over the microcontroller and microprocessor is that FPGA's have pipelined architecture which improves its versatility over the microprocessors and microcontrollers which have sequential approach. Other advantages of FPGA's are that these are reprogrammable and reconfigurable approaches. The time delay is an important factor in different applications of modern power system schemes such as relays, energy meters, and PMU. Reduced time delay is obtained with the FPGA due to its pipelined architecture.

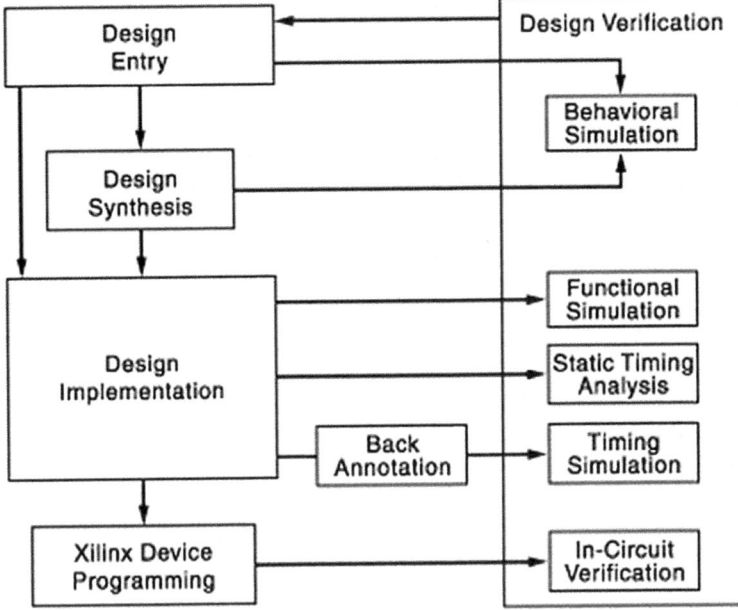

Fig. 2 FPGA design flow [13]

4 Implementation Details

FPGA-based various modules have been implemented for digital energy meter which can further be used in the field of modern power system schemes such as relays and PMU.

4.1 ADC Module

All of the FPGA chips work on digital data. This module is designed to change analog signal into digital signal. ADC modules start converting when chip select is activated and start of conversion of signal and conversion completes at the end of conversion. A 12-bit dual-channel analog to digital converter AD7476A is used [14]. The ADC7476A uses advanced design techniques to achieve very low power dissipation at high throughput rates.

4.2 Zero Crossing Detector

This module is used to calculate the phase, time period, and frequency of given signals. Phase is calculated by finding difference between zero crossing of voltage and current. Frequency and time period are calculated by finding difference between two consecutive zero crossings of given signal.

4.3 Counter Module

Different modules are working with different time delays. This module creates different delays for creating different clocks for ADC, IP cores, and communication modules. This module counts and collects samples from zero crossing.

4.4 Peak Detector

To measure different types of electrical quantity, it is necessary to find maximum voltage and current. Thus, a peak detector can be used for determining peak value of these signals by comparing present samples from ADC to previous sample of ADC. This module is not developed only for electrical measurements, but it can also be used in automatic application like air conditioners, water level detectors with the help of transducers with FPGA.

4.5 Float to ASCII Conversion

To communicate the data, at some other places, it is converted into ASCII format. After processing different modules, result may be transferred to different places. In this module, the floating data format is converted in ASCII form and then it can easily be communicated to LCD and also to hyper-terminal.

4.6 Communication Module

Hyper-terminal is used to display the results in ASCII format with help of serial communication Universal Asynchronous Receiver and Transmitter (UART) interface. Results are communicated by sending start bit, data bits, and stop bits. Different baud rate can be selected for communicating data with the help of clock divider circuits which generates different clock frequencies. This can be achieved by different delays in clock divider circuits. Different parameters of digital energy meter such as VMAX, IMAX, and angle (in degrees) have been communicated on hyper-terminal.

5 IP Cores

Handling of floating-point numbers is a difficult task in FPGA. Xilinx provides facility of IP cores to deal or computation of floating-point numbers for different conversion, arithmetic operation, trigonometric functions, comparator, communication (ethernet, wireless), etc. The various IP cores used for implementing different FPGA modules are as follows.

5.1 Floating-Point Core

Floating-Point IP cores are used for different arithmetic operations, viz., multiply, divide, float to fixed conversion, fixed to float conversion, float to float conversion, addition, subtraction, square root, and compare.

(1) *Fixed to Float Conversion*

Input for this core is fixed-point number, and output is floating-point number. Different custom sizes for inputs and outputs are considered. The binary representation of a fixed-point number contains three fields, viz., sign, integer, and fraction as shown in Fig. (3).

The binary representation of a floating-point number contains three fields, viz., sign, exponent, and fraction as shown in Fig. (4).

(2) *Float to Fixed conversion*

Input for this core is floating-point number, and output is fixed-point number.

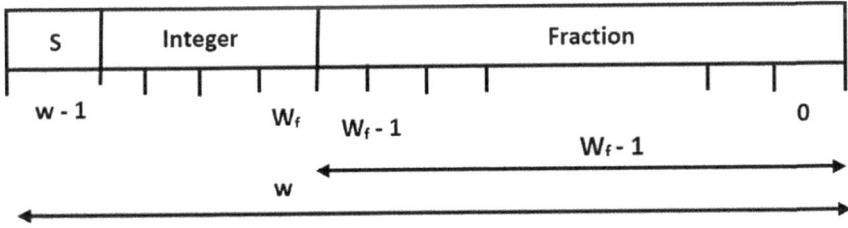

Fig. 3 Fixed-point number representation

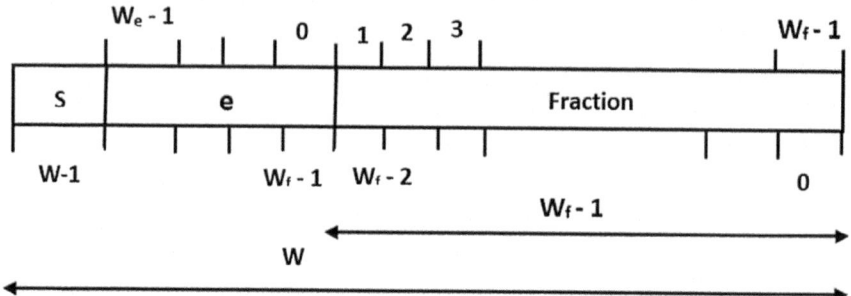

Fig. 4 Floating-point number representation

(3) *Multiply and Divide*

Two floating-point numbers can be multiplied and divided with the help of this core.

5.2 CORDIC

This IP core implements a generalized Co-Ordinate Rotational Digital Computer (CORDIC) algorithm [15]. Functions performed by this core are vector rotation (polar to rectangular), vector translation (rectangular to polar), Sin, Cos, Sinh, Cosh, ATan, Atanh, and square root. Sin and Cos values of angles are used for measurement of different powers and can be used to implement different power system schemes such as different relay, energy meters, and PMU. When the Sin or Cos functional configuration is selected, the unit vector is rotated, using the CORDIC algorithm, by input angle. It generates the output vector (Cos, Sin). The input/output width is set to 10 bits.

6   Test Results

Peak voltage of the signal is calculated by peak detector module and communicated to hyper-terminal with RS232 interface. Table 1 shows the percent error between actual maximum voltage and measured maximum voltage.

Figure 5 shows the graphical representation for Table 1.

Peak current of the signal is calculated by peak detector module and communicated to hyper-terminal with RS232 interface. Table 2 shows the percent error between actual maximum current and measured maximum current.

Similar to the voltage graph in Figs. 5 and 6 shows graphical representation of Table 2.

Table 1 Percent error in voltage

S. No.	Actual voltage (max) (in volts)	Measured voltage (max) (in volts)	Error (in percent)
1	0.75	0.73	2.66
2	1.15	1.12	2.61
3	1.47	1.46	0.68
4	1.86	1.85	0.54
5	1.94	1.90	2.06
6	2.26	2.24	0.88
7	2.60	2.58	0.77
8	2.72	2.73	0.37
9	3.00	3.02	0.67
10	3.04	3.07	0.99

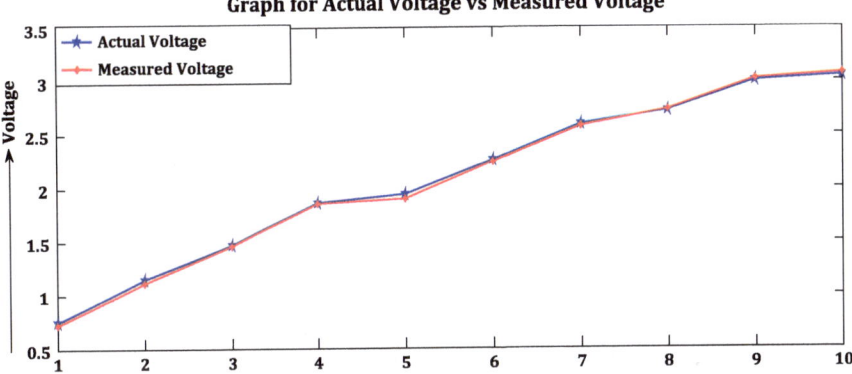

Fig. 5 Actual voltage and measured voltage (calculated on GENESYS XILINX VIRTEX 5 XC5VLX50T FPGA board)

Table 2 Percent error in current

S. No.	Actual current (max) (in Amp.)	Measured current (max) (in Amp.)	Error (in percent)
1	0.70	0.68	2.86
2	1.06	1.07	0.94
3	1.39	1.36	2.16
4	1.76	1.73	1.70
5	1.84	1.80	2.17
6	2.12	2.10	0.94
7	2.46	2.44	0.81
8	2.56	2.58	0.78
9.	2.84	2.83	0.35
10.	2.88	2.88	0

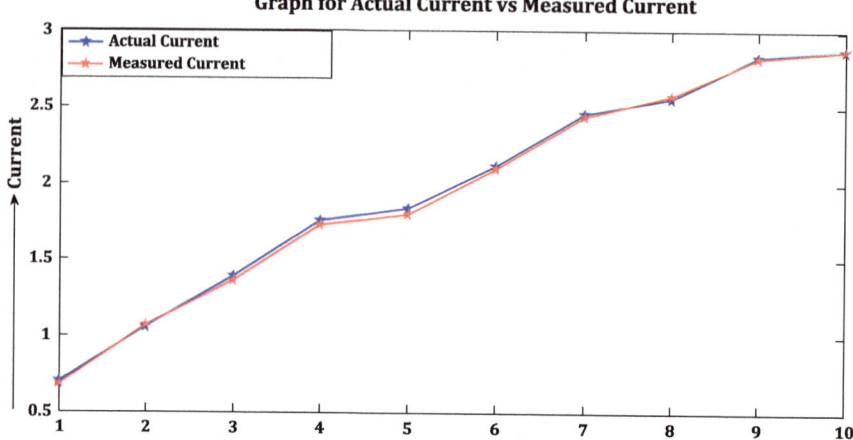

Fig. 6 Actual current and measured current (calculated on GENESYS XILINX VIRTEX 5 XC5VLX50T FPGA board)

Angle between voltage and current is calculated by counting samples between voltage and current zero crossing with the help of zero crossing detector and counter module. Angle is also communicated to hyper-terminal with RS232 interface. Table 3 shows percent error between actual angle and measured angle. After calculating angle CORDIC IP core is used to measure different operations on these angles.

Figure 7 shows measured maximum voltage (VMAX), measured maximum current (IMAX), and measured angle [ANGLE (dG)] communicated serially to hyper-terminal at a baud rate of 38,400 with UART interface.

This paper presents FPGA-based concurrent architecture modules, viz., sense, process, and communication cycles for implementing Digital Energy Meter. Table 4 shows the different parameters/modules in different pipelines along with time delay in the pipelines. Clock divider circuit is implemented on FPGA for generation of different clocks in sense and communication cycles, whereas process cycle works on system clock. Delay for generation of different clocks is summarized in Table 4.

Table 3 Percent error in angle

S. No.	Count between zero crossing of voltage and current	Actual angle (in degree)	Measured angle (in degree)	Error (in percent)
1	12	17	16.83	1
2	22	30	30.89	2.97
3	32	45	44.92	0.18
4	42	60	58.95	1.75
5	53	75	73.04	2.61
6	64	90	89.12	0.98

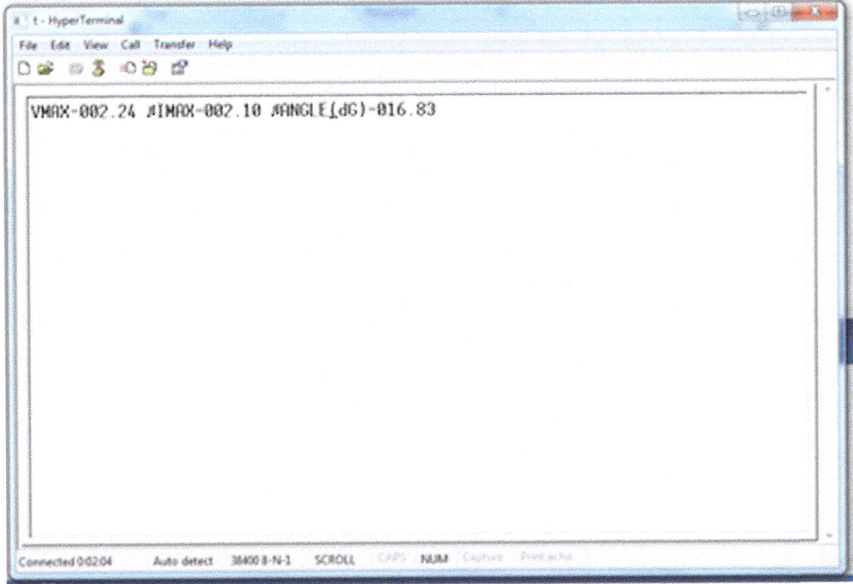

Fig. 7 Results communicated to hyper-terminal

Table 4 Table for parameters and time delays in different pipelines

Attributes	Sense	Process	Communication
Parameters/ modules	ADC module, peak detector, and ZCD for voltage and current samples	Voltage (VMAX), current (IMAX), angle and float to ASCII module	VMAX, IMAX, angle (degree) on hyper-terminal
Clock generation delay	186	(no delay as it works on system clock)	1302
Time delay	9.99 ms	1.23 µs	9.37 ms

Table 4 shows the time delays and different modules in different FPGA-based pipelines. The three pipelines, viz., sense, process, and communication, are working concurrently. Thus, it is observed that the FPGA-based modules consume a total time of 9.99 ms which is the maximum time taken by the FPGA modules in concurrent architecture, viz., in the sense cycle. On the contrary, comparing the microcontroller-/microprocessor-based modules, the total time consumed will be the sum of the total time consumed during sense, process, and the communication cycles, i.e. 19.36 ms, as different modules work sequentially. Therefore, total 51.6% time is reduced in FPGA-based concurrent architecture as compared to microprocessor/microcontroller-based sequential architecture.

Table 5 Device utilization summary of the proposed modules

S. No.	XILINX VIRTEX 5	Used	Total available	Utilization (in percent)
1	BUGs	3	32	9.37
2	External IOBs	15	480	3.12
3	LOCed IOBs	15	15	100
4	Logic	7168	28,800	24.89
5	Memory	408	7680	5.31
6	Slices	2770	7200	38.47
7	Slice registers	6985	28,800	24.25
8	Flip-flops	6985	–	
9	Bonded IOBs	15	480	3.12

Table 4 represents FPGA based sense and communicate cycles consume time delay in msec whereas process cycle consumes total delay in μsec therefore additional functionality viz. PMU's (Phasor measurement Units), Measurement of different powers i.e. true power, apparent power and reactive power, different relays and other function of the modern power system schemes can be added in the process cycle.

Different FPGA modules are implemented on GENESYS XILINX VIRTEX 5 XC5VLX50T FPGA Board. ISE 14.1 software is used for VHDL programming. Table 5 shows the device utilization summary of the proposed modules.

7 Conclusion

Microprocessors and microcontrollers are the first preference of professionals in the field of designing Digital Energy Meters. However, these devices have a drawback of time delay due to their sequential approach. This paper demonstrates implementation of different types of FPGA modules for implementing Digital Energy Meter. These modules also work together in pipelined architecture for different applications of modern power system schemes. The aim of implementing different modules is to reduce the time delay factor to improve functionality of the Digital Energy Meter efficiently and effectively. Different FPGA modules are implemented with the help of different IP cores. Test results are communicated serially to the hyper-terminal at baud rate of 38,400 with UART interface. Test results show that the maximum error is less than 3% which shows that the proposed modules are highly efficient and consistent in developing any power system schemes. Therefore, the proposed FPGA based concurrent architecture reduces total time delay 51.6% as compared to microprocessor/microcontroller based modules and additional functionality such as calculation of different powers i.e. true power, apparent power and reactive power, PMU's, relays etc. can be added in process cycle to make it more versatile. Therefore, proposed concurrent architecture-based modules are an alternative for replacement of microprocessor and microcontroller based modules which are having their sequential approach. The proposed modules and IP cores can be used to implement various kinds of modern power system schemes such as relays and PMU's.

Acknowledgements Authors gratefully thank Dr. M. K. Rawat (Principal, Faculty of Engineering and Technology (F.E.T), Agra College, Agra); Dr. R. K. Srivastava (Convener F.E.T), Agra College; Dr. V. K. Jain, (Dept. of Physics, F.E.T, Agra College, Agra); Er. Amit Srivastava, (Department of Electronics and Communication, F.E.T, Agra College, Agra); and Er. Amit Bhatnagar, (Department of Mathematics, F.E.T, Agra College, Agra) for their support and precious guidance. Authors are also thankful to the technical assistant Mr. Praveen Sharma for his valuable help.

References

1. Lai, M.-F., Wu, Y.-P., Hsieh, G.C., Lin, J.-L.: Design and implementation of a microprocessor- based intelligent electronic meter. In: IEEE Conference on Industrial Technology, pp. 268–272 (1994)
2. Zaidi, S.K.A., Masroor, H., Ashraf, S.R., Hassan, A.: Design and implementation of low cost electronic prepaid energy meter. In: IEEE Conference on INMIC, pp 548–552 (2008)
3. Vichitchot, M., Ghandakly, A.A.: Microcontroller based impedance relay. In: Industrial Applications Society Annual Meeting. pp. 1795–1801 (1991)
4. Sindhu, T.S., Sachdev, M.S., Wood, H.C.: Design of a microprocessor based overcurrent relay. In: IEEE Conference on Computer, Power and Communications System in Rural Environment, pp. 41–46 (1991)
5. Manzoul, M.A.: Interrupt-driven microprocessor-based overcurrent relay. IEEE Trans. Ind. Electron. **38**(1), 8–9 (1991)
6. Manzoul, M.A.: Multiple overcurrent relays using a single microprocessor. IEEE Trans. Ind. Electron. **37**(40), 307–309 (1990)
7. Fadal, F., Krahe, R.: Microprocessor based inverse time multiple overcurrent relays. Electr. Power Syst. Res. **35**(3), 207–211 (1995)
8. Li, J., Xie, X., Xiao J., Wu, J.: The framework and algorithm of a new phasor measurement unit. In: IEEE International Conference on Elecric Utility Deregulation, Restructuring and Power Technologies (DRPT 2004), vol. 2, pp. 826–83 (2004)
9. Ouadi, A., Bentarzi, H., Maun, J.C.: A new computer based phasor measurement framework. In: IEEE 6th International Conference on Systems, Signals and Devices (SSD'09), pp. 1–6 (2009)
10. Maheshwari, V., Devulapalli, B.D., Saxena, A.K.: FPGA-based digital overcurrent relay with concurrent sense-process-communicate cycles. Int. J. Electr. Power Energy Syst. **55**, 66–73 (2014)
11. Pedroni, V.A.: Circuit design with VHDL. vol. 3, MIT Press, Cambridge, MA, U.S.A (2004)
12. Ahuja, S., Kothari, L., Vishwakarma, D.N., Balasubramanian, S.K.: Field programmable gate arrays based overcurrent relays. Elecric Power Compon. Syst. **32**, 247–255 (2004)
13. [XILINX]: FPGA design flow overview. http://www.xilinx.com/itp/xilinx10/isehelp/ise_c_fpga_design_flow_overview.htm
14. [ANALOG]: Analog to digital converter datasheet. http://www.analog.com/media/en/technical-documentation/data-sheets/AD7476A_7477A_7478A.pdf
15. [XILINX]: Xilinx intellectual property cores. http://www.xilinx.com/products/intellectual-property.html

Design of a Hypothetical Processor Using Re-configurable Logic in VHDL

Ravinder Nath Rajotiya

Abstract The twentieth century was century for inventions, and the field of electronics and computer was at boom. The size of computer drastically reduced to portable size. Lot of automated EDA tools appeared that simplified the design and development efforts of the engineers. Evolution of the re-configurable logic devices, such as PLA, PAL, CPLD, and FPGA, helped the designers to burn the design in programmable chips and get the functionality of the hardware, and allowed to test and verify before the product could be custom designed and mass fabricated. This paper attempts to design an 8-bit processing element that accepts 8-bit data and produce the desired result. The implementation has been done using the Xilinx ISE Web Pack, and simulations are carried out using ISE simulator.

1 Introduction

It is well known that transistor, invented by William Shockley, John Bardeen, and Walter Brattain in 1947, was the best invention of the twentieth century [1]. It permitted the first wave of electronic miniaturization, and it was followed by the invention of ICs in the same century. All this brought down both the weight and size [2] of the systems from room to a table and then from table to our palm.

We have seen the things changing at every level from manual and very tedious design procedures to automated methods with the help of computer-based software approaches. These days various EDA tools are available to engineers. To address

R. N. Rajotiya (✉)
Department of ECE, JIMSEMTC, 48/4 Knowledge Park-III,
Greater Noida 201306, Uttar Pradesh, India
e-mail: ravinder.rajotiya@gmail.com

© Springer Nature Singapore Pte Ltd. 2018
S. K. Muttoo (ed.), *System and Architecture*, Advances in Intelligent Systems
and Computing 732, https://doi.org/10.1007/978-981-10-8533-8_27

the design complexly issue, after the design specifications are complete almost all the other steps are automated using CAD tools [2]. Now, the user has a choice to use either the fixed logic devices such as PLD, CPLDs or re-configurable ICs such as FPGA, MPLDs [3–5]. The choice for selections of a particular IC depends on many factors including market [4, 6] where one type of market eat the market of the other type, other factor being the cost and functionality. Also, it is well evident that the fixed logic ICs functionality remains static during its lifetime, whereas the programmable IC provides dynamic functionality [7, 8] meaning its functionality can be changed by reprogramming it and are the only way to achieve the required, real-time performance without fabricating custom integrated circuits [9]. The top level of any microprocessor system consists of the ports through which it communicates with the real-world environment which may be capturing the data from real world using transducers or device like keyboard and mouse.

The processor consists of pins for interfacing it with power supply, clock source, interrupt request, reset, address, data, and control lines so that it can communicate with the external devices. A processor performs three basic types of functions [1, 2, 10]; internal operations such as arithmetic, logical operation, external (or peripheral)-initiated operations in the form of request from the i/o devices, and microprocessor-initiated operations in the form of fetching instructions and data from memory, reading or writing data to/from memory or i/o devices. To communicate with the devices, the processor identifies the peripheral by generating its address, transfers data to/from the peripheral by generating proper control signals, and finally provides necessary timing and synchronization signals. The basic block diagram of a general-purpose microprocessor is given in Fig. 1. It shows the

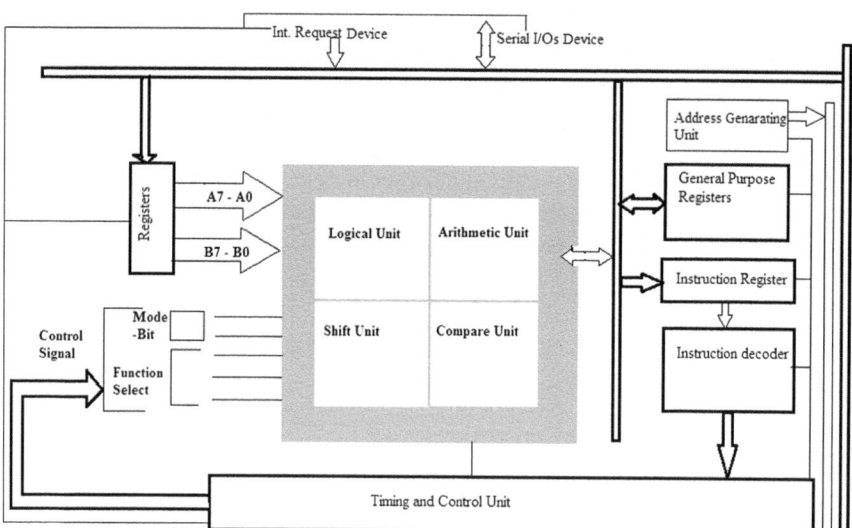

Fig. 1 Block diagram of a general microprocessor

internal architecture [1–3, 5, 10] of a processor consisting of register set, instruction register, instruction decoder, timing and control unit, ALU, address generator and interrupt and serial I/O.

The rest of the paper is organized as follows. Section 2 discusses the design of a hypothetical 8-bit processor and its various components. Section 3 gives the implementation of the various components in Xilinx ISE Web Pack using VHDL [3, 11–13] and the simulations of the components, and finally Sect. 4 concludes the paper.

2 Design of Processor

By definition, a processor is a programmable electronic device that is used to accept data and process it as per the instructions stored in memory and transfers the result to output devices or memory [10]. The hypothetical processor in our design consists of an ALU to operate on the operands, an accumulator used to store one of the operands to be processed by ALU and also to store the partial result and a temporary register, register file containing four general-purpose registers. We have not built the control unit whose purpose to generate the timing and control signals for the instructions read from the memory, instead, the control signals will be assumed to be available in binary format and will be passed to the system manually at the simulation time, the instruction register, its decoding and generation of the control task has not been completed in the present design, and hence the control signals in the form of various signals will be manually provided at runtime (during simulation).

2.1 Arithmetic, Logical, and Shift Unit

The AL&S unit performs the arithmetic ADD, SUB, INC, and the logical operations available are the AND, OR, NOT, NOR, XOR operations. The shifter unit provides operations such as Parallel Load, Shift Left, Shift Right, Rotate Left, Rotate Right, Clear the Register, and Set the Register to all 1s. Figure 2 shows the data path of the arithmetic, logical, and shift unit. Sel_unit signal is used to select

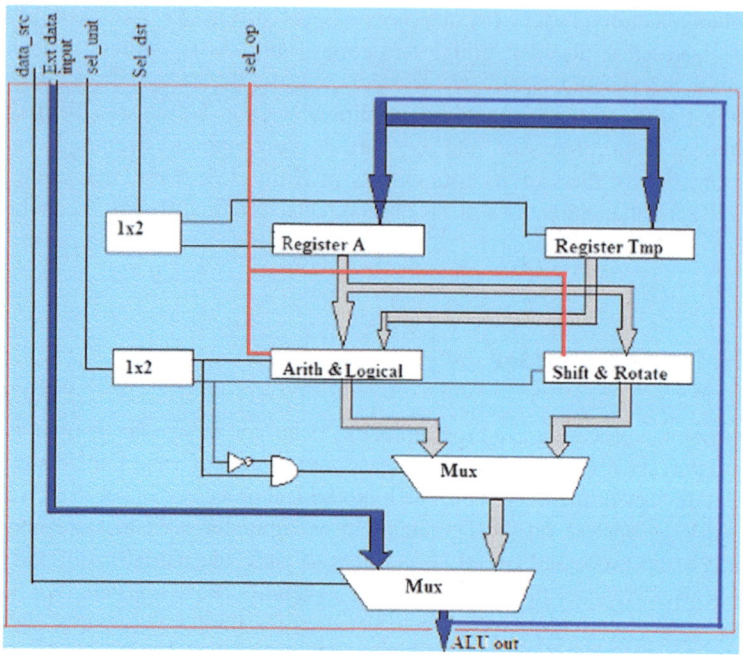

Fig. 2 Data path design of the arithmetic, logical, and shift operations

either the arithmetic unit or the shift unit, and the respective operation in the
selected unit is provided by a three-line sel_op signal.

```
entity arith_new is
   Port ( in_a : in STD_LOGIC_VECTOR (7 downto 0);
        in_b : in STD_LOGIC_VECTOR (7 downto 0);
        res : out STD_LOGIC_VECTOR (7 downto 0);
        sel_op : in STD_LOGIC_VECTOR (2 downto 0);
        sel_unit : in STD_LOGIC);
end arith_new;
architecture Behavioral of arith_new is
begin
process (sel_op,sel_unit, in_a, in_b)
begin
-- ADD, SUB, OR, AND,NOT,XOR,NOR, INC operation definitions
end process;
end Behavioral;
```

Table 1 shows the control signals (Sel_unit and Sel_op) used to select the functional units for performing an operations on the operands (Input_1 and Input-2).

Table 1 Arithmetic and logical operations

Sel_unit	Sel_op	Input-1	Input-2	Result
0	"XXX"	"XXXXXXXX"	"XXXXXXXX"	"ZZZZZZZ"
1	000	In-1	In-2	R ← in-1 + in-2
1	001	In-1	In-2	R ← in-1 − in-2
1	010	In-1	In-2	R ← in-1 OR in-2
1	011	In-1	In-2	R ← in-1 AND in-2
1	100	In-1	In-2	R ← NOT in-1
1	101	In-1	In-2	R ← in-1 XOR in-2
1	110	In-1	In-2	R ← in-1 NOR in-2
1	111	In-1	"XXXXXXXX"	R ← INCREMENT in-1
1	Others	"XXXXXXXX:	"XXXXXXXX"	R ← "ZZZZZZZ"

2.2 Shifter Unit

The purpose of the shifter unit is to perform the logical shift and rotate operations and the various operations are shown in Table 2. The VHDL declaration is given below.

```
entity shift_unit is
PORT ( reset :  IN std_logic;
        clk: IN std_logic;
            data_in : IN std_logic_vector (7 DOWNTO 0);
        sel_unit: std_logic;
            sel_op : IN std_logic_vector (2 DOWNTO 0);
            parout : OUT std_logic_vector (7 DOWNTO 0));
end shift_unit;
architecture Behavioral of shift_unit is
SIGNAL shift_reg : std_logic_vector(7 DOWNTO 0);
   --SIGNAL rot : STD_LOGIC;
begin
PROCESS (clk,reset, sel_op, data_in, shift_reg, sel_unit) BEGIN
if (sel_unit = '0') then
    IF (reset = '1') then
        shift_reg <= (others => '0');
        elsif (clk = '0' AND clk'EVENT) THEN
--LOAD,
SHIFT LT, SHIFT RT, ROTATE LT, ROTATE RT, CLR, SET operation definitions
    end if;
    END PROCESS;
    parout <= shift_reg ;
end Behavioral;
```

Table 2 Shift and rotate operations

Sel_unit	Clock	Sel_op	Input	operation
1	X	XXX	XXXXXXXX	Q ← "UUUUUUUU"
0	1	000	data_in	Q ← data_in
0	1	001	data_in	Q ← SHIFT LT (data_in)
0	1	010	data_in	Q ← SHIFT RT (data_in)
0	1	011	data_in	Q ← ROTATE LT (data_in)
0	1	000	data_in	Q ← ROTATE RT (data_in)
0	1	000	data_in	Q ← CLEAR 'Q' to all 0s
0	1	000	data_in	Q ← SET 'Q' to all 1s

2.3   Register File

The register file provides mechanism for reading and writing operations on various internal registers of the processor. The data path is shown in Fig. 3. The various operations are shown in Table 3, the data path provide for the read write operations on registers, for writing the result to the registers 2-bit sel_dst signal is used for selecting one of the four registers. For reading the register values for performing arithmetic, logical, or shift operations, src_A and src_B are used when RD signal is '0'. The VHDL entity is given in the following code.

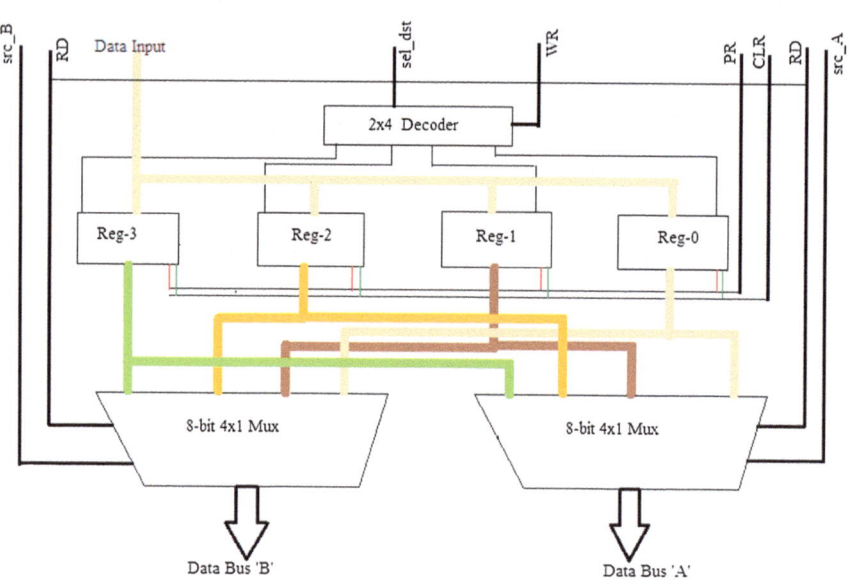

Fig. 3 Register file data path

Table 3 Register file operations

Sel_dst	Src_A	Src_B	Pr	Clr	RD	WR	Operation
00			0	0		1	Reg-0 ← input data
01			0	0		1	Reg-1 ← input data
			0	0		1	Reg-2 ← input data
			0	0		1	Reg-3 ← input data
	00	00	0	0	0		BUS_B ← Reg-0; BUS_A ← Reg-0
	00	01	0	0	0		BUS_B ← Reg-1; BUS_A ← Reg-0
	00	10	0	0	0		BUS_B ← Reg-2; BUS_A ← Reg-0
Different values select different combinations of registers for read–write operations							
	11	11	0	0	0		BUS_B ← Reg-3; BUS_A ← Reg-3

The entity for the register file is written below. It declares various ports through which the register file will communicate with the rest of the circuit.

```
entity Register_File is
Port ( input1 : inout STD_LOGIC_VECTOR (7 downto 0);
    sel_src_1 : in STD_LOGIC_VECTOR (1 downto 0);
    sel_dst, sel_src_2 : in STD_LOGIC_VECTOR (1 downto 0);
    rd, wr, pr, Clr : in STD_LOGIC;
    data_out_A : out STD_LOGIC_VECTOR (7 downto 0);
    data_out_B : out STD_LOGIC_VECTOR (7 downto 0));
end Register_File;
```

3 Simulation

The simulation of various units was carried out under different selection values and is shown in Figs. 4, 5 and 6.

The arithmetic and logical operations "ADD", "SUB", "OR", "AND", "NOT, "XOR", "NOR", and "INC" correspond to sel_op signals 000, 001, 010, 011, 100, 101, 110, 111, and the result is seen to be correct and verified for different inputs. The shift and rotate operations are performed on a single register, and this register will be implied in the instruction and will be the accumulator. The simulation result is shown in Fig. 5.

The operations performed on accumulator are Rotate Rt, Rotate Lt, Load, Shift Lt, Shift Rt, Clear, and Set corresponding to 3-bit sel_op signal values. The simulation result in Fig. 6 shows that the designed unit performs the desired behavior.

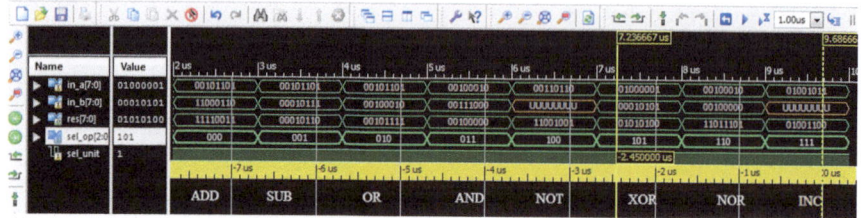

Fig. 4 Simulation of arithmetic, logical unit

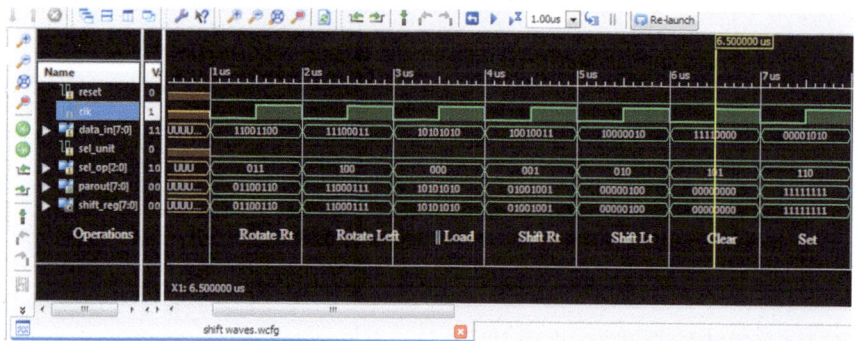

Fig. 5 Simulation of shifter unit

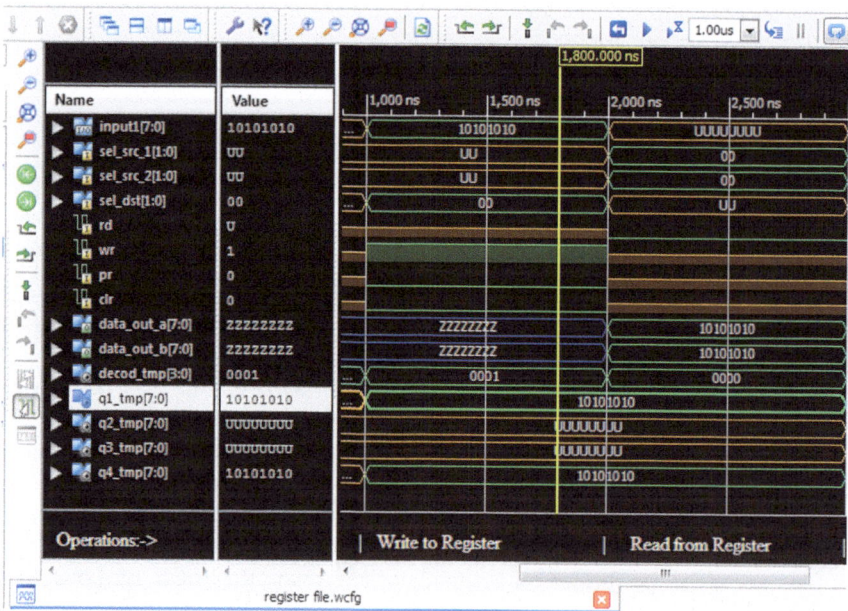

Fig. 6 Simulation of the register file

4 Conclusion

The invention of the transistors and subsequently the different re-configurable chips and the software tools such as HDL (Verilog and VHDL) has simplified the task of the designers to a great extent. Learning the HDL is not a big issue, but the programmer needs to be careful in various declarations and usage. The design of the 8-bit processor in this paper was a challenge to the author and as such has some limitations on its functionality. Some of the limitation as stated in Sects. 1 and 2 is that it is short of two major components, and these are the instruction decoder and the timing and the control unit design. We have decoded the instructions manually and assigned these codes directly to the processing unit. Leaving these the processor behaved as desired and was satisfactory.

References

1. Introduction to digital VLSI design flow. http://nptel.ac.in/courses/106103116/handout/mod1.pdf
2. Gaonkar, R.S.: Microprocessor Architecture, Programming, and Applications with the 8085. Prentice Hall (2002)
3. Mano, M.M, Ciletti, M.D.: Digital Design. Pearson Education (2014)
4. Sabeghi, M., Bertels, K.: Current Trends in Resource Management of Reconfigurable Systems. Computer Engineering Laboratory, Delft University of Technology (2008)
5. Brown, S., Rose, J.: FPGA and CPLD architectures: a tutorial. IEEE Des Test Comput. 0740-7475/96/ © 1996 IEEE
6. The Official Web Site of Nobel Prize. http://www.nobelprize.org/educational/physics/transistor/history/
7. Balaji, E., Krishnamurthy, P.: Modeling ASIC memories in VHDL. LSI Logic Corporation
8. Hauck, S.: The future of reconfigurable systems. In: Keynote Address, 5th Canadian Conference on Field Programmable Devices, Montreal, June 1998
9. Tessier, R., Pocek, K., DeHon, A.: Reconfigurable Computing Architectures. ISSN: 0018-9219. In: IEEE invited paper, Proceedings of the IEEE, vol. 103, No. 3, Mar 2015
10. Brey, B.B.: Intel Microprocessors, Architecture, Programming and Interfacing, 8th edn. Prentice Hall (2008)
11. Bhaskar, J.: A VHDL primer, 3rd edn. Pearson Education (2009)
12. Ercegovac, M., Lang, T., Moreno, J.H.: Introduction to Digital Systems. Wiley, New York (2014)
13. Navabi, Z.: VHDL Modular Design and Synthesis of Cores and Systems, TMH, 3rd edn. (2008)

Aspects Involved in the Modeling of PV System, Comparison of MPPT Schemes, and Study of Different Ambient Conditions Using P&O Method

Mohammed Aslam Husain, Asif Khan, Abu Tariq, Zeeshan Ahmad Khan and Abhinandan Jain

Abstract Discussion of almost all major aspects involved in the study and design of a solar photovoltaic (PV) stand-alone system has been incorporated in this paper. Detailed modeling of a photovoltaic cell and maximum power point tracker in MATLAB/Simulink environment has been shown. Initially, the precise model of a solar cell is made in Simulink, and then, how a solar module, array, and panel are obtained using that cell is shown clearly. All the existing methods for maximum power point method of solar PV power have been tabulated, and a comparative table is included in this article. Finally, a detailed study of the PV system with perturbation and observation MPPT method has been done.

Keywords SPV array · Insolation · MPPT · P&O · MATLAB simulation

1 Introduction

With the rising call on electrical power, the inadequate storage, and growing rates of conventional sources, a hopeful substitute is photovoltaic (PV) energy, which is becoming viable universally because of its free availability and least pollution concerns. The elementary device of SPV system is solar PV cell. Many SPV cells are grouped together to form modules. SPV array may be either a module or a group of modules arranged in series and parallel configurations. The output of SPV system may be directly fed to the loads or may use a power electronic converter to

M. A. Husain (✉)
Department of Electrical Engineering, REC, Ambedkar Nagar, India
e-mail: mahusain87@gmail.com

A. Khan
Department of Electrical Engineering, Aligarh Muslim University (AMU), Aligarh, India

A. Tariq · Z. A. Khan
University of Electronic Science and Technology of China, Chengdu, China

A. Jain
Department of Electronics Engineering, Aligarh Muslim University (AMU), Aligarh, India

© Springer Nature Singapore Pte Ltd. 2018
S. K. Muttoo (ed.), *System and Architecture*, Advances in Intelligent Systems and Computing 732, https://doi.org/10.1007/978-981-10-8533-8_28

285

process it. To study the converters and other connected performances, it is necessary to properly model the SPV systems [1]. An effective maximum power point tracking (MPPT) procedure is essential which is likely to follow MPP during various conditions of the environment and then compel the PV system to work near or at maximum power. It is a vital part of PV systems. Numerous techniques of MPPT along with their comparison are stated in this work.

The main task of this paper is to make aware of the basics required for the study of solar PV system. For this purpose, starting with the development of simulation model of SPV cell, module, and array to replicate/match the characteristics with those of existing SPV systems, selection of proper converter and proper MPPT scheme has been discussed in detail. Various curves of developed models have been shown for changed atmospheric conditions. This article presents in detail all the equations that are used for modeling and study almost all elements involved in a solar PV system. The main objective of this article is to offer the reader with all needed material, data, and equations to make photovoltaic models, converter, and MPPT scheme that can be used in the simulation and implementation of the hardware circuitry.

2 Mathematical Model of Photovoltaic Cell

2.1 Photovoltaic Cell

The elementary equation from the principle of semiconductors [2–6] that scientifically defines the I–V characteristic of the ideal photovoltaic cell is:

$$I_C = I_{Ph} - I_0 \left(e^{\frac{qV_C}{kT_C}} - 1 \right) \tag{1}$$

where I_{ph} is the short-circuit current that is equal to the current due to the photons.

$$I_d = I_0 \left(e^{\frac{qV_d}{kT_C}} - 1 \right) \tag{2}$$

I_d is the diode current which can be obtained using Shockley's diode equation (2); k represents Boltzmann constant, voltage drop across the diode is given by V_d, I_0 is reverse saturation current, T_C is reference temperature of the PV cell (25 °C), and q represents electron charge. Figures 1, 2, and 3 represent the basic diagrams related to PV cell.

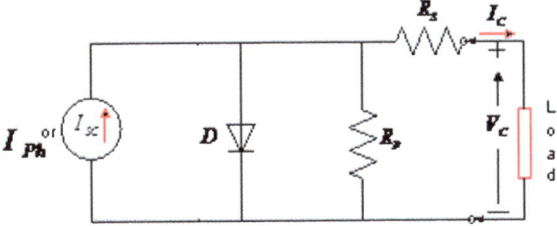

Fig. 1 One-diode model of the theoretical PV cell

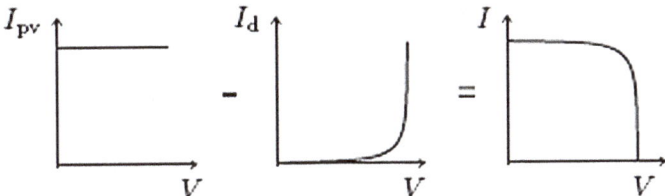

Fig. 2 Establishment of *I–V* curve of the cell

Fig. 3 A typical, current–voltage, *I–V,* curve for a solar cell for different loads and the three *remarkable points*: short circuit (0, I_{sc}), maximum power point (V_{max}, I_{max}), and open circuit (V_{oc}, 0)

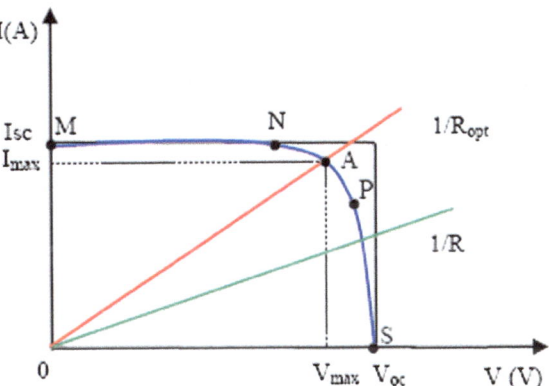

2.2 Modeling the Photovoltaic Array

Additional parameters are incorporated in the basic equations for obtaining proper characteristic of a practical PV array as it is composed of numerous linked PV cells [2].

Though, even when small load *R* is there, the operating zone of the cell is in *M-N* of the curve in Fig. 3, here the PV source behaves as a constant current source with a value of short-circuit current nearly. Else, for large values of *R*, the operating region is P-S and the PV source acts as a constant voltage source with a value of nearly open-circuit voltage.

Overall cell current (I) includes both I_{pv} and I_d, i.e., light-produced current and diode current, respectively.

$$I_C = I_{ph} - I_0 \left[e^{q\left(\frac{V_C + I_C R_S}{AKT_C}\right)} - 1 \right] - \left(\frac{V_C + I_C R_S}{R_P}\right) \tag{3}$$

where I_{ph} is the PV array current, I_0 is saturation current, $V_t = N_s\, k\, T/q$ is the thermal voltage of the array, N_s = number of series-connected cells, R_s = equivalent series resistance of the array, and R_p = Equivalent parallel resistance.

This equation invents the I–V curve shown in Fig. 3. Equation (3) signifies the practical SPV cell. Here, the five parameters are I_{ph}, I_0, V_t, R_S, and R_P. This equation can also be used to represent a series-/parallel-connected module by suitably modifying its parameters [1, 4, 5, 7].

Figure 1 is the representation of Eq. (3) used to define the single-diode PV model. Several authors have projected more refined prototypes that give improved accuracy. As a case in [7–10], the authors have used an additional diode signifying the carrier's recombination effect. Similarly in [9–11], additional two diodes were used and much better results were obtained. In this paper, simple single-diode model is used for the study, as this scheme provides a good settlement concerning accuracy and simplicity [1, 12–14].

Details provided by the manufacturers are not sufficient, and the data required for tuning of the model of PV array are not there. Data like reverse saturation current, ideality factor, shunt and series resistances are not provided. I–V curve provided by some manufacturers makes the validation and adjustment of the model possible.

Any electrical power source can be either current source or voltage source, but PV cell is a hybrid of both. Datasheets give the value of nominal short-circuit current (I_{sc}, n) and it is the full current obtainable by the practical device. The supposition $I_{sc} \approx I_{pv}$ is used in PV simulations as the real devices have a low value of series resistance and a high value of parallel resistance. There is linear dependence of light-generated current on the solar irradiation, and its value is also dependent on the temperature. This is shown in Eq. (4).

$$I_{pv} = \left(I_{pv,n} + K1\Delta T\right) \tag{4}$$

where $I_{pv,n}$ [A] is the light-generated current at the nominal condition (usually 25 °C and 1000 W/m^2), $T = T - T_{n,G}$ [W/m^2] is the irradiation on the device surface, and G_n is the nominal irradiation.

$$I_0 = \frac{I_{sc,n} + K1\Delta T}{\exp\left(\frac{V_{oc,n} + Kv\Delta T}{aVt}\right) - 1} \tag{5}$$

I_0 is dependent on the saturation current density of the semiconductor (J_0, generally given in [A/cm^2]) and on the effective area of the cells. J_0 depends on several physical factors such as the life span of minority carriers, the diffusion coefficient of electrons, and the intrinsic carrier density [11]. Figures 4, 5, 6, 7, and 8 show the Simulink model of the PV cell and array. The value of the diode constant "a" lies generally between 1 and 1.5, and this selection depends on various factors of the I–V model. Few values of "a" were obtained in [15] using empirical analysis. The value of "a" represents the extent of ideality of diode, and any value in the above range can be selected initially; then, further modified value can be used to improve the model [12]. The curvature of the I–V curve is affected by the value of constant "a". A proper selection of this constant improves the accuracy of the model.

The practical solar PV cells have a series resistance R_{se} and a parallel resistance R_{sh}. R_{se} has greater impact when the operating point is near the voltage source region, and R_{sh} has more effect on the current source region. R_{sh} has a high value and can be neglected as it is in parallel [6, 14, 16, 17]. R_{se} has a very low value, and

$$L_m = \frac{(1 - D^2)DR}{2f}$$

Fig. 4 Mathematical modeling implementation for I_o

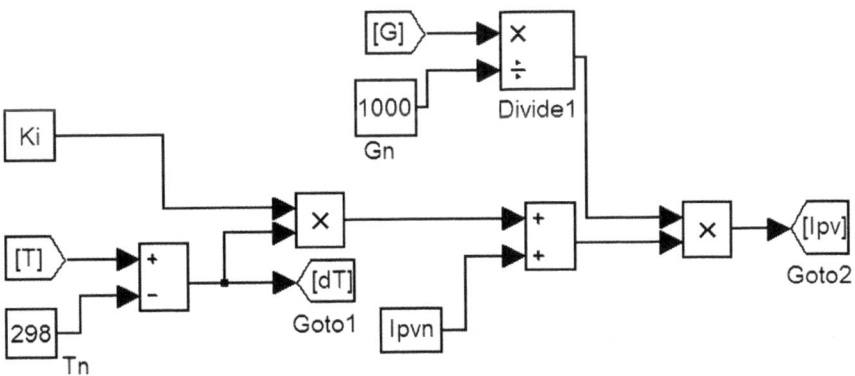

Fig. 5 Mathematical modeling implementation for I_{pv}

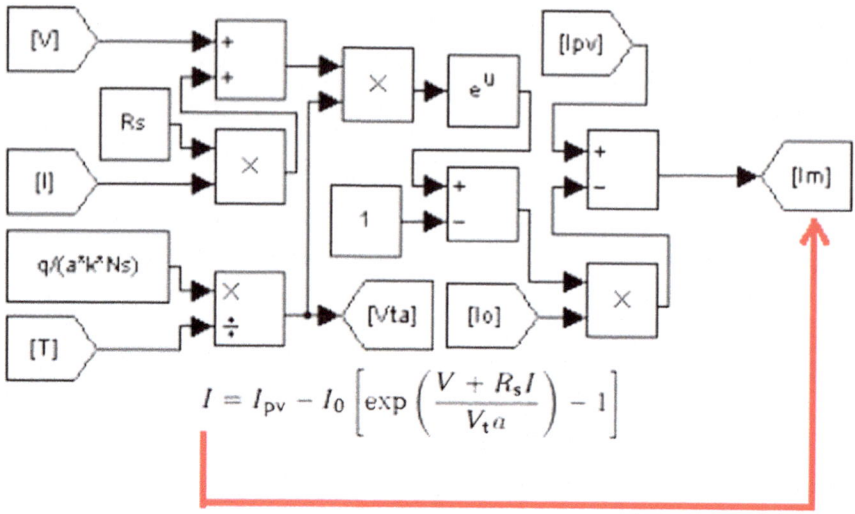

Fig. 6 Mathematical modeling implementation for model current I_m

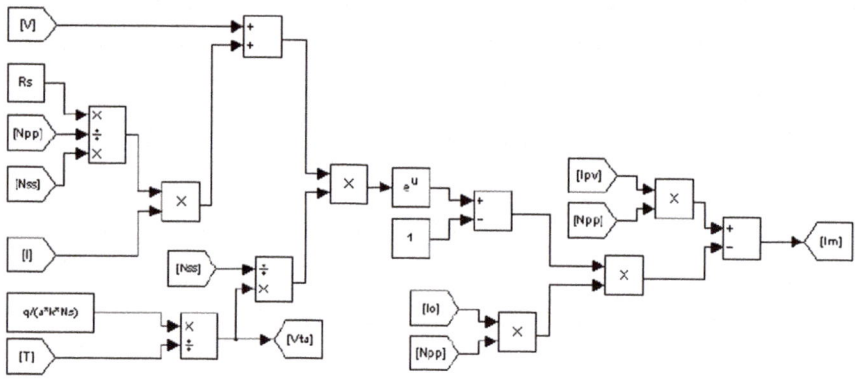

Fig. 7 PV array modeling

sometimes it can also be neglected [16, 18]. The value of R_se can be obtained using the V–I characteristics. Equation (6) can be used to obtain the value of R_sh. This equation is obtained experimentally and by curve fitting technique.

$$R_\mathrm{SH} = 3.6/(G - 0.086) \qquad (6)$$

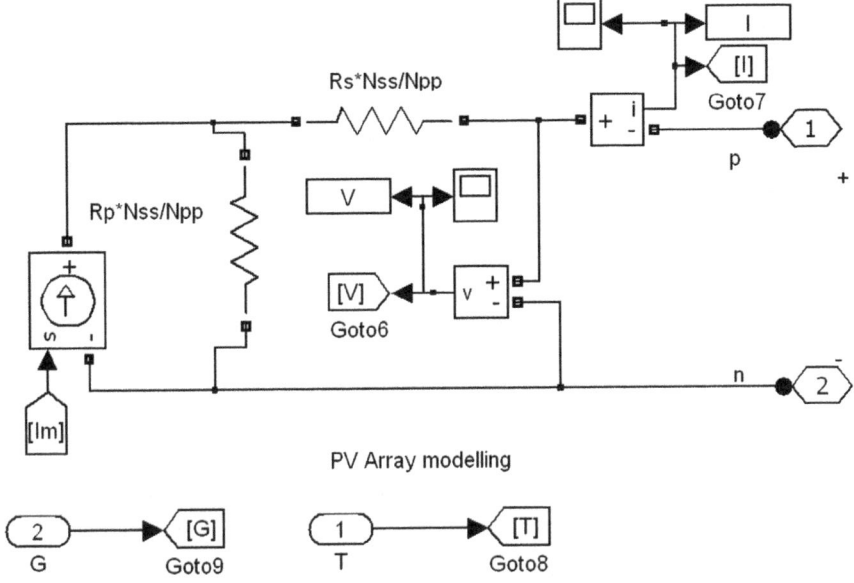

Fig. 8 Circuitry design for PV array

3 Maximum Power Point Tracking and Converters Used in PV System

3.1 Need of MPPT and Converters

Many procedures have been suggested for finding MPP. The purpose of any procedure is to govern the duty ratio (D) of the converter used in such a style that the load seen by the PV array corresponds with a load against the maximum power that can be obtained from the panel. For this purpose, a DC–DC converter is mainly used. Various converters used are given in Table 1 [19].

Figure 9 shows the schematic diagram of a PV system with DC–DC converter [20–22]. R_{in} is the input resistance of the converter, and R_0 is the output resistance or load resistance. In Fig. 10, the approximate range of R_{in} for different DC–DC converters have been shown; depending upon the value of R_0, the correct choice of converter can be made [21–23].

3.2 MPPT Schemes and Their Comparison

Various MPPT schemes used in PV system and their comparison have been shown in Table 2. Direct control strategies do not use any prior information of the PV

Table 1 Various converters used in PV system

Buck converter	Boost converter
Buck–boost converter	Boost–buck Converter
Cuk converter	SEPIC converter
ZETA converter	Canonical switching cell converter
Flyback converter	Interleaved dual boost converter
Interleaved zero current switching boost converter	Interleaved zero–voltage switch boost converter
Interleaved soft switching boost converter	Interleaved flyback converters

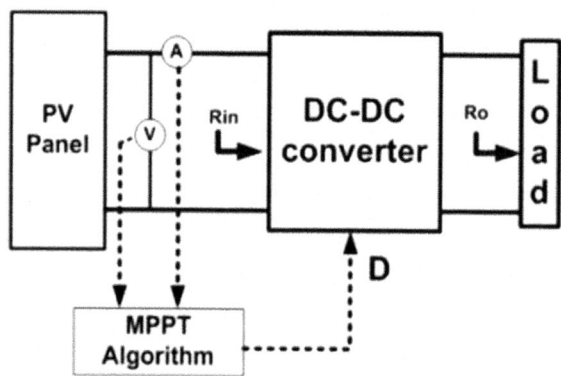

Fig. 9 Complete PV system representation

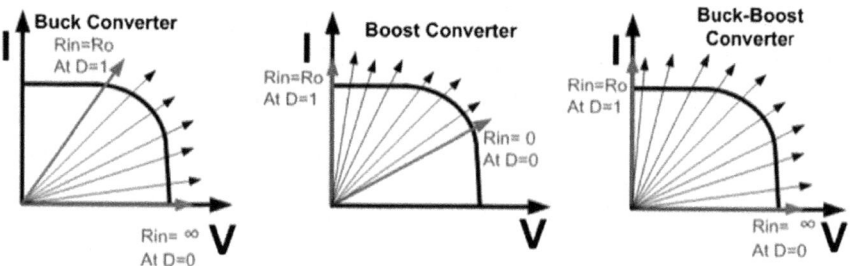

Fig. 10 Range of R_{in}

panel characteristics and directly seek MPP by sensing the variations of the PV panel operating points [24], whereas indirect control uses prior records that consist of information such as the PV panel I–V characteristic for different operating conditions. In case of probabilistic control, information based on probabilistic study is used. Complexity includes the algorithm and hardware implementation/circuit complexity. True MPP should be tracked in case of multiple peaks during partial

Table 2 Comparison of various MPPT schemes

MPPT	Control strategy	Circuit used	Complexity	True MPPT	Sensors	Cost	Accuracy/efficiency	Speed
Fractional short-circuit current	Indirect	Both	Medium	No	Current	Cheap	Low	Medium
Fractional open-circuit voltage	Indirect	Both	Simple	No	Voltage	Cheap	Low	Medium
Perturbation and observation method/hill climbing method	Sampling	Both	Simple	Yes	Current, voltage	Expensive	Medium	Varies
Incremental conductance method	Sampling	Digital	Medium	Yes	Current, voltage	Expensive	Medium	Varies
Array reconfiguration	Indirect	Digital	Complex	Yes	Current, voltage	Expensive	Varies	Slow
Steepest descent method	Sampling	Digital	Medium	Yes	Voltage or current	Expensive	High	Medium
Fuzzy logic	Probabilistic	Digital	Complex	Yes	Varies	Expensive	Very high	Fast
Neural network	Probabilistic	Digital	Complex	Yes	Varies	Expensive	Very high	Fast
Droop control	Modulation	Both	Simple	No	Voltage	Expensive	Medium	Medium
ASO-based MPPT	Probabilistic	Digital	Complex	Yes	Varies	Expensive	High	Fast
CFA-based MPPT	Probabilistic	Digital	Medium	Yes	Varies	Expensive	High	Fast
Switching ripple correlation control method	Modulation	Analog	Complex	Yes	Current, voltage	Expensive	High	Fast
Genetic algorithm-based MPPT	Probabilistic	Digital	Complex	Yes	Varies	Expensive	High	Fast
Computational/lookup table	Indirect	Digital	Medium	No	Irradiation, Temp.	Cheap	Varies	Fast
Sweep MPPT method	Modulation	Digital	Complex	Yes	Irradiation	Expensive	High	Slow
PSO-based MPPT	Probabilistic	Digital	Medium	Yes	Varies	Expensive	High	Fast

shading, and analog or digital circuit can be used to implement the circuitry of MPPT techniques depending on the skill of user and resources available. Accuracy of a MPPT technique can be analyzed by obtaining the efficiency of the MPPT technique. Efficiency [25, 26] of MPPT is given by Eq. (7)

$$\eta = \frac{\text{Obtained Power}}{V_{mp} I_{mp}} \tag{7}$$

3.3 DC–DC Boost Converter—Designing

The layout of the converter, represented in Fig. 11, comprises of a source V_S (DC), diode D, inductor L, controllable switch S, filter capacitor C, and R as load. Figure 12 shows inductor voltage and current waveform of boost converter in steady state.

As the switch S gets ON, the current through inductor L linearly rises and at the same time capacitor C is supplying the load current and it gets partially discharged. As the switch S gets OFF, the diode D gets forward biased and the inductor L starts supplying the load and also charges the capacitor.

Balance principle of inductor voltage is used to obtain the output voltage in steady state, which yields:

$$V_s \cdot T_{on} + (V_s - V_o) \cdot T_{off} = 0 \tag{8}$$

$$\frac{V_o}{V_s} = \frac{T_{SW}}{T_{off}} = \frac{1}{1 - D} \tag{9}$$

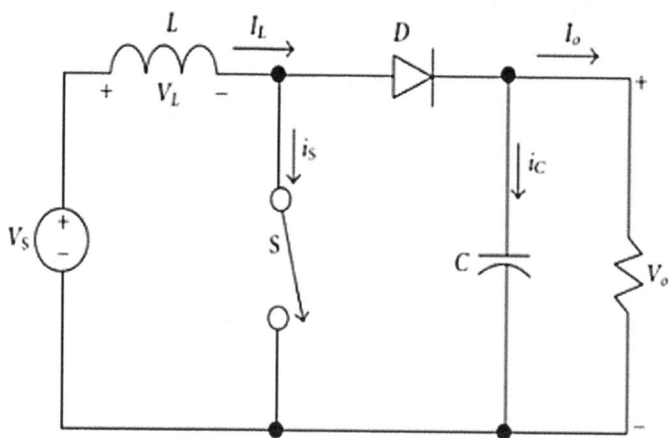

Fig. 11 Converter [boost, DC–DC]

Fig. 12 Steady-state inductor voltage and current waveform of boost converter

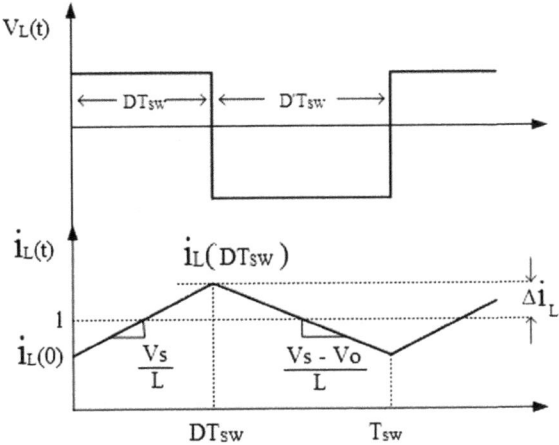

For a particular D (duty), voltage gain of the given can be written as:

$$M_v = \frac{V_o}{V_s} = \frac{1}{1-D} \tag{10}$$

where V_s = input voltage and V_o = output voltage.

The boost converter will operate in the continuous conduction mode if the inductance L has a value greater than L_m where

$$L_m = \frac{(1-D^2)DR}{2f} \tag{11}$$

where L_m = minimum value of L required for continuous conduction.

A large filter capacitor ($>C_{min}$) is required to limit the output voltage ripple due to discontinuous current supplied to the output RC circuit. C_{min} is the minimum value of the filter capacitance required to give the output current to the load when D is OFF, and this is given by Eq. (12).

$$C_{min} = \frac{DV_o}{V_r RF} \tag{12}$$

where V_r = ripple voltage.

4 Perturbation and Observation Technique

Maximum power point depends on the extent of insolation and on the temperature of the PV cell. To attain the desired MPP, a good algorithm is needed, which should be fast, has to be real time, and should adjust MPP with the change in temperature and insolation. Many algorithms for achieving MPP are proposed and are available, but the most operative and mostly used is called the perturbation and observation method [27].

P&O method works by giving a small disturbance by decreasing or increasing the voltage of array and then analyzing the power variation due to the above disturbance. When MPP is achieved, the system voltage oscillates around V_{MPP}. Figure 13 summarizes the P&O method control.

There is power loss associated with the oscillation at MPP, and its value depends on the step change in voltage of the PV panel. The noise level due to switching of the converter can be reduced by increasing the amplitude of the modulating signal, and thus, signal-to-noise ratio improves. But this increases the oscillation at MPP and causes more power loss. The flowchart used for this purpose is given in Fig. 14.

5 Model of Used Flowchart in Simulink

This model is represented in Fig. 15. V_{in} and I_{in} are taken as input for the P&O block, and duty cycle is obtained as the output. P&O block has been taken V and I as an input and then sends it to sample and hold block, which is used as a delay block because in actual measurement, the system has a measurement delay; therefore, it will be used for mentioning this delay. Moreover, at the output of the sample and hold circuit, the present-state voltage signal is $V(n)$. After this step, signal goes to memory block, where hold and delay operation takes place.

Fig. 13 Perturbation and observation (P&O) control action

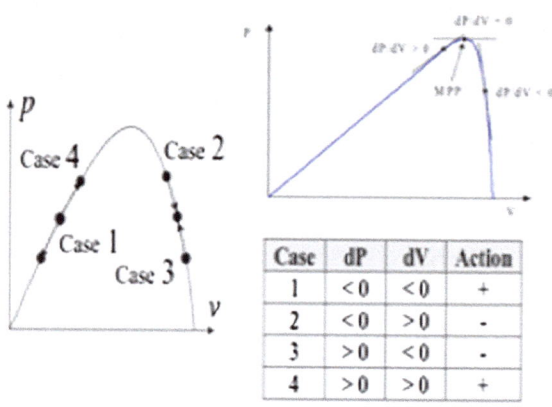

Case	dP	dV	Action
1	<0	<0	+
2	<0	>0	-
3	>0	<0	-
4	>0	>0	+

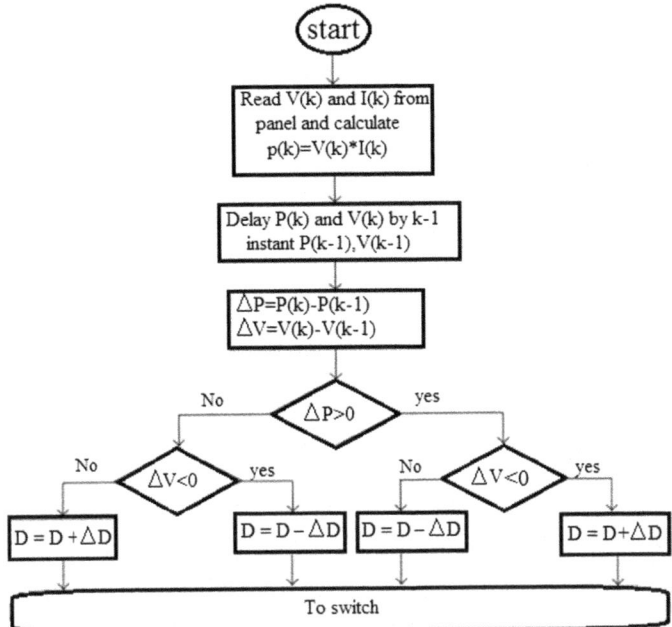

Fig. 14 Flowchart of perturbation and observation

Likewise, the product of V_{in} and I_{in} will be processed to provide p where P_n and P_{n-1} represent power at the current cycle time and power at the pervious cycle time of MPPT, respectively. Subtracting P_n and P_{n-1} is created ΔP, and subtracting V_n and V_{n-1} is created ΔV. In the next step, by using product block and multiplying ΔV and ΔP, if both have a same sign, the output will be positive and if the sign of one of these two signals were negative, the output will be negative. Afterward by the use of switch block, based on input second, it goes over the input one or to the input three. Data inputs are first and third inputs, and control input is the second input. The next step if $\Delta P * \Delta V < 0$ output of the switch will be negative and ΔD will be negative by multiplying the output of switch by a constant value of perturbation step and in the next step value of D will be added to the previous value, which is stored in memory block and will be decreased and vice versa. This new value of D will be sent to the next block for creating PWM signal.

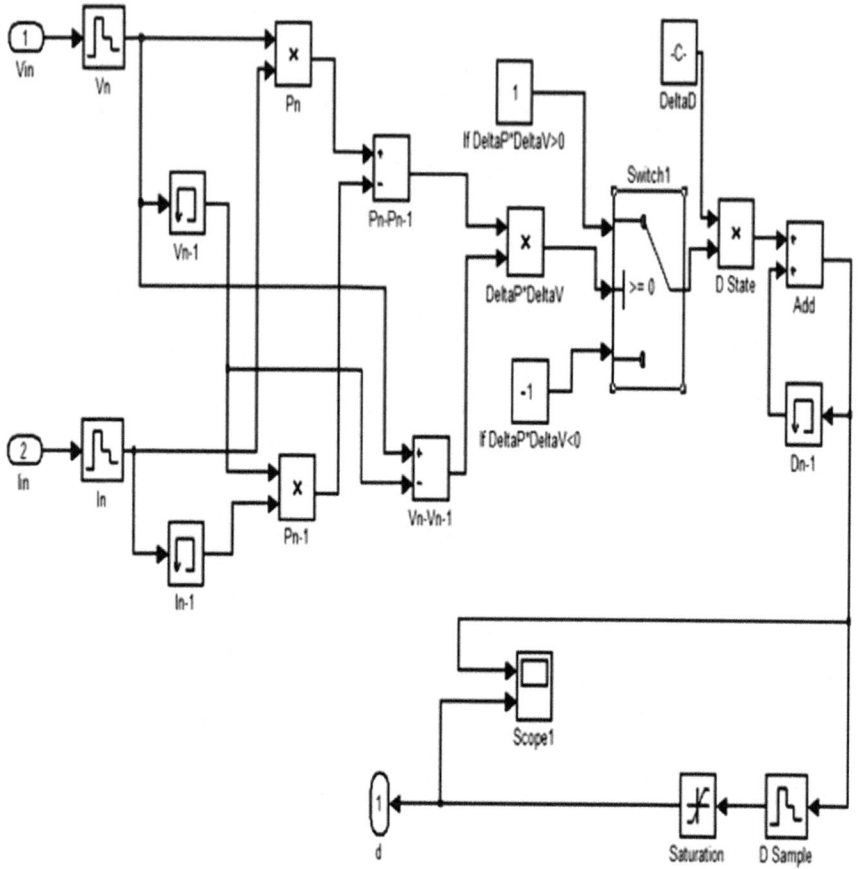

Fig. 15 Simulink model for P&O MPPT algorithm

6 Simulation Result

Different *I–V*, *P–V*, *P–t*, and *V–t* characteristics for varying insolation and temperature have been obtained and shown in Figs. 16, 17, 18 and 19 for the model whose parameters are shown in Table 3.

Figure 20 shows the simulation result of whole PV system incorporating P&O-based MPPT for varying insolation for the model of Table 4. In Fig. 20, at time *t* = 60 s, the insolation changes from 1000 to 500 W/m^2 while the temperature is maintained at 25 °C; simultaneously, the output of panel varies and MPP tracking is achieved.

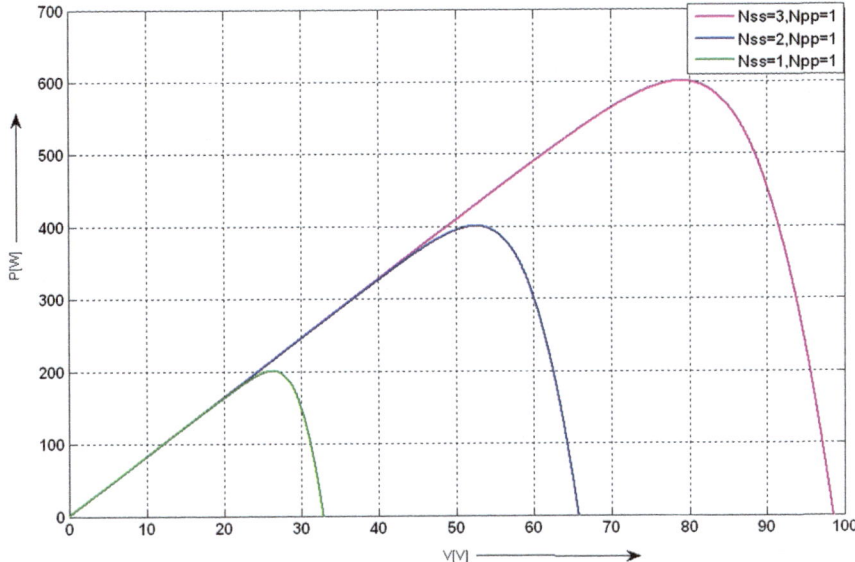

Fig. 16 P–V curve shows the comparison for $N_{ss} = 3$, $N_{pp} = 1$, $N_{ss} = 2$, $N_{pp} = 1$, $N_{ss} = 1$, $N_{pp} = 1$

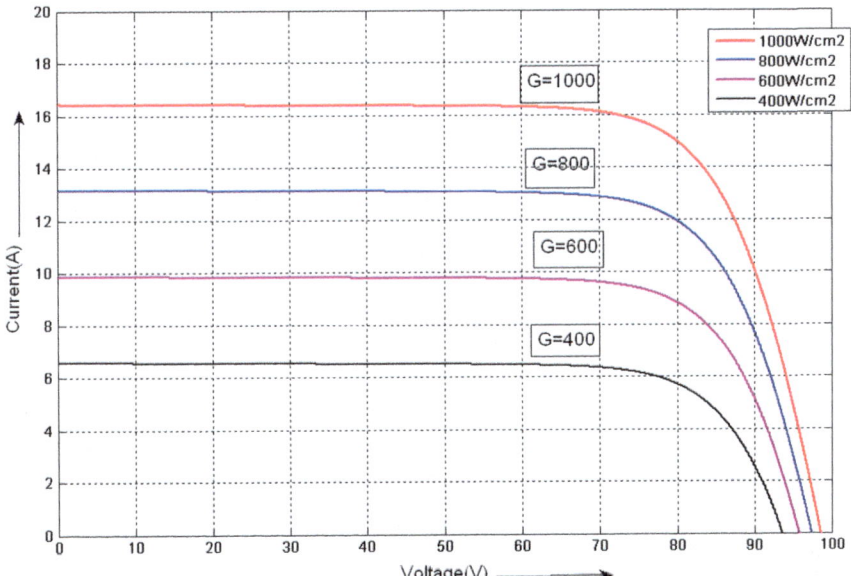

Fig. 17 I–V curve for $N_{ss} = 2$, $N_{pp} = 3$ at different insolation

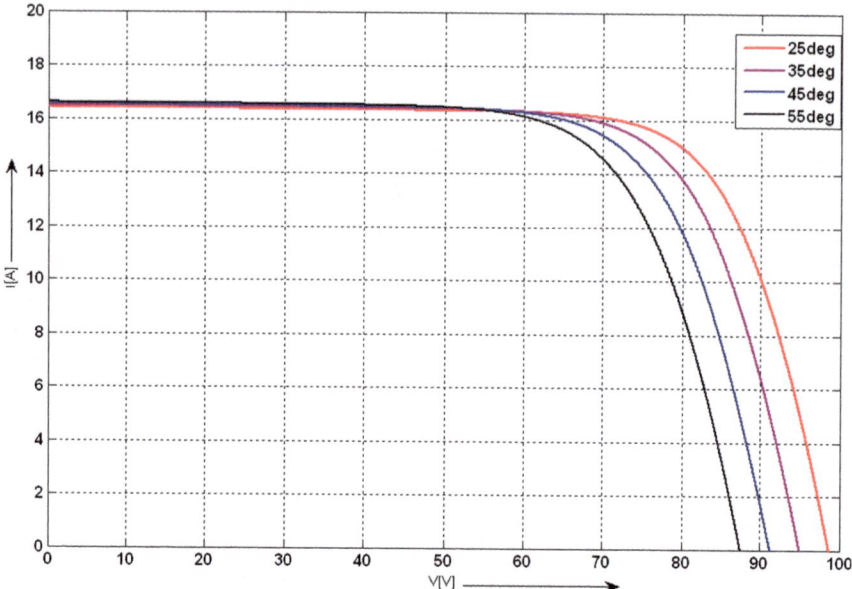

Fig. 18 *I–V* curve for $N_{ss} = 2$, $N_{pp} = 3$ at different temperatures

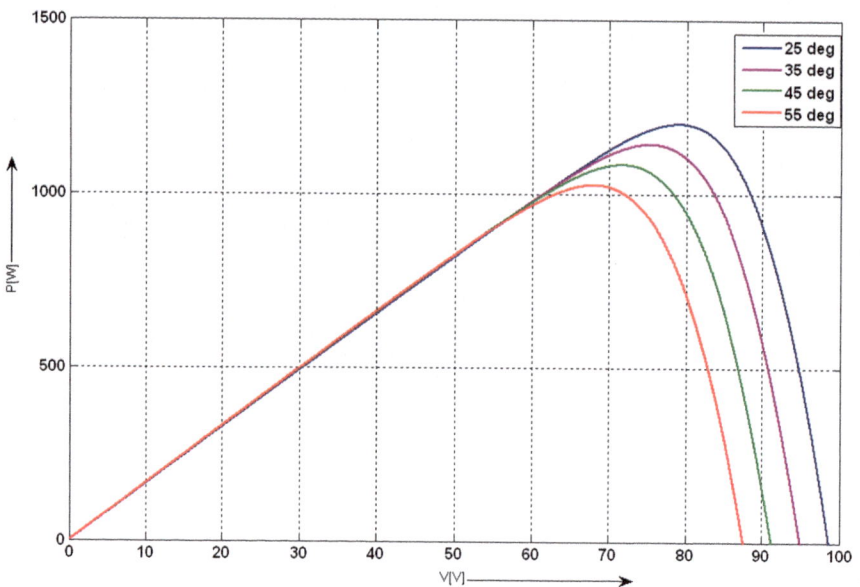

Fig. 19 *P–V* curve for $N_{ss} = 2$, $N_{pp} = 3$ at different temperatures

Table 3 Parameters of the model at nominal operating conditions

I_{mp}	7.61 A
V_{mp}	26.3 V
$P_{max,m}$	200.143 W
I_{sc}	8.21 A
V_{oc}	32.9 V
10, n	9.825×10^{-8} A
I_{pv}	8.214 A
a	1.3
R_p	415.405
R_s	0.221

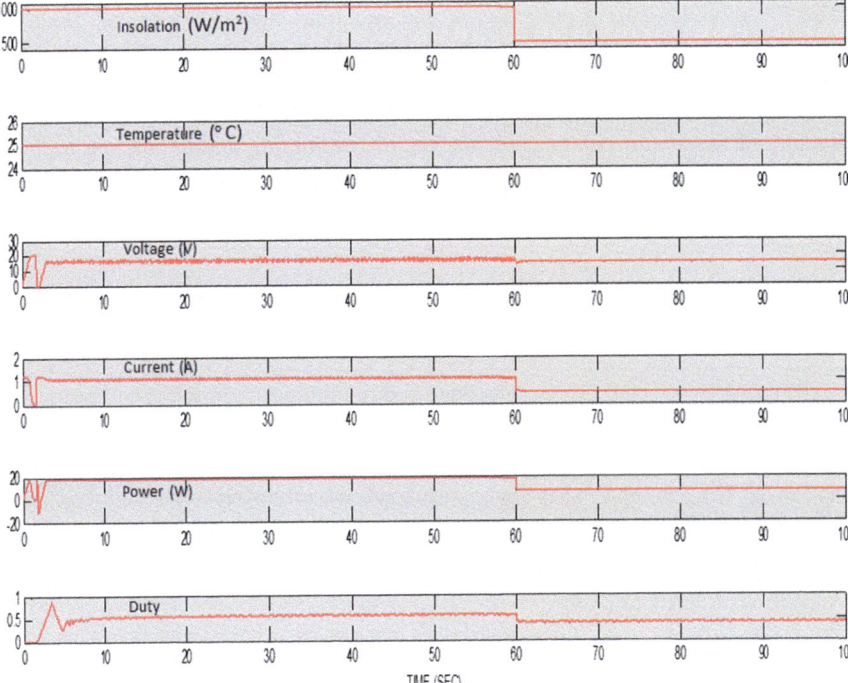

Fig. 20 Simulation result for varying insolation for model of Table 4

Table 4 Parameters of the
model KM-0018 at 25 °C and
1000 W/m² conditions

I_{mp}	1.05 A
V_{mp}	17 V
$P_{max,m}$	18 Wp $\pm$ 3%
I_{sc}	1.25 A
V_{oc}	21 V

7   Conclusion

This paper has explored the method used to mathematically model the photovoltaic arrays. Direct method has been suggested to apt the mathematical V–I curve to the significant points without guessing or estimating any parameters. This projected method is very useful for finding the parameters of the five-parameter model of a solar PV module. This paper gives all the equations that represent one-diode PV model, the process needed to attain the factors required by the governing equations, and reproduction of maximum power point tracker.

This paper offers all the compulsory information to develop a one-diode PV model and maximum power point tracker for examining and simulating a photovoltaic array. The proposed simulated PV model can be used for further analysis of PV stand-alone, in micro-grid and grid synchronized systems.

References

1. Ramaprabha, R.: Ph.D. Thesis. Maximum energy extraction from solar photovoltaic array under partial shaded conditions, Faculty of Electrical Engineering, Anna University, Chennai (2011)
2. Rauschenbusch, H.S.: Solar Cell Array Design Handbook. Van Nostrand Reinhold (1980)
3. Husain, M.A., Tariq, A.: Modeling of a standalone wind-PV hybrid generation system using matlab/SIMULINK and its performance analysis. Int. J. Sci. Eng. Res. 4(11) (2013)
4. Faridi, S.N.H., Husain, M.A., Tariq, A., Khair, A.: MATLAB based modeling of a PV array and its comparative study with actual system for different conditions. Int. J. Electr. Eng. Technol. 5(5), 19–27 (2014)
5. Husain, M.A., Tariq, A.: Modeling and study of a standalone PMSG wind generation system using MATLAB/SIMULINK. Univers. J. Electr. Electron. Eng. 2(7), 270–277 (2014). https://doi.org/10.13189/ujeee.2014.020702
6. Husain, M.A., Jalil, M.F., Beg, M.T.S., Naseem, M., Tariq, A.: Modeling and study of a standalone PV system using Matlab/Simulink. i-Manager's J. Electr. Eng. 5(4) (2012)
7. Pongratananukul, N., Kasparis, T.: Tool for automated simulation of solar arrays using general-purpose simulators. In: Proceedings of IEEE Workshop on Computers in Power Electronics, pp. 10–14 (2004)
8. Gow, J.A., Manning, C.D.: Development of a model for photovoltaic arrays suitable for use in simulation studies of solar energy conversion systems. In: Proceedings of 6th International Conference on Power Electronics and Variable Speed Drives, pp. 69–74 (1996)

9. Chowdhury, S., Taylor, G.A., Chowdhury, S.P., Saha, A.K., Song, Y.H.: Modelling, simulation and performance analysis of a PV array in an embedded environment. In: Proceedings of 42nd International Universities Power Engineering Conference, UPEC, pp. 781–785 (2007)
10. Hyvarinen J., Karila, J.: New analysis method for crystalline silicon cells. In: Proceedings of 3rd World Conference on Photovoltaic Energy Conversion, vol. 2, pp. 1521–1524 (2003)
11. Nishioka, K., Sakitani, N., Uraoka, Y., Fuyuki, T.: Analysis of multicrystalline silicon solar cells by modified 3-diode equivalent circuit model taking leakage current through periphery into consideration. Sol. Energy Mater. Sol. Cells 91(13), 1222–1227 (2007)
12. Carrero, C., Amador, J., Arnaltes, S.: A single procedure for helping PV designers to select silicon PV module and evaluate the loss resistances. Renew Energy (2007)
13. Koutroulis, E., Kalaitzakis, K., Tzitzilonis, V.: Development of a FPGA-based system for real-time simulation of photovoltaic modules. Microelectron. J. (2008)
14. Walker, G.: Evaluating MPPT converter topologies using a matlab PV model. J. Electr. Electron. Eng. Aust. 21(1) (2001)
15. De Soto, W., Klein, S.A., Beckman, W.A.: Improvement and validation of a model for photovoltaic array performance. Sol. Energy 80(1), 78–88 (2006)
16. Glass, M.C.: Improved solar array power point model with SPICE realization. In: Proceedings of 31st Intersociety Energy Conversion Engineering Conference (IECEC), vol. 1, pp. 286–291 (1996)
17. Kuo, Y.C., Liang, T.J., Chen, J.F.: Novel maximum-power-point tracking controller for photovoltaic energy conversion system. IEEE Trans. Ind. Electron. 48(3), 594–601 (2001)
18. Elhagry, M.T., Elkousy, A.A.T., Saleh, M.B., Elshatter, T.F., Abou-Elzahab, E.M.: Fuzzy modeling of photovoltaic panel equivalent circuit. In: Proceedings of 40th Midwest Symposium on Circuits and Systems, vol. 1, pp. 60–63, Aug 1997
19. Manimekalai, P., Harikumar, R., Aiswarya, R.: An overview of converters for photo voltaic power generating systems. In: International Conference on Advances in Communication and Computing Technologies (ICACACT) (2012)
20. Parisi, A., Curcio, L., Rocca, V., Stivala, S., Cino, A.C., Busacca, A.C., Cipriani, G., La Cascia, D., Di Dio, V., Miceli, R.: Photovoltaic module characteristics from CIGS solar cell modelling. In: Proceedings of International Conference on Renewable Energy Research and Applications (ICRERA), pp. 1139–1144 (2013)
21. Guerrero, J.M., Blaabjerg, F., Zhelev, T., Hemmes, K., Monmasson, E., Jemei, S., Comech, M.P., Granadino, R., Frau, J.I.: Distributed generation: toward a new energy paradigm. IEEE Ind. Electron. Mag. 4(1), 52–64 (2010)
22. Xiao, W., Ozog, N., Dunford, W.G.: Topology study of photovoltaic interface for maximum power point tracking. IEEE Trans. Ind. Electron. 54(3) (2007)
23. Katiraei, F., Agüero, J.R.: Solar PV integration challenges. IEEE Power Energy Mag. 9(3), 62–71 (2011)
24. Patel, H., Agarwal, V.: MPPT scheme for a PV-fed single-phase single-stage grid-connected inverter operating in CCM with only one current sensor. IEEE Trans. Energy Convers. 24(1) (2009)
25. Subudhi, B., Pradhan, R.: A comparative study on maximum power point tracking techniques for photovoltaic power systems. IEEE Trans. Sustain. Energy 4(1), 89–98 (2013)
26. Zainudin, H.N., Mekhilef, S.: Comparison study of maximum power point tracker techniques for PV systems. In: Proceedings of 14th International Middle East Power Systems Conference, Egypt, 19–21 Dec 2010
27. Femia, N., Petrone, G., Spagnuolo, G., Vitelli, M.: Optimization of perturb and observe maximum power point tracking method. IEEE Trans. Power Electron. 20(4), 963–973 (2005)

A Novel Approach for Data Classification Using Neutrosophic Entropy

Kanika Bhutani and Swati Aggarwal

Abstract Fuzzy classification is very necessary because it has the ability to use interpretable rules. It has got control over the limitations of crisp rule-based classification. This paper mainly deals with classification using fuzzy probability and Neutrosophic probability. Classification based on Neutrosophic probability employs Neutrosophic logic, Neutrosophic probability, and Neutrosophic entropy for its working and is compared with classification based on fuzzy probability on the basis of parameters such as probability and ambiguity in the results. Classification based on fuzzy and Neutrosophic probabilities is implemented on appendicitis dataset from knowledge extraction based on evolutionary learning.

Keywords Classification · Fuzzy probability · Fuzzy entropy · Neutrosophic probability · Neutrosophic entropy

1 Introduction

Classification is defined as a process in which various objects are acknowledged, distinguished, and inferenced [1]. There are many techniques which are used for classification of data that give a realistic solution for all feasible inputs [2]. Fuzzy mapping of input and following fuzzy handling is a current research region which has been effectively applied to various areas from control theory to artificial intelligence [3, 4].

Fuzzy logic is of great interest because of its ability to deal with non-statistical ambiguity. In decision analysis, uncertain information is treated probabilistically in numerical form. An another methodology in which a more realistic hypothesis is

K. Bhutani (✉)
Department of Computer Engineering, NIT Kurukshetra, Kurukshetra, India
e-mail: kanikabhutani91@gmail.com

S. Aggarwal
COE, NSIT, Dwarka, India
e-mail: swati1178@gmail.com

© Springer Nature Singapore Pte Ltd. 2018
S. K. Muttoo (ed.), *System and Architecture*, Advances in Intelligent Systems and Computing 732, https://doi.org/10.1007/978-981-10-8533-8_29

made is fuzzy probability in which it is known imprecisely as fuzzy and is exemplified by the perceptions of possibility labeled as very probable, improbable, not very probable, etc. [5] Uncertainty due to fuzziness is sometimes correlated with probabilistic uncertainty [6]. For example, in case of coin, the occurrence of head supports the fuzzy event HIGH more than a tail does. Entropy is uncertainty. It permeates discourse and systems. It connects with information and learning. Fuzzy entropy was introduced by Luca and Termini [7]. Fuzzy entropy is the entropy of fuzzy sets representing the information of uncertainty. Let E be a set to point mapping such that $E: F(2^x) \to [0, 1]$. Here, E is a fuzzy set defined on fuzzy sets. E is an entropy measure if it satisfies the four rules [7]:

$$E(Y) = 0 \quad \text{iff } Y \in 2^x (Y \text{ non fuzzy}), \tag{1}$$

$$E(Y) = 1 \quad \text{iff } m_Y(x_i) = 0.5 \text{ for all } i, \tag{2}$$

$E(Y) \le E(Z)$ if Y is less fuzzy than Z, i.e. if $m_Y(x) \le m_Z(x)$ when $m_Z(x) \le 0.5$ and $m_Y(x) \ge m_Z(x)$ when

$$m_Z(x) \ge 0.5, \tag{3}$$

$$E(Y) = E(Y^C). \tag{4}$$

Here, Y is a subset of set E. $m_Y(x)$ is the membership of element x in set Y. Y^c is the complement of Y.

Neutrosophic probability is simplification of the traditional and imprecise probabilities. Let X be a Neutrosophic space, and Σ a σ-Neutrosophic algebra over X [8]. A Neutrosophic measure v is defined for Neutrosophic set $Z \in \Sigma$ by

$$v: X \to R^3 \tag{5}$$

$$v(Z) = (m(Z), m(neutZ), m(antiZ)) \tag{6}$$

where $antiZ$ = opposite of Z and $neutZ$ = neutral(indeterminacy) neither Z nor $antiZ$. v is a function that satisfies the property of null set and countable additivity. $m(Z)$ means measure of determinate portion of Z, $m(neutZ)$ is measure of indeterminate portion of Z, and $m(antiZ)$ is determinate portion of $antiZ$ [8].

So, flipping a coin on a cracked surface, there is a chance that coin gets struck on its edge and then the sample space is:
{Head, Tail, indeterminacy}.
The Neutrosophic probability for head and tail is described as:

$$NP(\text{Head}) = NP(\text{Tail}) < \frac{1}{2} \tag{7}$$

Generally, $P(\text{Head}) = P(\text{Tail}) = \frac{1}{2}$, but here indeterminacy is involved which is also having some probability so the probability of head and tail is less than half. Neutrosophic entropy was introduced by Majumdar and Samanta [9]. Let $N(X)$ be a Neutrosophic soft set on X. An entropy is a function $E_N: N(X) \rightarrow [0, 1]$ that satisfies the following rules [9]:

$$E_N(Y) = 0 \quad \text{if } Y \text{ is crisp set}, \tag{8}$$

$$\begin{aligned} E_N(Y) = 1 \quad &\text{if } (T_Y(x), I_Y(x), F_Y(x)) \\ &= (0.5, 0.5, 0.5) \quad \text{for all } x \in X, \end{aligned} \tag{9}$$

$$\begin{aligned} E_N(Y) \geq E_N(Z) \quad &\text{if } Y \subset Z, \text{ i.e., } T_Y(x) \leq T_Z(x), \\ F_Y(x) &\leq F_Z(x) \text{ and } I_Y(x) \leq I_Z(x) \text{ for all } x \in X, \end{aligned} \tag{10}$$

$$E_N(Y) = E_N(Y^C) \quad \text{for all } Y \in N(X). \tag{11}$$

The remaining of the paper is organized as follows: Sect. 2 gives the details of dataset used. Section 3 describes the fuzzy probability and fuzzy entropy for classifying dataset. Section 4 elaborates the Neutrosophic probability and Neutrosophic entropy for classifying dataset. Section 5 presents implementation of fuzzy and Neutrosophic probabilities and entropy on appendicitis dataset. Section 6 presents discussion of results. Section 7 outlines the conclusion and future work.

2 Dataset Details

In this research, appendicitis dataset from knowledge extraction based on evolutionary learning (KEEL) [10] is selected for fuzzy classifier and Neutrosophic classifier. The dataset has different seven attributes which are multiplied by 100 for simplicity, so all the attributes are in the range of 0–100.

Different attributes to be experimented:

Attribute 1—WBC1
Attribute 2—MNEP
Attribute 3—MNEA
Attribute 4—MBAP
Attribute 5—MBAA
Attribute 6—HNEP
Attribute 7—HNEA

Classes to be classified:
0 means the patient is not suffering from appendicitis.
1 means the patient is suffering from appendicitis.

Appendicitis dataset contains 106 instances out of which 96 instances are used for training and 10 instances for testing. Ninety percent of the instances are used for training, and 10% of the instances are randomly selected for testing.

3 Classification Based on Fuzzy Probability

Fuzzy probability is a component of standard information theory. It shows vague probabilities with ties to concepts of random sets. It shares the frequent attribute of all imprecise probability models, and the uncertainty of an event is characterized with a set of possible degree in terms of probability or with bounds on probability.

3.1 Basic Criteria for Determining Fuzzy Probability

Classification based on fuzzy probability is done on the basis of fuzzy logic. As overlapping is expected in fuzzy logic, suitable rules are designed for all the appendicitis dataset attributes and output classes. It can be observed that the outputs produced after defuzzification in inference system can be of three types as shown in Fig. 1.

Case 1: If the output lies in the range of 0–a, then it supports HIGH fuzzy event for class A and LOW fuzzy event for class B.

Case 2: If the output value lies in the overlapping range, then there is some degree of indeterminacy. There is imprecise value of LOW and HIGH fuzzy events, so Neutrosophic probability is applied in this region to get more realistic results.

Fig. 1 Criteria for assigning fuzzy values

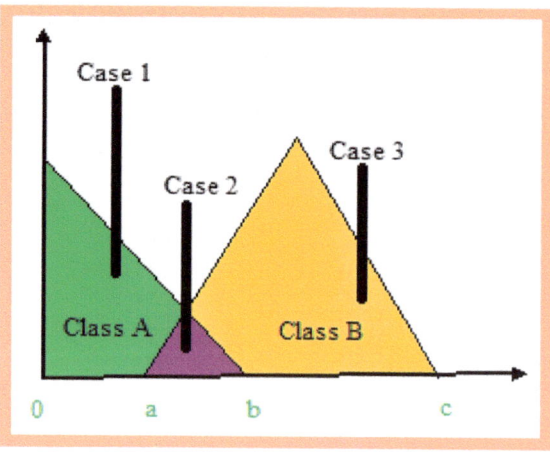

Case 3: If the output lies in the range of b–c, then it supports HIGH fuzzy event for class B and LOW fuzzy event for class A.

After assigning fuzzy linguistic variables to all the outputs in a particular class, fuzzy probability is calculated for fuzzy events as

$$FP(\text{HIGH}) = \frac{\sum_{i=1}^{n} \mu_i(\text{HIGH})}{n} \tag{12}$$

where HIGH is the fuzzy linguistic variable of a class, n is the total number of samples available in the class, and $FP(\text{HIGH})$ is the fuzzy probability of fuzzy variable HIGH.

Similarly, fuzzy probability for all the fuzzy events is calculated in a particular class.

3.2 Basic Criteria for Determining Fuzzy Entropy

In fuzzy entropy, all the instances of appendicitis dataset are considered as sets and entropy is calculated by the rules given by Luca and Termini. If the fuzzy output value is 0.5, then entropy will be 1. If the fuzzy output value belongs to power set of [0, 1], then entropy is 0. Entropy of two instances can be compared using Eq. (3). As it is fuzzy entropy, it will always provide the value in the range of 0–1.

4 Classification Based on Neutrosophic Probability

In real life, indeterminacy can be seen everywhere. If a die is tossed on a cracked surface, then there is no clear face to see. Thus, it is indeterminacy. If weather reports say that the probability of rain tomorrow is 70%, then it does not mean that the probability of not raining is 30% because there are some hidden weather factors that the reporters are not aware of. So, there is some ambiguity that leads to indeterminacy. Indeterminacy occurs due to defects in creation of physical space or defective making of physical items involved in the events.

Thus, Neutrosophic probability considers both random variables and indeterminacy variables. Neutrosophic probability is a specific case of Neutrosophic measure. It is an approximation of an event together with estimation of indeterminacy involved [8, 11]. Neutrosophic probability that an event X occurs is

$$NP(X) = (ch(X), ch(neutX), ch(antiX)) = (T, I, F) \tag{13}$$

It can also be represented as

$$NP(X) = \big(ch(X), ch(\text{indeterm}_X), ch(\overline{X})\big) \tag{14}$$

T is the chance that X occurs denoted by $ch(X)$, I is the indeterminate chance related to X denoted by $ch(\text{indeterm}_X)$, and F is the chance that X does not occur denoted by $ch(\overline{X})$.

4.1 Basic Criteria for Determining Neutrosophic Probability

Neutrosophic probability works on the same concept like fuzzy probability, but after defuzzification, output value is represented in the triplet format, i.e., truthness, indeterminacy, and falsity [12]. Designing of Neutrosophic components is shown in Fig. 2 [13].

The following steps are followed for classifying data using Neutrosophic probability:

(1) First of all, create the training and testing sets for every class. Here, 96 instances are used for training and 10 instances are used for testing.
(2) Neutrosophic probability is expressed in terms of three components: Neutrosophic truth, indeterminacy, and falsity component.
(3) Neutrosophic truth component is designed as follows:

   (a) Memberships functions are designed for all the variables, i.e., input and output variables such that no overlapping exists between the two membership functions.
   (b) Suitable rules are created using rule editor.

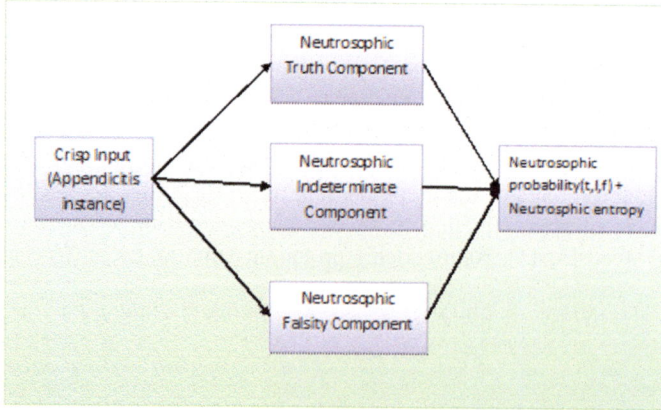

Fig. 2 Block diagram of Neutrosophic components

(4) Neutrosophic indeterminacy component is designed as follows:

    (a) Memberships functions are designed for all the variables, i.e., input and output variables such that no overlapping exists between the two membership functions. Indeterminacy and falsity components are designed only for overlapping regions of two membership functions.

    (b) Suitable rules are created using rule editor.

(5) Neutrosophic falsity component using training set is designed in the same way as it is done for indeterminacy component, but height of every membership function is 0.5.

(6) After training is done, all the components are tested independently using the testing data.

(7) At the end, Neutrosophic probability$(t + i + f)$ will be categorized into complete, incomplete, or paraconsistent probability.

4.2 Basic Criteria for Neutrosophic Entropy

The entropy can be calculated as [14]

$$E_N(Y) = \frac{1}{n}\sum_{i=1}^{n}\left(1 - \frac{1}{b-a}\int_{a}^{b}|T_Y(x_i) - F_Y(x_i)||I_Y(x_i) - I_Y(x_i)|dx\right) \quad (15)$$

Here, $E_N(Y)$ is the Neutrosophic entropy of any instance. N is the total number of instances. $T_Y(x_i)$ is the truth component value, $I_Y(x_i)$ is the indeterminate component value, and $F_Y(x_i)$ is the falsity component value. a and b are the lower and upper limits.

5 Implementation of Fuzzy Probability and Neutrosophic Probability on Appendicitis Dataset

The designing of fuzzy and Neutrosophic components for appendicitis dataset is described as:

(1) The input variable 1 range from 0 to 100 is composed of trapezoidal membership functions as shown in Fig. 3.

(2) Similarly for all other attributes, input membership is defined.

(3) Design output membership for two classes, i.e., 1 and 0 represented by A and B as shown in Fig. 4.

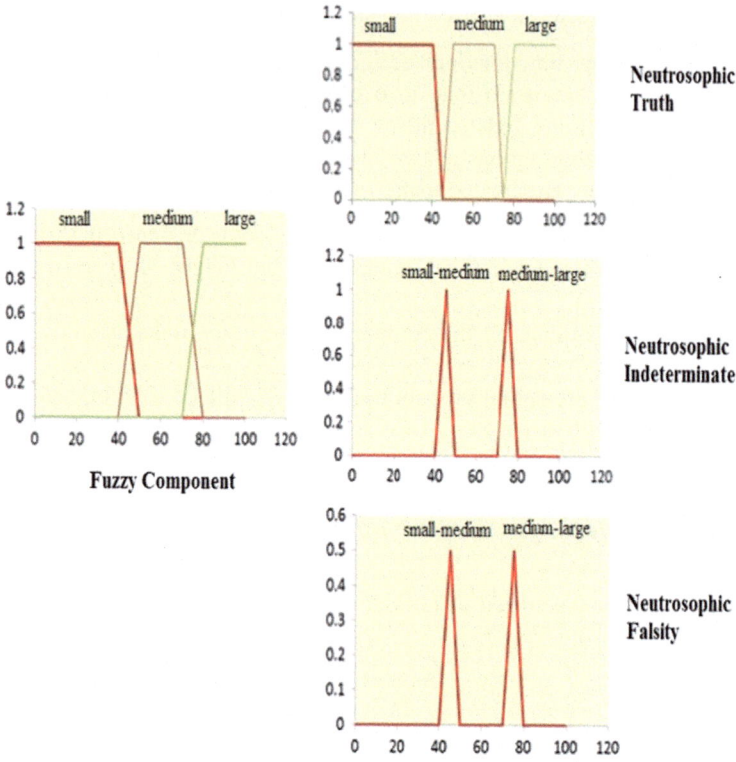

Fig. 3 Membership function for input 1

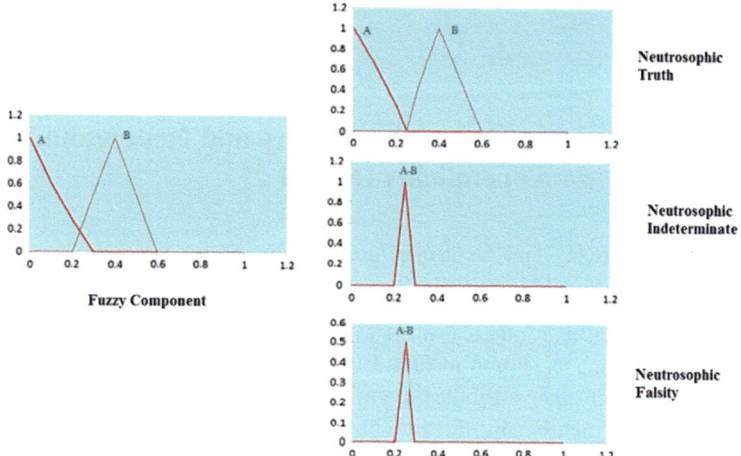

Fig. 4 Membership function for output class

(4) The rule base of the fuzzy component contains 35 if-then rules. The rule base of Neutrosophic truth, indeterminate, and falsity component contains 40, 11, and 11 rules.

6 Experiments and Results

Table 1 shows the rules formed and training and testing samples for fuzzy and Neutrosophic components.

Table 2 shows the details of the testing instances for fuzzy component on appendicitis dataset.

Here, if the membership value is 0.5, then the entropy is 1. If it lies in the power set of [0, 1], i.e., other than 0.5, then the entropy is 0. Table 3 shows the details of testing instances using Neutrosophic probability and entropy.

Here, entropy is calculated using Eq. (15). If the Neutrosophic value of instance is crisp, then the entropy is 0, otherwise it is 1. Authors have analyzed the following cases from Table 3:

(a) If $t + i + f = 1$, then it means it is complete probability; i.e., it is normalized probability which can be seen in second instance of class B.

Consider a real-world situation; there are two parties A and B; on the basis of previous records, if both parties have 50% chance of winning, then $NP(A$ wins over $B) = (0.5, 0, 0.5) = 1$.

Table 1 Details of training and testing data

Component	Training samples used	Testing samples used	Number of rules
Fuzzy	96	10	35
Neutrosophic truth	96	10	40
Neutrosophic indeterminate	96	10	11
Neutrosophic falsity	96	10	11

Table 2 Details of testing instances using fuzzy probability and entropy

Appendicitis classes	Instance	Output	Analysis of the output	Fuzzy probability	Entropy (E)
Class A	[21.3 55.4 20.7 0 0 74.9 22]	HIGH	Both cases indicate clear belongingness to class A	FP(HIGH) = 1 FP(LOW) = 0 FP(L/H) = 0	0
	[5.8 58.9 8.7 58.3 19.6 57.6 6]	HIGH			0

(continued)

Table 2 (continued)

Appendicitis classes	Instance	Output	Analysis of the output	Fuzzy probability	Entropy (E)
Class B	[39.6 46.4 32.2 61.1 50.6 36.6 27.4]	HIGH	Six cases indicate clear belongingness to class B Two cases generated results lying in overlapping zone of class A and class B	FP (HIGH) = 0.75 FP(L/ H) = 0.25 FP(LOW) = 0	1
	[53.8 73.2 54.9 5.6 5.8 88.2 55.8]	HIGH			1
	[32.9 66.1 33.4 15.3 11.2 67.4 30.4]	L/H			0
	[75.1 82.1 79.7 29.2 39.2 74.7 70]	L/H			0
	[68 71.4 67 1.4 1.7 85.1 68.1]	HIGH			1
	[51.6 76.8 54.4 13.9 13.9 66.7 46.2]	HIGH			1
	[47.1 83.9 53.1 11.1 10.4 84.5 48.1]	HIGH			1
	[62.2 75 63.5 26.4 30.6 78.7 60.1]	HIGH			1

Table 3 Details of testing instances using Neutrosophic probability and entropy

Appendicitis classes	Instance	Truth probability	Indeterminate probability	Falsity probability	Neutrosophic probability (t, i, f)	Entropy (E_N)
Class A	[21.3 55.4 20.7 0 0 74.9 22]	0.08	0.5	0.5	$t + i + f = 1.08$	0
	[5.8 58.9 8.7 58.3 19.6 57.6 6]	0.08	0.5	0.5	$t + i + f = 1.08$	0

(continued)

Table 3 (continued)

Appendicitis classes	Instance	Truth probability	Indeterminate probability	Falsity probability	Neutrosophic probability (t, i, f)	Entropy (E_N)
Class B	[39.6 46.4 32.2 61.1 50.6 36.6 27.4]	0.4216	0.5	0.5	$t + i + f = 1.4216$	0
	[53.8 73.2 54.9 5.6 5.8 88.2 55.8]	0.20	0.4	0.4	$t + i + f = 1.0$	1
	[32.9 66.1 33.4 15.3 11.2 67.4 30.4]	0.2901	0.25	0.25	$t + i + f = 0.7901$	1
	[75.1 82.1 79.7 29.2 39.2 74.7 70]	0.42	0.25	0.25	$t + i + f = 0.92$	1
	[68 71.4 67 1.4 1.7 85.1 68.1]	0.4204	0.5	0.5	$t + i + f = 1.4204$	0
	[51.6 76.8 54.4 13.9 13.9 66.7 46.2]	0.2865	0.5	0.5	$t + i + f = 1.2865$	1
	[47.1 83.9 53.1 11.1 10.4 84.5 48.1]	0.2841	0.5	0.5	$t + i + f = 1.2841$	1
	[62.2 75 63.5 26.4 30.6 78.7 60.1]	0.2877	0.5	0.5	$t + i + f = 1.2877$	1

(b) If $t + i + f < 1$, then it means it is an incomplete probability; i.e., there exists some indeterminacy. It can be seen in third and fourth instances of class B.

Consider a real-world situation; there are two parties A and B; if both parties do not perform well, then there is 20% chance of winning of A or B. On the basis of previous records available, there is 30% chance of both parties having equal votes.

Therefore, $NP(A$ wins over $B) = (0.2, 0.3, 0.2) < 1$.

(c) If $t + i + f > 1$, then it means it is paraconsistent probability. It means there is some inconsistent data which can be seen in many cases discussed above.

Consider a real-world situation; there are two parties A and B; according to their previous history, A is 70% favorable to win. But according to last year election results, B is showing better performance so B has 80% chance to win. Other people think that A was generally better than B, so there is 10% chance that both parties will get equal votes (tie).

Therefore, $NP(A$ wins over $B) = (0.7 + 0.8 + 0.1) > 1$.

Table 4 Ambiguous results

Class	Instance	Fuzzy probability result	Neutrosophic probability result	Analysis
A	[32.9 66.1 33.4 15.3 11.2 67.4 30.4]	L/H	(0.2901, 0.25, 0.25) $t + i + f < 1$	The result of fuzzy probability indicates that it lies in the overlapping region of class A and class B. It just gives the probability of overlapping. Thus, authors cannot surely say to which class this instance belongs to. But Neutrosophic probability can handle this overlapping region because it gives the percentage of truth, percentage of indeterminacy, percentage of falsity to which it belongs to class B. Also these two instances show incomplete probability that means there is some indeterminate attribute available in the dataset. Hence, it shows that Neutrosophic probability can deal with such ambiguous situations in a better way
B	[75.1 82.1 79.7 29.2 39.2 74.7 70]	L/H	(0.42, 0.25, 0.25) $t + i + f < 1$	

(d) Entropy is calculated using Eq. (15); if the Neutrosophic value of instance is crisp, then the entropy is 0, otherwise it is 1. Neutrosophic entropy basically helps us to deal with the indeterminate values present in the real world.

Table 4 shows the details of ambiguous results found using fuzzy and Neutrosophic probabilities.

7 Conclusion and Future Scope

Classification using Neutrosophic probability and entropy provides more practical results as compared to fuzzy probability. Neutrosophic probability and entropy involve indeterminate sample space that exists in the real world. It provides results in the triplet form, i.e., truth, indeterminate, and falsity. It also categorized the results into complete, incomplete, and paraconsistent probability: complete probability when there is no indeterminate or ambiguous instance; incomplete probability when there is some indeterminate instances present in the dataset; and paraconsistent probability when there is some contradiction among various attributes of an instance. It can be seen in Sect. 6 that some instances are showing results in overlapping section, i.e., indeterminacy which can be handled with Neutrosophic probability.

It is a sample study as it is implemented on 106 instances. In future, it can be extended on complex datasets or those datasets which contain more overlapping regions which can be dealt with Neutrosophic logic. A real-time application can be created using Neutrosophic logic and Neutrosophic probability that could replace the existing fuzzy-based applications. Also hybridization of other soft computing techniques with Neutrosophic logic can be done to analyze the indeterminacy present in the data.

References

1. National Diabetes Data Group: Classification and diagnosis of diabetes mellitus and other categories of glucose intolerance. Diabetes **28**(12), 1039–1057 (1979)
2. Rahman, R.M., Afroz, F.: Comparison of various classification techniques using different data mining tools for diabetes diagnosis. J. Softw. Eng. Appl. **6**(03), 85 (2013)
3. Adlassnig, K.P.: Fuzzy set theory in medical diagnosis. IEEE Trans. Syst. Man Cybern. **16**(2), 260–265 (1986)
4. Zimmermann, H.J.: Fuzzy set theory. Wiley Interdisc. Rev. Comput. Stat. **2**(3), 317–332 (2010)
5. Zadeh, L.A.: Fuzzy probabilities. Inf. Proc. Manag. **20**(3), 363–372 (1984)
6. Pal, N.R., Bezdek, J.C.: Measuring fuzzy uncertainty. IEEE Trans. Fuzzy Syst. **2**(2), 107–118 (1994)
7. Kosko, B.: Fuzzy entropy and conditioning. Inf. Sci. **40**(2), 165–174 (1986)
8. Smarandache, F.: Introduction to neutrosophic measure, neutrosophic integral, and neutrosophic probability (2013)
9. Majumdar, P., Samanta, S.K.: On similarity and entropy of neutrosophic sets. J. Intell. Fuzzy Syst. **26**(3), 1245–1252 (2014)
10. Retrieved appendicitis dataset on 10 Oct 2014 from http://sci2s.ugr.es/keel/dataset.php?cod=183
11. Smarandache, F.: Proceedings of the First International Conference on Neutrosophy, Neutrosophic Logic, Neutrosophic Set, Neutrosophic Probability and Statistics, University of New Mexico, Gallup Campus, Xiquan, Phoenix (2002)
12. Smarandache, F.: A unifying field in logics: neutrosophic logic. Multiple-Valued Logic/An Int. J. **8**(3), 385–438 (2002)
13. Ansari, A.Q., Biswas, R., Aggarwal, S.: Neutrosophic classifier: an extension of fuzzy classifer. Appl. Softw. Comput. **13**(1), 563–573 (2013)
14. Şahin, R., Küçük, A.: On similarity and entropy of neutrosophic soft sets. J. Intell. Fuzzy Syst. Appl. Eng. Technol. **27**(5), 2417–2430 (2014)

SDN Layer 2 Switch Simulation Using Mininet and OpenDayLight

Vipin Kumar Rathi and Karan Singh

Abstract Software-Defined Networking is a separation of control plane and data plane where control plane controls several devices https://www.opennetworking. org/sdn-resources/sdn-definition [1]. SDN provides a programmable network protocol that can virtualize whole network infrastructure. Networking reached to threshold point in driving next-generation network architecture. In this paper, simulation of Layer 2 Switch based on SDN using OpenDaylight and Mininet Emulator is performed. SDN is implemented by OpenvSwitch (OVS) as a data plane and OpenDaylight as a Control Plane both Mininet and OpenDaylight is installed on different Instances of an IBM Server. Then analyzes the architecture of the Layer 2 Switch with OVS and OpenDaylight that can successfully run Loop Remover, Arp Handler on ODL Controller which prevents broadcast storms (McKeown et al in ACM SIGCOMM Comput Commun Rev 38:69, 2008 [2]; Nunes in Commun Surv Tutorial-s 16(3):1617–1634, 2014 [3]; Open Networking Foundation 2014 [4]).

Keywords Software-defined networking · OpenFlow · OpenvSwitch
OpenDaylight · Loop Remover · Mininet

1 Introduction

Everyday networks are becoming more complex, loads on these networks are also increasing and availability is also important. Today, network design is not sufficient to fulfill this kind of demand, due to this networks becoming more complex, making [2–4] the administration of these networks more difficult. Therefore, we

V. K. Rathi (✉) · K. Singh
School of Computer and Systems Sciences, Jawaharlal Nehru University,
New Delhi, India
e-mail: vipin68_scs@jnu.ac.in

K. Singh
e-mail: karan@mail.jnu.ac.in

© Springer Nature Singapore Pte Ltd. 2018
S. K. Muttoo (ed.), *System and Architecture*, Advances in Intelligent Systems
and Computing 732, https://doi.org/10.1007/978-981-10-8533-8_30

need next generation of networking that can manage such high demand and utilize the bandwidth at its maximum. Due to new trends in computing like a cloud, Big Data, and Internet of Things, a new design for networking is needed that is fulfilled by Software-Defined Networking (SDN). SDN helps to detach control plane from data plane which helps the administrator to manage the network centrally and can utilize bandwidth at its maximum, resulting in great flexibility [5].

The conventional network architecture where data plane and control plane remain in the same device which cannot fulfill these high demands and solution to this problem is Software-Defined Networking (SDN). The network paradigm separates data plane and control plane [6]. The network can be dynamically managed; for example, whenever there is a change in topology due to loops or any other causes, then the network can be managed dynamically. Mininet is a lightweight container or virtualization-based emulator. Mininet provides a rapid development for SDN, it is flexible and creates easily configurable topologies such as switches, controllers, virtual hosts and configurations starts a network in few seconds and also supports the OpenFlow protocol that can be used for network based SDN simulation. Mininet includes a command–line interface (CLI) that is topology-aware and OpenFlow-aware [7].

This paper uses Mininet Simulator for simulation of SDN. SDN network consists of data plane as OVS and control plane in the form of OpenDaylight controller. OpenDaylight controller functions as Loop Remover, Arp Handler, Packet Handler, Host Tracker, and Address Tracker.

1.1 Problem Definition

In legacy Layer 2 Switch, there is no intelligence and capability to learn network topology and forward packets from source to destination.

2 Theory

This section discusses OpenFlow, architecture, OpenDaylight with brief details of the same as follows.

2.1 OpenFlow

The communication between the OpenFlow controller and switch takes place using the OpenFlow protocol. By using OpenFlow protocol, a OpenFlow controller can do CRUD (Create, Read, Update, Delete) operation on flow entries, e.g.,

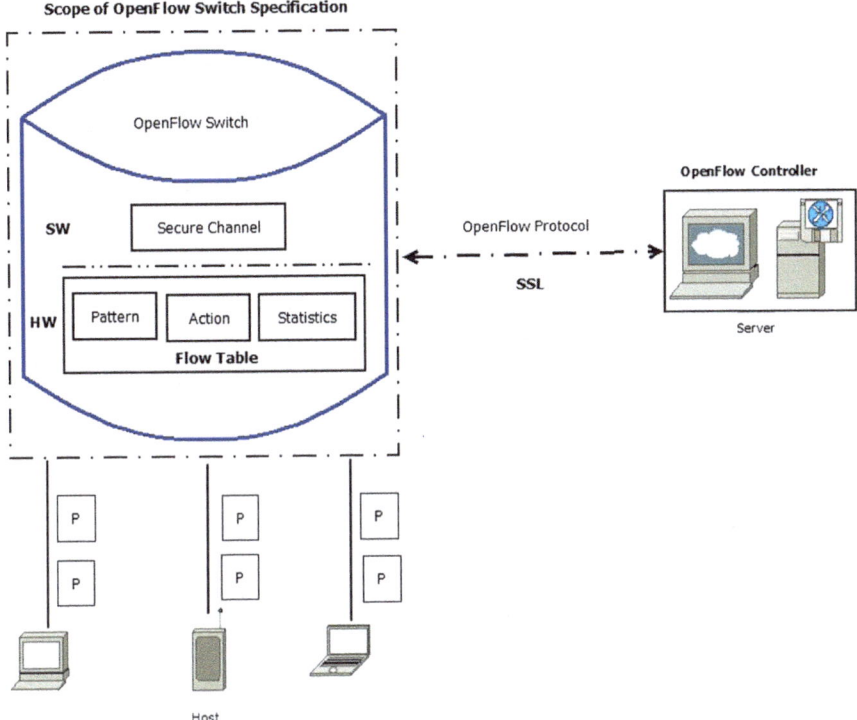

Fig. 1 OpenFlow architecture

FLOW MOD (ADD) to create a flow entry, FLOW MOD (MODIFY) to modify a flow entry, FLOW REMOVED to remove a flow entry [8]. Figure 1 illustrates the architecture of OpenFlow, in which we have OpenFlow Switch, OpenFlow controller, Hosts, and Servers. Communication between controller and switch takes place securely by using Secure Socket Layer.

OpenFlow Switches are expected to process all 802.1D Spanning Tree Protocol (STP) packets locally before performing lookup; e.g., in layer 2, OpenFlow Switches forward broadcast traffic which may result in loops. Spanning tree helps to provide loop-free topology but when link fails there is exchange of BPDU between switches and then they take an alternative path which takes some time. However, in SDN, controllers do topology discovery and link fault detection. In SDN, Spanning Tree Protocol is comparatively easier. Whenever there is a change in topology, it simply computes a STP from the topology using prims algorithm.

OpenFlow Switch maintains the flow table according to pattern, action, priority and counter for e.g. pattern, action, and priority and counter values are Dst IP address (10.5.2.1), Port 1, 15 and 105 respectively. The complete table and their values are given below in Table 1.

Table 1 OpenFlow flow table

Pattern	Action	Priority	Counter
Dst IP Addr=10.5.2.0	Port 1	15	105
TCP/UDP Dst Port=25	Drop	25	310
Dst IPAddr=192.*	Port 2	10	200
*	Controller	0	116

The failure of links in Software-Defined Networking based on OpenFlow will result in the need to converge on a new topology which will be the same at layer 2 or 3 since OpenFlow seems to merge the control and data planes resulting in unified logical topologies. Since OpenFlow utilizes flow tables, the concept of feasible successors can be applied to flow tables by inserting alternate paths as less preferred flow entries. The use of successor routes will result in no need to contact a controller on link failures. In SDN based on OpenFlow when there is failure of links, it will result in a new topology which will be same at layer 2 or 3.

2.2 OpenDaylight

The OpenDaylight can deliver the benefits of SDN to the Internet of Things or control Ethernet switches using the OpenFlow protocol. OpenDaylight provides a Model-Driven Service Abstraction Layer (MD-SAL) that allows users to write apps that can work easily across a wide variety of hardware and south-bound protocols [9].

OpenDaylight aims to accelerate the adoption of Software-Defined Networking and creates a solid root for Network Function Virtualization. Newest version of OpenDaylight is Lithium. OpenDaylight not only supports OpenFlow but also supports other south-bound protocols like NETCONF, OVSDB, SNMP. For north-bound Protocols, Representational State Transfer (REST) APIs are used.

OpenDaylight runs on Java Virtual Machine (JVM), and it is platform independent that can be run on any Operating System. OpenDaylight makes use of the following tools Maven, OSGi, Java Interfaces, and REST APIs. Figure 2 shows a high-level network view of the OpenDaylight controller. In which SDN apps talk to Northbound API according to request the corresponding API is activated now at next layer we have two functions Service Functions and Base Network Functions which contain different modules like Statistics Manager, Device Man- ager, Topology Discovery, Inventory Manager then request reaches the Service Abstraction Layer and then through Southbound API which can be it reaches to Network Device.

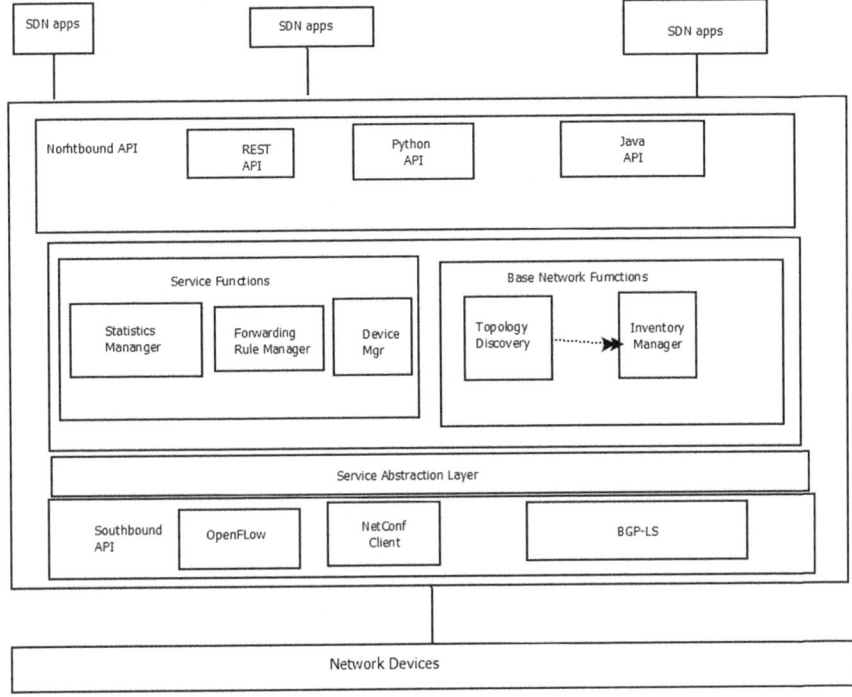

Fig. 2 High-level network view of the OpenDaylight controller

2.3 Layer 2 Switch

The Layer 2 Switch gives Layer 2 functionality. There are various modules present in Layer 2 Switch like Loop Remover which removes the loop in the network and updates the corresponding STP Status of networks ports. In the operational inventory data store, Host Tracker tracks the location of the host relatively to the network. Switch Manager Component holding the inventory information for all the known nodes in the controller, Topology Manager Component holding the whole network graph, Statistics Manager Component in charge of using the Service Abstraction Layer Read Service to collect several statistics from the Network, Arp Handler which handles the decoded ARP packets, either by installing proactive flood flows or by dispatching packets back to network, based on the configuration, Layer 2 Switch Main installs flows on each switch, based on network traffic and address learned by address tracker [10]. This allows the switch to learn the network topology and be aware to changes. Thereby, when a packet is received it is directly redirected to the destination instead of flooding to every other host. This results in very high efficiency as compared to current switching methodology in layer 2.

3   Simulation Design

This section briefly discusses network design and SDN controller as follows.

3.1   Network Design

Our study used IBM server which contains 32 GB RAM, 1 TB hard disk on which we have place Kernel-based Virtual Machine (KVM) as a Hypervisor and upon it we have placed two instances: One instance contains Mininet with 192.168.56.103 as ip address, and another instance putting OpenDaylight as controller with the following ip address 192.168.56.101. The network simulation contains three switches and three hosts; one host is connected with one switch in Mesh Topology. The network topology of simulation is shown in Fig. 3.

3.2   SDN Controller

In this simulation, SDN controller is OpenDaylight which is installed on one of the instances of IBM server that contains Ubuntu 14.03 LTS Controller which disables some links with the help of Loop Remover internally.
Running Spanning Tree Protocol.

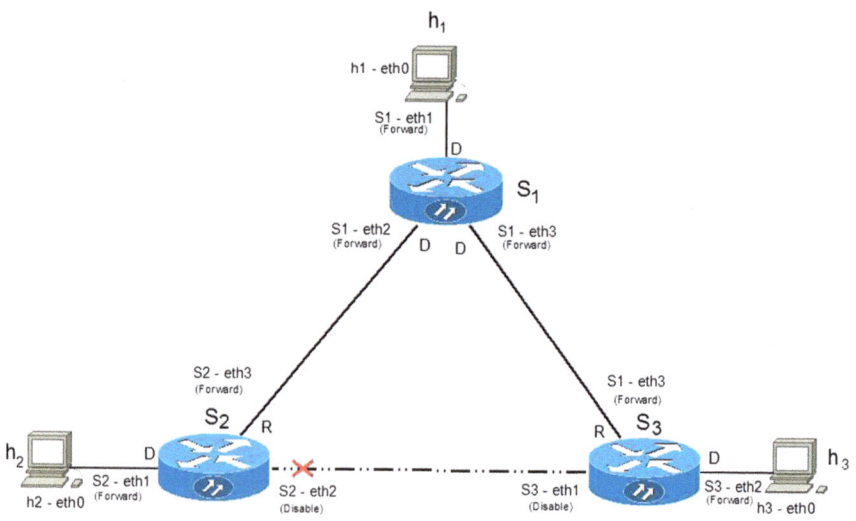

Fig. 3 Network topology

3.3 Procedure for Simulation

We are using Mininet, add a custom topology in Custom Directory, and create a python file called as meshtopology.py, which contains the following algorithm

1. Initialize topology
   Topo. init (self)
2. Add hosts and switches

   leftHost = self.addHost('h2')
   rightHost = self.addHost('h3')
   leftSwitch = self.addSwitch('s2')
   rightSwitch = self.addSwitch('s3')
   aboveHost = self.addHost('h1')
   aboveSwitch = self.addSwitch('s1')

3. Add links

   self.addLink(leftHost, leftSwitch)
   self.addLink(leftSwitch, rightSwitch)
   self.addLink(rightSwitch, rightHost)
   self.addLink(aboveHost, aboveSwitch)
   self.addLink(aboveSwitch, leftSwitch)
   self.addLink(aboveSwitch, rightSwitch)

4 Result

On Mininet, we have to run the following command sudo mn –controller=remote, ip=192.168.56.101 –custom /mininet/custom/meshtopology.py –topo mytopo. After running the following command, controller creates Mesh Topology as shown in Fig. 4, as we can see in figure there are three switches connected in Mesh Topology. Now on Mininet run h2 ping h3 and sudo WireShark & so that result can be seen on Wireshark Window as shown in Fig. 5. On Wireshark we can filter arp packets and path follow by packets are from host2 to Switch2, Switch1, Switch3 and finally it reach to host3. Because link between Switch2 and Switch3 is in Blocking State to prevent packet to not go in to loop.

We can verify the above result by running the tcpdump command on Switch1 and listening on eth2 interface, and all nodes are able to ping each other as shown in Fig. 6.

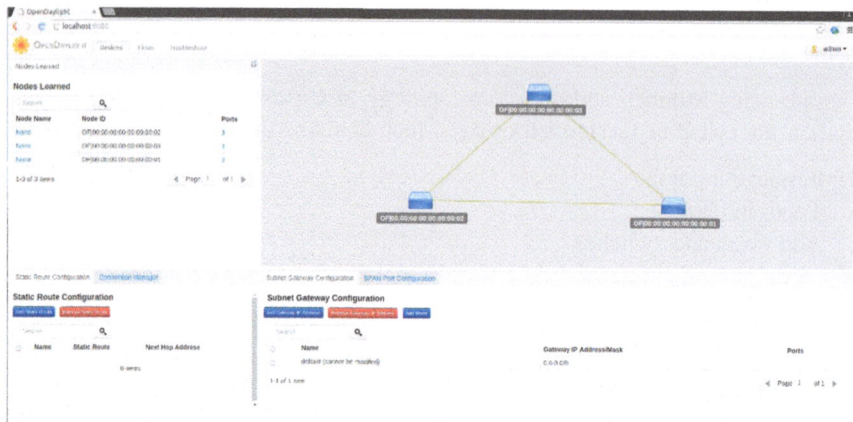

Fig. 4 OpenDaylight dashboard

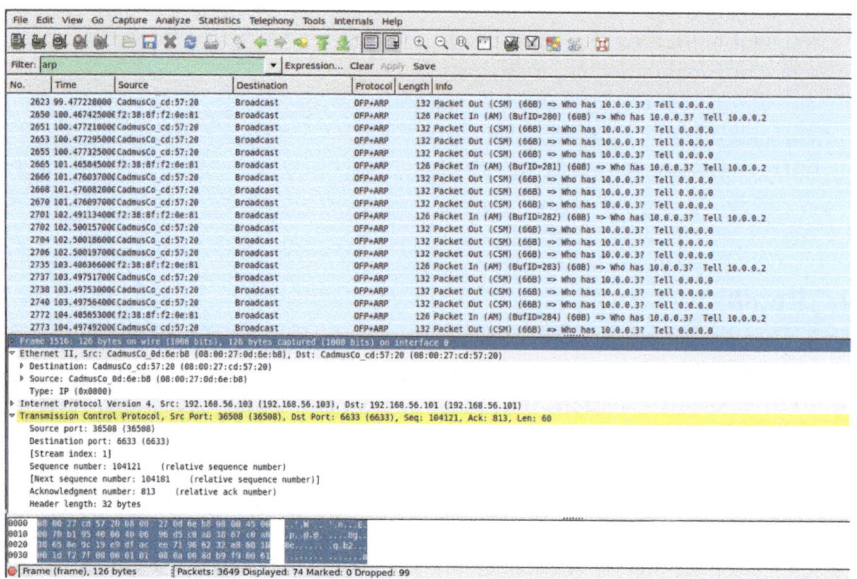

Fig. 5 Capture results form Wireshark

5 Conclusion

SDN Layer 2 Switch is introduced in a brief manner in this research paper. SDN has risen as a way to enhance programmability within the network to fulfill the dynamic nature of future network functions. SDN keeps on making progress within large enterprise and cloud service provider for data center networking. SDN offers a wide

Fig. 6 ARP reply

determination of competing architectures, yet at its most simple. In this paper, we have done the simulation of the SDN with OpenFlow Switch and OpenDaylight controller successfully and test Loop Remover, Arp Handler. OpenDaylight controller can perform STP. STP stops broadcast storm on network and prevents from flooding. In future works, new topologies like leaf-spine and Trill (instead of STP) may be tested.

References

1. What is SDN ? https://www.opennetworking.org/sdn-resources/sdn-definition
2. McKeown, N., Anderson, T., Balakrishnan, H., Parulkar, G., Peterson, L., Rexford, J., Shenker, S., Turner, J.: Open-flow: enabling innovation in campus networks. ACM SIGCOMM Comput. Commun. Rev. **38**(2), 69 (2008)
3. Nunes, B.A.A., Mendonca, M., Nguyen, X.-N., Obraczka, K., Turletti, T.: A survey of software-defined networking: past, present, and future of programmable networks. Commun. Surv. Tutorials **16**(3), 1617–1634 (2014). https://doi.org/10.1109/surv.2014.012214.00180. 13 Feb 2014 (IEEE)
4. Open Networking Foundation: Software-Defined Networking (SDN) Definition, 2014, available at https://www.opennetworking.org/sdnresources/sdn-definition. Accessed Jan 2015
5. Kim, H., Feamster, N.: Improving network management with software defined networking. IEEE Commun. Mag. **51**(2), 114119 (2013)
6. Open Networking Foundation: SDN Architecture 1.0, 2014, available at: https://www.opennetworking.org/sdn-resources/technical-library. Accessed Jan 2015 (Django, Django: the Web framework)
7. MININET. An instant virtual network on your laptop (or other pc).http:// mininet.org/
8. FOUNDATION, O. N. OpenFlow specification 1.3. https://www.opennetworking.org/images/stories/downloads/sdn-resources/onfspecifications/openflow/openflow-specv1.3.0.pdf
9. OpenDayLight: Open source network controller. http://www.opendaylight.org/
10. L2 Switch: https://wiki.opendaylight.org/view/L2_Switch:Helium:Developer_Guide
11. ONF, Open networking foundation. https://www.opennetworking.org/. (2015)

An Architectural Design for Knowledge Asset Management System

H. R. Vishwakarma, B. K. Tripathy and D. P. Kothari

Abstract Knowledge assets (KAs) are the main focus for knowledge management as these are considered most valuable in this knowledge-driven economy. However, the tasks of understanding, valuation, and management of knowledge assets have been daunting in contrast to their physical counterparts. There have been no generally agreed frameworks for carrying out the above tasks. Organizations strive to minimize the cost of creating and managing knowledge assets and to maximize value addition from knowledge assets. Also, they provide knowledge services to its internal and external customers using knowledge assets and processes with the help of knowledge workers. Hence, efficient management of knowledge assets is often the central theme in most organizational knowledge management (KM) programs. In this paper, we discuss knowledge asset management from multiple perspectives. We propose a set of generic steps involved in knowledge asset management (KAM) and also propose an architectural design for managing knowledge assets in organizational settings.

Keywords Knowledge management · Knowledge workers · Knowledge process
Knowledge assets · Knowledge artifacts · Knowledge services
Knowledge asset management system

H. R. Vishwakarma (✉) · B. K. Tripathy · D. P. Kothari
VIT University, Vellore 632014, Tamil Nadu, India
e-mail: hrvishwakarma@vit.ac.in

B. K. Tripathy
e-mail: tripathybk@vit.ac.in

D. P. Kothari
e-mail: dpk0710@yahoo.com

© Springer Nature Singapore Pte Ltd. 2018
S. K. Muttoo (ed.), *System and Architecture*, Advances in Intelligent Systems
and Computing 732, https://doi.org/10.1007/978-981-10-8533-8_31

1   Introduction

In today's economy, organizations are focusing more on knowledge assets (KAs) rather than physical assets. Knowledge management programs are being adopted by many organizations in order to gain competitive advantage in market increasingly dominated by knowledge-based products and services. Articulating knowledge vision and developing knowledge management strategy is one of the top agenda points in boardroom discussions in most organizations. Knowledge vision and strategy drive the knowledge processes used and services provided by organizations. Knowledge processes represent internal perspective of knowledge management, whereas knowledge services are external perspectives typically catering to needs of customers. Many organizations have begun to convert internally generated knowledge into knowledge-based products, processes, and services that can be used by business associates and customers. An organization has to consider seven aspects related to knowledge management so as to ensure leverage of its knowledge resources. These aspects are knowledge strategy, knowledge structure, knowledge workers, knowledge process, knowledge services, knowledge assets, and finally knowledge systems.

Many researchers have established links between knowledge management strategies and knowledge creation processes as well as overall innovativeness of organizations. Choi and Lee [1] derive a model showing alignment of KM strategies with knowledge creation process models. Ferraresi et al. [2] show how knowledge management influences strategic orientation even without affecting business performance. Bosua and Venkitachalam [3] propose a framework explaining key enablers and approaches to align KM strategies with workgroup knowledge processes.

Knowledge asset management (KAM) is the heart of any knowledge management program. It involves several steps such as identification, categorization, auditing and mapping of knowledge assets that are available, acquiring or creating assets that are needed, etc. Knowledge assets and knowledge processes are inextricably linked.

Kans [4] discusses knowledge assets and processes in the context of maintenance process including planning and control aspects to achieve business goals.

Naftanaila [5] presents perspectives of knowledge asset management in project environment suggesting a few strategies to address management challenges. Carlucci and Schiuma [6] propose a framework giving guidelines for planning, implementing, and evaluating knowledge management initiatives. They also illustrate how to identify knowledge assets and their interdependencies.

Rebentisch and Ferretti [7] propose an integrated framework for technology transfer process that involves the transfer of embodied knowledge assets between organizations. The framework considers organizations embodying three aspects technology, operational, and structural.

Smuts et al. [8] mention how learning opportunities and business gains are lost owing to unintentional fragmentation of knowledge assets in information system outsourcing scenarios. According to them, organizations need to aim at optimizing critical knowledge assets and at improving knowledge-sharing mechanism.

According to Heredia et al. [9], interactive knowledge asset management helps in acquiring the experiences of individual knowledge workers. It also facilitates utilization of existing knowledge assets and sharing accumulated knowledge among all concerned. Further, they also find that such an approach helps in improving ability of individuals and in enhancing quality of products.

Whelan and Carcary [10] show how talent management concepts help in knowledge worker identification, knowledge creation, sharing, competency development, and knowledge retention. Lerro et al. [11] describe various aspects that help decide strategies for assessing knowledge assets. They discuss the organizational value, the processes, approaches, and evaluation architectures. Schiuma et al. [12] propose a system thinking-based framework for analyzing and developing mechanisms that support evolution of knowledge assets and knowledge flow dynamics. They show knowledge assets are interdependently and dependently related and are translated into organizational value. Marr et al. [13] emphasize on the importance of measuring knowledge assets as these enhance organizational capabilities and competencies. They further suggest the knowledge asset dashboard considering dynamic actor/infrastructure relationship and nature of these assets. According to Le Dinh et al. [14], an integrated approach for organizational content management should be developed to support knowledge creation and collaboration processes. They present a framework for knowledge-based content management to transform organizational content into knowledge assets.

An innovative architecture for organizational knowledge management was proposed in [15]. In this proposal, it is considered that knowledge management initiative begins at the top management level in an organization by articulating knowledge vision and strategic goals. Knowledge processes and knowledge services are defined subsequently. The focus of knowledge processes is efficient knowledge management. On the other hand, knowledge services are meant for efficient utilization and sharing of knowledge with an objective of maximizing return on invest and gaining competitive advantage.

Knowledge asset management and knowledge networks play crucial role in dynamic evolution as well as assessing and enhancing the values of knowledge assets. In this paper, we primarily focus on the above aspects, analyze it, and provide a comparison with the existing approaches wherein the proposed approach is superior to these approaches.

The outline of remainder part of the paper is as follows:

Section 2 discusses knowledge asset management processes and actors. Section 3 presents the architecture of knowledge asset management system. Section 4 lists the advantages of the system.

2 Knowledge Asset Management Processes and Actors

Organizations provide knowledge services to its internal and external customers using a variety of knowledge processes and with the help of knowledge workers. Knowledge workers are workers whose main capital is knowledge. They are persons employed to produce or analyze ideas and information. They can assume the role of knowledge producer (i.e., author, owner) or consumer (i.e., user, seeker) or both. A few super-knowledge workers may assume the role of active managers for organizational knowledge. Sometimes, they play the role of neutral facilitators of knowledge sharing among individual peers.

Knowledge workers and the knowledge networks formed by them contribute significantly in managing knowledge assets and impact knowledge flow dynamics. We incorporate various roles knowledge workers play in knowledge asset management (KAM) as follows.

Individual knowledge workers create and/or own knowledge asset as well as use and/or edit knowledge assets using various knowledge processes. Further, they publish and share knowledge assets with co-workers. They may store knowledge assets at their respective workstations or at a centralized repository.

Figure 1a illustrates use case diagram pertaining to individual work processes.

Knowledge workers use domain-specific knowledge processes, for example, requirements engineering, architectural design, etc., in the case of software development project. They may also use generic processes, e.g., interview, workflow, meeting. Knowledge assets are used, created, and modified in the above collaborative processes.

Figure 1b illustrates use case diagram pertaining to collaborative work processes.

A knowledge asset may be comprised of several knowledge objects and may be associated with a set of keywords. Further, knowledge assets may have two types of attributes: system-defined and user-defined, in order to facilitate search by multiple search criteria.

Knowledge asset management typically involves the following processes: identification, categorization, mapping, acquisition, creation, editing, merging, splitting, copying, storing, retrieving, indexing, searching, sharing, auditing, etc., of knowledge assets. Some of the above processes are applicable for existing knowledge assets, e.g., searching, editing, while some of the processes are applicable only for new knowledge assets, e.g., creation, storing etc. Each of the above processes has distinct characteristics, say; searching process is characterized by accessibility and responsiveness, acquisition and creation are characterized by validation, and so on.

Figure 1c, d illustrate use case diagrams pertaining to supervisory processes and SME processes, respectively.

The following section describes an architectural design incorporating the above processes and actors.

Fig. 1 a Use case diagram for individual work processes, **b** use case diagram for collaborative processes, **c** use case diagram for supervisory processes, and **d** use case diagram for SME processes

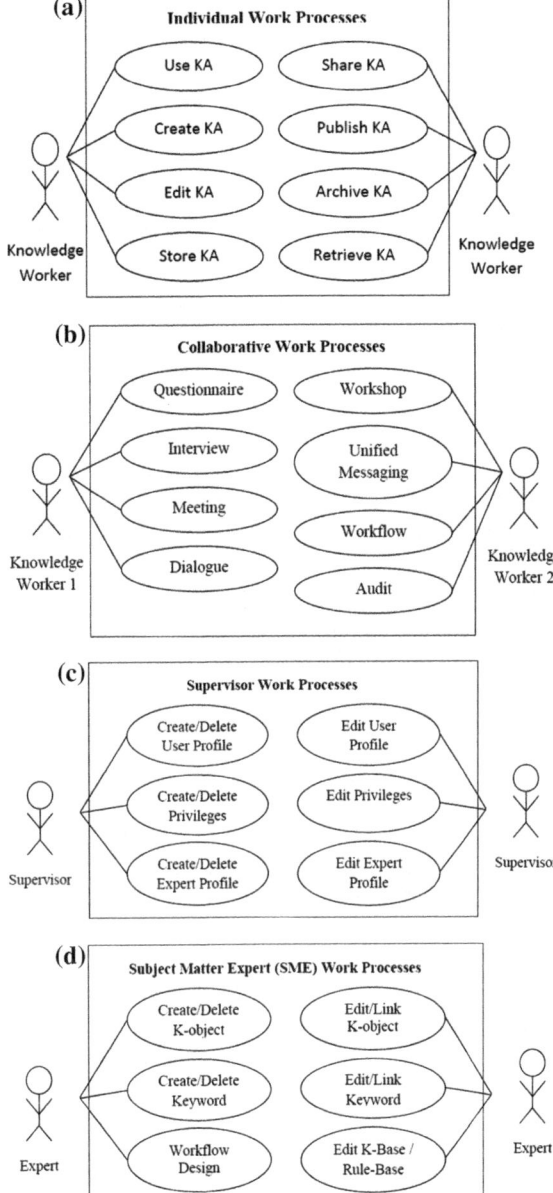

3 Architecture of Knowledge Asset Management (KAM) System

In this paper, we consider knowledge assets (KAs) as the base on which knowledge management initiatives are taken up by organizations. We have used the term "knowledge asset (KA)" to represent a knowledge product or artifact that may be a set of documents or a single document. However, in a broader context, a KA is considered as any type of knowledge including insight, know-how, experience, competence, and relationship capital, intellectual capital such as a copyright or patent. Knowledge-based organizations such as software development companies and education and research institutions deal with a variety of knowledge assets. For such organizations, efficient management of knowledge assets is of paramount importance. We consider the knowledge asset management as the key capability required to survive in this knowledge-driven world.

In this section, we discuss an architectural design for knowledge asset management (KAM) system that is an amalgamation of multiple perspectives. Figure 2 illustrates context model for the proposed KAM system along with its enclosing environment.

We consider that a KAM system needs to manage knowledge assets residing in the intranet and knowledge warehouse of organization/team concerned and in the Internet. Knowledge workstations (KWS) are the systems designed to cater to the needs of knowledge workers helping them in carrying out individual work processes and collaborative work processes as well as managing process flows and services deliveries. There are also two special types of KWS, one each for subject matter expert (SME) and supervisor.

Unified messaging system (UMS) provides a single mailbox for each knowledge worker to handle voice, fax, and regular text messages as objects. Some of these messaging objects may constitute or augment a knowledge asset.

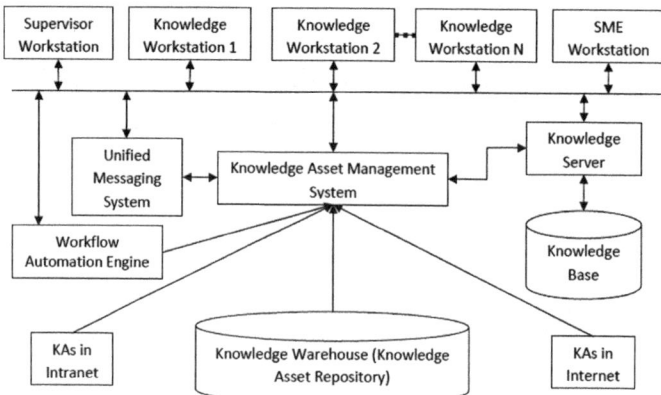

Fig. 2 Context model for knowledge asset management system

Workflow engine helps knowledge works in managing various process flows involving their peers and/or superiors. However, the aspects of workflow design/ administration and applications remain with SME/supervisor workstation and knowledge workstations.

Knowledge server supports knowledge workers using its knowledge base that also grows dynamically overtime. It guarantees that processes followed and services delivered are in accordance with the rules. Knowledge server also facilitates SME to edit its knowledge base.

Figure 3 illustrates the architectural design of knowledge asset management (KAM) system. We describe here only the major modules of the system.

Knowledge user module consists of query processor, KA browser, KA converter, and KA editor. Knowledge asset directory and map (KADAM) maintains the list of knowledge assets along with the usage and location maps. It enhances the visibility of knowledge assets among potential users. A user with the help of query processor, knowledge asset directory and map (KADAM), and knowledge asset browser can find a desired knowledge asset and use it. A knowledge asset can be browsed, converted from one form to another, and/or edited via KADAM.

Knowledge asset analyzer and processor (KAP) examines whether a knowledge asset meets certain criteria and rules. It also extracts objects, keywords, and attributes from a knowledge asset. It stores the above in a database and sends the knowledge asset for storing it through KADAM module.

A knowledge asset resides either in main storage or auxiliary storage of KAM system depending on its frequency of usage. Supervisor can modify attributes and storage locations of knowledge assets. An expert (i.e., domain or subject matter expert) can modify objects and keywords of knowledge assets.

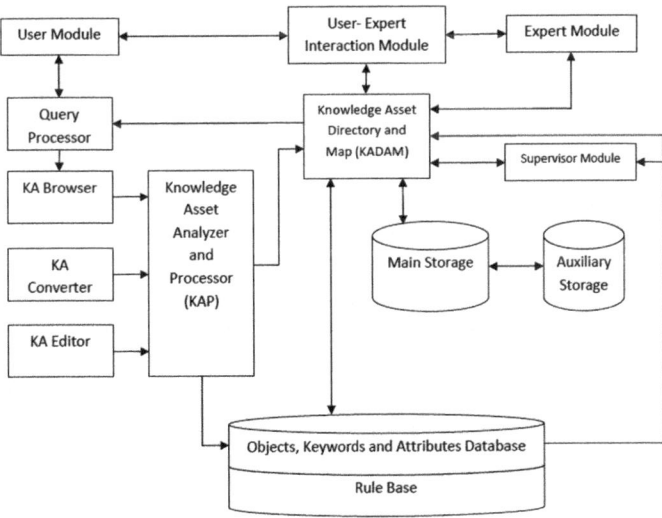

Fig. 3 Architectural design of knowledge asset management

The user–expert interaction module helps in direct interaction addressing some of the needs that are not otherwise being facilitated. Such interactions might help in discovery of new knowledge assets as well as new application scenarios of existing knowledge assets. These direct interactions might also help in quick evaluation of knowledge assets and in identifying scope for evolution of knowledge assets.

4 Comparative Analysis and Advantages of the Proposed System

The performance of the proposed system is compared with that of the existing systems in this section. The proposed system offers the following advantages:

(1) The architecture facilitates capturing explicit knowledge documented by individual knowledge workers as well as conversion tacit knowledge into explicit knowledge through collaborative processes interviews, meetings, etc.

(2) It supports both the types of repositories of knowledge assets—local repositories for individual knowledge workers and a centralized repository.

(3) It supports both the task-specific knowledge processes and generic organizational processes that use, create, and modify knowledge assets.

(4) It supports leveraging of knowledge assets available within project teams, within an organization, and with external sources.

(5) It automatically archives less frequently accessed knowledge assets from main storage to auxiliary storage, thus improving overall performance.

(6) It helps in evolution of knowledge assets as these are shared among knowledge workers and updated through various knowledge processes, e.g., inclusion of new sources of knowledge, re-application of knowledge in different contexts, optimization by feedback loops, etc.

(7) It promotes knowledge harvesting as ideas are generated and captured in formal and informal interactions among knowledge workers.

(8) It provides an integrated user interface, where document creation, editing, filing, retrieving, and mailing functions are available as efficient sequential operations.

(9) The system maintains the list of knowledge assets along with usage and location maps, thus enhancing the visibility of knowledge assets among potential users.

(10) The system supports versatile search-based multiple options including keywords, objects, system, and user-defined attributes of knowledge assets.

From a broad perspective, the proposed system is distinguished from the existing systems using 10 major criteria grouped into two categories, viz., knowledge assets and knowledge processes as shown in Tables 1 and 2.

Table 1 Knowledge assets

Criteria	Existing systems	Proposed system
Repositories	Mostly support centralized repositories	Supports both local and centralized repositories
Format conversion	Not supported	Supports conversion of knowledge assets from one format to another
Searching assets	Only search using name and keywords of knowledge assets	Versatile options for search including names, keywords, objects, and attributes of knowledge assets
Leveraging assets	Only internal sources of knowledge assets	Both internal and external sources of knowledge assets
Tools support	Mostly support filing and retrieving of knowledge assets	Integrated support for creating, editing, filing, retrieving, and mailing of knowledge assets

Table 2 Knowledge processes

Criteria	Existing systems	Proposed system
Knowledge evolution	Limited scope	Wide scope as assets are shared among knowledge workers and updated through multiple processes
Tacit-to-explicit knowledge conversion	Not supported	Supports via collaborative processes such as interviews and meetings
Processes support	Mostly support organizational knowledge processes	Supports both task-specific and generic organizational processes
Automatic archival	Not supported	Supported based on frequency of usage
Knowledge harvesting	Not supported	Supported as ideas are generated and captured in user–expert interaction

5 Conclusion

This paper considered knowledge assets as foundation stones of organizational knowledge management and the reviewed literature pertaining to knowledge asset management. It described the processes and actors involved in knowledge asset management. It presented a context model for knowledge asset management and proposed an architectural design for managing knowledge assets in organizational settings. Further work can be carried out to assess quality of knowledge assets and value addition from knowledge assets to organizations.

References

1. Choi, B., Lee, H.: Knowledge management strategy and its link to knowledge creation process. Expert Syst. Appl. **23**(3), 173–187 (2002)
2. Ferraresi, A.A., Quandt, C.O., dos Santos, S.A., Frega, J.R.: Knowledge management and strategic orientation: leveraging innovativeness and performance. J. Knowl. Manag. **16**(5), 688–701 (2012)
3. Bosua, R., Venkitachalam, K.: Aligning strategies and processes in knowledge management: a framework. J. Knowl. Manag. **17**(3), 331–346 (2013)
4. Kans, M.: Knowledge asset management in the maintenance context. In: COMADEM 2013, International Congress of Condition Monitoring and Diagnostics Engineering Management, 11–13 June 2013, Helsinki. KP media Oy (2013)
5. Naftanaila, I.: Managing knowledge assets in project environments. J. Knowl. Manag. Econ. Inform. Technol. **2**(1), 64–73 (2012)
6. Carlucci, D., Schiuma, G.: Knowledge asset value spiral: linking knowledge assets to company's performance. Knowl. Process. Manag. **13**(1), 35–46 (2006)
7. Rebentisch, E.S., Ferretti, M.: A knowledge asset-based view of technology transfer in international joint ventures. J. Eng. Tech. Manag. **12**(1), 1–25 (1995)
8. Smuts, H., Kotzé, P., Van der Merwe, A., Loock, M.: Knowledge asset management pertinent to information systems outsourcing. New Contributions in Information Systems and Technologies, pp. 43–55. Springer International Publishing, (2015)
9. Heredia, A., Garcia-Guzman, J., de Amescua, A., Sanchbez-Segura, M.I.: Interactive knowledge asset management: acquiring and disseminating tacit knowledge. J. Inf. Sci. Eng. **29**(1), 133–147 (2013)
10. Whelan, E., Carcary, M.: Integrating talent and knowledge management: where are the benefits? J. Knowl. Manag. **15**(4), 675–687 (2011)
11. Lerro, A., Iacobone, F.A., Schiuma, G.: Knowledge assets assessment strategies: organizational value, processes, approaches and evaluation architectures. J. Knowl. Manag. **16**(4), 563–575 (2012)
12. Schiuma, G., Carlucci, D., Sole, F.: Applying a systems thinking framework to assess knowledge assets dynamics for business performance improvement. Expert Syst. Appl. **39**(9), 8044–8050 (2012)
13. Marr, B., Schiuma, G., Neely, A.: Intellectual capital-defining key performance indicators for organizational knowledge assets. Bus. Process Manag. J. **10**(5), 551–569 (2004)
14. Le Dinh, T., Rickenberg, T.A., Fill, H.G., Breitner, M.H.: Enterprise content management systems as a knowledge infrastructure: the knowledge-based content management framework. Int. J. e-Collab. (IJeC) **11**(3), 49–70 (2015)
15. Vishwakarma, H.R., Tripathy, B.K., Kothari, D.P.: A five-layer framework for organizational knowledge management. Paper presented in the international congress on information and communication technology (ICICT–2015), Udaipur, 9–10 October 2015

Printed by Printforce, the Netherlands